THE NIGERIAN MILITARY

AFRICAN STUDIES SERIES

General Editor: DR J. R. GOODY

1 *City Politics: A Study of Léopoldville, 1962–63* – J. S. LA FONTAINE
2 *Studies in Rural Capitalism in West Africa* – POLLY HILL
3 *Land Policy in Buganda* – HENRY W. WEST
4 *The Nigerian Military: A Sociological Analysis of Authority and Revolt, 1960–67* – ROBIN LUCKHAM

THE NIGERIAN MILITARY,

A SOCIOLOGICAL ANALYSIS OF AUTHORITY & REVOLT 1960-67

by ROBIN LUCKHAM

Lecturer on Sociology, Harvard University

CAMBRIDGE   707885

AT THE UNIVERSITY PRESS, 1971

Published by the Syndics of the Cambridge University Press
Bentley House, 200 Euston Road, London NW1 2DB
American Branch: 32 East 57th Street, New York, N.Y.10022

Library of Congress Catalogue Card Number: 73-152643

ISBN 0 521 08129 7

Printed in Great Britain
at the University Printing House, Cambridge
(Brooke Crutchley, University Printer)

In memory of Agbo and to my parents, in gratitude

I hope some day
Intent upon my trade of living, to be checked
In stride by *your* apparition in a trench,
Signalling, I am a soldier. No hesitation then
But I shall shoot you clean and fair
With meat and bread, a gourd of wine
A bunch of breasts from either arm, and that
Lone Question – do you friend, even now, know
What it is all about?

From poem 'Civilian and Soldier'
by Wole Soyinka

Wole Soyinka, *Idanre and other poems* (London: Methuen, 1967), p. 53.

CONTENTS

List of tables   *page* ix

Preface   xi

Map   xiv

INTRODUCTION   I

PART ONE: TWO MILITARY COUPS

  I January 1966: the Majors' coup   17

 II July 1966: the junior officers' and NCOs' coup   51

PART TWO: THE NIGERIAN MILITARY AS A SOCIAL SYSTEM

Introduction   83

 III The Nigerian Army: composition and structure   88

 IV Officers and gentlemen: the image of an elite   109

  V Peer groups: solidarity and cleavage   131

 VI Of heroism and hierarchy: the dilemmas of discipline   145

 VII Nigerianisation: the legacy of haste   163

VIII Tribe and region: the activation of primordial identities   177

PART THREE: THE MILITARY AND POLITICS

Introduction   201

 IX The political background   206

  X Civilian control of the military, 1958–66   230

 XI The Ironsi regime: the army as a government, January to
      July 1966   252

 XII Military image and political beliefs   279

XIII The way to secession   298

Contents

APPENDIX 1. Origins, training and promotions up to 1966 of officers in 1944 to 1961 seniority cohorts   *page* 343

APPENDIX 2. Extracts from documents concerning meeting of the Nigerian military leaders held at Peduase Lodge, Aburi, Ghana, 4th and 5th January 1967   347

Index of names   357

Index of authors   363

Index of subjects   365

TABLES

1   Distribution of ranks: January 1966 conspirators   *page* 29

2   Comparison of qualifications of January 1966 conspirators with their peer groups   37

3   Number of senior officers killed and surviving coup of January 1966   43

4   Fate of officers in key command and staff appointments, January 1966   45

5   Comparison of ethnic distribution of January coup leaders with peers and Sandhurst course-mates   48

6   Attrition in the higher levels of the officer corps, January 1966   54

7   Comparison of ethnic/regional origins of fifty most senior officers before and after coup of January 15   55

8   Comparison of ethnic balance of upper ranks, January and May 1966 (before and after January coup)   56

9   Rank levels of officers with role in July coup   72

10   Rank of leaders and followers among officers with operative roles in July 1966   73

11   Training of July coup officers   74

12   Ethnic and regional origin of victims of July coup   76

13   Cultural/ethnic affiliations of July coup participants   78

14   Comparison of Nigeria's military resources with selected African and Asian countries   89

15   Combat officers absented from military duties as a result of January and July 1966 coups   91

16   Disposition of officers surviving events of 1966 in August 1967   92

17   Militarily active officers in Federal and Biafran armies (August 1967) as a per cent of January 1966 officer corps   93

18   Comparative educational levels of Nigerian elite groups   96

19   Age structure of Federal government bureaucracies in January 1966   98

20   Experience levels of Federal government bureaucracies in January 1966   98

21   Numbers of officers with experience in staff and top command posts, January 1966   100

22   Sandhurst years of January 1966 coup figures   133

List of tables

23 Military training of different generations of army officers *page* 134
24 Military training of officers of different ranks 135
25 Military postings of January coup leaders, 1961–5 141
26 Shape of command hierarchy, January 1966 155
27 Indigenisation of the officer corps, 1960–6 163
28 Age structure of the Nigerian officer corps, 1966 164
29 Average seniority differentials at points in Nigerian Army hierarchy 165
30 Succession in selected military command posts, 1962–4 169
31 Median times of promotion from rank to rank, 1963–6 172
32 Comparison of median speeds of promotion of officer seniority cohorts 175
33 Cultural origins of Northern combat officers 183
34 School origins of Northern combat officers 184
35 Numbers of officers of tribal/regional groups commissioned, 1944–65 187
36 Regional/ethnic origins of officer seniority cohorts 189
37 Regional/ethnic origins of officers at different rank levels 190
38 Population size of regions and main tribes, 1963 208
39 Trend of military expenditures, 1958–66 235
40 Nigerianisation of command posts, 1960–5 239
41 Comparison of career origins of senior officers and January 1966 conspirators 240
42 Regional/ethnic distribution of officers commissioned up to 1961 245
43 Organisation chart of the National Military Government at 31 March 1966 255

MAP

Location of main military installations in Nigeria, January 1966 xiv

PREFACE

This book is about a human tragedy of terrible proportions. There have been times when I have wondered whether I should have written about it at all, making grim events the subject of the intellectual games played by a social scientist. I cannot pretend to have resolved this issue for myself; and perhaps all I have done has been to make it more complicated. So-called objective or value-free social science has come under attack from many quarters, sometimes quite rightly, but all too often, one suspects, by those who wish to keep their political morality simple, to protect their predilections from being undermined by wayward facts. In this study I hope I may help to demonstrate the utility of a relatively value-free approach to an emotionally and politically charged series of events. I have not sought, however, the kind of objectivity which limits itself to the recording of facts and of the simple correlations or relations between them, but rather that which is guided by theory, which attempts in the tradition established for sociology by Marx and Weber to understand events and institutions in terms of their inner logic, which thus fuses empirical observation with theory. (By a value-free social science Weber did not mean the total absence of values: rather that the basic terms of a social theory should not be value judgements; though the selection of problems to be studied might appropriately be the subject of moral choice and the empirical predictions of a theory might result in the rearrangement of a scholar's hierarchy of values.)

To be sure, my analysis of events is bound to be influenced to some extent by my political biases. But I have tried to keep these to the minimum, or at the very least to make them explicit when they do occur. This is all the more necessary because in Nigeria extremely violent and sometimes disgraceful deeds were perpetrated. Ordinary men – in some cases really good men – were either responsible or condoned what happened, although apologists of both the Federal and the Biafran sides in the recent civil war have all too often tried to discredit the motives of the other side, to ascribe to simple human wickedness what need not be so explained.

Personally I am inclined to feel that the somewhat intangible political goals of the perpetrators of both of Nigeria's military coups and of the leaders of both sides in the subsequent civil war did not justify the human cost, and this is the message of Soyinka's poem, an extract of which is quoted above. But that unfortunately does not help me – or anyone else – to understand how politics works in this imperfect world. Above all it does not help us to understand how intelligent and honourable men like Nzeogwu, Ifeajuna, Ironsi, Hassan Katsina, Akahan, Gowon or Ojukwu acted like they did or took the decisions they did. What were the specific social and organisational pressures to which they were exposed, and how did they react to them?

In some respects the Nigerian officers of this story are like the heroes of Greek tragedy. Their *hubris* in entering politics so violently brought the wrath of the gods upon them – unlocking further terrible conflicts over which they could have little control, and in which so many of them were destroyed. As Max Weber put it, 'whosoever contracts with violent means for whatever ends – and every politician does – is exposed to its specific consequences'.[1]

Weber's stricture was not upon the use of violence as such, but on the *irresponsible* use of violence for ends – however desirable in themselves – without calculation of the specific consequences. Yet the consequences of political actions are hard to predict, especially for persons with a less than adequate grasp of the institutional structure or of the likely reactions of other persons and groups to their own actions. The warning seems to be of particular relevance to the officers and men who staged the two military coups of 1966. But for those who led Nigeria into the civil war it is less clear-cut. Given the political situation after the July 1966 coup and the nature of their commitments, it was difficult for either Gowon or Ojukwu and their advisers to avoid a recourse to force in order to resolve the conflict between the Federal and Eastern Region governments – except, I suppose, by casting aside the assumptions and constraints of an institutional system in which authority in both army and government was based on the legitimate control of the means of violence.[2]

I owe an enormous debt to all my friends and acquaintances in the Nigerian Army – dead and alive – and hope I have done them justice, though for obvious reasons I cannot mention them all by name here. The Nigerian Army of which I have written, of course differs quite markedly from the army now, because of five years of military government, the civil war, heavy casualties among previously serving officers and the rapid expansion in the number of men under arms.

The book was first written as a Ph.D. dissertation for the University of Chicago. I am grateful to members and fellows of the Committee for Comparative Study of New Nations, the Center for Social Organisation Studies and the Committee on African Studies at Chicago for their help; and to colleagues at Ahmadu Bello and Manchester Universities. The topic was

[1] In his essay on 'Politics as a vocation', *From Max Weber: essays in sociology*, H. H. Gerth and C. Wright Mills (eds.) (London: Routledge and Kegan Paul, 1948).
[2] My own preference, but not one that one could expect the army leaders to endorse!

suggested to me by Morris Janowitz, who has encouraged – and sometimes cajoled – me with considerable persistence over the past four years and to whom I am particularly grateful for assistance. Suggestions and encouragement were given at various stages by Glenys Luckham, Keith Panter-Brick, Chester Hunt, Brian Chapman, Dan Aronson, Mahmud Tukur, Ibrahim Tahir, Sam Richardson, Alan Milner, James O'Connell, John Ballard, John de St. Jorre, Michael Wolfers, John Colas, Billy Dudley, Martin Dent, Norman Miners, Francis Idachaba, Tony Kirk-Greene and J. Carnochie (the last six named have all assisted me, among other things, in ascertaining the regional/ethnic origins of the Nigerian Army Officers). Different versions of the manuscript have been read by Morris Janowitz, Philip Foster, Donald Levine, Billy Dudley, Sammy Finer, John Dunn and Dennis Austin, and I have benefited from their comments and suggestions for improvement. I am especially grateful to Dennis Austin for going carefully through my final draft and clearing up many inelegancies of style and presentation. Thanks are also due to Mrs L. Gissop, Mrs Lucille McGill and Mrs Pat John, who typed successive versions of the manuscript.

ROBIN LUCKHAM

Legon, Ghana
May 1971

Location of main military installations in Nigeria, January 1966

1	HQ Nigerian Army, HQ Nigerian Navy, Lagos Garrison Organisation, Federal Guard	Lagos
2	2nd Brigade HQ	Apapa
3	2nd Battalion	Ikeja
4	2nd Recce Squadron (Armoured Cars)	Abeokuta
	2nd Field Squadron (Engineers)	
5	1st Battalion	Enugu
6	4th Battalion	Ibadan
7	HQ Nigerian Air Force, Nigerian Defence Academy, Nigerian Military Training College, 1st Brigade HQ, 3rd Battalion, 1st Recce Squadron (Armoured Cars), 1st Field Squadron (Engineers)	Kaduna
8	Depot (Training)	Zaria
9	5th Battalion	Kano

INTRODUCTION

A STATEMENT OF THE PROBLEM

The colonial government in Nigeria created a military organisation in Nigeria which was modelled on the British army in organisational format and professional training. Yet on 15 January 1966, less than six years after Independence, a small group of army officers carried out a military coup against the civilian regime, violating the Sandhurst formula of the political neutrality of the military. What is more, the army then began to fragment and discipline to break down under pressure from the primordialisms of tribe and region. In July 1966, a conflict broke out which aligned officers of different regions and ethnic groups against each other and had the undertones of a populistic revolt of junior officers and NCOs against the high command. Many officers and men were killed in an outburst of mass behaviour within the military organisation itself. Army and nation then split into hostile parts, leading to the secession of Biafra at the end of May 1967 and to the civil war in July 1967.

These are the historical events examined in this book. They are of interest not only in their own right, but also because they raise a number of more general issues of sociological enquiry.

First there are problems connected with the transfer of institutions from one socio–political context to another – battalions, regulation boots and beer in the mess on Saturdays in countries where these never existed before. The concept of institutional transfer is notoriously vague; and there are still remarkably few good descriptions of how new organisations and procedures actually become established in the newly independent states. It is hoped that a case study in depth will help to suggest a number of the variables which are relevant for the comparative analysis of an immeasurably difficult process.

It might for instance seem as if the apparently chaotic train of events in Nigeria confirms the contention that since there is such a wide divergence between the organisational models and reality in Africa such models have very little meaning, if any at all.[1] The implications one might draw from this

---

[1] For example A. R. Zolberg, 'The structure of political conflict in the new states of Tropical Africa', *American Political Science Review*, LXII, 1 (1968), argues 'constitutional arrangements' have 'had little reality beyond their physical existence as a set of written symbols deposited in a government archive'; 'in the civil service the usual bureaucratic norms are so rare that it is perhaps better to speak of government employees as a categoric group'; trade unions 'are

I

kind of radical scepticism about whether institutions or modes of organisation are in fact genuinely transplanted are of two kinds. First, one could stress that modern African states are all process and no structure, a kaleidoscope of unrelated events: that they can tolerate a degree of flux, chaos and violence which might seem catastrophic anywhere else, because nothing that goes on in the government or in the so-called 'modern' sector is all that important anyway. The second implication that might be drawn, therefore, is that it is the non-modern or 'traditional' institutions of these states which control most of the important allocations;[1] that shape political alliances; that determine recruitment into the elite; and are the main influence on patterns of action in modern organisational contexts, in so far as one can speak of patterns at all. The *reductio ad absurdum* of this would be the view held by some social scientists that patterns of action in the recently transferred institutions are distorted to such an extent that it is more meaningful to study the behaviour of the new politicians, civil servants, army officers and businessmen in the light of childrearing patterns and the social values of the traditional societies from which they emerge than in terms of the occupational roles they have learned or the structural contexts within which these roles are played.[2]

Both types of approach have their merits. To emphasise process rather than structure is a useful corrective to some of the less critical analyses that have been made of written constitutions, formal party structures and bureaucratic organisation charts. It takes into account the influence of rapidly changing and sometimes unique definitions of the situation on events. And it draws attention to the unplanned or anomic aspects of political behaviour, which are of clear importance in explaining the breakdown in authority in the army and in political life in Nigeria from May to October 1966. Again – though the distinction between traditional and modern institutions in present-day Africa is a very elusive and confusing one – there is little doubt that behaviour in modern organisational contexts is shaped in a number of ways by traditional residues from the wider social environment. In the Nigerian Army, for instance, there were differing attitudes of the main ethnic groups to military recruitment; and there were the patron–client relations between officers and NCOs developed on paradigms from status contexts external to the army.

The main thrust of argument in this book, however, will be that military institutions even in new states which faced a fundamental threat to their

---

more by way of a congeries of urban employed and unemployed intermittently mobilised for a street demonstration'; and the army 'which far from being a model of hierarchical organisation, tends to be an assemblage of armed men who may or may not obey their officers'.

[1] Zolberg, 'The structure of political conflict'.

[2] A good example is the fascinating book on Burmese bureaucrats and politicians by L. W. Pye, *Politics, personality and nation-building* (New Haven, Conn.: Yale University Press, 1962).

authority and existence, as in Nigeria, can be seen to have a structure, pattern and vitality of their own. Chester Barnard wrote that the significant fact about authority in all organisations is the extent to which it is ineffective in specific instances.[1] It would be premature, therefore, to allow the revolts and apparent chaos in the Nigerian Army during 1966 to lead us to the conclusion that it was in any sense a 'non-organisation', or totally ineffective in all situations.

On the contrary, indeed, the organisational model of a professional military is crucial to the understanding both of the Nigerian military revolts and of the army's role in politics. The erosion of discipline and the outbursts of collective revolt can themselves be seen as arising from strains that are inherent to varying degrees in most modern military organisations. The bitter hostility between ethnic and regional groups in the army, it will be argued, had organisational roots to the extent that primordial identities of this kind were used to symbolise cleavages between the ranks in the army hierarchy. From one point of view, then, it may still be possible to talk of 'success' as well as 'failure' in the transfer of institutions. Even when discipline was most seriously challenged during the coup of July 1966 the fictions of military status were sedulously maintained; so that after the coup it was possible for authority to be routinised back along the normal channels of command within a matter of months.

The criteria of 'success', however, are ambiguous: the creation of a British-style military organisation also had a number of undesirable latent functions or consequences. The somewhat rigid traditions of discipline learned from the British, for example, made it less easy to cope realistically with tensions between the ranks. The political doctrines of the Majors who started the January 1966 coup had clear affinities with the anti-political outlook of British officers; and some of the military leaders' inflexibility when in power themselves also may have come partly from the same source.

A cogent reason why the transfer of institutions did not have the expected results was that the replacement of the British by Nigerians in the officer corps had to be effected in haste because of the political priorities of Independence. There is little doubt that Nigerian officers at Sandhurst, Mons, Fort Benning, Quetta or the Staff College, Camberley, learned their jobs well and acquired all the correct social rituals to accompany them. But they returned to play their newly acquired role in an army the social structure of which had been distorted. For the normal relations of command and control were undermined because there was little difference in age and experience between officers at upper and lower levels of the hierarchy; and career expectations had to be adjusted to a situation in which promotions were alternately very fast

---

[1] C. L. Barnard, *The functions of the executive* (Cambridge, Mass.: Harvard University Press, 1938), Chapter XII.

and then very slow,[1] in which mobility from posting to posting was very rapid and organised career lines difficult to establish. It was the pace at which military institutions were transferred and the structure of the situation in which this took place, rather than the failure of African officers to internalise their roles, or the lack of vitality of modern organisations in new contexts, which were largely responsible (it will be argued) for the apparent breakdown of military institutions which took place in Nigeria in 1966.

A second set of general issues that this book may help to clarify concern the models which are or are not appropriate for the analysis of civil–military relations in new nations. There are two somewhat divergent traditions in the analysis of civil–military relations upon which one can draw, the first of which tends to emphasise the political environment in which the military operates and the second the organisational and professional characteristics of the military itself.

As an exponent of the first view one may take Finer who in *The man on horseback* suggested that the level of military intervention in a nation is negatively related to the 'level of political culture' or the degree of public attachment to civil institutions.[2] The latter is a *parameter* of military intervention in that the constraints *against* military rule are stronger in countries of 'mature' or 'developed' political culture. And it is also a *cause* of intervention in that a high degree of conflict over basic values in a society tends to bring in the military as a strategically placed arbiter in the area of social dissensus. The argument is related to the view already examined that structures are so weak in countries of low or minimal political culture and boundaries so poorly maintained that military organisations themselves are shaped and permeated by the political environment; caught up in uncontrollable social processes, they are unable to maintain either their structural integrity or their capacity for independent action.

There are a number of limitations inherent in this kind of approach. For instance, a high level 'political culture' as defined by Finer includes a complex of different but interrelated dimensions including publicly accepted procedures for the transfer of power, legitimacy for the holders of public office, and the existence of large and well mobilised private associations. These ought to be – and in fact are – capable of independent variation.

Secondly, there is the implication of a developmental sequence from a high degree of military intervention at lower levels of political culture to

---

[1] The highest positions in the hierarchy were not completely filled by Nigerians until 1965, so that promotions had only just started to slow up: nonetheless, the *expectations* of most officers in 1966 were of very slow promotions indeed in the future.

[2] S. E. Finer, *The man on horseback* (London: Pall Mall Press, 1962). Although the main thrust of Finer's argument concerns the importance of the civil culture as a determinant, he does bring other variables into his analysis.

civilian control at the higher levels. But the range of variation in political culture that exists between countries in which military intervention has taken place is extremely wide: there is a world of difference, for example, between countries with relatively powerful civilian institutions such as Argentina and Greece, and those where public attachment to such institutions is relatively feeble such as the Congo and the Dominican Republic. It may be said, moreover, that the greater strength of civil institutions in the former type of country has itself been a factor which tends to *widen* the extent of military intervention, because the army has only been able to obtain the kind of political influence it has desired by smashing down the powerful institutions that oppose it.

Thirdly – and most important here – any close empirical examination of civil–military relations in the case of any specific country will reveal an *interaction* of political and organisational or professional variables. To be sure, in the Nigerian context, it will be shown that conditions for military intervention were provided by the weakening in legitimacy of the civilian authorities during the first years of Independence. It is also true that the changing political context after the army assumed power provided the necessary conditions for the activation of regional and ethnic ties in the military. But it was not a sufficient condition. For one might have expected the military to have been insulated from the currents of mass behaviour by virtue of its tightly organised normative framework. One needed to know, therefore, at the very least, why organisational controls were not effective against environmental pressures. Was it simply because the army was a disorganised assemblage of armed men without discipline in the first place? Or can one specify the problem in terms of more explicit organisational and professional factors of the kind suggested by Janowitz and Huntington in their extensive theoretical statements on the military?[1]

The second main approach to civil–military relations emphasises the importance of the military profession and the types of organisation with which it surrounds itself. In *The soldier and the state* Huntington suggests that civilian supremacy over the military may be assured in one of two ways: either by 'subjective control', the permeation of the military by civilian values and interests; or by 'objective control' in which the officer corps is disciplined by its own professionalism and corporate commitment to the military organisation. His argument that an adequate professionalism secures civilian supremacy, however, as Finer points out, has shaky empirical foundations. Professionalism may actually lead to direct confrontation with

[1] S. P. Huntington, *The soldier and the state* (Cambridge, Mass.: Harvard University Press, 1967) and M. Janowitz, *The military in the political development of new nations* (Chicago: University of Chicago Press, 1964).

civil institutions as in the Weimar Republic in Germany, Japan between the two World Wars and in Turkey. In Nigeria, the Majors who effected the coup of January 1966 clearly belonged to the professional elite in the officer corps, most of them having alternated between training and staff appointments. Similarly, a thorough permeation of the army by civilian society (or different sections thereof) may pull it into politics as the ally of different political groups or ethnic factions, as in Syria. In Nigeria the opening of ethnic and regional cleavages in the army during 1966 reduced the latter's control over events but it did not end military rule.

Huntington's approach is capable of reformulation. Professionalism, it can be argued, provides a distinctive contribution to the civil–military balance, though it cannot be assumed in advance that the outcome will be civilian control. One must also recognise that there may be more than one thread of military doctrine both as between different armies and within the same military organisation itself. Janowitz, for example, suggests that profession and career lines in the armies of new nations may develop strong political motivations such as nationalism, anti-communalism and 'the politics of wanting to be above politics'.[1] These motivations are sharply at variance with the more narrow professionalism of Huntington's formulations, and are of the kind which led to military expansionism among the Majors of January in Nigeria.[2]

Huntington also tends to regard professionalism as being all of a piece with the social cohesion of the officer corps to which it is related, but these strands should be disentangled. The tragedy of the Nigerian conflict was that solidarity was highly *valued* but not easily *maintained*, brotherhood being replaced in the two coups of 1966 by suspicion and fratricide. Doctrine can be taught in military academies like Sandhurst and is fairly readily transferable from one set of military institutions to another. Cohesion is a more difficult quality to assure. It depends to a larger extent on the social and political environment in which institutions are transplanted; or on *how* the transfer is effected; and on the complex interplay of structural variables like organisational format, status relations, discipline and career lines. Cohesion, as Janowitz points out, gives armies a greater self-steering capacity.[3] They are better equipped to follow consistent policies, to intervene under the 'legitimate' high command on the one hand, or to accept civilian supremacy if they so wish on the other. Lack of cohesion on the other hand tends to lead

---

[1] Janowitz, *The military in the political development of new nations*, pp. 63–7.
[2] See Chapter I and the discussion of the political outlook of Nigerian army officers in Chapter XII below.
[3] Janowitz, *The military in the political development of new nations*, pp. 67–74, and K. W. Deutsch, *The nerves of government* (New York: Free Press, 1966).

to unstable and fragmented involvement and the likelihood of counter-coups d'etat after the seizure of power, as in Nigeria.

The military role, then, is not the product of any single factor or set of factors. There is a complex interplay of changing pressures from the political and social environment; the professional doctrine and political ideas of the officer corps;[1] and the cohesion of the military, this in turn itself being determined by the interaction of a number of structural and environmental variables.

The multiplicity of factors that may be relevant, however, is confusing,[2] and it is useful to have a heuristic device to specify and fit together the variables and combinations of variables that are likely to be of interest. As an overall conceptual frame for the book, therefore, the Nigerian Army like other military organisations is taken to be a social system in its own right, with definable boundaries, across which transactions with its political and social environment take place.[3] This is intended as no more than a convenient shorthand to simplify thinking about the very complex relations between army, politics and society. By calling the army a system one need not be committed to anything ambitious or make pretensions to a holistic theory in which events and relationships fit all too neatly together with logically closed symmetry.[4] There are merely three basic and simple conditions to be satisfied, namely:

1. That there are structural elements or variables – the shape of the hierarchy, recruitment patterns, training, the age structure, and discipline – which are related to each other in a coherent way. In social science it is rarely possible to portray the relations and interactions of more than two or three

---

[1] The precise effects of professional doctrine and the political ideas of the officer corps are difficult to pin down and in any case are probably not as important in the Nigerian Army as in many other militaries. Thus our analysis boils itself down in the main to the interplay of environment and the organisational cohesion of the military (though the effect of political ideas is also discussed in Chapter XII below).

[2] Except perhaps in a multivariate statistical analysis, if suitable indicators for the relevant variables could be found, for in the study of a single case, like the Nigerian Army, it is impossible to isolate particular factors or combinations of factors to control for the effects of others. There are few good indicators of the organisational state of armies on a cross-national basis, so that multivariate analyses usually focus mainly on the effects of the social and political environment: see, for example, R. Putnam, 'Towards explaining military intervention in Latin America', *World Politics*, xix (October 1967), who found the extent of military intervention in Latin America to be negatively related to indicators of social mobilisation like education, literacy, etc. and positively related to economic development, controlling in each case for the other factor.

[3] For a very lucid discussion of the ideas of system and boundaries as used in social science, see D. Easton, *A framework for political analysis* (Englewood Cliffs, N. J.: Prentice Hall, 1965), especially Chapter V.

[4] Indeed, if we were to call the Nigerian Army a system, under such assumptions we would definitely be assuming one of the things we wish to demonstrate, namely that the organisational attributes of the army can be used to help understand the social and political behaviour of Nigerian soldiers.

variables at a time; or to set out an overview of 'the system', of the complete set of all relations and variables that make it up; nor will this be attempted here. Although some of the variables and relations between them must be functional to the maintenance of the system – in this case to the authoritativeness of military institutions – others may be entirely dysfunctional and yet others again combine benefits and disadvantages. There is no need to commit oneself to a functionalist position any further than this.[1]

2. The system should have roughly definable boundaries.[2] Those of a military organisation may seem to be a common sense social fact, they are the gates of the barracks or mess, the sartorial barrier that divides uniformed men in the street from those who are not. But the idea becomes more problematic when one discovers relatives trading from a soldier's quarters, or officers prepared as in Nigeria to kill their commanders in furtherance of purely political goals, which they have discussed with civilian friends. For the boundaries of social systems are hardly ever watertight, which makes it difficult to say in a precise manner where they end and something else begins.[3] Again, however, few of the generalisations one is likely to make will be so elegant as to require more than a crude approximation as to what their boundaries are and where they lie.

3. It should be possible to talk meaningfully of transactions or influence flowing across these boundaries to an environment and back. The nature and extent of these can be said to depend on four things. Firstly, on the internal state of the system itself: an unstable system like the Nigerian Army, as will be argued later, is more likely to succumb to external influences. Secondly, on the characteristics of the boundaries themselves; whether, for example, an organisation is permeable, like the majority of police forces, which are usually structurally decentralised and permit or require a lot of trafficking between individual policemen and complainants, criminals or politicians; or whether, like most armies – including the Nigerian – they possess a high degree of unity in format and do not put soldiers in day-to-day official contact with the citizenry.[4] Thirdly, on the nature and consequences of the actual transactions which take place, for example the bargaining between military leaders and

---

[1] Except to make the rather obvious point that functions must balance and in the long run prevail over dysfunctions, if one is to be able to continue to say the system exists.

[2] For an attempt by the author to develop a theory of civil–military relations around the notion of military organisations and their boundaries, see A. R. Luckham, 'A comparative typology of civil–military relations', *Government and Opposition*, VI, 1 (1971).

[3] For analytical purposes, boundaries may be defined as the tantological converse of systems: boundaries can be said to be established towards the point where the variables which one chooses to include in the system cease to be related to each other in a coherent and predictable way.

[4] See some of the implications of unity in format drawn for the Nigerian Army in Chapter III below.

politicians over military expenditures, patterns of recruitment into the army or the exchange of political ideas between officers and other members of the intelligentsia. Fourthly, on the state of the social and political environment itself, including both the long-standing social values of civil society (or societies in a plural nation like Nigeria) and the immediate political and social context. The latter, of course, is highly responsive to the political behaviour of the military itself, especially when the latter enters politics, as in Nigeria, and creates a direct feedback from its political acts upon its boundaries.[1]

There is, however, an extra complexity which may reduce the elegance of this overall framework of system/boundaries/transactions/environment. This is the time-scale of different transactions between organisation and environment – a time-scale which may vary considerably. One must distinguish very approximately between those transactions which build themselves – or their consequences – into the system itself and those which are a part of the immediate definition of the situation, the kaleidoscope of events that pass. For example, the pattern of recruitment into the Nigerian Army led to a concentration over the years of particular ethnic/regional groupings at certain levels of the hierarchy, a high concentration of Ibos towards the top and of Northerners towards the bottom. The military system was accordingly out of balance. But this was of relatively little practical consequence until shafts of illumination from the immediate political environment – the sequence of political events from 1964 to 1966 – brought into focus the ethnic and regional identities in the army, investing them with a political significance and potentiality for fratricidal conflict between the soldiers that they had not had before.[2]

This book, therefore, falls into three parts. In Part One, the two military coups of January and July 1966 are looked at in detail. They are a good starting point, because they illustrate the crisis of authority in the Nigerian Army in its most critical phases. The coups are described as unique historical events, but from this description we hope to convey a sense of how military norms and structures conditioned or influenced behaviour in the midst of rebellion, the points of strain around which revolt arose, how tribal and regional identities became enmeshed with organisational cleavages and how shifting political events transformed both organisational and primordial relations.

Part Two departs from these historical events. The time dimension is frozen to produce a synchronic picture of the structural or systemic conditions

---

[1] The idea of feedback in relation to social systems is also developed in Easton, *A framework of political analysis*, but is dealt with especially well in Deutsch, *The nerves of government*.
[2] See the detailed analysis in Chapter VIII below.

of the collapse of authority and boundaries in the Nigerian military. We do this by detailing the army's format and overall structural characteristics; the processes of socialisation and their effect on military and elite images; the nature of cohesion and cleavage based on organisational identities (peer group ties); the strains within the disciplinary system and the effects of the indigenisation of the officer corps; and the nature of the cleavages on tribal and regional lines emerging within the military establishment. Each of these in turn is related to the breakdown and survival of the military system. Chapter VIII on primordialism, with which Part Two ends, is central to the argument of the book, as it is here that it is shown how organisational strain and cleavage became linked with conflict on regional and ethnic lines, and how the pressures of the political and social environment were transmitted into the military itself.

Part Three describes the army's political environment and the pattern of civil–military relations which emerged from it. First an attempt is made to delineate some of the more enduring patterns of Nigerian politics under the civilian regime and after. Then we move to the evolution of civil–military relations under the civilians, and the specific political influences to which the military was subject. Next we examine the political performance of the army when in power and the pressures for the allocation of political values to which it became exposed as the country's ruling group; first under Major General Ironsi's brief regime from January to July 1966; and then during the aftermath of the coup of July 28–29 1966, the implications of the fragmentation of the army into two parts and the events leading to the civil war of 1967–70.

SOURCES AND METHODS

The study was begun in January 1967 while the writer was teaching in a university in Nigeria.[1] An attempt was made to obtain official clearance for it from the Ministry of Defence and the university authorities, but this was not given. It was therefore not possible to adopt the normal procedures of interviewing and data collection. In July 1967 the civil war against Biafra broke out, which increased security precautions and virtually cut off the writer from his observational sources until he left Nigeria in January 1968.

The most important sources of information, therefore, were freely obtainable documentary materials – newspapers, pamphlets, *Official Gazettes* and telephone directories. As a result of the events of 1966–7 both sides were anxious to discredit each other and made a very considerable amount of information public concerning the manner in which the two military coups of 1966 had occurred, the conduct of negotiations and so on. Some of this

---

[1] The writer was also in Nigeria in the same capacity from 1963 to 1965.

published material – like the Eastern Region pamphlet *January 15th: before and after*[1] and the verbatim report of the Aburi discussions between the military leaders in Ghana in January 1967 – is quite extraordinary in its detail. Much of it, however, is secondary rather than primary source material and might therefore be regarded with disfavour by the professional historian.[2] The fact that much of it was issued with polemic intent also serves to produce distortions and bias. Where possible, therefore, criteria of historical accuracy have been stringently applied, based both on the levels of specificity of the items included and on the extent to which they cross-check with other sources. For example, *January 15th: before and after* both accuses Lt Colonel Gowon in the most general and vaguely formulated terms of organising the coup of July 29 1966; and provides some very specific details as to the manner in which the coup was carried out by junior Northern officers. Much of the latter is also confirmed by independent sources and is acceptable by both kinds of criterion; but the allegations about Gowon seem to be substantiated neither in specificity and consistency of detail, nor by cross-checking.

Historical materials not only provide the facts about historical events, they are also a mine for various kinds of sociological information. First, there are large numbers of speeches, press conferences and personal interviews (e.g. those of the editor of the *Daily Times* with various of the Military Governors in 1966) which are an invaluable source for the personal opinions, political values and biographies of military figures; and for statements of their own perceptions of their role in events.

Secondly, the documentary materials are rich in symbolic content. In the period prior to army rule, for example, they played a very important role in diffusing stereotypes of ethnic groups and regions. The various documents put out by the two sides in the conflict after July 1966 also give some indication of the way in which the different groups in army and government came to perceive one another. On the other hand, the absence of serious information in the newspapers in the first twelve months of army rule in 1966, was one factor in the growth of rumours. For the latter sought both to supply the information that was not freely available and to reinterpret these fragments of fact in highly charged symbolic terms.

Thirdly, it was possible to develop indicators of the organisational characteristics of the military and of changes therein in the available documentation. From *Official Gazettes* and office and telephone directories supplemented by personal acquaintance with officers and linguistic analysis of officers' names, a comprehensive picture of the training, ethnic composition,

---

[1] *January 15th: before and after* (Enugu: Ministry of Information, Eastern Region, 1966).
[2] See the discussion by Gottschalk in L. Gottschalk *et al.*, *The use of personal documents in history and sociology* (New York: Social Science Research Council, 1945), pp. 35–47.

turnover, age structure of the officer corps and other like indicators of organisational variables could be built up.

These historical sources were supplemented by observational data obtained from informal association with army officers, drinking in the mess, attending military parades, chatting with student friends or other acquaintances of theirs, and so on. The writer also talked informally with former British officers who served in Nigeria and with expatriate journalists and academics who had some contact with the army. There were no interviews with officers, nor were they questioned directly on military or political matters, both because of the suspicions this would arouse and because of the ethical problems associated with the collection and use of such information. Nevertheless, association with Nigerian officers was extremely useful in building up a participant 'feel' for the working of military organisation and the beliefs and behavioural dispositions of the officers.

Serious problems arise, however, on the validity of the data obtained from observation.[1] It may be argued that some of the behaviour observed (e.g. the rules of behaviour before ladies in the mess and the prescribed rituals of deference to senior officers) can be said to be similar for information obtained by anthropologists from 'key informants' about the norms and customs of their communities in that it does not depend for its validity on the frequency with which it is observed, because of its essentially prescriptive character. Even then the problem arises as to how effectively institutionalised these official norms are; and one thus becomes interested in how often the official practice is observed, whether *in fact* officers behave like the gentlemen that key informants say they should be. Still more problematic are other types of behaviour which are not a part of the official scheme of values, for example, the informal relations between officers and NCOs of the same ethnic group. On the basis of observation, it is possible to suggest the way in which these relations may be shaped by traditional norms of reciprocity. But it is impossible to determine how general or well established a pattern this is without much more thoroughgoing observation than the writer was able to undertake, without having some means of reaching an assessment of the *frequency* of such transactions.

The diffuseness of both the observational and the historical materials of the study require that they both be carefully coordinated. Like the archaeologist, it is necessary to piece a whole set of fragments or snippets of data together. In these circumstances it is particularly useful to develop multiple indicators of sociological variables[2] and to use different fragments of both

---

[1] See the discussions of such problems in H. S. Becker, 'Problems of inference and proof in participant observation', *American Sociological Review*, XXIII, 6 (December 1956).

[2] E. J. Webb *et al.*, *Unobtrusive measures: non-reactive research in the social sciences* (Chicago: Rand McNally, 1966), Chapter I.

historical and observational data to support the same conclusions. A very good example of this is the chapter on peer groups[1] where an attempt is made to coordinate:

(*a*) historical data on the role of peer groups in the two military coups in 1966,

(*b*) statistical data from the Gazettes, etc., on common training and criss-crossing of careers of the coup participants,

(*c*) observation of the manner in which officers associate with their peers, go out drinking with them, chat about their friendships among their course-mates, and show deference towards their senior officers.

Both types of data, however, pose problems as to how particular historical sequences or observed behaviours are to be fitted into generalisations about the overall structure and functioning of military institutions. Examination of the historical record of the two coups, for instance, reveals the continuing effectiveness of certain military authority norms. But what one concludes from this is very much a matter of judgement. Did the violation of military authority in many other respects in the coup show that military authority norms were not adequately internalised and that those norms that continued to be effective were only trivial or only had lip service paid to them? Or that the retention of some of these norms was genuine and the violation of others derived from organisational dilemmas rather than inadequate socialisation? Similarly, one can recount all the solidarity rituals of mess life, the complex of social activities like riding, drinking, shooting, mess nights and the like. All of which clearly contribute to the solidarity of the officers – though it is by no means clear what all the relevant mechanisms are, nor how much such practices *in fact* develop cohesion in the officer corps.

Under these circumstances, a certain amount of interpretative understanding of events becomes an inevitable part of the analysis. Not that we should necessarily regret this. The detailed study of a single case generates a richness in the interpretation of events which is impossible to achieve in a cross-sectional or comparative study of the kind which keeps to the quantitative indicators of organisational characteristics. For not all the relevant factors are equally easily quantified. Both historical and field-observation methods attempt to describe a total social situation in all its complexity, rather than isolated variables out of context. Unique events are analysed in terms of a multiplicity of causes. Moreover, a case study of this kind will, it is hoped, uncover relations between variables that may be amenable to comparative analysis at some later stage.

The use of history in this kind of study requires interpretation in two directions. First, inference from particular historical events to social

---

[1] Chapter V below.

structures, as in Part Two, for instance, when the military coups are used as a point of departure for generalisation about peer grouping and the maintenance and breakdown of military authority. Secondly, from social regularities to the analysis of how particular events took place (as in Parts One and Three). There is an evident danger of circularity of explanation here, in that events which have been used to infer the operation of structural principles will seem to fall in place too easily when explained by the latter, or *vice versa*. This danger must be balanced against the gain in understanding both of the historical processes and of the social structure of the military, as well as the interaction between them.[1] It will be for the reader to judge how well the trap has been avoided by comparing the synchronic analysis in Part Two with the sequential account of the remaining chapters. One important safeguard is, of course, the use of observation to supplement the historical data when we seek to infer social structure, though it is impossible to avoid some degree of circularity in the explanation.

[1] For an interesting discussion of the use of history to account for structural change in social systems and an application of this to the Hausa–Fulani Emirate of Zaria, Nigeria, see M. G. Smith, *Government in Zazzau* (London: Oxford University Press for the International African Institute, 1960), especially the methodological discussion in Chapter VIII.

PART ONE

TWO MILITARY COUPS

CHAPTER I

JANUARY 1966: THE MAJORS' COUP

THE BACKGROUND[1]

During the years after Independence many army officers came to share the growing disillusion with the ruling political class which was common among bureaucratic and intellectual elites in Nigeria. Members of that political class were riven with bitter internal conflict about the division of material and political resources between the regions and the ruling groups that controlled them. They were venal and did not hesitate to use coercion to maintain themselves in office. The gleam or shine of legitimacy they had acquired by winning independence was fading quickly.

The politicians had also contributed in some degree to the politicisation of the army – though this was still not very intense as far as the majority of the officers were concerned until the coup of January 1966. The internal security operations in which the military was asked to play a part – most notably in pacifying the Tiv in 1960 and 1964, maintaining essential services during the 1964 general strike and policing the Western Region after the regional elections of October 1965 – made it quite clear to those soldiers who cared to think about it that the survival of the existing political order depended upon them. And President Azikiwe's attempt to ensure for himself the allegiance of the military during the constitutional crisis after the 1964 Federal general election – though it failed – created troublesome ambiguities about where the soldiers' legal and political obligations lay. The first known political intrigues within the army indeed occurred during that crisis when Lt Colonel Ojukwu and other Headquarters officers of like seniority are said to have canvassed their military colleagues about an army intervention.

The officers who actually made the January coup do not seem to have begun to talk of action until some time in August 1965, when Majors Ifeajuna and Okafor and Captain Oji and a small group of intellectuals living around Lagos and Ibadan met and agreed to approach a number of military colleagues they felt they could trust. By November 1965, the inner circle seems to have been complete, consisting of Majors Ifeajuna, Okafor, Chukuka, Nzeogwu,

---

[1] This serves merely to introduce this chapter. A more detailed account of political events before the January coup is to be found in Chapters IX and X below.

Anuforo, Ademoyega and Captain Oji.[1] Planning began in earnest. Major Ifeajuna assumed the main responsibility for coordinating operations in the south and Major Nzeogwu in the North. The latter subsequently recruited Major Onwuatuegwu and Captains Ude and Gbulie at Kaduna to help him organise operations in the North. It is not clear how long before the coup he took them into his confidence, though it is thought that Onwuatuegwu and Ude, his colleagues at the Nigerian Military Training College, were apprised some weeks beforehand. The conspirators' civilian friends dropped into the background and so far as one can tell played no further part in planning the coup.

It is said that one of the Majors' first moves was to make soundings among certain senior officers.[2] Few of these would commit themselves, though apparently one or two lt colonels promised their support if the Majors took the first initiative and did all the hatchet work. These soundings were most likely the source of the intelligence reports that are said to have reached the Ministry of Defence late in November 1965. They were passed onto the Prime Minister, who was inclined not to take them seriously, perhaps because Major General J. T. U. Aguiyi-Ironsi, the General Officer Commanding, played down their importance.[3] Consequently some of the conspirators remained in highly strategic posts – notably Ifeajuna as Brigade Major of the 2nd Brigade and Okafor as Officer Commanding the Federal Guard – from which they would certainly have been removed had the reports not been discounted.

One explanation may be that more than one conspiracy in the army was reported, and the authorities were waiting for the various groups of plotters to show their hand more clearly before moving against them. The army's own intelligence section, moreover, was very small and quite unsuited to the collection and evaluation of political intelligence.[4] The times were uncertain and reliable information hard to come by.

[1] These are the officers said by the Police Report on the coup to be the organisers. A shortened version of this report was prepared for publication, but was never published for political reasons. The draft of this chapter was written before reading it, but has not been altered, except for the addition of one or two bits of detail from the report.

[2] The source for this assertion and one or two others that follow is an interview with a senior Nigerian newspaper editor whose information is thought to be fairly reliable.

[3] Not necessarily for any sinister reason. Rumours were so rife that Ironsi could well have thought it was a matter of crying wolf. There are indications that Brigadier Maimalari, the commander of the 2nd Brigade, who was killed in the coup, took a similar line. Indeed, the latter is said to have chided Major Ifeajuna with plotting a coup, half in jest. It is quite possible he was one of the senior officers approached by the conspirators, and believed they would not go ahead after they had been discouraged by senior officers like himself.

[4] Being geared, on British lines, to the collection of the more traditional types of military and strategic information. In so far as political intelligence was collected at all, it was by the Special Branch of the Police, which did not have easy access to a corporate British-style officer corps. An interesting discussion of the importance of intelligence in a coup is to be found in E. N.

This situation was much exacerbated by the eruption of large-scale civilian violence in the West in the last months of 1965 after the region's blatantly rigged elections. Many of the soldiers and Federal police who were brought in to restore order sympathised quite openly with the Action Group against the ruling party of the region, the Nigerian National Democratic Party. Rumours grew and three or four different cliques of army officers were at one time or another suspected of plotting. One indication of the confusion that resulted is that a number of highly placed persons in the North thought at first that the coup was the handiwork of Brigadier Ademulegun, the Commander of the 1st Brigade at Kaduna, who was in fact one of the coup's most important victims. Extra encouragement to all this talk about army plots was given by a sequence of military coups elsewhere in Africa (in the Congo (Kinshasha) and Dahomey in November 1965, the Central African Republic on 1 January 1966 and the Upper Volta on 4 January 1966).

The soldiers were not the only ones to be tangled in this web of suspicion. The government was also receiving reports of a rumoured civil uprising planned in the Western Region for the middle or late January 1966. And various members of the ruling elite – in particular the premiers of the North and West, the Sardauna of Sokoto and Chief Akintola – were themselves suspected of planning some kind of a political *putsch*, put together from the following elements in varied combinations:[1] the removal of the GOC Major General Ironsi who was to be placed on indefinite leave and be replaced by a senior non-Ibo officer; massive deployment of troops in the Western Region to end the violence there; the arrest of the NNDP's main opponents in the West; and an externally stimulated uprising in minorities areas of the East, leading to a declaration of a state of emergency in that region by the Federal

Luttwak, *Coup d'état: a practical handbook* (London: Allen Lane. The Penguin Press, 1968), pp. 94–8.

[1] The booklet published by the Eastern Nigeria government after the events of 1966, *January 15th: before and after*, (Enugu: Ministry of Information, 1966), claims that an insurrection was to be started in the Niger Delta area, which would be the pretext for a declaration of a state of emergency in the Eastern Region; that a number of leading opponents of the regime in the Western Region were to be liquidated: that the Sardauna of Sokoto was to take over as prime minister: and that a number of the leading officers killed on 15 January (e.g. Brigadiers Maimalari and Ademulegun, and Lt Colonel Largema) were involved. There is no evidence to suppose that any of these propositions were true. Moreover, it hardly seems plausible that the Sardauna would find it necessary to resort to such tactics while able to control the political life of the Federation by more 'legitimate' means; or that highly professional military figures would allow themselves to be dragged into such intrigues. These allegations could be written off as merely *ex post facto* self-justification for the behaviour of the Eastern Region leaders after the coup of July 29 1966, were it not for the fact that rumours of this kind were definitely current in January 1966. See *West Africa* (London), 22 January 1966, and a series of reports in the *Guardian* (London) by the British journalist Patrick Keatley, who was in Lagos at the time (summarised in *Africa Research Bulletin* (Exeter), January 1966). Keatley was able to interview civilian friends of the conspirators who were clearly convinced of the existence of a 'Hausa–Fulani' plot. Nzeogwu's statements quoted elsewhere in this chapter also show that the Majors themselves also shared such beliefs.

government. Among the many people who shared in and propagated these collective beliefs were, as we shall see, the officers who staged the coup themselves.

THE COUP

It is likely that developments in the political arena were crucial in the timing of the coup, to take place in the early hours of 15 January 1966. The preference of some of the conspirators seems originally to have been for a later date which would have given them time to recruit additional associates and rehearse more thoroughly.[1] But in the end such considerations were disregarded for three reasons. First, in order to prevent any further information as to their intentions leaking out. And second, because of their suspicions about the purpose of discussions then taking place between the military and political leaders. These began soon after the arrival of the Sardauna of Sokoto back from Mecca on 13 January. On the 14th Chief Akintola, premier of the Western Region, had talks with him at Kaduna along with Lt Colonel Largema, the Commanding Officer of the 4th Battalion, Ibadan, in order to discuss the West's deteriorating security position. After this Lt Colonel Largema flew to Lagos for discussions at Headquarters, one purpose of which may have been to organise a larger and more effective military presence in the West to bring the disturbances there to a halt.

Thirdly, at that particular moment of time the command structure of the army was very vulnerable to attack. For two of the army's five battalion commanders were tied up in Lagos, Lt Colonel Largema and Lt Colonel Kurobo of the 3rd Battalion, Kaduna, who had followed the former down, arriving at Lagos in the early morning of 15 January. Another of the battalions temporarily lacked a commander because of changes in postings.[2] The commander of the Abeokuta Garrison, Lt Colonel Fajuyi was on leave in his home town. There were thus only five combat units of the Nigerian army under the immediate control of their designated commander, and most of these were considered by the Majors to be on their side or neutral: the Federal Guard, Lagos, was under the command of Major Okafor himself;

---

[1] Interview between Major Nzeogwu and Tai Solarin in *Nigerian Tribune* (Ibadan), 2 July 1967: 'in every military exercise you cannot be expected to succeed if you do not practice...Practice was therefore demanded from every centre of operation, but had the original date not been *advanced* and fixed for January 15th the necessary rehearsal throughout the country would have been meticulously carried out.' This conflicts with Nzeogwu's earlier assertions, just after the coup, to the effect that it was postponed a few days because of the Commonwealth Prime Ministers' Conference, taking place in Lagos up to 13 January. The latter statement, however, may have been made mainly for public relations purposes and in any case does not mean that the *original* plans for a coup were not made for some time later in 1966.

[2] The 1st at Enugu, which was to be taken over by Lt Colonel Ejoor from Lt Colonel Fajuyi, who had already left for his new posting at Abeokuta.

the 2nd Battalion at Ikeja and the 5th at Kano were in the hands of Lt Colonels Njoku and Ojukwu, whose friendly neutrality the conspirators – in the event rather rashly – counted on; and they may also have hoped for the neutrality or friendship of Majors Hassan Usman Katsina and Obienu, who controlled the 1st and 2nd Recce Squadrons at Kaduna and Abeokuta respectively, though it seems that the former at least did not know of the coup until he was recruited at gun-point by Major Nzeogwu on the morning of the 15th and the latter gave little positive support when the time came.

The conspirators in Lagos held a clandestine meeting at Major Ifeajuna's house on 14 January after a cocktail party given by Brigadier Maimalari, which most of them attended. They asked a number of junior officers to this meeting, invited them to join them and threatened them with death if they broke their confidence. They divided themselves into six or seven squads which were each assigned specific tasks such as the assassination of important military figures, the arrest and/or murder of the Prime Minister and other political personalities and the seizure of strategic key points like the Army and Police HQs, the Nigerian Broadcasting Corporation, the telephone exchange and the Nigerian External Telecommunications building. The troops involved in the south were to be drawn almost entirely from the Headquarters units – the 2nd Brigade HQ, Lagos Garrison Organisation and the Federal Guard at Dodan Barracks, supplemented by a small contingent from the Abeokuta Garrison led by Captain Nwobosi, a last-minute recruit to the coup. Significantly, they did not include the main fighting unit in the environs of Lagos, the 2nd Battalion, which was sixteen miles away from the capital at Ikeja.

Early in the morning of the 15th things were set in motion. After a rendezvous at the 2nd Brigade HQ, Apapa, at 2.00 a.m. the squads set out in private cars, army Mercedes and landrovers. Most of the strategic key points were quickly seized and the commander of the 2nd Brigade, Brigadier Maimalari, the Chief of Staff, Colonel Kuru Mohammed, the Adjutant General, Lt Colonel Pam, the Quartermaster General, Lt Colonel Unegbe and Lt Colonel Largema were speedily eliminated. The Federal Prime Minister, Sir Abubakar Tafawa Balewa, and the Minister of Finance, Chief Okotie-Eboh were kidnapped and eventually assassinated after the Majors had been forced to retreat from Lagos. Meanwhile, Captain Nwobosi's small detachment from Abeokuta moved into Ibadan and killed Chief Akintola before being forced to withdraw.

The conspirators in Lagos reassembled at the rendezvous at the Federal Guard officers mess at the Dodan Barracks, only to find that the rest of the army was by now being mobilised against them. For Major General Ironsi and a few of his senior officers had managed by one means or another to evade capture or assassination. Ironsi appeared at the Police HQ, pistol in hand, at 3.20 a.m., and ordered the troops on guard there to return to barracks because they were engaged on an 'unlawful operation'. He found his way up to Ikeja, where he was able to rally the 2nd Battalion to him with the help of Lt Colonel Njoku; and by the time one of the conspirators, Captain Oji, arrived there at 4.00 a.m. to reconnoitre, it was too late. Meanwhile fragments of the Federal Guard under Northern officers and NCOs broke loose from their commander, Major Okafor; and rampaged against Eastern officers and men supporting the coup. Lt Colonel Gowon, just back from a course in the UK, also escaped the assassination squads. He was able to get in touch with Ironsi and some Northern officers of the Federal Guard with their RSM, and to rally pockets of troops from all the various Lagos units around the legitimate command.[1]

The insurgents were eventually forced to abandon Lagos. Majors Okafor and Ifeajuna drove in the latter's car out onto the Abeokuta road. They took with them the Prime Minister, whom they murdered by the roadside. They were followed by a small group of the other conspirators who carried in their jeeps the bodies of the dead senior officers and Chief Okotie-Eboh, still alive who was led into the bush to be killed. Okafor and Ifeajuna decided to proceed independently to Enugu in the East. They did not arrive there until early afternoon and by that time it was too late to activate the 1st Battalion there or to assassinate the regional premier, Dr Okpara, if indeed that was their intention. Major Okonweze, the battalion second in command, an Ibo major who was not in the conspiracy, had received signals from Lagos to arrest Dr Okpara, but had become suspicious and did no more than to throw up a cordon round the latter's house, where he was entertaining Archbishop Makarios after the Commonwealth Prime Ministers' Conference. By the time Ifeajuna and Okafor arrived in Enugu Ironsi's signals had reached the battalion and their new Commanding Officer Lt Colonel Ejoor was on his way from Lagos to take over. There appears to have been some disagreement among the officers of the battalion about what they should do. Ifeajuna was permitted to have an interview with Dr Okpara after which he escaped to Ghana. The latter was arrested by two or three angry young officers at the airport after he had seen off Makarios but was released after only a few hours' detention.

By mid-morning of the 15th, the GOC was in complete control of Lagos and had been able to obtain assurances of support over the phone from the 1st, 4th and 5th Battalions at Enugu, Ibadan and Kano. At 2.30 p.m. the Nigerian Broadcasting Corporation announced the kidnapping of the Prime

---

[1] The activities of Gowon and the Federal Guard troops in turning the tide against the insurgents, are treated in somewhat more detail by M. J. Dent in his interesting book draft on the Nigerian crisis, parts of which the writer has had the privilege of reading.

Minister by 'a dissident section of the army', but stated that the remainder of the army had 'stayed loyal'.

Nevertheless Ironsi did not as yet control the whole army. For Major Nzeogwu, unlike his colleagues in the south, had been completely successful in Kaduna. He had recruited his main associates – Major Onwuatuegwu and Captain Ude – not very long before the coup actually took place, but he had also been able in his capacity as Chief Instructor, Nigerian Military Training College, to organise for some weeks previously a series of night exercises. These permitted him to move troops about at night without suspicion; and gave him control of soldiers from operational units, the 3rd Battalion, the 1st and 2nd Field Squadrons of the Nigerian Army Engineers and the 1st Field Battery, which he would not otherwise have had. After Exercise Damissa, as the last of these operations was called, had finished at about 1.30 a.m., Nzeogwu called a meeting of the officers taking part in the exercise, addressed them in patriotic terms and asked for their cooperation. He then assigned them tasks and set them in motion. Nzeogwu himself led a party to kill the Sardauna of Sokoto, the regional premier, while his subordinates were to eliminate Brigadier Ademulegun and Colonel Shodeinde, the commanders of the 1st Brigade and Nigerian Military Training College respectively;[1] to arrest politicians; and to seize strategic points. When these things had been done, the officers in charge of the 3rd Battalion[2] and the 1st Recce Squadron, the two largest operational military units in Kaduna, and members of the staff of the 1st Brigade[3] were quickly won over; Major Hassan Usman Katsina, the Officer Commanding the 1st Recce Squadron, was enlisted by Nzeogwu who appeared at his house and asked him at gun-point whose side he was on.[4] Other officers both in the military units and the Nigerian Air Force whose opposition was anticipated were placed under restriction.

At the Depot, Zaria, the second in command, Major Akagha, believed to be an associate of Nzeogwu's took command, the Commanding Officer,

---

[1] Colonel Shodeinde was also second in command (to an Indian brigadier) of the Nigerian Defence Academy.

[2] Major Okoro, the second in command, in the absence of the commander, Lt Colonel Kurobo.

[3] Captain Gbulie was apparently delegated the task of calling together Major Keshi, the Brigade Major, the staff captains and other officers shortly after the operation began in order to explain the position and ask for their cooperation.

[4] In the light of subsequent controversies, Nzeogwu's account at a press conference of how he recruited Hassan Katsina, is of interest: 'After the attack on the Premier's house on Saturday morning, I went to the home of Major Hassan. I had a gun in my hand. When I saw him standing outside I said "what side are you on. Are you with me or are you with them?" Major Hassan replied, "Don't bother, I'm on your side." ' *New Nigerian* (Kaduna), 20 January 1966. Major Hassan Katsina's own comments on the same occasion are: 'As you see I am still alive. I will be here for many years yet. I am proud to have a chance to help save my country. We respect each other. I have been able to help Major Nzeogwu with some of his problems during the past few days. I am his good friend and I am sure that he will now help me. We will work together for the betterment of our country.'

Lt Colonel Bassey, having escaped with the help of expatriate friends after receiving a warning that he was to be assassinated. It has been alleged that the Commanding Officer of the 5th Battalion at Kano, Lt Colonel Ojukwu, also pledged his support and took measures to secure the city as soon as news of the coup came through.[1] Even if this is true, however, this support was very much dependent on the course of political events. After the tide had turned in Lagos and both Ironsi and Gowon had spoken to him on the phone, he committed himself to the 'legitimate' command, as eventually did Major Akagha at Zaria.

Thus, fairly early on the 15th, Nzeogwu found himself isolated, controlling Kaduna alone. There was a somewhat confused period during which he threatened to march down to the south to complete the job his associates had left unfinished, made a somewhat disordered radio broadcast, locked up senior Northern civil servants and policemen and even threatened to kill one or two of them; he was persuaded later to release the civil servants and to set up an interim administration under Alhaji Ali Akilu, the head of the Northern civil service, whom he had earlier been threatening to kill. He then began to negotiate with Lagos, where Major General Ironsi was himself in process of taking over political power.

A COUP WITHIN A COUP

The Majors' coup, though it failed, created a vacuum in authority which had to be filled. Hurried consultations took place between Ironsi, two senior Northern People's Congress ministers, the Attorney General and the Deputy Inspector General of Police. These were followed by two meetings of the rump cabinet, one on the evening of the 15th and one the next day. At the first of these, Dr Orizu, President of the Senate who was acting for the President of the Republic, Dr Azikiwe, then away in London, was asked to appoint an acting prime minister, but refused, saying he was trying to get in touch with Azikiwe; in any case the cabinet was unable to agree on whom to appoint. At the second meeting Ironsi asked that power be handed over to the armed forces. The ministers were by now divided and demoralised, and they abdicated authority without too much argument. The constitution had contained a set of emergency provisions which might have enabled them to

---

[1] *Nigeria 1966* (Lagos: Federal Ministry of Information, 1967). This is not an impartial document and in reviewing it the editor of *West Africa* (London), 21 January 1967 and 18 February 1967, suggests that Ojukwu's actions may have been justified as a normal security precaution without his being privy to the coup. Yet the fact remains that he acted *before* Ironsi took control; that unlike Northern civil servants who cooperated with Nzeogwu he was not under duress; that he may (according to some Northern sources) have been in Kaduna in the early morning of the 15th; and that Gowon had to warn him quite strongly on the telephone to desist from supporting the dissidents.

deal with a situation like the one that had arisen by assuming extra powers and devolving some of them on the Commander in Chief.[1] But apparently Ironsi insisted he could only deal with the situation if he were given complete power and the constitution abrogated. In a late-night broadcast at 11.50 p.m. on the 16th, Dr Orizu announced the cabinet's decision to hand over power to the armed forces; and Ironsi then announced decrees setting up a Federal Military Government of which he was to be Head, with Regional Military Governors in each region.

There is some controversy about Major General Ironsi's motives for taking power. Some sources state or imply a pattern of conspiracy or wheels within wheels, namely that the GOC was privy to the coup beforehand; that he was not marked out by the conspirators for their assassination squads; that when he saw the Majors' coup was failing he decided either to make sure it was successful or to take advantage of a confused situation to seize power for himself; and finally that all the protestations of loyalty to the Federal government and consultations with the cabinet were a front to gain both time and legitimacy for his assumption of power.[2] This is almost certainly a distortion of the true picture. Ironsi probably did know something about the coup beforehand, though not necessarily any more than officers, like Brigadier Maimalari, who were killed in it. His sources of information were presumably officers like Lt Colonel Njoku, whose sympathies the Majors tried to secure, rather than the latter themselves. This may account for the speed with which he moved up to the 2nd Battalion at Ikeja on the early morning of the 15th. There is little evidence as to whether he favoured the coup to start with, though his actions at Police HQ and Ikeja do not seem to suggest he did.[3] And even if he did, he would clearly not have wanted the Majors to succeed completely with their plans, as this would have jeopardised his own control over the army.

Once the Majors' attempt had actually taken place, it is doubtful whether anything less than the complete seizure of power would have enabled Ironsi to regain control of the army. The revolt left the latter exposed to conflicting pressures which required firm leadership. On the one hand, many Northern troops were reluctant to accept orders. In Lagos they did so after persuasion from Lt Colonel Gowon, though it was a day or two before they would hand over Major Okafor, whom they held prisoner after his arrest and gave a

---

[1] *Constitution of the Federal Republic of Nigeria* (1963), Chapter V.

[2] This is the general picture which is conveyed by *Nigeria 1966*, as well as by M. J. Dent and Dr B. J. Dudley in their manuscripts on the crisis.

[3] It is significant that he began action to halt the coup *before* he could have known anything about the fate of the Prime Minister and other politicians. As we shall show in Chapter XI, he obviously thought it was time the regime was overthrown, but this did not mean he felt it was the army's job to do it, nor that he would have gone along with a coup organised by the methods, at the time and with the personnel that the Majors used.

beating.[1] In Ibadan the NCOs of the 4th Battalion refused to accept orders from Major Nzefili, an Ibo who took over after Largema's death. Even in Kaduna some of the soldiers became disorderly for a few hours, before Majors Nzeogwu, Hassan Katsina and Okoro between them restored order. On the other hand, there were many middle-ranking officers, who, though they knuckled under to threats or calls to discipline from Major General Ironsi after he had shown his hand, were said to have been sympathetic to the political objectives of the Majors. Among these were officers like Lt Colonels Ojukwu and Banjo, Majors Akagha, Keshi and Obienu, who probably reneged on earlier assurances to the Majors, mainly because the latter were not successful. Such men could only be expected to remain loyal if Ironsi showed that he was authoritative and that he would not hand power back to the politicians.

Finally, Major Nzeogwu would certainly not have surrendered willingly unless Ironsi had been able to give the assurance that there would be no return to the political *status quo ante*; and if he had not surrendered the General would have faced open conflict within an army whose discipline he could not be certain of. From all accounts, Ironsi was always strongly committed to the maintenance and enhancement of the army as an organisation – in one officer's words, 'the Federal Army is his pride and joy'.[2] Under normal conditions, this would have implied defining the boundaries of the army as an organisation, so as to minimise its political commitments, and thus its vulnerability to political interference. Paradoxically, the revolt of the junior officers necessitated quite the opposite, in other words a rapid expansion in the political role of the army in order to ensure its survival as an effective organisation.

Moreover, the General was in a very good position to dictate his own terms to the cabinet. He was the only person who could hope to reach a settlement with the insurgents still ensconced at Kaduna. The assassination of Northern and Western senior officers temporarily left virtually all the combat commands in the army in the hands of officers on whose cooperation in any clash with Northern ministers he could have counted. The operative control of the five battalions, the Depot, Zaria and the Federal Guard was in the hands of the southern officers, all but one of whom were of Ibo origin.[3] The strategically

---

[1] Details in Dent's manuscript.

[2] Quoted in the *Guardian* (London), 19 January 1966.

[3] The Depot, Zaria, under Major Akagha, its second in command after Lt Colonel Bassey had fled; the Federal Guard under an Ibo captain who had not followed Okafor; the 1st Battalion under Major Okonweze and Lt Colonel Ejoor (non-Ibo Mid-West), the latter being sent to take control on the 15th; the 2nd Battalion under Lt Colonel Njoku; the 3rd under Major Okoro (its CO Lt Colonel Kurobo, a non-Ibo Easterner, was in Lagos and then appointed CO of the Air Force); the 4th under Major Nzefili, until the appointment of Lt Colonel Akahan a few weeks later; and the 5th under Lt Colonel Ojukwu (shortly to be made Military Governor of the East). The only

placed 2nd Battalion at Ikeja was now under the control of two officers who had served with him in the Congo.[1] Without necessarily implying that he consciously used ethnic ties, Ironsi had an excellent power base from which which to stage his coup within a coup.

Following the announcement at midnight on 16 January that the Commander in Chief was taking over power, Major Nzeogwu offered his 'surrender' and negotiations with Ironsi began over the phone. As Nzeogwu said in a subsequent interview: 'I was being sensible. The last thing we desired was unnecessary loss of life. If I had stuck to my guns there would have been a civil war and as official head of the army he (Ironsi) would have split the loyalty of my men'.[2] At Kaduna he had direct control over only two combat units, the 3rd Battalion and the 1st Recce Squadron; even his control over these was precarious; and he was by now aware that Lt Colonel Ojukwu was no longer with him.[3] In a press conference at 1.00 p.m. on the 16th, Nzeogwu announced that he had reached agreement with Ironsi; and that he had received guarantees of safety and of freedom from legal prosecution for himself and his associates; and an assurance that 'the people whom we fought to remove will not be returned to office'.[4] On the 18th, he handed over to Major Hassan Usman Katsina, the newly appointed Military Governor of the North: and on the 19th he allowed himself to be taken into custody in Lagos by another Ibo officer, Lt Colonel Nwawo.

THE CONSPIRATORS

It is possible to distinguish five levels of direct or indirect complicity in the coup. First, it appears that Major Nzeogwu in the North and Major Ifeajuna in the south were the key planners and coordinators for their respective

Northerner with an operative command was Major Katsina of the 1st Recce Squadron, shortly to be appointed Military Governor of the North by Ironsi. Lt Colonel Gowon had not yet taken control of the 1st Battalion, Ikeja, which he was due to take over from Lt Colonel Njoku; and instead was asked by Ironsi to be his Chief of Staff (Army).

[1] Lt Colonel Njoku and Major Igboba, his second in command, who took over the battalion when the former was appointed by Ironsi to take over the 2nd Brigade soon after the coup.

[2] Interview with Nzeogwu by Dennis D. Ejindu in *Africa and the World*, III, 31 (May 1967). This interview was subsequently repudiated by Nzeogwu. There is every reason, however, to believe that the interview was authentic. Nzeogwu probably either felt it necessary to repudiate it or was compelled to do so by Lt Colonel Ojukwu, because (*a*) it contained some fairly strong criticism of his associates and an admission that tribal considerations may have crept in on the course of the operations in Lagos; and (*b*), in the interview he expressed himself strongly against the secession of the Eastern Region; a few weeks later, Nzeogwu was fighting in the secessionist army.

[3] It is said, for example, that on 15 January Kaduna was short of cash. Nzeogwu requested Ojukwu to send funds from Kano, but the latter procrastinated about doing so until after Nzeogwu's surrender.

[4] *New Nigerian* (Kaduna), 18 January 1966.

areas[1]. Secondly, there was a wider group of planners with some active and prior responsibility for the organisation of the coup and of subsequent operations, including Majors Nzeogwu and Onwuatuegwu at the Nigerian Military Training College, Kaduna, Major Ifeajuna, the Brigade Major at the 2nd Brigade HQ, Apapa, near Lagos, Major Okafor, the commander of the Federal Guard, Lagos, Majors Chukuka and Anuforo, both in staff positions at Army HQ, Lagos and Major Ademoyega and Captain Oji, also in Lagos.[2] In addition Captains Gbulie and Ude in Kaduna, Udeaja in Lagos and Nwobosi in Abeokuta helped to organise operations, though they were not brought into the picture until a matter of days (in Nwobosi's case only one day) before the coup took place. These officers might fit equally well into the third category, namely the active subordinates in the coup. Those who were subordinates also included some thirteen lieutenants and 2nd lieutenants, most of whom were not apprised of the coup until an hour or two before operations began.[3] Fourthly, there were five direct service officers from the technical wings who gave technical and logistic support. The spread of these officers amongst the ranks is summarised in Table 1.[4]

In addition, there was an outer circle of officers who were kept informed and were prepared to give a certain amount of tacit support without committing themselves to active involvement. In its nature such a group is hard to define. The version of events which sees them as a gigantic Ibo plot[5] would put all senior Ibo officers in this category, including Major General Ironsi himself. It is more likely, however, that the boundaries of this group were defined more in ideological than ethnic terms. Lt Colonel Ojukwu, an Ibo, and Lt Colonel Banjo – non-Ibo – who both appear to have belonged to

---

[1] Major Ifeajuna has written a draft of a book (not seen by this writer) which apparently denigrates Major Nzeogwu's claims to overall leadership, and suggests that the northern and southern sections of the conspiracy were each to determine their own tactical scheme of operation, though coordinating in timing and strategy.

[2] Chukuka was the Deputy Adjutant General II and Anuforo General Staff Officer II (Training). It has not been possible to ascertain the postings of Ademoyega or Oji, although it is believed that both were in one or other of the Lagos Headquarters organisations.

[3] According to Major Nzeogwu in the *New Nigerian* (Kaduna), 18 January 1966.

[4] There is a careful analysis of the January conspiratorial group in J. N. Colas, 'The social and career correlates of military intervention in Nigeria: a background study of the January 15th coup group', unpublished paper prepared for the Inter-University Seminar on Armed Forces and Society, October 1969, which did not reach the writer until this book was in final draft. Colas' figures differ slightly from those shown here for two reasons: first, he included names given in *January 15th: before and after* who cannot be traced to any officer list (presumably officers who had only just been commissioned in 1966 and still not gazetted); and secondly, he includes the names of four more officers not named either in *January 15th* nor in *Nigeria 1966*, who, according to his informal sources, were arrested after the coup. It is interesting that he mentions two Northerners, Captain Omananyi and Lieutenant A. S. Wali. There were, however, several mistaken arrests after the coup and the writer thinks it unlikely that either was involved, at least in the effective coup-making group, both from acquaintance and because if they were arrested it was only for a few days and they were back in their military postings (unlike the others) shortly after the coup.

[5] *The Nigerian situation: facts and background* (Zaria: Gaskiya Corporation, 1966).

TABLE I. *Distribution of ranks: January 1966 conspirators*

	Combat commissions	Direct commissions
Major	7	1
Captain	5	0
Lieutenant	3	4
2nd Lieutenant	10	0

Sources: January 15th: before and after (Enugu: Ministry of Information, Eastern Region, 1966) and *Nigeria 1966* (Lagos: Federal Ministry of Information, 1967).

it, had radical political views and are known to have openly expressed a desire for military intervention against the regime in the period before the coup.[1] Banjo, the Director of the Electrical and Mechanical Engineers, was arrested on suspicion of attempting to assassinate Ironsi three days after the coup. His actions were strange[2] and gave rise to the supposition that he was either an associate of the conspirators, or disgruntled at the predominance of Ibo officers in Ironsi's coup within a coup, or both. One or two other officers at the lieutenant colonel level, may also have been given information of what was to happen; though some appear to have used this to keep the army command or Major General Ironsi informed; others to keep out of the way when it came; and others to actually commit themselves to friendly support if the coup came off. Some other middle-ranking officers below lieutenant colonel may also have had some degree of complicity. Major Akagha of the Depot, Zaria, certainly did, and it is possible that the subsequent cooperation of middle-ranking officers in the Kaduna units such as Major Okoro, second in command of the Third Battalion, or Major Hassan Katsina, commander of the Recce Squadron, could have been partly sounded out beforehand and not wholly

[1] In an interview with the editor of the *New Nigerian* (Kaduna), 16 August 1967, Gowon states that during the election crisis of 1964 he met Banjo discussing politics with Ojukwu, both of them holding that the army should take over.

[2] It seems that in the confusion an attempt by Lt Colonel Banjo to obtain an audience with Ironsi may have been mistaken for an assassination attempt. Major General Gowon's account of Banjo's arrest in the interview with the editor of the *New Nigerian* in August 1967 is of some interest: 'I met Banjo on the 16th. He was arrested on the orders of Ibo officers. He denied completely any knowledge of the coup. True I had reservations that an officer of his calibre, with so much interest in politics, could be ignorant about it. I could not help recalling the 1964 episode. Anyhow as the Adjutant General I ordered his release. Even so, in the two days following the coup, Banjo was very fidgety. This may have been due to two factors. Either he did not get the place planned for him, if he knew about the plans, or he was simply upset because he did not know. However, three days after the coup Banjo came to the police headquarters, General Ironsi was there, Kurobo, and Anwunah and myself were there. So were several Ibo officers, Anwunah came and reported that Banjo had come armed to kill the General. As a result he was disarmed and put under arrest. Suspicion was, at that time, sufficient to lead to his arrest in order to avoid unsettling the situation further. Since he was not subsequently interrogated there was no opportunity to obtain the facts.'

obtained under duress. Major Obienu was believed by the Northern officers who staged the July coup to have been an accomplice; and it is certainly true that three Ferret scout cars from the 2nd Recce Squadron which he commanded joined the remnants of the conspirators on the Abeokuta road after they had retreated from Lagos, although they do not seem to have played a role in operations up to that point.

Members of the inner group are said to have been discussing the need for political intervention though not the specifics of it for about two years. The more senior conspirators had developed a number of linkages with one another as a result of their careers. Majors Nzeogwu, Chukuka, Anuforo, Onwuatuegwu and Captains Udeaja, Gbulie and Nwobosi overlapped each other at Sandhurst.[1] In addition, the postings of the more senior conspirators had intersected frequently between 1960 and 1966, during which time most members of the group spent a large part of their service in units in the North, especially the 5th Battalion (at Kaduna until 1965), the Nigerian Military Training College, Kaduna, and the Depot, Zaria.[2] Some of them had in addition served in proximity to each other in staff postings in Lagos.

It is interesting to note, moreover, that the distribution of responsibility in the active conspirational group was effected on traditional military lines. First, Majors Nzeogwu and Ifeajuna exceeded all of the others in seniority of promotion to major. The former had been in the senior year at Sandhurst[3] at the same time that those of his associates who had also been at the Royal Military Academy had been cadets in the junior year. The second layer of officers with a hand in the planning and responsibility for operations were at the level of junior major or captain. Tactical leadership at the platoon level fell, thirdly, to lieutenants and 2nd lieutenants. Officers who exceeded the Majors in seniority either did not take part in the coup at all or stayed in the background, open to approaches from the Majors, but unwilling to commit themselves at all until the coup had been effected.[4] (This too – as we will argue in detail in Chapter V – reflects a basic characteristic of military authority relations, namely the unwillingness of senior officers to cooperate *directly* with their juniors in any other capacity than that of superior: if the original impetus or initiative did not come from their own peers, they would not take part even though they might stand ready to legitimate it afterwards rather as Lt Colonel Gowon did in July 1966 or as General Ankrah did in

---

[1] See the tabulation of the Sandhurst training and career patterns of the conspirators in Chapter V, pp. 133 and 141.

[2] It is important to note that Zaria is only some fifty miles from Kaduna, and communication between officers in the two garrisons was easy.

[3] The senior year at Sandhurst has rights to privileges, command and deference over the junior year.

[4] Even the middle-ranking officers said to be neutral but friendly, like Majors Akagha, Okoro, Obienu and possibly Katsina, were senior to the Majors in promotion dates.

February 1966 in Ghana.) Even if their purpose, therefore, was to destroy the military command, the coup participants still kept up the normal command relationships between each other.

This is also reflected in the fact that Northern Other Ranks – except a number of Federal Guardsmen – accepted their officers' orders even when they were to kidnap the Prime Minister or to kill the Sardauna of Sokoto. As Major Nzeogwu put it:

On Saturday morning the other officers and men thought they were going out only on a night exercise. It was not until they were out in the bush that they were told the full details of the plan...Any man had the chance to drop out. More than that, they had bullets. They had been issued with bullets but I was unarmed. If they disagreed they could have shot me...most of the Other Ranks were Northerners but they followed...all the same...it was a truly Nigerian gathering. Only in the army do you get true Nigerianism.[1]

(He may, however, have been a little too sanguine in thinking that his soldiers understood and accepted the *political* implications of what they were doing as opposed to just following orders. Nor did he tell them that senior Northern officers in Lagos were to be killed.)

There was also anxiety among the conspirators to legitimise the coup in military terms, to reintegrate themselves afterwards into the hierarchy against which they had struck. This is shown in Nzeogwu's desire to reach a negotiated settlement with Ironsi and to avoid a military conflict, even if this meant he had to surrender himself for possible punishment.[2] On 17 January, before he had reached agreement with Ironsi, he was complaining:

I am anxious to hand over command to a superior officer, but none has appeared. We have let it be known that we will grant safe conduct to any high ranking officer who wishes to speak to us. We think that some staff officers are not passing on our messages to the Supreme Commander. We wanted to change the government for the benefit of everybody also. We were concerned with what was best for Nigeria. Our action made the Supreme Commander and he should recognize us.[3]

TACTICS AND STRATEGY OF THE COUP

The operation was both well planned and extraordinarily simple-minded in its ruthlessness. The basic idea was concisely expressed by Major Nzeogwu in a subsequent interview: 'We had a short list of people who were undesirable for the future progress of the country or who by their positions at the time had to be sacrificed for peace and stability.'[4] In the first such category came the premier of the North, the Sardauna of Sokoto, the Western Region

---

[1] *New Nigerian* (Kaduna), 18 January 1966.
[2] Similarly in Ifeajuna's wish to return from Ghana to face possible punishment.
[3] *New Nigerian* 18 January 1966.
[4] *Africa and the World*, III, 31 (May 1967).

premier, Chief Akintola, and possibly a number of officers with connections with the existing regime.

In the second category came virtually all those officers holding key staff or command appointments in the army. The list of officers killed included among others the two brigade commanders, Brigadiers Ademulegun and Maimalari, the Chief of Staff, Army Headquarters, Colonel Kuru Moham-med, the Adjutant General, Lt Colonel Pam, and the Quartermaster General, Lt Colonel Unegbe. At the battalion and unit commander level, the killing was in practice less inclusive, though it seems that the intention may have been to kill most officers at this level too. Of the five battalion commanders and four other unit commanders, only Lt Colonel Largema of the 4th Battalion, Ibadan, (who was shot in the corridor of his Lagos hotel) and Colonel Shodeinde, commander of the Nigerian Military Training College, were murdered. It seems that at least two other officers at this level were on the list, namely Lt Colonel Bassey of the Depot, Zaria and Lt Colonel Gowon, both of whom had lucky escapes.

Major Nzeogwu claimed afterwards that the intention was to kill Major General Ironsi and the premiers of the East and Mid-West, Chief Osadebay and Dr Okpara, as well. He blamed the failure to achieve a clean sweep of the command structure and to remove Major General Ironsi on his associates in the south, especially Major Ifeajuna.[1] There seems to have been some con-fusion amongst the conspirators themselves as to the specific targets to attack, for Ifeajuna has argued that the intention was for the conspirators in each major centre to decide themselves whom it would be necessary to eliminate.[2] The Police Report on the coup, indeed, suggests that the intention was to arrest the politicians in the first instance (unless they resisted), rather than to kill them; and that Nzeogwu was exceeding his instructions in hastening to kill the Sardauna of Sokoto in Kaduna in spite of the fact that he did not resist arrest. The Prime Minister and Minister of Finance (unlike the senior army commanders) were not killed until after the conspirators had been forced out of Lagos; and Chief Akintola was killed at Ibadan after firing a sub-machine gun at the party led by Captain Nwobosi which came to arrest him.

What was the object of such a ruthless *blitzkrieg* on all these major military and political figures? A look at a statement by Major Nzeogwu made in a British television interview will help:

We wanted to get rid of rotten and corrupt ministers, political parties, trades unions and the whole clumsy apparatus of the Federal system. We wanted to gun down all

[1] *Africa and the World*, III, 31 (May 1967).
[2] This is apparently his argument in the unpublished manuscript which he wrote on the coup, mentioned earlier.

the bigwigs on our way. This was the only way. We could not afford to let them live if this was to work. We got some but not all. General Ironsi was to have been shot. But we were not ruthless enough. As a result he and the other compromisers were able to supplant us.[1]

This statement suggests both tactical and strategic reasons for shooting the 'bigwigs'.

In tactical terms the important factor was that the conspirators were only a very small group, some thirty officers and 100 to 150 men in an army of over 500 officers and over 10,000 men. The effective infiltration of the group was confined to the Nigerian Military Training College, Kaduna, the Federal Guard, Lagos, and one or two officers and NCOs at the 2nd Brigade Head-quarters, Apapa, the Lagos Garrison Organisation and the Abeokuta garrison. The conspirators were thus clearly over-extended from the start. The deft timing of the coup, which caught the commanders of the majority of the battalions away from their posts, was still not enough to offset this dis-advantage.

In Kaduna Major Nzeogwu acted swiftly enough to obtain the benefit of surprise. But in Lagos and Abeokuta the situation was more complex. The Federal Guard – or those bits of it which would obey orders – and the various headquarters troops were simply too few to carry out the tasks required of them – to capture or kill key military and political figures, hold the Nigerian Broadcasting Corporation and Army and Police HQs, establish an effective presence in Lagos and neutralise potentially hostile military forces like the 2nd Battalion, only sixteen miles away in Ikeja. Their transport was inadequate. The assassination squads had to operate in private vehicles as well as army landrovers and staff cars. Some of the detachments posted to guard key points were left stranded without transport of their own and there are rather pathetic stories of soldiers having to catch buses home from their guard points when they finally heard that their leaders had deserted Lagos. The tiny detachment under Captain Nwobosi which left from Abeokuta to kill Chief Akintola had difficulty in scraping up any transport at all: in the end it managed to obtain a jeep and a three-ton truck but was soon forced to leave Ibadan because of the absence of support from the 4th Battalion there. The last-minute recruitment of most of the junior officers taking part was another disadvantage as it meant that they were inadequately briefed. Captain Nwobosi failed, for instance, to cut off the telephones at Ibadan because he did not realise that dismissing the Posts and Telegraphs workers would not in itself halt the operation of the automatic exchange. And the lieutenant originally detailed to kill Colonel Shodeinde at Kaduna failed to do so because he did not know where his house was. The complete failure to infiltrate the

[1] The interview is reprinted in the *Daily Telegraph* (London), 22 January 1966.

2nd Battalion at Ikeja, the 4th at Ibadan or the 1st at Enugu – the major operational units in the south – was probably the most crucial weakness of all.

In this situation there were tactical advantages in killing rather than capturing military and political leaders. To kill them meant that thinly spread military resources would not be tied up in guarding prisoners. There was then no possibility of the latter escaping to rally counter-coup forces. The ruthless elimination of all the major military and political figures would have utterly disrupted the lines of authority. The army, like a chicken which had been beheaded, might have been able to manage a few spasmodic movements, but would have been unable to take coordinated action to stop the seizure of power. It is significant that it was in the first instance the army leaders rather than the politicians who were to be killed. Such tactical arguments gain some cogency from the fact that Major General Ironsi and the one or two senior officers, who in the event escaped the conspirators' net, were able to organise effective counter-measures within a very few hours of the time that the Majors struck.

As a matter of *strategy*, the object was to bring down the whole edifice of political authority by attacking it at key points. In the Nigerian context, this implied the neutralisation of the most powerful political personages, especially the Sardauna of Sokoto and Chief Akintola. Even if one or two other strategic figures escaped, the authority of the old political order would have been destroyed. This could not have been reversed even though the coup itself failed: thus Nzeogwu was willing to take Ironsi's assumption of power as second best and to surrender to him.

This logic ultimately led to the assassination of the Federal Prime Minister, Sir Abubakar, after the conspirators had been forced to leave Lagos when it was taken over by the 'legal forces'. They were obviously not going to be able to seize power themselves. To hand the Prime Minister back or to surrender with him still alive would involve the risk that the civilian regime could re-establish itself; to kill him was one way of preventing this even though the Majors themselves did not get hold of the levers of power.

The subsequent bickering between Nzeogwu and his associates over the failure to achieve a clean sweep of the military and political leaders in the south may thus have arisen from differences in the interpretation of their strategy. It is evident from Nzeogwu's statement above that he envisaged a total killing, whereas his associates in the south were a bit more apprehensive of the consequences of a total destruction of the army high command and political leadership.

One interesting feature of the coup was the amount of violence and hostility towards constituted authority that was brought to the surface. Even if the killings were a tactical necessity – which is by no means certain in spite of what has just been said – some of them were carried out in a way that suggests either uncontrolled dislike of authority or simple animosity to the victims. At Kaduna, Major Nzeogwu is said to have riddled the Sardauna's body with bullets, fired at the women of the household with a machine gun as they ran and destroyed the house with mortar fire, though little of this was necessary. He was in such a state of excitement for some days after the coup, that he threatened to kill one or two of the senior Northerners he had in custody; he wanted Major Ifeajuna shot for escaping to Ghana and said he would march south to finish off the job his associates had left unfinished by not assassinating Dr Okpara and Chief Osadebay. Chief Akintola was shot after he had actually surrendered to Captain Nwobosi, apparently because the latter was angry that Akintola had earlier shot at him and wounded him with his sub-machine gun. Chief Akintola, the Sardauna, Brigadier Ademulegun, and Colonel Shodeinde, were all shot before members of their families; the Sardauna's senior wife and Ademulegun's wife were killed with them, whilst Shodeinde's wife was shot in the legs because she screamed. Nzeogwu and Onwuatuegwu were reportedly jointly responsible for the death of their commanding officer, Colonel Shodeinde (after a more junior officer had failed to kill him). Major Ifeajuna also shot his own commander, Brigadier Maimalari, after the latter had waved down his car to find out what was afoot (having earlier escaped from his house where Major Okafor had been sent to hunt him out). Ifeajuna had been Maimalari's Brigadier Major and was regarded by him as a friend, though relations between them are said to have taken on a degree of ambivalence in the months before the coup. The victims of the Lagos operation were tied up and put in the car boots of the assassination squads, though for what reason it is not clear. There are also stories that some of the victims – in particular Chief Okotie-Eboh – were beaten or tortured before their deaths, though these are not very well substantiated.[1]

At other times, however, there was a curious mixture of violence with the forms and courtesies of military life; as when Colonel Kuru Mohammed was granted permission by Major Anuforo to pray before his death; or when Lt Colonel Pam's protests were met by Anuforo and Chukuka with the statement that they had their orders to kill him; or when Captain Nwobosi told Chief Akintola he was 'for lawful arrest by the army on orders from HQ, 2nd Brigade'.

There is little doubt that murder of respected senior officers did much to turn the Northern NCOs and men in the Lagos units against the Majors to

---

[1] There were also reports of the torture and mutilation of the Prime Minister, Sir Abubakar, though these were most likely simply a part of the mythology that developed among Northerners afterwards.

the latters' immediate tactical disadvantage. It also set the stage, as will be shown in the next chapter, for the much bigger outburst of violence which occurred in the July 1966 coup.

POLITICAL MOTIVES

The Majors' strategy of carrying out a clean sweep of the political order suggests that they had a clearer, more definite sense of political purpose than the makers of most other West African military coups. There was also, however, as we suggest below, a sense in which the coup was a response to the direct pressure of civilian groups which sought to coopt and enlarge the role of the military.[1] These pressures from a disorganised civil arena provided officers of an expansionist political outlook with an appropriate occasion to intervene.

More than most officers in the Nigerian Army, the planners could justly be considered 'intellectuals', both in respect of their professional qualities and in regard to their wider interests. Majors Nzeogwu, Onwuatuegwu, Okafor and Chukuka all held training appointments at various times, either in the Nigerian Military Training College, Kaduna, the Depot, Zaria or the Nigerian Military School, Zaria. At the time of the coup, Nzeogwu was Chief Instructor at the NMTC and Onwuatuegwu the Chief Instructor of the Infantry Wing there. Two of the six combat-status officers in the army who held university degrees or equivalent were in the inner group of conspirators (Majors Ifeajuna and Ademoyega) and two provided tacit support (Lt Colonels Ojukwu and Banjo).[2] In addition all five direct-service commissioned officers playing a supporting role are believed to have had a degree or comparable professional qualifications.

It is possible to compare the leading figures in the coup with their peers by dividing the officer corps into annual entry cohorts of more or less equivalent seniority as they enter the army. (These cohorts are a device used to standardise officer entrants into groups of more or less equivalent seniority, taking into account their differing length of training and previous experience. The basis for assignation into cohorts is shown in Table 23. For Sandhurst-trained officers the year of their cohort corresponds roughly to the year they entered Sandhurst.) The Majors and Captains involved in the January 1966 coup all fall in the 1957 to 1961 cohorts; the Majors alone all within the 1957 to 1959

---

[1] Janowitz, *The military in the political development of new nations*, p. 16, makes a distinction between 'designed' and 'reactive' militarism, corresponding roughly to intervention by conspirators with a clear political purpose of their own on the one hand, and by those who merely respond to pressures from the civilian area on the other. What we are in effect saying here is that this dichotomy is too simple, as the January 1966 coup appears to have been a composite of both elements.
[2] Lt Colonel Banjo had received the equivalent of a university degree course at the Royal Military College of Science, Shrivenham, England.

cohorts. The Majors all had either university[1] or Sandhurst training, with one exception, Major Okafor, an ex-NCO who had received a short service training at Mons Officer Cadet School. All but one of the Captains were Sandhurst trained. The contrast in the training of the main conspirators with their peers is a marked one as will be clear from Table 2. Thus the conspirators included two out of the three graduates among the combat officers of the 1957–61 cohorts, a little under twenty per cent of the Sandhurst graduates but only two out of fifty of the short-service entry.[2] Seven out of the twenty-three officers entering Sandhurst (or a little under a third) in the years 1958 and 1959 played an active role in the coup.

TABLE 2. *Comparison of qualifications of January 1966 conspirators with their peer groups*

| Type of training | January 1966 | | Total |
	Participant	Non-participant	
Breakdown all types of training, 1957–61 cohorts			
Short service (ex-NCO)	1	20	21
Short service (cadet entry)	1	30	31
Sandhurst	7	31	38
Short service (graduate entry)	2	1	3
	11	82	93
Sandhurst and graduate versus short service, 1957–61			
Short service	2	50	
Sandhurst + graduates	9	32	
$\phi = 0.28$ X^2 significant at 0.01 level			
Sandhurst and graduate versus short service, 1957–9			
Short service	1	21	
Sandhurst + graduates	7	16	
$\phi = 0.36$ X^2 significant at 0.05 level			

Sources: as for Table 1, and also Federation of Nigeria, *Official Gazettes* (1960–5).

The January Majors and Captains therefore belonged to the elite of the officer corps. For only the best of each year's cadet entry went to Sandhurst; and the professional training given there was longer, more intensive and at a higher educational level than the short-service training at Mons Cadet School. By contrast, all thirteen junior officers who were subordinates in the coup (lieutenants and second lieutenants) were in later cohorts (1962 to 1964) and none had either a university degree or attended Sandhurst.

[1] University graduates were normally given three years' seniority and sent to short-service cadet school at Mons, it being assumed that their university background would make the more academic training given at Sandhurst redundant.
[2] Excluding the graduates.

In their careers, however, the conspirators were neither more nor less successful than their peers of equivalent training. Nzeogwu's promotion to major was held up for some months, his promotion through to that rank[1] being slower than that of any other officer entering Sandhurst the same year as he. Chukuka, Onwuatuegwu and Udeaja were all promoted slightly less fast than the median for their Sandhurst year – but only slightly so. Up to 1966 six officers of the 1957–9 cohorts had been picked out for staff training at the Staff College, Camberley or equivalent; but only one of these (Major Nzeogwu)[2] was in the January group. On the other hand, Anuforo's promotion was faster than all his Sandhurst course-mates. And Okafor's was higher than the median for the other ex-NCOs of his cohort.[3] These data do not therefore provide much basis for generalisation on the effect of career success or failure on the political motivations of the Majors as a group. It may be true in one or two purely individual cases that political interest widened as disappointment in careers increased. The frequency with which some of the Majors were posted to training units may here have a double meaning. For though such appointments normally went to officers of professional skill and promise, it is possible that they were also a way of keeping 'difficult' officers out of the way. It is said in particular that Nzeogwu was appointed to the Nigerian Military Training College both because of his undoubted talents as an officer and because it was felt he could not be fully trusted in an operative command.[4]

Speculation as to the relation between the personalities of the conspirators and their political activities is equally inconclusive. Ifeajuna is said to have been strong willed and not to have taken kindly to military authority, because he considered himself a cut above the average military type in education and intelligence. Early in his career he apparently disgraced himself by assaulting a British officer in a dispute over accomodation. Both Anuforo and Nzeogwu are also said by some of their acquaintances to have been aggressive. But this is not compatible with other reports of Nzeogwu's abstemiousness, his shyness with women and the pains he took to entertain his brother officers' children. Equally, a British course-mate of Ontwuatuegwu's at Sandhurst was of the opinion that he was the last person he would expect to stage a coup, because he was such a 'dull, parade-ground, goody-goody soldier'.

The civilian involvements and intellectual interests of the two most

---

[1] Both from lieutenant to captain and from captain to major.
[2] Who went to staff college in India or Pakistan.
[3] We omit Ifeajuna and Ademoyega because there are too few other graduates to compare them with in respect of promotion.
[4] According to one good source, this was Major General Welby-Everard's reason for having him posted there.

important conspirators, Nzeogwu and Ifeajuna were especially far-reaching. Nzeogwu, who was a product of Sandhurst, was widely read with a library which apparently included such writers as Mao Tse Tung and Marx as well as the usual military histories; he was both a socialist of sorts and an extremely devout Roman Catholic. Ifeajuna was a graduate of the University of Ibadan, where he had been a star athlete, and had wide contacts with radical intellectuals in the civil service and universities, including a number of Northerners. In the broader circle of tacit supporters, Lt Colonel Ojukwu is a graduate of Oxford University, had connections through his family with major figures in the NCNC and had also been a civil servant (a district officer in the Eastern Region) before joining the army; and Lt Colonel Banjo had contacts with the Action Group intellectuals in the Western Region, being brother-in-law and business associate of an influential Action Group lecturer at the University of Ibadan.

The conspirators had an explicit set of political objectives though it is difficult to reconstruct these adequately from the few public statements attributed to them, which were mostly made by Major Nzeogwu in his brief period of control at Kaduna. Their political code had points of similarity to Franz Fanon's analysis of revolutionary violence in the colonial and post-colonial situation, although the resemblance may be no more than accidental.[1] The political institutions which had emerged after the period of colonial rule were illegitimate and corrupt, and could only be destroyed by violent means: in Nzeogwu's words 'elections are always rigged. It is impossible to vote out a Nigerian Minister.'[2] In so doing they would be expressing both a radical popular will and their deep-seated shame in the existing state of affairs. A broadcast read over the Nigerian Broadcasting Corporation's transmitters on the early morning of the 15th announced that the military had taken over power 'to bring an end to gangsterism and disorder, corruption and despotism' and ended 'my compatriots, you will no longer be ashamed to be Nigerian'.[3] The violent elimination of the representatives of a corrupt moral and political order would create conditions in which a new and purified institutional structure could emerge. It was never made clear – except in terms of a few highly simplistic statements of value – what shape this reconstruction would take. Drastic measures would be taken against all kinds of corruption and decadence. The first broadcast made by Nzeogwu in the name of the 'Supreme Council of the Revolution of the Nigerian Armed Forces' during his brief period of ascendance in Kaduna stated that 'the aim of the Revolutionary Council is to establish a strong united and prosperous nation, free from

[1] F. Fanon, *The wretched of the earth* (New York: Grove Press, 1966).
[2] *New Nigerian* (Kaduna) 17 January 1966.
[3] *West Africa* (London), 22 January 1966.

corruption and internal strife' and proclaimed Extraordinary Orders of the Day, which decreed that: 'looting, arson, homosexuality, rape, embezzlement, bribery or corruption, obstruction of the revolution, sabotage, subversion, false alarms and assistance to foreign invaders are all offences punishable by the death sentence'.[1] Steps would be taken to eradicate 'tribalism and regionalism' and other sectional interests that might be obstacles to national unity. For the army was in power because it was the institution which most truly expressed the unity of the nation.

The standard military themes of nationalism, anti-tribalism and anti-corruption were commingled with a certain amount of poorly digested Marxism, deriving partly from left-wing civilian intellectuals among whom the group had contacts. A letter from Major Nzeogwu to Dr Tunji Otegbeye, the leader of the Nigerian Socialist Workers and Farmers Party, published in *Advance: The Nigerian Worker's Own Newspaper*, conveys some of the flavour of these attitudes. The letter was written at the outset of the civil war and deplores the fragmentation of the nation which has led up to the war:

I am writing to you at a momentous occasion in our country's history but with sadness at the turn of events in the political arena. Whilst the forces of progress are being knocked about by the whims of reactionary nationalism, I have hopes in the determined efforts of the progressive peoples of this country to forge a strong and united nation...The control of all information media by the local capitalists and national bourgeoisie, who manipulate feuding war lords, has sublimated the sins of national disintegration and a return to tribe...My sadness lies in the fact that our control of the information media is nil, our contact with the masses is apparently not real and our general efforts are academic not pragmatic. In our lethargy we shall be witnesses to the renting of our national fabric and the biting away of large chunks of our territory by monarchs of reaction and tribal mob leaders.[2]

So far as can be told, the Majors were to remain remarkably consistent in their political position throughout the political upheavals of 1966–7 in comparison to many other groups. The letter just quoted shows Nzeogwu opposed to the disintegration of Nigeria at the time of the Biafran secession in May 1967. Although he subsequently fought on the secessionist side, he was killed in strange circumstances, which indicated that he may have been defecting to the Federal army.[3] Major Ifeajuna and Lt Colonel Banjo supported Lt Colonel Ojukwu in the war only so long as this was consistent

[1] The full text of this broadcast is reprinted in S. K. Panter-Brick (ed.), *Nigerian politics and military rule: prelude to the civil war* (London: Athlone Press, University of London, 1970), pp. 184–6.

[2] The letter to Dr Tunji Otegbeye is dated 30 May 1967, and is reprinted in *Advance* (Lagos), 13–19 August 1967.

[3] Though it must be said that there is more than one version of his death, and it is impossible to be certain which is the correct one.

with their overall aim of destroying the power of the North and setting up a radical regime based on the south: hence Banjo's attempts to intrigue with Lt Colonel Ejoor and Chief Awolowo shortly after he had led the invasion of the Mid-West in August 1967; and the abortive plot by Banjo and Ifeajuna against Ojukwu's life, for which they were executed in September 1967.[1]

The political objectives of the coup must also be understood in the context of the prevailing balance of political power in January 1966. The coup was clearly aimed at destroying the political dominance of the North. Many army officers, like other groups of southern intellectuals, tended to attribute all of the political shortcomings of the regime to the Northern Peoples Congress's control of the political life of the Federation. The Western Region crisis of 1965 and the Federal government's failure to deal with it were (with justification) viewed as the outcome of the NPC's desire to maintain allies compliant to itself in the south. We have already pointed out that the Majors were among those who believed that the Sardauna of Sokoto and Chief Akintola were about to stage a political *putsch* of their own to remove or neutralise the Federal government (especially the NCNC element), manipulate key appointments in the army and police and use the military to crush any dissidence ensuing in the Eastern and Western Regions. As Major Nzeogwu stated it:

the public is still largely unaware of the fact that a gigantic military operation over the Western Region was to swoop down on that territory on January 17. The incident that is associated with January 15 today was to take place sometime later, that is the following month. When therefore the significance of the state of emergency due to be proclaimed on January 17 was made known to us, it became inevitable that the operation of January 15 must necessarily take place before the dawn of January 17.[2]

There is no evidence that anything more sinister than a routine increase in the military presence in the Western Region was being planned. But the existence of beliefs in such a plot is of importance both in accounting for the motives and behaviour of the conspirators and the later reactions of Ibo officers to subsequent events. They served to make a coherent, focused picture out of a confused and disturbing set of political phenomena – namely the weakness of civilian institutions, the rise in political conflict and the attempts of Northern politicians to expand their influence in the military establishment.[3] They served to justify the Majors' actions to the outside world. Finally, they may have helped to reduce whatever dissonance they felt between their own conduct in the coup and professional norms proscribing

---

[1] These events are described in more detail in Chapter XIII below.
[2] Interview with Tai Solarin in *Nigerian Tribune* (Ibadan), 2 July 1967.
[3] See Chapter X below.

interference in politics and disobedience to senior officers, still less their murder. It is significant that the killing of Brigadier Ademulegun tended to be justified in terms of his personal friendship with the Sardauna of Sokoto which earned him the contempt of a number of his subordinates, Nzeogwu among them; and that Brigadier Maimalari was suspect among other things for the role he had played as Commanding Officer of the 2nd Battalion during the Western Region crisis of 1962.

To what extent can it be said that the insurgent officers were coopted by external political groups? Were they hand in glove with the politicians of the United Progressive Grand Alliance which had lost the 1964 Federal election, as other commentators have alleged?[1] The evidence unfortunately is very threadbare. The Majors undoubtedly had a range of contacts among radical intellectuals in the universities and the civil service, with the Action Group and among members of the Zikist movement, a radical fringe of the NCNC; but none of these were established figures in the main parties of the UPGA opposition. Nevertheless, their political ideas were strongly influenced by their contacts among the intelligentsia, and the original idea for a coup also seems to have emerged during discussions with civilian friends, though these were aggrieved at not being let into the Majors' later plans.[2] They also claimed that they intended to install hand-picked politicians in power after the coup, rather than governing themselves.[3]

It is unlikely, however, that civilian political groups had anything to do with the specifics of the coup, with its organisation and timing. Military intelligence was much preoccupied in January 1966 with rumours of an impending civilian uprising in the Western Region. There is indeed some suggestion that the Action Group may have been organising the same kind of conspiracy against the Federal government as it allegedly planned in September 1962, though there is at present no evidence to connect this with the January coup.[4] There is little reason to suppose the Majors would have

[1] Both M. J. Dent and B. J. Dudley make much of their contacts with politicians of the NCNC or Ibo State Union, like Dr Okpara, though their evidence is highly circumstantial.

[2] J. P. Clark, *Casualties* (London: Longman, 1970), p. 57. He and his fellow-poet Christopher Okigbo brought Ifeajuna back from Ghana. Wole Soyinka, the playwright and lecturer, Chike Obi the mathematician and S. G. Ikoku and Dr Tunji Otegbeye, the radical politicians, were other friends of the Majors.

[3] In his *Nigerian Tribune* interview with Solarin, Nzeogwu claimed the intention was to install Chief Awolowo as executive president. At his press conferences just after the coup in January 1966, he also stated quite explicitly that the intention had been to hand over to 'honest' politicians.

[4] M. J. Dent, 'The military and politics: a study of the relations between the army and the political process in Nigeria', unpublished seminar paper (London: Institute of Commonwealth Studies, 1967). A revised version of this paper has been published in K. Kirkwood (ed.), *African Affairs, Number Three*, St Anthony's Papers no. 21 (Oxford: Oxford University Press, 1969). Dent suggests that it is significant that S. G. Ikoku was arrested on the night of the coup attempting to smuggle arms over the Dahomey border into the Western Region; and that Major Ifeajuna

wished to put their security in pawn by *direct* coordination with the radical politicians. The coup itself was organised on military lines. And its timing was dictated by information of army movements to which civilian groups had no access at all.

THE SPECTRE OF TRIBALISM

It is striking that almost all of the conspirators came from the same ethnic group, the Ibos. All of the seven Majors but one (Major Ademoyega, a Yoruba) were Ibo; and nineteen of the other twenty-three active participants were also of the same tribe. None of the group were Northerners,[1] although some Northern Other Ranks had taken part under orders.

Moreover the pattern of killings seems selective in regional and tribal terms. Both of the regional premiers to survive – Osadebay of the Mid-West and Okpara of the East – were Ibos. The small group of senior Northern officers was virtually obliterated whilst almost all senior officers of Mid-West and Eastern origin – more than two-thirds of whom were Ibo – survived. Table 3 analyses the impact of the killings on the officers at rank of Lt Colonel and above.

TABLE 3. *Number of senior[a] officers killed and surviving coup of January 1966*

		Survived		
Region of origin	Killed	Absent from Nigeria	In Nigeria	Total
North	4	0	1	5
West	2	2	2	2
Mid-West	1	1	1	3[b]
East	0	0	7	7[c]

Notes:
[a] Rank of substantive lt colonel and above, 1 January 1966.
[b] Two of these were Ibos, Lt Colonel Unegbe, who was killed, and Lt Colonel Nwawo, who was absent from the country at the time of the coup.
[c] Of whom five were Ibos.

These figures are all the more remarkable when it is considered that of the five Northern and Western officers of this seniority to survive, three were out

fled to Ghana after the coup. These events were not necessarily linked with the coup. Nkrumah, moreover, was embarrassed by Ifeajuna's presence in Ghana and put him under restriction, to be released and brought back to Nigeria by Clark and Okigbo following the intercession of the Nigerian High Commission.
[1] Though see the review of evidence as to whether two Northern officers were involved, on p. 28 above.

of reach (Brigadier Ogundipe and Colonel Adebayo abroad on courses, Lt Colonel Fajuyi on holiday in his home town), one was searched for but had a lucky escape (Lt Colonel Gowon) and the fifth (Lt Colonel Banjo) was thought to be sympathetic by the conspirators.

It is hardly surprising that many drew the conclusion that 'the event of 15th January, 1966 was not a mutiny as such, but a premeditated and carefully projected plan by the Ibos to impose themselves on other tribes of Nigeria',[1] and there was no intention to kill Major General Ironsi, who was allegedly in on the plot from the beginning. Yet this is an over-simple interpretation of events. It is difficult to reconcile with the account previously given of the motives and actions of both the conspirators and the Commander in Chief himself. In particular it would mean that we would find it difficult to take at face value any of the statements given by the conspirators of their political beliefs and intentions.

It can be argued that perfectly good alternative explanations both for the ethnic composition of the group of conspirators and for the pattern of killing are available. Though these do not completely rule out explanations in terms of the Ibo tribe, they do make such explanations less compelling.

The pattern of killings may have derived from the conspirators' scheme of political and strategic priorities or from setbacks in execution or both. In the context of the political events of 1964 and 1965 the priority given to the neutralisation of the Federal Prime Minister, the premier of the North and the premier of the Western Region is quite intelligible. Major Nzeogwu's allegation that they failed to wipe out major political figures in Eastern and Mid-Western Nigeria because of the incompetence of his associates in the south was rather harsh, as the logistics of the operation were much more complex than in the North. As we have already observed, Majors Ifeajuna and Okafor did not reach Enugu, the capital of the Eastern Region until it was too late and Ironsi had re-established control over the army. By this time they were on their own and in no position to arrest Dr Okpara, whom, as we have seen, they paid a visit on the afternoon of the 15th.[2]

The apparent selectiveness of the killings among senior officers is partially explained by the fact that the Northerners and Westerners were very well represented in the key command and staff positions which were the object of the rebels' assault, as the tabulation in Table 4 should make clear.[3] In general, the main deviations from the principle of eliminating all officers in

---

[1] *The Nigerian situation: facts and background*, p. 2.

[2] Some commentators have seen this as evidence of Dr Okpara's complicity in the coup, though in the writer's opinion it is too slender to put such an interpretation upon it.

[3] Compare the proportion of Northerners and Westerners in this table with that in Table 3. The weighting of the senior command posts in the Northerners and Westerners favour as against the Ibos occurs mainly because the former were more senior in the rank of Lieutenant colonel and above, the Ibos having not started to join the officer corps in large numbers until the late 1950s.

TABLE 4. *Fate of officers in key command and staff appointments, January 1966*

Rank and name	Post	Regional/ ethnic origin	Fate	Notes
Major General Aguiyi-Ironsi	GOC	East (Ibo)	Survived	Listed for killing?
Brigadier Ademulegun	CO, 1st Brigade	West	Killed	—
Brigadier Maimalari	CO, 2nd Brigade	North	Killed	—
Colonel K. Mohammed	Chief of Staff	North	Killed	—
Lt Colonel Y. Pam	Adjutant General	North	Killed	—
Lt Colonel Anwuna	Acting General Staff Officer (I)	East (Ibo)	Survived	?
Lt Colonel Unegbe	Quartermaster General	Mid-West (Ibo)	Killed	Federal document *Nigeria 1966* claims was killed for not handing over keys of armoury. Almost certainly on list anyway.
Lt Colonel Banjo	Director, Electrical and Mechanical Engineers	West	Survived	An associate of the conspiracy.
Lt Colonel Effiong	Director of Ordinance and Supplies	East (non-Ibo)	Survived	Technical post–not listed?
Lt Colonel Trimnell	Director of Signals and Transport	Mid-West (Ibo)	Survived	Technical post–not listed?
Lt Colonel Ejoor	Just appointed CO, 1st Btn (Enugu)	Mid-West	Survived	In Lagos night of 14/15 January. Same hotel as Largema. Out when assassins visited?
Lt Colonel Njoku	Just handing over 2nd Btn (Ikeja)	East (Ibo)	Survived	Was ill and in process of handing over command to Gowon. Informed?
Lt Colonel Gowon	CO-designate, 2nd Btn	North	Survived	Listed. Arrived back from UK 2 days before coup.
Lt Colonel Kurobo	CO, 3rd Btn (Kaduna)	East (non-Ibo)	Survived	In Lagos early morning, January 15
Lt Colonel Largema	CO, 4th Btn (Ibadan)	North	Killed	Killed in Lagos Hotel.
Lt Colonel Ojukwu	CO, 5th Btn (Kano)	East	Survived	Informed by conspirators?
Lt Colonel Bassey	CO, Depot (Zaria)	East (non-Ibo)	Survived	Escaped with help from friends. Listed?
Colonel Shodeinde	CO, Nigerian Military Training College and Deputy CO, Nigerian Defence Academy	West	Killed	—
Lt Colonel Fajuyi	CO, Abeokuta Garrison and All Arms Battle Group	West	Survived	On leave in home town.

45

TABLE 4. (*cont.*)

Rank and name	Post	Regional/ ethnic Origin	Fate	Notes
Lt Colonel Imo	CO, Lagos	East (Ibo)	Survived	Shunted off to this job in disgrace. Therefore not a key figure on the Majors' list?
Major Katsina	OC, 1st Recce Squadron (Kaduna)	North	Survived	Persuaded on 15 January by Nzeogwu at gun-point to support him.
Major Obienu	OC, 2nd Recce Squadron (Abeokuta)	East (Ibo)	Survived	Informed by conspirators?
Major Okafor	OC, Federal Guard (Lagos)	East (Ibo)	Survived	One of the conspirators.

strategic positions can be explained in terms of alliance with the Majors (e.g. Lt Colonels Ojukwu and Banjo) or inaccessibility (Lt Colonel Fajuyi), though it is possible that friendliness with the conspirators may have protected some of the Eastern and Mid-Western Lieutenant Colonels, like Njoku, Anwuna, Kurobo, Ejoor or Imo.

The main difficulty seems to surround the survival of Major General Ironsi. The story of his escape is told earlier in this chapter. Was he just a little too lucky? Did the Majors ever intend to kill him? Was he, as some have suggested, privy to the plot? Most of the evidence tending to implicate him is both circumstantial and inaccurate. Ironsi did not help his own case by putting about more than one story of how he escaped. Before the coup he was believed to have been strongly opposed to military intervention in politics, an attitude which was epitomised by his terse reply of 'I hope not' when asked two days after the coup by a journalist whether he would remain in charge of the government after things had been normalised. He did not show favouritism towards his own tribe in appointments and promotions; and indeed surrounded himself with Northern aides.[1] Northern ministers present at the first meetings of 15 January vouchsafed that Ironsi was in tears and appeared genuinely upset by the whole affair. Thus the most convincing reason for his seizure of power on the 16th must still be his organisational loyalties rather than personal ambition or 'tribal' politics.

If Ironsi was not implicated, how did he then survive? It may simply have been bad planning: it was a mistake, for example, to start killing Ironsi's

[1] As is clear from Table 4, many of the senior staff and command positions under Ironsi were held by Northerners. Of Ironsi's ADCs only one (the air force ADC) was from the South; his police ADC was the brother of Lt Colonel Pam who died in the January incident.

staff before the General himself. Alternatively it has been suggested that those responsible for the operation in Lagos (Majors Ifeajuna and Okafor) 'faced with the brutal task of killing not only Northerners but their own compatriots...warned Ironsi of what was about to happen and deliberately went through the motions of trying to kill him, rather than actually carrying out the deed'.[1] There is no evidence either way, beyond Ironsi's own role in events, and Nzeogwu's statement that he was disappointed with the way the plan had been carried out by his colleagues in the south. Major General Ironsi's actions, as we pointed out earlier, seem consistent with the view that he may have had some advance warning (though not necessarily intentionally) through Lt Colonel Njoku or some other source; but do not suggest he condoned the coup or its methods. And it is hard to see why the Majors in Lagos should have deliberately stopped short of killing Ironsi when the logic of their plan required the elimination of the whole high command and when they showed no apparent hesitation in killing Lt Colonel Unegbe who was also an Ibo.[2]

The interpretation of the pattern of killings also depends on what meaning we give to the ethnic composition of the rebels' group. First, it must be noted that Ibos predominated in the middle ranks of the officer corps. At least twenty of the thirty-two officers at the ranks of substantive major as of January 1966 were Ibos and around fifteen of the fifty-four substantive captains were also of the same tribe. Of the 1957–61 entry to which all of the Majors and Captains implicated in the coup belonged, some thirty-eight out of ninety-two were Ibos. In the 1957–9 cohorts which included just the Majors alone twenty-one out of forty-four were Ibo. Chance considerations alone therefore might lead one to expect Ibos to play a leading role in *any* group based on the middle ranks of the officer corps.

Nevertheless, one can show that the ethnic bias of the conspirational group exceeded chance expectations. In Table 5, the Captains and Majors participating in the coup are compared first with other members of their seniority cohorts and second with other officers passing through Sandhurst with them. In all of the four comparisons of Table 5 participation in the January coup is associated beyond a chance level with ethnicity. Moreover, if we use the phi coefficient as a measure of relationship, the association between participation and tribe is *higher* within the Sandhurst group than in the 1957–61 cohorts as a whole. This suggests an additive effect of training upon tribe: namely that Sandhurst created the right conditions for the formation of peer group

[1] Dent, 'The Military and politics'.
[2] *Nigeria 1966* alleges that Unegbe was killed only because he held the keys of the armoury as Quartermaster General. Yet the conspirators had already armed themselves before killing him. It thus seems much more likely that Unegbe *like other key staff officers* was killed *ex officio*, because he might endanger the success of the coup.

associations amongst course-mates; and the cliques that formed in this way tended to take shape on ethnic and regional lines. The single peer group in which this is most marked is that of 1959. All four Ibo officers entering Sandhurst in that year became implicated in the conspiracy, but none of the non-Ibo officers of that year were involved. Fifteen officers of that entry-cohort were of non-Sandhurst background and only one of these (Major Ademoyega, a Yoruba university graduate) was in the January group.

TABLE 5. *Comparison of ethnic distribution of January coup leaders with peers and Sandhurst course-mates*

	January leaders	Non-participants		January leaders	Non-participants
	A 1957–61 entry cohorts			B 1957–9 entry cohorts only	
Ibo	10	28		7	14
Other	1	53		1	22
	$\phi = 0.37$ and X^2 significant at 0.01 level			$\phi = 0.38$ and X^2 significant at 0.05 level	
	C 1957–61 Sandhurst entry			D 1957–9 Sandhurst entry only	
Ibo	7	10		5	4
Other	0	20		0	10
	$\phi = 0.52$ and X^2 significant at 0.01 level			$\phi = 0.63$ and X^2 significant at 0.01 level	

Source: as for Table 2, plus data on ethnicity contained in Chapter VIII.

There is no need to adopt sinister explanations for the appearance of a revolutionary clique based mainly on a single ethnic group. Theorists of interpersonal dynamics,[1] for instance, would predict that patterns of inter-action among military colleagues, particularly those of the same rank, would tend to cluster around ethnic lines, if only because of unconscious similarities in values and outlook among members of the same ethnic group.

If the single hypothesis of a tribal plot is not accepted, the possibility that ethnic group interest may have shaped the motivation and objectives of the plotters at some less self-conscious level needs serious examination. In the case of the Ibos, it is particularly difficult to sort out group-interest from 'modernising' political ideology, because universal and achievement-centred values have in general been highly conducive to their own interests.[2] Within the army the Ibos were among the groups most likely to be adversely affected by the interference of Northern Ministers of Defence. If the blockages in promotion that were building up in the army were to lead to redundancy and political interference in promotions – as many officers feared – the Ibos

[1] F. Heider, *The psychology of interpersonal relations* (New York: Wiley, 1968), Chapter VII.
[2] See R. LeVine, *Dreams and deeds: achievement motivation in Nigeria* (Chicago: University of Chicago Press, 1966) and the discussion in Chapters VIII and IX below.

believed they would be the first group affected.[1] The precedent of the ejection of Ibos from the Nigerian Railway Corporation and the University of Lagos in early 1965 was not auspicious. Redundancies of serving officers and discrimination in promotions in favour of particular regions could probably only be created by an amendment to the Nigerian Military Forces Act and a major political row. Yet there is little doubt that members of the January group considered this a real possibility. Thus concern among Eastern and Mid-Western officers for their own career security became tied up both with distaste in principle for particularist restrictions on occupational mobility, and with hostility towards the political regime for its political conservatism and its domination by the North.

There are, finally, the organisational requirements of a revolutionary group as analysed by theorists from Lenin onwards.[2] They include such characteristics as secrecy, ease of communication and group cohesion, all of which would tend to be maximised in a single ethnic group. Thus, we should not be surprised that the Majors should take on the appearance of a tribal clique, even if their self-conscious objectives were political and ideological in nature.[3] It may indeed be that the only reason their coup came subsequently to be regarded as tribalistic was that they failed to seize power, meaning they were unable to carry out their programme of reform, to develop sources of support outside the narrow clique which effected the coup, or to counteract attempts by opponents to define them in terms of selfish factional interests. In like fashion, Ironsi's coup within a coup came to grief within a brief seven months because of his government's lack of political dynamism, its inability to resolve ambiguity and thus to escape identification by its opponents with narrow ethnic and regional interest. The contrast with the Ghanaian coup of February 24 1966, is a pertinent one. The original conspirators were also predominantly of one tribe, the Ewes. But there the coup succeeded, members of other groups were in the majority in the National Liberation Council and a successful political programme was embarked upon.[4]

[1] The role of Northern Ministers of Defence is discussed in Chapter X; the promotion blockage in Chapter VIII; and its ethnic implications in Chapter IX. It is of interest that Major Nzeogwu's father lost his job as a PWD carpenter in the North shortly before the coup.

[2] V. I. Lenin, *What is to be done* (Moscow: Foreign Languages Publishing House).

[3] As Luttwak puts it in his recipe for a coup; 'We will therefore make the fullest use of the ethnic matrix, without, however, aligning our coup with any particular ethnic faction. In terms of petty tactics, we will match each potential recruit with a recruiter who shares his affiliation and, if necessary, the image of the coup will be presented in a similar vein...But, if, in the operational phase of the coup, we are at any stage delayed, then our essential weakness will be shown: we shall probably acquire a definite political coloration, and this in turn will lead to a concentration of forces which oppose the tendency we represent (or are thought to represent). As long as the execution of the coup is rapid, and we are cloaked in anonymity, no particular faction will have either a motive, or an opportunity, to oppose us.' *Coup d'état*, p. 72 and p. 54.

[4] Accusations of Ewe domination in the army and police did arise later, but only when the NLC had begun the return to civilian politics.

Major Nzeogwu himself clearly perceived the dynamic relation between tactical success, effective political initiative and the capacity to escape charge of partiality or tribal bias. Had the original coup succeeded, he said, 'the suggestions that now fill the air about the apparent partiality of the operation would have been impossible of invention'.[1]

[1] Interview between Nzeogwu and Solarin, *Nigerian Tribune* (Ibadan), 2 July 1967.

CHAPTER II

JULY 1966: THE JUNIOR OFFICERS' AND NCOS' COUP

ALIENATION OF THE NON-COMMISSIONED OFFICERS

The January coup left a legacy of shock and mistrust among the soldiers, especially sharp among Northern Other Ranks. We have already described the quasi-mutinous state of many of the Lagos troops, particularly the Federal Guard during the morning of 15 January 1966. At Ibadan, the Other Ranks in the 4th Battalion are said by one of their officers to have been 'rolling on the ground in sorrow' when they got to hear of the death of their Commanding Officer, Lt Colonel Largema. A major who was passing through Ibadan and suspected of taking part in the coup was shot.[1] It was, it is said, several days before the officers – with some exceptions – dared to go near their men. The position was not calm until the appointment of Lt Colonel Akahan, a Northerner, to be the new commander of the battalion. The assassination of high-ranking officers in the January coup, in sum, breached military authority norms and violated the identification of Other Ranks with leading military figures like Brigadiers Maimalari and Ademulegun, Colonels Kuru Mohammed and Shodeinde and Lt Colonels Largema and Pam. Reactions were probably strongest in the 4th Battalion because it was the only one to have lost its Commanding Officer, Largema, as well as a previous commander, Colonel Kuru Mohammed: and this unit was to be one of the most important centres of activity in the July mutiny.

Myths soon grew up to dignify these resentments. The officers and politicians who had died began to assume heroic status, the manner of their deaths being said to have been miraculous. At the same time all the Ibo officers came to be cast in sinister conspiratorial roles; and it was widely put about that Major General Ironsi had himself played a nefarious part behind the scenes in January. The myths around Brigadier Maimalari, the most senior Northern officer killed, were especially fertile. At first it was said that Maimalari was alive and in hiding. A number of Northern NCOs in Lagos were able to keep up this belief for a while, because his name remained posted

[1] Major S. Adegoke, a Yoruba officer. The circumstances of his death are obscure, though there is no conclusive evidence as to his having taken part in the January conspiracy.

on official notice boards around the Brigade HQ: and they verged on a revolt when his name was removed. Or if his death was accepted, it was believed that he could only have been killed by trickery, for only trickery could have evaded the miraculous forces that protected him like a saintly, military Rasputin. It was rumoured that he had fled to Ghana, that he had arranged to negotiate with Ironsi on the border between Dahomey and Nigeria a fortnight later, but had been shot dead by the latter with forty-nine bullets. Alternatively, it was said that Maimalari escaped from the conspirators on 15 January but encountered Ironsi on the road who ordered his guard to arrest him and shoot him. The bullets somehow did not penetrate and attempts to use a bayonet also failed. Finally Ironsi was alleged to have ordered his driver (a Northern NCO) to tie Maimalari up and run over him in his car.

It was possible for such rumours to flourish and grow because of the high command's simple lack of public recognition of what had happened. They did not announce what they intended to do about the January conspirators, nor whether they were to be punished. Nor did they ever say who had been killed in the coup, let alone make arrangements for an honourable military burial: it was as if they had simply disappeared from the face of the earth. It seems that the new military rulers could not face up to the political consequences of saying what had happened to the army's top Northern and Western officers. As Lt Colonel Hassan Katsina argued at the Aburi discussions in January 1967, when advocating that the deaths of Ironsi and Fajuyi in July be confirmed:

This is what happened after the January coup. We agreed to announce the names of all the senior officers killed, but there was fear all over. Let us combine the whole story ready, do the whole thing respectably (this time) and solve the problem.[1]

Informally, of course, the salient facts about the assassins and of their victims were quite well known, especially in the army itself. Under these conditions, withholding information was dangerous. With little publicly available evidence to the contrary, there were few constraints against the development of a generalised belief defining events in terms of an Ibo plot.[2] In absence of information to distinguish between the roles played on 15 January and afterwards by Major General Ironsi and Lt Colonels Njoku, Imo, Anwuna, Okonweze and other senior Ibo non-participants on the one hand, and the Majors on the other, it is understandable that the Northern officers and NCOs tended to assimilate the two in their definition of the situation. The absence of a firm decision to prosecute the Majors and their

---

[1] *Meeting of the Nigerian military leaders held at Peduase Lodge, Aburi, Ghana, 4th and 5th January 1967* (Lagos: Ministry of Information, 1967), p. 14.
[2] For the role of generalised beliefs in legitimising hostile outbursts of the kind described in this chapter, see N. J. Smelser, *Theory of collective behaviour* (New York: Wiley, 1966).

collaborators similarly encouraged the belief that all Ibos were in it together.

Why was this allowed to happen? For two reasons: first, because the military's own decision-making machinery was slow and creaky. Investigations under the Chief of Staff (Army), Lt Colonel Gowon, took until May to complete, and the Supreme Military Council did not for one reason or another get round to considering the findings.[1] Secondly, there was ambiguity in the supreme command's own undertakings about the surrender of the January insurgents. Major Nzeogwu had publicly claimed when he announced his surrender that Ironsi had agreed not to prosecute the group for their actions. Yet there is little doubt that such an undertaking could have been overridden had Ironsi established a firm set of political priorities. One reason the Military Government found it difficult to act was that it faced conflicting pressures on the issue which it was unable to reconcile. On the one hand, radical elites in the universities, the civil service and the army and certain Lagos newspapers wanted the Majors to be released and given public recognition as heroes for sweeping the corrupt politicans out of power. On the other, there were pressures for punishment from the North as well as from the lower ranks of the army. It was primarily because the Ironsi government lacked political courage that it failed to take decisive action to dispel these uncertainties.

ORGANISATIONAL STRAINS

Feelings of disorientation generated by the coup and the conditions of ambiguity which surrounded it were augmented by a number of strains of a specifically organisational nature. First of all, there were the organisational strains resulting from the rapid indigenisation of the officer corps, to be discussed further in Part Two. A poorly institutionalised authority structure like that of the Nigerian Army was badly placed to absorb either the dislocation in discipline brought about by the January coup or the political pressures put upon it now that its leaders governed the country.

The situation was made worse by changes in the distribution of authority in the army that resulted specifically from the elimination of many of the officers at the top of the command hierarchy during the coup. Table 6 shows

[1] See *January 15th: before and after.*
This document suggests that: 'In meeting after meeting of the Council Lt Colonel Gowon was asked about his report and each time his reply was that he had had no time and that he was still collecting evidence.' It also states that the council never received Gowon's final report after being promised it as soon as possible after the investigation ceased in May. It alleges deliberate prevarication by Gowon. The writer is inclined to think that the delay was either due to the general staff's lack of time and resources; or because the Supreme Commander, Ironsi himself, kept it off the council's agenda because it was a delicate subject and because there were other issues to be settled at the relatively infrequent council meetings after May. The latter receives some support from Lt Colonel Hassan's statement quoted above.

TABLE 6. *Attrition in the higher levels of the officer corps,[a] January 1966*

	Number killed	Number imprisoned	Number in Military Government[c]	Total number	Per cent attrition
A Impact on ranks[b]					
Brigadier and Major General	2	—	1	4	75[d]
Colonel	2	—	—	3	67
Lt Colonel	3	1	3	14	50
Major	1	4	1	32	19
B Impact on seniority cohorts[e]					
Before 1952	3	—	1	7	57
1952–3	2	—	1	5	60
1954–5	2	1	2	13	38
1956–7	—	1	1	16	13
1958–9	1	7	—	35	23

Notes:
[a] Combat officers only.
[b] Substantive not temporary or acting ranks.
[c] Head of Military Government and the four Military Governors.
[d] Major General Ironsi combined a political role as Head of Military Government with a military one as Supreme Commander. The figure is therefore 50% if we count him as the latter.
[e] For the basis of the establishment of these see Chapter V below.

quite clearly how the killings depleted the upper military ranks of the hierarchy and the more senior age groups. Thus the gap in experience and in ascriptive qualities such as age and seniority between the upper and lower ranks of the officer corps, between commanders and subordinates, was made still narrower than it had been before.[1] Talking of this time, young officers say it was one in which they felt quite distinctly that the social distance between themselves and their superiors had decreased; that both familiarity and hostility between high- and lower-ranking officers were greater; and that particularistic relations of friendship and clientage, tribe and region tended to develop at the expense of organisational ties. Discipline weakened and it became more common for subordinate officers to answer back, query orders and stand by their rights. It is difficult, however, to pin down at all precisely how much of this was a simple result of demographic adjustments in the officer corps; how much because the January coup tarnished the charisma of command; and how much because political tensions were transmitting themselves through the army.

Important changes in the ethnic composition of the officer corps were also brought about by the January events. This can be seen clearly if we compare the fifty most senior officers before the army took power (approximately the

[1] See the discussion of the youthfulness of the officer corps' age structure even before the coup took place, in Chapter VII below.

most senior fifteen per cent of all the combat officers) with the fifty most senior officers remaining after the killings, imprisonment and political changes of January. The effects of mortality, etc. are seen most clearly in Table 7, where it can be seen that the Ibos moved automatically from a position of numerical inferiority among the most senior twenty or thirty officers to a position of numerical dominance, though suffering a slight decline in the middle-level positions from which they moved up.

TABLE 7. *Comparison of ethnic/regional origins of fifty most senior officers[a] before and after coup of January 15*

| | Number in each ethnic/regional category | | | | | | | |
| | Before January 15 | | | | After January 15 | | | |
	Ibo	Non-Ibo E or MW[b]	Yoruba[c]	North[c]	Ibo	Non-Ibo E or MW	Yoruba	North
1–10 most senior	2	1	5	2	4	2	2	1
11–20 most senior	4	2	1	3	8	2	1	0
21–30 most senior	7	2	0	1	6	1	2	1
31–40 most senior	8	0	1	1	5	2	3	0
41–50 most senior	4	1	5	0	4	1	2	3

Increase of Ibo percentage share of senior officers in military

| Numbers of most senior officers (cumulative) | Per cent Ibo in each cumulative group of officers | | |
	(a) before January 15	(b) after January 15	before/after January 15 (b–a)
10 most senior	20	40	+20
20 most senior	30	60	+30
30 most senior	43	60	+17
40 most senior	52.5	57.5	+5
50 most senior	50	54	+4

Notes:
[a] Seniority ratings derived from promotional dates in Federation of Nigeria, *Official Gazettes* (1960–6) and *British Army List* (1955–60).
[b] It is impossible to distinguish in practice between non-Ibo groups in the Western and Mid-Western Regions from the data available.
[c] It is impossible to distinguish Northern and southern Yorubas, so the North will be taken to exclude the former.

The Ibos were thus well placed in demographic or seniority terms to step into dead men's shoes. And this they did. Twelve officers were gazetted lieutenant colonel in May 1966 to fill the gaps created by the January coup.[1]

[1] Twelve names appeared in the gazette, though one of these, Lt Colonel Kurobo, had substantive promotion dating from 1965. His promotion is therefore omitted from Table 8.

Of these eight were Ibos and only one, Lt Colonel Hassan Katsina, a Northerner. The effect of this on the rank structure was to transfer the numerical predominance of the Ibos at major up to lieutenant colonel, as will be clear from Table 8.

TABLE 8. *Comparison of ethnic balance of upper ranks, January and May 1966 (before and after January coup)*[a]

	Ibo	Non-Ibo E or MW	Yoruba	North	Total	per cent of total Ibos	per cent of total North
A January 1966							
Colonel and above	1	0	4	2	7	14	29
Lt Colonel	5	4	2	3	14	36	20
Major	21	2	7	2	32	66	6
B May 1966							
Colonel and above	1	0	2	0	3	33	0
Lt Colonel[b]	12	5	2	2	21	59	9
Major[c]	10	1	5	1	17	59	5

Notes:
[a] Substantive ranks of combat officers and gazetted rank changes only.
[b] Includes Military Governors (one from each region). If we exclude these, the per cent Ibo at lieutenant colonel (11 out of 17) goes up still further to 65% and the North reduces to 6% (1 out of 17). Total figure also includes only ten out of the eleven promotions made to lieutenant colonel, May 1966 because the other one was of an officer in a non-combat branch.
[c] Total number reduced because of (i) promotions to lieutenant colonel, (ii) imprisonment of January Majors. There were no gazetted promotions to major from January to July 1966.

The consolidation of Ibos in the main command and staff positions was almost as impressive. During the first month after the January 15 coup, Ibo officers held every post of any importance in the army except Chief of Staff (Army) (Lt Colonel Gowon) and commander of the 1st Brigade (Lt Colonel Bassey). All the five Battalions, one of the two Recce Squadrons, the artillery field battery and all three training units were under the command of Ibo officers.[1] In February and March 1966, Major General Ironsi made some attempt to redress the regional balance, including the appointment of two

[1] After the drafting of the four Military Governors and of Lt Colonel Kurobo to be head of the Air Force, the 2nd, 3rd, 4th and 5th Battalions and the 1st Recce Squadron were all in charge of their second in commands, Majors Igboba, Okoro, Nzefili, Okafor and Isong, respectively; so too was the Depot, Zaria, under Major Akagha. Obienu remained in command of the 2nd Recce Squadron. The 1st Battalion, the NMTC and the Abeokuta garrison were put under Majors Ogunewe, Kalu and Okonweze, respectively. All these officers with the exception of Isong were Ibo. All except Nzefili and Okafor, who were later replaced by Akahan and Mohammed Shuwa, retained their positions until July. The brigade commanders were Njoku (Ibo) and Bassey (Eastern non-Ibo); and the CO, Lagos Garrison, Imo (Ibo).

Northerners to command the 4th and 5th Battalions, Lt Colonels Akahan and Mohammed Shuwa. The appointment of the former was presumably aimed at placating the Northern soldiers of the 4th Battalion who were still in ferment after the killing of Lt Colonel Largema. Even after these changes, however, the Ibos continued to be conspicuous in the top levels of the command structure.

Perceptions of such changes are shaped by the perspective from which one views them. If one's starting point is the normal working of the promotional system according to the principles of seniority and merit then there is little or no evidence of systematic discrimination in favour of the Ibos as a group. As far as the promotions to lieutenant colonel in May 1966 are concerned, for example, a case-by-case analysis of the promotional dates of the individuals concerned shows that *none* of the seven Ibos of combat status[1] promoted were advanced above non-Ibo officers of equivalent or greater seniority. For only four of the fifteen substantive majors of the longest standing seniority were not Ibos, and all four of them were promoted. Nor did postings show evidence of discrimination. True an Ibo protege of Major General Ironsi's, Major Igboba, who had served with him in the Congo was very lucky to stay on as the Commanding Officer of the 2nd Battalion, Ikeja – of which he had been second in command up to January, for he was only a substantive captain and there were at least a dozen officers who had precedence over him. Nevertheless, two Northern officers, Lt Colonels Mohammed Shuwa and Muritala Mohammed, received even more preferential treatment, the former being appointed to command the 5th Battalion and the latter to be Inspector of Signals. Both were substantive captains at the time and from ten to thirty-five (the former) and twenty-two (the latter) other officers had the precedence in seniority over them. This clearly suggests a deliberate attempt at regional balancing designed to placate the North, the more so as both the Mohammeds came from the 'dry' or Moslem far North.

Yet the changes that were salient in the eyes of the junior Northern officers and NCOs were the gross overall changes towards greater Ibo numerical dominance at the higher levels. Though few *individual* Northern officers or men had fallen behind in promotions as a result of the January coup – and some had clearly gained – the alterations in composition at the upper levels were thought of as a symbolic deprivation for the Northerners as a group. This impression was perhaps heightened by the fact that most of the new postings put Ibo officers into command assignments rather than into staff or specialist positions. Thus by March 1966, Ibo officers held ten out of thirteen unit command positions (commanders of the battalions, training units, recce squadrons and artillery battery); whereas in January they had held only five

---

[1] The eighth Ibo promoted, Lt Colonel Morah, was head of the Pay Corps.

out of twelve. This was important because the battalion (or equivalent group)[1] was the effective unit for day-to-day operative command in the army, and any change in command at this level was more likely to come to the notice and concern of the average soldier. The conspicuous position of Ibo officers in the hierarchy also fitted in with the Northerners' understanding of the new political position, namely that the North had lost power and the East had gained it. Thus it was easy to believe that conspiratorial design rather than the demographic characteristics of the officer corps itself had placed Ibos in command.

ACTIVATION OF THE NORTHERN OFFICERS

Many young Northern officers were unsure to start with how they should regard the military's assumption of power. On the one hand, they often shared the simplistic belief in nationalism and a distaste for the politics and corruption of the politicians that prevailed in the officer corps. On the other hand, they were uneasy about the methods by which power had been seized, and at the killings of their senior officers. As one of them put it: 'I knew there would be trouble as soon as I heard soldiers had been killing soldiers.'

Yet in general it seems that they were not as badly alienated as their Other Ranks. Perhaps the younger officers' smaller commitment to organisational norms disposed them to be less enraged at the latters' violation than were the longer-serving NCOs. The extent to which they identified politically with the North, moreover, was initially not uniform, some of those from the Middle Belt areas being as hostile to the political dominance of the Sardauna of Sokoto and the Hausa–Fulani elite in Federal and regional politics as their southern counterparts.

As events unfolded after January, however, the political alternatives evoked for Northern officers became increasingly circumscribed, and the differences among them began to fade into the background. The Military Government's clumsy handling of the political situation[2] in the months after the coup was for them one critical factor. Their turning point came later than that of the NCOs and was probably marked by Decree no. 34 of May 1966 which purported to do away with Nigeria's federal constitutional structure and make the country a unitary state. The decree confirmed the Northerners' fears that the military regime aimed at depriving them of power and a separate identity. The student demonstrations at the end of May and the riots which followed them in the Northern cities demonstrated compellingly the

---

[1] The Recce Squadrons were equivalent to infantry companies rather than battalions. They were, however, independent units in the same sense as the battalions for command purposes, coming directly under the brigade command.
[2] Described in detail in Chapter XI below.

regime's loss of legitimacy in the region. The unease of the young Northern officers was brought into direct political focus.

They were urged on by their Northern Other Ranks. The latter, it is said, remonstrated with them constantly for doing nothing, using the multiple ties of reciprocity between officers and NCOs[1] to persuade them to act. The officers were also influenced by their contacts among groups outside the military. Northern university students, especially those at Ahmadu Bello University, seem to have had some influence on them, many of the officers with the rank of second lieutenant through to captain having been contemporaries of the students at secondary school.[2] Such links, however, seem to have served to shape the officers' overall political perspective rather than to generate specific plans for intervention; and it seems doubtful if any student groups had prior knowledge of or complicity in the coup itself.[3]

Similarly, one or two Northern officers may have had links with former Northern (and also perhaps former Western NNDP) politicians. There is plenty of evidence that the politicians *wanted* to obtain access to groups in the military.[4] But it is difficult to determine whether in fact they did so, and even if they did, it is not certain whether this had specific consequences for the organisation of the coup that followed: whether, that is, those officers who were 'accessible' in one way or another were in fact the coup makers. It is possible that the conspiratorial group contained a mixture of officers like Lt Colonel Muritala Mohammed with political ties and others without such links. The writer's impression,[5] however, is that the majority of the officers involved were unlikely to have been seriously enmeshed with the former politicians, both because this would have created security problems for a coup d'etat[6] and because it would have been inconsonant with the high value most of them placed on probity and an anti-political outlook. The fusion of organisational stress and political conflict through belief in an Ibo conspiracy

[1] See below, pp. 166–8.

[2] Most officer cadets were accepted for training after passing their West African School Certificate examinations at secondary school. Their colleagues would have stayed on at least another two years, in order to pass their Higher School Certificate, before going to university. Thus a 2nd lieutenant with one year of training and one year of experience would be the school contemporary of a first-year university student.

[3] Students who were close friends of some of the main conspirators say that the whole thing was kept secret from them.

[4] See, for example, the facts cited in M. J. Dent, 'The military and the politicians', in *Nigerian politics and military rule: prelude to the civil war*, ed. S. K. Panter-Brick (London: Athlone Press, 1970). There were ties of kinship between Lt Colonel Muritala Mohammed and the ex-Minister of Defence, Alhaji Inuwa Wada. Dent suggests that the latter was using his private wealth and/or NPC funds to increase his support in the military.

[5] Based on personal acquaintance with one or two of the young officers who staged the July coup.

[6] See Luttwak, *Coup d'état*. Even now the participants are still very careful to whom they talk about the coup. Student friends of two conspirators assert that they preferred not to take married officers or most of the senior Northern officers into confidence because of the wish to minimise security risks.

was enough in itself to motivate a revolt, independent of whatever transactions may have taken place with political figures. Such contacts may have hastened things along, though it is the writer's contention that alliances within the army itself, such as that between junior Northern officers and NCOs, were of more direct relevance than outside contacts.

From the May 1966 riots onwards, all officers were increasingly caught up in a spiral of mutual fear and suspicion. Hostility between regional and ethnic groups began to come out in the open. Feelings of distrust were all the more salient because they were dissonant with previous sentiments of affection and solidarity, particularly among peers. As one young Northern officer subsequently expressed the growth of his fears, the Ibos

know how to talk and pretend to be brothers. We discovered their treachery late. Most countries have one Judas Iscariot for every one hundred of their people. The Ibos are ninety-nine per cent Judas'. My best friend in the army was an Ibo. I discovered afterwards that even he had misbehaved.

The rumours gathered through June and July. As is normal on such occasions, it becomes very difficult to make an adequate analytic distinction between the underpinning social facts and the web of myth surrounding them both at the time and in subsequent reinterpretations of events. For myths become a part of each group's definition of the situation, influencing their present actions as well as their beliefs. The cycle of mutual reaction and anticipation thus turned the fears of the Ibos and Northerners alike that they were being conspired against into a self-fulfilling prophesy.

A number of Ibo officers began reacting to the May riots, and to the belief that a number of highly placed Northerners had had some hand in them, by advocating a greater centralisation of power, circulating names of persons considered untrustworthy and advocating a review of the position of the January conspirators, if not their release. Major General Ironsi himself was probably not among these, but he was exposed to increasing pressure from them. He came to rely to an increasing extent on informal contact with Ibo unit commanders in the North, like Lt Colonels Okoro and Akagha, for his information on political developments in the region, in preference to the official Northern Region administration.[1] This gave further impetus to Northern fears, particularly after Ironsi's decision (announced rather precipitately in mid-July 1966), to appoint military prefects at a provincial level, to post the military governors away from their regions of origin, and to rotate

[1] The writer has seen documentary evidence of the kind of political advice Ironsi was getting from Lt Colonel Akagha, who was now the Commanding Officer of the Depot, Zaria. There were also a number of occasions in this period when Ironsi took decisions affecting the North without consulting Lt Colonel Hassan Katsina or the head of the Northern civil service, Alhaji Akilu, at all.

the battalions. Each of the decisions would have had the effect of tightening central control over the regions still further.[1]

In their turn the Northerners came to believe in specific plans for some kind of coup or master plan aimed against them. This was to take place (in different versions) at some specified date in August, 1966, to involve (in some versions but not others) the replacement of Ironsi by a more dynamic leader, and to be accompanied by the dismissal of prominent Northerners both in the army and in civilian life, and by the deportation of certain expatriates sympathetic to the North; the names being contained in a master list supposedly in circulation among the Ibos. This list was clearly an evocative symbol of the Northerners' personal fears for their own safety and of the breakdown of trust between them and their Ibo confreres. (It is of significance that the Ibos also conceptualised their insecurities in the same way.[2]) These beliefs in nefarious activity against them permitted the Northerners to justify their own clandestine preparations for the coup which took place on July 28–29 1966.

THREE DIFFERENT VIEWS OF THE COUP

What makes it particularly difficult to reconstruct events is that beliefs of the kind described above are of continuing importance in providing legitimacy after the event, a bias which badly impairs the truth of the main documentary evidence. Northern sources tend to emphasise the preemptive nature of the coup and the supposed conspiracy of the Ibos. A Northern document[3] alleges that:

Ironsi and his Ibo clique had in fact planned to do more than just conquer the North. But unfortunately for them...THE GOD OF AFRICA...did not permit the execution of the next part of the plan – 'operation annihilation of Northern Nigerians'. A plan designed to annihilate completely certain categories of Northern Nigerians, including Chiefs, Commissioned and Warrant officers of the Nigerian Army and senior civil servants. The plan was spear-headed by zealous and over-confident Ibos who felt that Ironsi was not fast enough. Lt. Colonel Ojukwu was to be the new leader.

To implement the plan a group of Ibo Army Officers in Abeokuta in the early hours of July 29, 1966 attempted to disarm the Northern soldiers of the same unit. But after a scuffle the tide turned against the Ibos and by the end of the second day the Army personnel of Northern origin were in complete control all over the country...

---

[1] See the account of the political situation between January and July 1966 delineated in Chapter XI below.

[2] They also believed that the Northerners had a list of prominent citizens to be killed in the North as well as the military figures killed in July. See *January 15th: before and after*, p. 35.

[3] *The Nigerian situation: facts and background*, p. 8.

On the other hand the Federal government's account[1] places a greater emphasis on the spontaneous and almost accidental course of events:

There were wildly circulating rumours that the 'uncompleted' job of January 15 was to be finished by eliminating the remaining officers of non-Eastern origin. . . . There were also rumours of a counter-coup planned by some Northern elements in the Army with the assistance of civilians. On July 28 there was strong evidence that one group or another would attempt something but the details were not available to the senior officers. The Supreme Headquarters and the Army Head-quarters took the normal military precautions of warning all units to remain alert. It appears from the investigations that an officer in Abeokuta went beyond the pre-cautionary measure and armed some men drawn from Southern rank and file. When those of Northern origin got wind of this they became apprehensive of such a move, thinking a repeat of January 15, 1966 was in the offing. They also took their weapons. These latter men shot three of their officers on the spot and in-fighting within the Army spread to Ibadan, Ikeja and then the units stationed in the North followed. . .

In contrast to this emphasis on spontaneous social processes through which there was in some sense a contagion of revolt from one military unit to another, Eastern Nigerian sources have attempted to depict a malevolent grand design. According to the document *January 15th: before and after*,[2] there was a huge conspiracy which took the following form:

Just as the pogrom of May 29, 1966 and after was largely a civilian affair so the holocaust of July 29 and after at least began as largely a military affair. In accord-ance with the decades-old policy of the North, the aim of the July 29 massacres was clearly two-fold: to split the country and establish an independent REPUBLIC OF THE NORTH; or to re-establish |the dominance of the North (in cooperation with some elements in the West) over the rest of Nigeria. . .

As available evidence indicates the details of the second phase of the pogrom which started on July 29 are as follows: selected Northern Army officers and men were to be organised in formations at strategic military centres and given assign-ments for capturing various military installations, particularly armouries and maga-zines, and creating a situation which would make it appear that Eastern soldiers were on the offensive. At this point senior Northern Army officers would signal to their men in the various centres to commence operations on the pretext of crushing this 'Eastern Offensive'. The D-Day was given the code name 'ARABA (Hausa for "SECESSION") DAY'. On that day all arms and ammunition in all military units and installations were to be seized from Eastern soldiers and given to Northern soldiers. Eastern soldiers on guard duty would likewise be replaced by Northern soldiers. All this would leave the Easterners totally defenceless. In Lagos Lt. Col. Yakubu Gowon (Chief of Staff, Army) was to install himself in the Central Opera-tions Room to enable him to discharge his overall responsibility for co-ordinating

---

[1] *Nigeria 1966.*   [2] *January 15th*, pp. 41–3.

the operations throughout the country. In the North the Military Governor Lt. Col. Hassan Usman Katsina, was to disappear so that no authority could have access to him to direct any counter-move. In the East the Military Governor, Lt. Col. Odumegwu Ojukwu was to be killed as early as possible. Most important of all, the Supreme Commander and Head of the National Military Government, Major-General J. T. U. Aguiyi-Ironsi, was to be captured, wherever he might happen to be at the time, and killed. Finally, in all military centres all Eastern Officers were to be annihilated and any skilled Non-Commissioned Officers (NCOs) and other soldiers of Eastern origin were to be detained and killed...

As was the case with the pogrom of May 29 among the leading personalities involved in the initial planning of the broad outlines of the operations were the discredited Northern ex-politicians and the Northern civil servants...

Among the Northern Army officers involved, the most prominent were Lt. Col. Gowon (Chief of Staff, Army) Lt. Col. Katsina (Military Governor, North) Lt. Col. Mohammed (Inspector of Signals), Major T. Y. Danjuma, Major Alao and Major Kyari. But, generally speaking all officers and men of Northern origin were eventually involved at one stage or the other in the planning, supervision or execution of the operations, for non-cooperation on the part of any one of them was deemed inimical to Northern interests and was punishable by DEATH.

It is the writer's belief that all three sources give an over-simple and distorted interpretation of events. A major problem, however, is the lack of reliable and independent sources of information, so that rather like in certain novels or films[1] one or two facets can be changed, suppressed or manipulated to produce widely different Gestalts. It is nevertheless possible even with available data to disconfirm some of the key assumptions of each of these competing 'pictures' of events. In particular the description of the coup that follows will show on the one hand that the coup of July 28–29 did not lack prior organisation, but on the other that it was not as tightly organised as Eastern sources make out, nor did certain of the key Northern figures mentioned, such as Lt Colonel Hassan Katsina or Lt Colonel Gowon play the behind-the-scenes coordinating role attributed to them. A guiding assumption that will be useful in understanding the pattern of events is that in a situation in which alignments are fluid and the mechanisms of authoritative control are ineffective, it requires only a small increase in organisation to achieve appreciable results.[2] As in other hostile outbursts, some degree of prior organisation may have been required to mobilise participants for action. But this need only have been organisation of the most fragmentary and informal kind.

[1] For example, the novels of Alain Robbe-Grillet and Kurosawa's film *Rashomon*.
[2] Similarly A. R. Zolberg, *Creating political order* (Chicago: Rand McNally, 1966), suggests that the early African political parties were able to reap large political dividends with little organisational effort because the political systems of emergent African states were organisational vacuums.

THE COUP OF JULY 29TH: THE PATTERN OF EVENTS[1]

It appears that during most of July, Northern soldiers were already in a semi-mutinous state. Late in June there had been a minor revolt of NCOs in Kaduna.[2] It was left to the officers however to establish the organisational frame of revolt, and to legitimise the outright rejection of authority. It seems that specific plans were not made until two or three weeks before the coup, and it is probable that detailed contingency plans were made only at the level of individual command units such as the battalions and training garrisons. Coordination between units seems to have been sketchy, being achieved through a series of assignations in cars and other private places. Lt Colonel Muritala Mohammed may also have been able to play a strategic role through his position as Inspector of Signals. Nevertheless it seems improbable that planning amounted to anything more than a series of understandings that each group would act in support of the other, in contrast to the coordinated series of operations in the January coup. Most of the advance activity was confined to the units in the Western Region and Lagos area[3] especially the 4th and 2nd Battalions at Ibadan and Ikeja, the Abeokuta Garrison and the Federal Guard in Lagos, because they were relatively near each other.

Coordination even between these was not very good. The revolt began late at night on 28 July in the Abeokuta Garrison, where Northern officers and men broke into a meeting in the officers mess, shot their commander, Lt Colonel Okonweze, Major Obienu of the 2nd Recce Squadron and another Ibo officer. Yet although their colleagues in Ibadan and Ikeja were alerted immediately it was (it seems) two or three more hours before they got themselves organised and were able to take over the armouries and disarm the Eastern troops.[4] In the event it gave time for the supreme command to

[1] A great deal of the source material for the following four sections is derived from the extremely detailed account of events issued at the end of 1966 by the Eastern Nigeria government in its document *January 15th: before and after*. Unfortunately this document was issued for propaganda purposes, and although it does include much useful material unobtainable elsewhere, it is marred by both unconscious biases and by deliberate distortions of fact. It is possible, however, to eliminate the worst of these by accepting only details that are specific enough to reduce the likelihood that they have been invented, by applying internal checks for the consistency of information and by cross-checking details as far as possible with the other sources available to the author.

[2] This occurred after the expulsion of a former British officer who had helped to organise a resettlement scheme for the Ex-Serviceman's Association, on trumped-up charges of anti-Ibo activity during and after the May riots.

[3] So much so that one of the planners of the coup had to drive for several hours in his private car from Ibadan up to Kaduna in the North immediately after the success of the revolt in the 4th Battalion in the early morning of the 29th in order to activate officers in the North.

[4] *January 15th: before and after* attempts to demonstrate that the operation was planned and coordinated in some detail beforehand. It asserts, for example, that the revolt began at both Ibadan and Ikeja, as well as Abeokuta before midnight on the 28th. Its evidence for this, however, appears to be inconsistent with other parts of its account. For example, the Supreme Commander's bodyguard is asserted to have been disarmed and Government House, Ibadan,

receive a warning in the early hours of the morning of the 29th and for the Chief of Staff (Army), Lt Colonel Gowon, to put all units on the alert. This seems to indicate either that the timing was not worked out properly or that the Northerners in Abeokuta acted precipitately, or possibly that 29 July was not the date orginally agreed upon, the Abeokuta revolt being an accident that triggered the whole revolt off in the fashion described by Federal sources.

By the time, however, that Army Headquarters were able to contact Major General Ironsi and his host at Government House, Ibadan, Lt Colonel Fajuyi, it was too late. At about 5.00 a.m. they were surrounded and their guard disarmed. An attempt was made to despatch Lt Colonel Njoku, the brigade commander of the 2nd Brigade (Lagos), who was in Ironsi's entourage, in civilian clothing to assume control in Lagos, but he was recognised by some of the arriving troops. He escaped wounded, but was unable to proceed. Ironsi himself was not confronted until 9.00 a.m. when Major Danjuma of the 4th Battalion went upstairs in Government House with an escort, saluted him, questioned him and ordered his arrest. Subsequently, Ironsi and Fajuyi were driven out of Ibadan under the guard of two junior Northern officers and a number of NCOs and taken to an isolated spot by the roadside where they were led into the bush, tortured, questioned and killed by the NCOs.

In the Lagos area Northern troops gained control of the Ikeja barracks and the nearby airport in the early morning of the 29th with little difficulty. A number of middle-ranking Northern officers from the Lagos and Apapa Headquarters organisations, like Lt Colonel Muritala Mohammed and Majors Adamu, Usuman and S. Alao then moved up to Ikeja to take charge.

In Lagos itself, Brigadier Ogundipe, the Chief of Staff (Supreme Headquarters) assumed overall command in Ironsi's absence. Early in the morning of the 29th, he sent Lt Colonel Gowon, the Chief of Staff (Army), up to Ikeja to parley with the rebels. They made Gowon stay there with them and asked him, as the most senior Northern officer in the army, to act as their spokesman. After some further discussions with the Northerners at Ikeja, Ogundipe unwisely sent troops from the Lagos Garrison Organisation to break through to the airport, but they were ambushed and routed. A later attempt to organise another contingent came to grief when a platoon of the Federal Guard and their officer refused to take orders. Although none of the units in the Lagos area other than the 2nd Battalion were in open revolt, it was clear that most of the troops could not be relied on. A number of the

surrounded before midnight on the 28th. Yet it was still possible for him to receive news of the 'mutiny' at Abeokuta at 3.30–4.00 a.m., and for Lt Colonel Njoku to leave Government House to encounter troops arriving from the barracks at this time. Although there was probably a certain amount of preplanning, the Eastern document is clearly stretching the evidence to attempt to prove a centrally organised conspiracy.

officers and NCOs of these units had already moved up to Ikeja, while other NCOs ran amok in Lagos looting and terrorising civilians and Ibo soldiers. Brigadier Ogundipe was visited by a delegation of Northern junior officers who asked if he would resign.[1] This he did and left Lagos secretly in civilian clothes for England.

The revolt in the North took some time to get moving, and it seems that the officers there had not been properly primed beforehand. Many officers in the North knew what was about to happen, but were not sure what their role in it was to be. In response to the first headquarters alerts, the customary security measures were taken, road blocks established and so on. The commander of the 3rd Battalion, Kaduna, Lt Colonel Okoro, addressed his troops in the early afternoon of the 29th, telling them that there had been a mutiny in the south and asking them to be loyal. But it was not until reports began to filter through – in BBC news broadcasts and from emissaries from the southern units – as to the nature and outcome of the revolt that the Northerners took action. They did not begin to move in any of the Northern units until late in the evening of the 29th, about twenty-four hours after the initial revolt at Abeokuta. It seems as if even then a number of the Eastern officers, thinking they had things in the North under control, were taken unawares. At Kaduna Lt Colonel Okoro was duped, for example, by his Northern RSM to an assignment in the guardroom, where he was questioned and shot by two of his young Northern officers. Control was established quite quickly, and by the morning of the 30th all units in the North were in Northern hands.[2]

The only military centre where the Northerners did not gain control was Enugu, capital of the Eastern Region. There the Commanding Officer, Lt Colonel Ogunewe, received an alert early enough to prevent the Northerners of the 1st Battalion – who were in the majority – from acting upon the signals they were already receiving from their colleagues elsewhere. A local truce was arranged and the arms depot put under a joint guard of Northern and southern troops. The Military Governor, Lt Colonel Ojukwu, fled to Police Headquarters where he was guarded by armed police of the Mobile Force. A stalemate ensued which could be broken neither by the Northerners nor by Lt Colonel Ojukwu. The latter was unable to persuade the Eastern Region Commissioner of Police to use his armed police to seize the armoury, without instructions from Lagos. This precarious balance, however, left

---

[1] This detail is from M. J. Dent's manuscript on the Nigerian crisis, Chapter V, 'The July coup'.

[2] The seizure of control implied different things in different units in the North. In the 3rd Battalion and the 1st Recce Squadron, control had to be seized by force and the commanders of these units assassinated. The brigade commander of the 1st Brigade, Lt Colonel Bassey, a non-Ibo Easterner, was left alone while the Northerners seized control from his staff. At the Depot, Zaria, the Commanding Officer fled, leaving the second in command to take over peacefully. The commander of the 5th Battalion, Kano, was a Northerner, so that the transfer of control was unproblematic, although a number of Eastern officers and men were subsequently arrested and killed.

Ojukwu in political control of the East, and gave him enough leeway to negotiate with Lagos, until the Northern troops were sent back to the North in exchange for Easterners, two weeks later.

NEGOTIATIONS: THE POLITICAL OUTCOME[1]

Fighting in the Lagos and Ikeja areas ceased before midnight on 29 July and negotiations began, continuing through to the morning of 1 August. Lt Colonel Gowon and the officers already at Ikeja were joined there by representatives of other military units.[2] A lively political debate among the officers ensued, in which one or two prominent Northern civil servants and policemen participated directly; the Military Governors of the regions were contacted by telephone; and many others were brought in indirectly on the telephone or through one of the many emissaries who plied between Lagos and Ikeja.

Initially it appears that the majority of the officers favoured a *de facto* secession of the North from Nigeria. The main spokesman for this view was Lt Colonel Muritala Mohammed, and he and other like-minded officers started to make arrangements for the immediate withdrawal of all Northern troops and civil servants in Lagos back to their region. Lt Colonel Gowon's stance in the early negotiations is not very clear, though it seems unlikely that he would have endorsed Northern secession as strongly as other officers did. A number of important civilian figures – including Sir Adetokunboh Ademola, the Chief Justice, Mr Justice Bello, a Northern judge of the Supreme Court, Alhaji Sule Katagum, the chairman of the Public Service Commission, and a number of the federal permanent secretaries – urged Gowon very strongly against secession. The British high commissioner and the American ambassador also gave similar advice, although it is difficult to assess their influence. Gowon responded to these urgings, and was also able to persuade his fellow-officers that some framework of common authority should be maintained. It is said that at one point, however, he had to insist he would not remain their spokesman if they did not shelve the arrangements they were making to withdraw Northern troops from Lagos. It is also clear that the only condition under which they would accept any alternative to secession was that Gowon himself, as the most senior Northerner in the army – and a

[1] There is a fuller account of the negotiations in Dent, 'The military and politics', to which the writer is indebted for one or two of the details given here.

[2] There is some discrepancy in available reports as to exactly who did and did not take part in the Ikeja negotiations. Major Danjuma certainly did come down from Ibadan to take part and it is probable that Lt Colonels Akahan and Mohammed Shuwa of the 4th and 5th Battalions at Ibadan and Kano, did too. The main figures mentioned as being already at Ikeja, namely Lt Colonels Gowon and Muritala Mohammed, Majors Adamu, Usuman and S. Alao all, of course, would have taken part.

widely respected officer – should take up the cloak of power himself. On
1 August Gowon went to Lagos and announced on the radio his assumption
of office as Supreme Commander and Head of the Military Government.

At this point there was still confusion about the shape of the political
settlement agreed on, for Gowon's statement in his first broadcast that he
intended to carry out a 'review of the issue of our national standing', on the
understanding that the basis no longer existed for a unitary constitutional
structure, was ambiguous and later gave rise to a certain amount of misunderstanding.[1] The most serious difficulty, however, was that Gowon was
not able to obtain the consent of the Military Governor of the East, Lt
Colonel Ojukwu, to his assumption of power. The latter went on the air
shortly after Gowon's broadcast to say that in his telephone conversations he
had pointed out that Ogundipe should have assumed control of the army and
the country as the most senior officer after Ironsi. Failing this, he had agreed
to accept the Northerners' original proposal to split the nation and its
military personnel into its component regional parts. He was not party to the
agreement that Gowon should take power and would not therefore accept his
authority. Thus the lines were drawn for the East's *de facto* withdrawal from
the political control of the centre, and the secession and civil war that followed
in 1967.

ORGANISATION AND DISORGANISATION IN THE COUP

The summary of events above shows them falling into shape in two ways
which at first glance do not seem consistent with each other. On the one hand,
it was suggested that control broke down in the army and that the coup took
the form of an uncontrolled outburst of hostile behaviour spreading by
contagion from one military unit to another. On the other hand, that there
was a definite pattern of organisation to the coup, and that some elements of
military authority survived. To understand how these two aspects were
combined one must look at the patterns of group behaviour in the last days of
July in somewhat sharper focus.

The hostile outburst aspect of the coup was most evident among the NCOs.
They were especially prone to collective beliefs defining the events of the
past seven months in terms of a cycle of conspiracy, miracle overcome by
evil forces and retribution. Major General Ironsi was tortured by the NCOs
of his escort in order to extract confessions about the part they supposed he

---

[1] For instance, the allegation made by Biafran supporters that in his statement that 'the basis for
unity is not there', he had committed himself to the eventual partition of the country: whereas
from the text of the broadcast reprinted in W. Schwartz, *Nigeria* (London: Pall Mall Press, 1968),
p. 211, it is quite clear that he intended this to mean that the basis no longer existed for the kind of
unitary constitutional structure Ironsi tried to impose.

had taken in the January coup and Maimalari's death. There were even a number of NCOs who apparently still believed that Maimalari and other senior officers had survived after the coup, and they demanded that the latter should either be released or information as to their whereabouts provided. In a number of instances the Other Ranks are known to have engaged in the ritual defacement of their adversaries of a kind designed to deprive them of their identities and render them powerless and no longer threatening in symbolic terms. At Ikeja, for instance, captives of Eastern origin are said[1] to have been flogged and made to lie in human urine and faeces, which were then converted into 'meals' that they were forced to eat; and others to have been slaughtered by Northerners in the same manner as goats are killed. One Ibo officer who was captured at Ikeja airport was tied to an iron cross, beaten and left to die in the guardroom. Another – Major Okafor, a January conspirator – was buried alive. There are also examples of rituals of rebellion in which the rejection of organisational authority which was difficult to express overtly was given expression in fantasy. It is reported, for instance, that Northern Other Ranks engaged in the pretence that they could assume the rank of the officer they had killed, wearing his insignia and assuming his name.[2]

The coup was used by some of the Other Ranks as an excuse to terrorise, rape and loot. Even the property of absent Northern officers was sometimes looted. On a number of occasions in August, Eastern officers and men were killed after specific assurance had been given that they would be guaranteed safety at their posts and repatriation to the East if they so wished. Often killings were entirely spontaneous acts of indiscipline, as when the Provost Marshall, Major Ekanem, was shot on 1 August when on an errand for Lt Colonel Gowon himself. Guarantees, therefore, did not operate mainly because the senior Northern officers were themselves unable to enforce them. In addition, however, some Eastern officers and men who were suspected of complicity in the January coup or who were thought to have 'abused Northerners' were on a definite list or lists for assassination. It is not known at what level the lists originated.[3] It is inconceivable that Lt Colonel Gowon sanctioned this kind of behaviour, though he lacked the effective power to

---

[1] *January 15th: before and after*, p. 51. Despite their origin, there is no reason to disbelieve these accounts, although one or two of the images (e.g., the killing of Ibos like sacrificial goats by Northern Moslems) may possibly have been invented in order to fit southern stereotypes of the Northerner.

[2] Information from Martin Dent.

[3] Nor how widely they circulated among Northerners: *January 15th: before and after*, pp. 49–55, contains an account of the sentencing and execution of Easterners on 1 and 2 August 1966. It also reports the arrest and shooting by firing squad of a number of Eastern soldiers of the 4th Battalion near Makurdi on 11–16 August under the direction of a Major. Whether or not one accepts the Eastern version of such events in its entirety, there is sufficient evidence from independent Northern sources to satisfy this author that a list or lists of Easterners who were to be killed was or were circulating among Northern NCOs and junior officers.

stop it. In all there were more than forty-one officers and 194 men killed in the course of the revolt or during the weeks that followed.[1]

Yet despite the undercurrent of revolt and rejection of controls, there was a degree of minimal adherence to military authority norms, even if it seemed at times as if the attachment was more to the form than to the substance of discipline. It is significant that the more senior of the Northern NCOs were on the whole able to maintain their leadership over the rank and file during the coup, this role not being preempted from them by new charismatic figures arising from below as is common in the literature on non-institutionalised conflict of this kind.[2]

Relations between Northern officers and men were a little more ambivalent. The Northern Other Ranks preferred, on the one hand, to have their officers initiate the coup on their behalf as this was more like legitimate military procedure. On the other hand, there were frequent occasions when officers' orders were disregarded. Yet even in the breach of authority, adherence to the proper forms was regarded as desirable. On one occasion, it is said that a Northern officer was respectfully asked by his NCOs to order them to shoot their captives or they might need to deal with him too. At times an unauthorised shooting could be given sanction as an 'accidental discharge, sah!'. Ironsi was killed after the officer in charge of his escort had apparently responded to the NCOs' demands (that they be allowed to deal with him) by returning to Ibadan to 'get his orders', on a half-implicit understanding that the NCOs could do what they liked while he was away.

Among the officers themselves there seems to have been a similar cycle of revolt from below, with legitimation later conferred from above, for those things that could be made to seem respectable, and silence concerning those which could not. To understand how this pattern worked, it is necessary to distinguish three separate levels of officers each with their distinctive role in the coup.

First, the operational side of the coup – the preparation of specific contingency plans, the seizure of control in the battalions and the capture of Ironsi – was mainly in the hands of junior officers at the platoon commander or company second in command level.

Secondly, there were the middle-ranking staff officers in Lagos, Lt Colonel Muritala Mohammed, Majors Martin Adamu, S.A. Alao and Baba Usuman, who pledged their support before the coup and who took over negotiations at Ikeja on the junior officers' behalf after it. These officers probably also

---

[1] *January 15th: before and after* gives these figures, though, as the document points out, this may be an underestimate owing to the incompleteness in sources of information (to be balanced against its tendency to invent details). The figure includes twenty-three detained in Kaduna prison, presumed dead, as well as 171 actually known to have been killed.

[2] See Smelser, *Theory of collective behaviour.*

played some part in coordinating operations, though it is difficult with the information presently available to say precisely what they did, except that if anybody in such a loosely structured situation could be said to have been the overall leader of the coup it was Lt Colonel Muritala Mohammed. As staff officers at HQ,[1] however, neither Mohammed nor any of the others had actual operational control of troops they could commit to the struggle, having to rely on officers in command of troops outside Lagos. Mohammed's position as the head of the army's signals unit was obviously strategic, though mainly in urging the units in the North and East to get moving after the initial revolts in Abeokuta, Ibadan and Ikeja had already taken place. Major Danjuma of the 4th Battalion at Ibadan was probably the only middle-ranking officer to take an active operational part as well as the symbolic role he played when he arrived to arrest Major General Ironsi, after the latter had been surrounded in Government House, Ibadan, for some hours by the junior officers of the Battalion.

Finally, the most senior Northern officers – Lt Colonels Gowon, Hassan Katsina, Akahan, Mohammed Shuwa – seem not to have been involved in the revolt itself, being brought in, in various capacities afterwards. Gowon, as we have seen, was coopted by the Northerners into assuming power as the most senior Northerner in the army, thus giving the seizure of control an air of respectability in terms of military authority norms. Hassan Katsina was on a tour of the North when the coup occurred and was first of all arrested, then brought in by telephone later for the discussions of 31 July–1 August. Akahan, though commander of the 4th Battalion, does not seem to have played a direct role in events at Ibadan and at one stage, indeed, was actually kept away from the barracks by his own troops. On the other hand, he did nothing positive to stop the revolt. He also lent dignity to Ironsi's arrest by appearing afterwards in order to make an apology for letting this happen to a guest, attempting to make events intelligible in military terms by saying that the Northerners had their orders.[2] Once events had run their course on 30 July, he ordered that the Northern troops should be disarmed, paraded them and offered his congratulations, saying there would be no more bloodshed 'since events had now balanced out'.[3] Lastly, all Lt Colonel Mohammed Shuwa had to do, since he was already in command of the 5th Battalion at Kano, was to make a declaration of support when the smoke had cleared in the south.

[1] Lt Colonel Muritala Mohammed was Inspector of Signals, Alao a staff officer at Air Force HQ, Major Usuman a Staff Officer II (Intelligence) at HQ and Major Adamu at Brigade HQ, Apapa.
[2] Dent, 'The military and politics'. From the Eastern point of view this might be further evidence of conspiracy. But this is at odds with what is known of Akahan's actions and views at the time. 'Having orders' is sometimes used as a euphemism in army circles for having no alternative but to take a certain course, as a way of apologising for doing something unpleasant.
[3] *January 15th: before and after*, p. 48.

In view of the different part each played in events it is interesting to note how sharply these groups were differentiated from each other in both seniority and rank. In Table 9 it may be seen that each role corresponds roughly to a distinct level in rank structure. The lines are especially well drawn if one considers substantive rather than temporary or acting ranks (for the rapid advancement in 'acting' capacities of some Northern officers after the January coup opened up a wide gap between their temporary commands and their gazetted ranks, the latter being a better indicator of their peer group standing than the former).

TABLE 9. *Rank levels of officers with role in July coup* (*substantive and temporary ranks*)

	Substantive (gazetted) rank	Temporary rank
A Officers in West/Lagos Operational role	10 Lieutenants 8 2nd Lieutenants	= 5 Captains 5 Lieutenants 8 2nd Lieutenants
Coordination and negotiation	5 Captains	= 1 Lt Colonel 4 Majors
Legitimacy after the event	2 Lt Colonels	= 2 Lt Colonels
B Officers in North Operational role	7 Lieutenants 5 2nd Lieutenants	= 1 Captain 6 Lieutenants 5 2nd Lieutenants
Undefined coordination or cooperation after the event[a]	3 Captains 4 Lieutenants	= 2 Majors 5 Captains
Legitimacy after the event	1 Lt Colonel 2 Captains	= 2 Lt Colonels 1 Major

Sources: Substantive ranks from Federation of Nigeria: *Official Gazettes*. Officers are allocated into the above categories in accordance with detailed descriptions provided in *January 15th: before and after* and revised and supplemented where required from other sources at the writer's disposal.
Note: [a] Available descriptions of roles of middle-level officers in the North are especially sketchy, so that it is impossible to place much reliance on them (e.g. A/Major Alabi who 'cooperated with the Northerners' according to *January 15th: before and after*, but this is hardly a very explicit description of his role). It is not possible in most instances to determine if middle-ranking officers coordinated happenings or just lent cooperation after the event, like Captain Sawntong, who temporarily took command of the 3rd Battalion.

In terms of substantive ranks the paradigm seems to have been lieutenants organising the operations, captains (acting majors or lt colonels) in the middle-level negotiation and coordination capacities, and lt colonels providing the blessing afterwards. Officers serving in units in the North are shown separately in the table from those in the Western Region and Lagos. The Northern revolt lacked a well-defined middle-level coordinating group, comparable to that which operated in the latter areas. This could either be because there was less advance planning there than in the south; or because there were fewer middle-ranking officers, the Northern HQ organisation being small; or because the Ikeja negotiations created a distinctive role for middle-ranking officers that was absent in Kaduna.

Again, it is possible to subdivide the more junior group of officers into those who played leading roles and who took some part in the advance planning of the coup; and those who played more subordinate roles (e.g. transporting and guarding prisoners, arranging firing squads, leading groups of troops at the platoon level) many of whom may not have joined the revolt until the day it took place. This subdivision can only be a rough one, depending as it does on descriptions of the activities of the officers in the various sources available. Yet it does indicate that the appropriate correspondence between rank and role also maintained itself *within* the group of active junior officers.

TABLE 10. *Rank of leaders and followers among officers with operative roles in July 1966 (West and Lagos only)*

	Substantive (gazetted) rank		Temporary rank	
	Leaders	Followers	Leaders	Followers
Captain	—	—	4	1
Lieutenant	7	3	3	2
2nd Lieutenant	2	6	2	6

Sources: As for Table 9. It is possible that these sources, and in particular *January 15th: before and after*, introduce a degree of bias in favour of our hypothesis that military status norms continued to operate during the coup. For this document has a tendency to *assume* that the more senior officers had by definition a leading role. We have attempted to correct for this bias by designating as 'leaders' only those officers whose leadership role is described with a minimum degree of specificity and/or when this checks with other sources at the writer's disposal. It is probable that a larger number of officers took part than indicated by any of the available sources.

These overall figures for all units in the Lagos/West area may even understate the degree to which rank and leadership went together. For leaders in the most junior ranks tended to emerge only in army units in which there were few or no participants of higher seniority than themselves, for instance the two 2nd lieutenants organising the rebellion at Ikeja.[1] It is interesting to note that the main organisers in each unit were of virtually identical rank and

[1] Before more senior officers from the HQ organisations came up to join them.

73

seniority. In Abeokuta two temporary captains are described as taking the lead, in Ibadan three lieutenants and a captain (temporary Major Danjuma) and at Ikeja two 2nd lieutenants.

Nevertheless, in contrast with the January clique, the formation and patterning of the group seems to have owed relatively little to fraternisation and common experience at cadet school. For the conspirators were very diverse in their training, apart from a strong Mons Officer Cadet School contingent. In this respect there was no significant difference from their peers in the 1961–4 seniority cohorts from which most of them were drawn. The short-service training at Mons, in India, the USA or Canada which the majority of them received, was by no means as intense a socialising experience as two years at Sandhurst. To say that the July officers as a group lacked a frame in common training is not, however, to deny that linkages between *individual* participants might have developed in cadet schools. The writer knows of at least one instance where such links were of practical importance – though it is impossible to generalise because of the paucity of evidence.

TABLE 11. *Training of July coup officers*

	Short-service courses	Operational role	Coordination/ negotiation
Mons OCS, England (cadet entry)		11	4
Mons OCS, England (ex-NCO entry)		—	3
India		2	—
USA		5	—
Canada		4	—
Australia		1	—
Academy			
Sandhurst, England		4	5
Other academies[a]		2	—
Not known		1	—

Note: [a] In India, Pakistan, Ethiopia.

Thus, to sum up, military patterns of behaviour and status were not only still of importance, but defined the appropriate interrelationships amongst the persons participating in the coup. This is all the more remarkable because the breakdown of organisational controls, the decrease in social distance between junior and senior officers that occurred after January, and the anomic character of the July 28–29 revolt, might have led one to predict the emergence of new status patterns superseding the old. It is true that the appropriate forms were sometimes used merely in order to put a gloss on the effective rejection of authority. There were also times when it did seem as if new patterns of charismatic leadership were emerging. For some weeks after July, Lt Colonel Muritala Mohammed apparently possessed an authority of this type, challenging that of Gowon.[1] But Gowon's position, based on 'legitimate' seniority principles in the Northern officer group, soon became formalised to such an extent that it was out of the range of challenges of this type, and the army settled down to the normal routines of command and control.

The failure of the coup in the 1st Battalion at Enugu makes an interesting comparison with the above, because the same basic elements of revolt and authority were combined somewhat differently, with the latter in the end prevailing over the former. The southern officers, having been alerted in time by calls from Abeokuta and headquarters, got to the barracks and found the Northerners already assembling. The latter were not yet armed but 'could not explain themselves' to their colleagues. It was possible to arrange a local truce largely because of the good personal relations between the Commanding Officer, Lt Colonel Ogunewe, Major Chude-Sokei, the second in command, and the junior Northern officers of whom the most senior, Captain Jalo, acted as the main spokesman. Ogunewe ordered all officers to sleep in the mess and all NCOs in the battalion office from the night of 30 July onwards, as well as having the arms depot locked and under joint guard.

Nonetheless, the truce was a precarious one. Signals kept arriving for the Northerners from Lt Colonel Muritala Mohammed and others in Lagos urging them to act, threatening them and promising a relief force within a week. The Northern rank and file went on the rampage in nearby villages and at one point some of them tried to break into the armoury, but were overpowered. A meeting of Ibo officers attended by Ogunewe, Chude-Sokei and Ojukwu had also proposed to break the stalemate by sending the Mobile Police in to seize the arms depot. But the Commissioner of Police, Mr Okeke, had refused to be a party to this, saying that the events were a 'fight internal to the army' and that he took orders from Lagos only.[2]

The departure of the Northern troops which was negotiated between the East and Lagos[3] took place on 10 August and was marked by an interesting display of military cameraderie. A photographer was brought up to the mess for a last group photograph of the officers of the battalion together. Then drinks were served and the officers toasted each other, washing away the fear of fratricide which had been ever present during the two preceding weeks.

[1] See the more detailed account in Chapter XIII, of the relative positions of Gowon and Muritala Mohammed during the three months after the coup.
[2] Mr Okeke, who was himself an Ibo, apparently was in fear of assassination by both sides until the final departure of the Northerners.
[3] The official seal to this agreement, however, being put by a meeting of the representatives of the National Military Government with those of all the Regional Military Governors on 9 August.

TRIBE AND REGION IN JULY

The victims of the coup were mainly Ibos from the Eastern and Mid-West Regions, though a scattering of non-Eastern Ibos were also killed, as can be seen in Table 12. In general, being an Ibo was sufficient grounds for slaughter during the seizure of power in army units at the early stages, though there was more selectivity later on in preparing lists of 'suspects' for killing. It appears that non-Ibos whether from the East, Mid-West or West were only killed if they got in the way during seizure of power, if they were in some way suspected of sympathy with the January coup, or if the particular Northern troops by whom they were confronted made the false assumption that they were Ibo. Some were also taken into custody alongside the Ibos at the early stages, but were subsequently released. The majority of the soldiers from the West and Mid-West (non-Ibo) went free throughout, and a handful participated in the coup themselves.

TABLE 12. *Ethnic and regional origin of victims of July coup*

Region	Deaths of		Ethnicity	Deaths of officers only
	Officers^a	Men^b		
East	31	154	Ibo	27
Mid-West	5	14	Non-Ibo Mid-West	2
West	3	3	Non-Ibo East	6
North	0	0	Yoruba	4

Source: January 15th: before and after. Obvious inaccuracies in this document allowed for, though estimates still subject to small margin of error.

Notes:
^{a} List of officers excluded two additional Ibo air force officers killed.
^{b} Excluded 23 Eastern Other Ranks imprisoned in July, fate unknown.

The officers who carried out the coup were almost entirely Northern, although there was one Yoruba (Temporary Major Alao) in the coordinating group and three among the active junior officers.[1] There were no Eastern and only one Mid-Western officer taking part. There was indeed some discontent against the regime and against Decree no. 34 among non-Ibo southerners – especially the Yorubas – but it was not strong enough to induce many to play an active part. Most – excepting a few non-Ibo Easterners who fled to the East with their Ibo confreres – remained in the main Federal army with their Northern colleagues after Gowon assumed power.

[1] Some of these, however, were Northern Yorubas. In addition, there were two middle-ranking Yorubas who are listed as playing an undefined role in the North.

Yet it would be wrong to regard this polarisation of conflict between Ibos on the one hand and Northerners on the other as a simple confrontation of primordial groupings. Tribal and regional ties never entirely superseded organisational relationships. This is clear both from the persistence of military status norms and from the fact that the conflict itself drew much of its energy from the tensions between the various levels of the military hierarchy, between NCOs and officers, between junior officers and their seniors.

Secondly, it could not be said that either the Ibos or the Northerners acted as a cohesively structured group, in the manner depicted by their mutual stereotypes of each other. The Northerners especially were diverse and fragmentarily organised. The direct participants themselves were a fraction, little more than thirty-two per cent of the total number of 112 or so Northern combat officers in the officer corps. Admittedly, this was more than the proportion of Ibo officers mobilised during the January coup – probably because of the disorganised 'mass' character of the July revolt. But even if the figure is an underestimate, it scarcely indicates that the Northerners were unanimous.[1]

In social and cultural terms, the participants – like the rest of the Northern officer group from which they were recruited – were a very mixed group. It is possible to make a very crude distinction[2] between (*a*) the inhabitants of the centralised Moslem Emirates of the far North (Hausa–Fulani and Kanuri); (*b*) persons from the largely Moslem diaspora of the pagan areas which had been subjected to conquest by the Emirates and cultural assimilation by the Hausa–Fulani (Niger Province, Bauchi, Southern Zaria, Adamawa, etc.); (*c*) the inhabitants of the 'Middle Belt', the culturally and religiously diverse peoples of the southern areas of the North; and (*d*) the Northern Yorubas whom it is impossible for practical purposes to differentiate from their compatriots in the Western Region. In Table 13, we show the approximate ethnic origins, both of those who took part, and of the seniority cohorts of Northerners from which they were recruited. The number of participants in all probability slightly exceeds the totals shown, because the sources are incomplete. The percentage distribution is in addition slanted slightly in

[1] It is interesting to compare this picture of the fragmentation of regional identification among the Northerners with the conspiratorial image put forward after the coup by the East. The latter was expressed in a press conference by Lt Colonel Ojukwu as follows: 'The point here and the crux of the whole matter is that the North wants to dominate...Gowon is not capable of doing anything. He is only a front man for the whole NPC/NNDP coalition...in fact the officers and men who took part in the July massacre were being used as tools. If you remember in the course of my first statement I said that the soldiers wanted secession. This is most significant. It is the soldiers not knowing what they were being used for, who wanted secession. But the NNDP/ NPC coalition which master-minded this pogrom definitely wanted to continue the old policy of the North, that is to dominate and dictate.' *Nigerian Outlook* (Enugu) 21 March 1967.

[2] For a full description of the procedure for assignation into the various cultural/ethnic/regional categories, see Chapter VIII below.

77

favour of the Moslem Emirates, because of the method of assignation of officers into the categories shown.[1]

TABLE 13. *Cultural/ethnic affiliations of July coup participants*

Roles of participants in coup	Cultural origins (per cent of total)			
	Dry North	Hausa–Fulani diaspora	Middle Belt	N =
Operational role	37	44	19	27
Coordination, etc.	33	56	11	9
All direct participants	36	47	17	36
Cultural origins of the Northerners in seniority cohorts to which participants belonged	36	33	31	108
Northern population (1963–, excluding the Yoruba areas)	54	27	19	—

Sources: as for Tables 9 and 33.
Note: This table excludes the Northern Yorubas because of the difficulty of separating them from the Yorubas of the Western Region. The six Yorubas taking part in the coup amounted to 11% of the total number of Yorubas (Northern and Western) in the coup-makers' seniority group.

The table shows that there were many participants from both the Emirate, the diaspora and the Middle Belt areas of the North. There were in addition six Yoruba participants, at least four of whom were Northern Yorubas from Kabba and Ilorin Provinces of the then Northern Region. It appears that the Middle Belt was slightly under-represented and the diaspora group slightly over-represented, relative to their share of the seniority cohorts from which coup participants were recruited. This may merely reflect biases in the data, especially as the relationships do not seem to be very strong. It is also possible that the Middle-Belt officers would have identified slightly less with the political interests and goals of the North. On the other hand, it is interesting that the subjugated lands of the Emirates (the diaspora) were better represented than the Emirates themselves.

Nevertheless, it is clear that common interests and goals were widely shared and mobilised a substantial proportion of the officers and men from *all* areas of the North, including those previously in political opposition to one another, ranging from the Tiv and Northern Yoruba on the one hand to the Hausa-Fulani and Kanuri on the other. The common political cause of

[1] Officers with purely Moslem or Hausa names are assumed to originate from the Emirates, unless other sources (personal acquaintance, historical sources, schools attended, etc.) indicate otherwise. This is likely therefore to swell the numbers in the first category. Fortunately this bias should not invalidate our conclusions because it runs against our hypothesis that the conspiratorial group – like the Northern officer group in general – are not drawn exclusively from the 'dry North'.

these groups was fashioned from the special political conditions prevailing in July 1966 which – as described later[1] – defined the situation in terms of regional sentiment, resistance to administrative and political unification and opposition to the real or supposed dominance of the Ibos both in the structure of central government and the military.

After the seizure of power, the consensus began to weaken almost immediately and the North no longer evoked the same loyalty. The new political balance created by the coup encouraged officers who had earlier wanted the North to secede to swing round behind a strong Federation, some even advocating within a few days of the coup the immediate invasion of the East, to bring it back under the common political framework by force rather than by negotiation.[2] Many of the diaspora and Middle-Belt officers came from September 1966 onwards to demand that the old North be broken up into a number of separate regions or states, and this division was eventually carried out by Lt Colonel Gowon in May 1967.

[1] In Chapter XI below.
[2] See the detailed summary of political events after the coup in Chapter XIII below.

PART TWO

THE NIGERIAN MILITARY
AS A SOCIAL SYSTEM

INTRODUCTION

Our portrait of the two military coups of 1966 aimed at bringing out the distinctive characteristics of each and the nature of the social process that led from one to the other. To start with there was the January coup, a classic *cuartelazo* or conspiracy by a small, well-organised group of officers aimed explicitly to capture power for defined ideological or political purposes (albeit rather simplistic ones). Then came a growth in political conflict in the army because it became the focus of all political allocations, the military leaders having become the government. This contributed to the spread of indiscipline and to a loss of solidarity between military 'brothers'. These trends acquired extra salience from the killing of Northern and Western officers in the January coup and the foreshortening of the hierarchy of command that resulted; both tending to generalise revolt from the tight knot of conspiracy to a wider circle of mass rejection of authority at all lower levels of command. The result was the July counter-coup, an outburst of revolt against authority from below by junior officers and NCOs in an attempt to effect a transfer of political power but also as an outburst of hostility against a particular ethnic group, the Ibos.

Yet despite each coup's unique character and place in a sequence of historical events, there were also important similarities between the two. It is worth summarising these very briefly here, as they begin to suggest how the revolts may have been related to the structure and functioning of the Nigerian Army as a distinct social system.

First, the remarkable power of military norms in the midst of rebellion. In both coups, the distribution of authority and tasks *within* the active conspiratorial group was effected on classic military lines with the more senior officers taking the lead. In both, the arrest and/or killing of military figures was sometimes justified under the cloak of the fiction that those carrying out the arrest 'had their orders'. In both, once the action was over, the participants sought to bring themselves back into the normal hierarchy of authority, to legitimate their position in military terms, Major Nzeogwu in wanting to surrender to Major General Ironsi once the latter had taken power, the Northern junior officers in bringing in first the more senior Northern officers to negotiate and then Lt Colonel Gowon, as the most senior Northerner, to assume power on their behalf.

Both coups, moreover, reveal similar sources of conflict. In both, peer

83

groups – majors in January, lieutenants and captains in July – were the frame of cleavage. In both, senior officers and the military hierarchy were the object of attack. There was a difference, however, in the importance of primordial – ethnic or regional – cleavages in the coups. In July, this element was much more explicit, the Northerners consciously organising among themselves as a group, planning first of all to secede from the Federation en bloc and focussing their attack almost entirely upon the Ibos and Easterners alone. In January, however, both the conspiratorial group and those whom they killed were patterned in ethnic/regional terms, but more as a result of the tactical and political requirements of the coup than through any self-conscious use of ethnic or regional ties of the type that was seen in July.

Thirdly, there was a strong element of non-rational behaviour in the revolts. Again, this was nearer the surface in the July coup. It could be seen in the collective belief in a gigantic Ibo plot, the saintly deaths of Northern figures, like Brigadier Maimalari in January, and the need for retribution against those who had caused them. And it was also evident in the indisci-plined and vicious circumstances in which large numbers of Easterners were defiled, tortured and killed. Similar features, however, were also present in January; as in the belief in conspiracy in high places to use the army to crush the Action Group and NCNC in the south which was among the precipitant factors for the coup; or the somewhat angry manner in which figures like the Sardauna of Sokoto, Brigadiers Ademulegun and Maimalari and Colonel Shodeinde were shot by the Majors.

There is a tradition in sociology which accounts for non-rational behaviour in social situations in terms of social strain, an imprecise concept which may be taken to mean that there are cleavages of interest or conflicting role expectations in a social context, which from the point of view of the actors in that situation cannot be resolved by the mutual adjustment of interests or roles.[1] In Nigeria, the two coups may be regarded, on the one hand, as a response to strains in the political arena – the collapse of civilian politics and the transfer of power away from the North implied in the first coup – which we leave aside for consideration in Part Three; and on the other hand, to the structural strains of the army itself.

[1] See Smelser, *Theory of collective behaviour* and T. Parsons, 'Social strains in America' in *Structure and process in modern society* (New York: Free Press, 1959), Chapter VII. Marxist critics of bourgeois social science argue that the idea of social strain conceals static social assumptions, for example, R. Blackburn, 'Brief guide to bourgeois ideology' in A. Cockburn and R. Blackburn, *Student power* (London: Penguin Books, 1969). The difference is that whereas the former see situations of social strain as leading to regressive irrational behaviour, the latter argue that when the correct social diagnosis can be found (revolution by some of the actors in the situation, namely the proletariat, etc.) social strain is not necessarily regressive or dysfunctional. In the present case there is a combination of both. Both coups aimed at the transfer of political power – from the actors' point of view a perfectly rational goal – though both had a very marked resonance of non-rational behaviour, of regressive responses to the situation of social strain.

The latter, the organisational strains of the military, which are analysed in detail in the chapters which follow, fall into two broad categories. The first of these again suggests itself from our examination of the two military coups of 1966, namely that both cohesion and cleavage often appeared to be linked with the same standard features of military organisation: the peer groups which played such a prominent role in both, were at one and the same time a source of cleavage and an indicator of the power of military status norms; the ethic of brotherhood accentuated each group's mutual bitterness about the 'treachery' of the others after the killing of colleagues; and military forms and rituals were used to clothe acts of rebellion, as when Northern NCOs forced their officers to give them orders to kill or in July pretended to assume the ranks of their victims. This combination of the elements of cohesion and cleavage springs, we may suggest, from common dilemmas of organisation,[1] the interplay between functions and dysfunctions, the fact that structural elements and behaviour which maintain a social system in some respects may undermine it in others.

The cohesion of an organisation – its ability to hold together and continue to function effectively – has, on the one hand, a horizontal dimension, to which the concept of solidarity more or less corresponds, if one is considering the internal workings of the system, and the maintenance of boundaries, if it is the relation of the organisation to its environment that is important. And there is secondly, a vertical dimension, that of authority or discipline in military terms (though this is not of course entirely independent of the horizontal dimension, for the authoritativeness of an organisation's leaders is increased if there is harmony among their subordinates[2] and if boundaries do not allow the cooptation of the latters' loyalties by external political or social groups). The functional dilemmas that characterised the Nigerian Army can therefore be set out as shown in Fig. 1.

To take these in the order they appear in the chapters which follow, we shall argue: (1) Unity in format makes it possible for the military to act swiftly and decisively: integral boundaries insulate it from external conflict and preserve the unity of command. Yet these features also made the army more prone to revolt and rebellion; to fratricidal conflict in which brothers

[1] The idea of dilemmas in bureaucratic organisation is discussed in P. Blau and W. R. Scott, *Formal organisations* (San Francisco, Calif.: Chandler, 1962), Chapter IX, and in the specifically military context (under the terminology of organisational strain) by M. Janowitz and Lt Colonel R. Little, *Sociology and the military establishment* (New York: Russell Sage Foundation, 1965), especially Chapter II. The classic treatment of the interplay of functions and dysfunctions is to be found in R. K. Merton's discussion of manifest and latent functions in *Social theory and social structure* (rev. 2nd ed., Glencoe, Ill.: Free Press, 1957), pp. 50–4.

[2] Or, as P. Blau, 'Critical remarks on Max Weber's theory of authority', *American Political Science Review* (1963), p. 312, suggests, one 'distinguishing criterion of authority...is that structural constraints rooted in the collectivity of subordinates rather than instruments of power or influence wielded by the superior himself enforce compliance with his directives'.

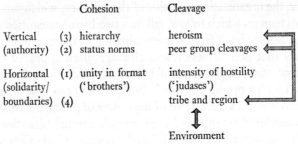

		Cohesion	Cleavage
Vertical	(3)	hierarchy	heroism
(authority)	(2)	status norms	peer group cleavages
Horizontal	(1)	unity in format	intensity of hostility
(solidarity/		('brothers')	('judases')
boundaries)	(4)		tribe and region

Environment

Fig. 1

became judases (Chapter III); and made it inflexible and unable to adjust to political conflict once it was embroiled in it (Chapters III and XII). (2) The military belief in the officer corps as a corporate brotherhood of 'officers and gentlemen' increased the solidarity of the army (Chapters IV and V); and the strongly enforced military norms of status (salutes, an order of precedence on on all public occasions and shouts of 'sah') buttressed discipline (Chapters V and VI). But the combined effect of them both gave rise to peer groups, a hierarchy of brotherhoods which became the nodal points of cleavage (Chapter V). (3) A simple military structure like the Nigerian Army must somehow combine the two elements of heroism and hierarchy, of initiative and discipline; indeed discipline itself, as we will show, depends on subordinate commanders at each level of the hierarchy being able to control a wide enough area of initiative to dominate their own subordinates (Chapter VI). The appropriate 'mix' of these two elements, however, is difficult to establish in *any* military organisation, the more so in one which is operating in unstable political and organisational conditions, as in Nigeria.

(4) In addition, there was the problem of reconciling the organisational identities of officers and men in the army with their latent identities of tribe and region (Chapter VIII). Though this is not a functional dilemma in the same way as the above, it is important for two reasons. First, because of the unique way in which tribe and region linked up with organisation strains, cleavages between such primordial groups coinciding with those between peer groups, the revolt against authority being legitimised in terms of the need to prevent one ethnic group (the Ibos in the July coup) from dominating the senior positions in the military hierarchy. And secondly, because ethnicity and region provide the main link with the social and political environment, conflicts between different groups in the army becoming vested with salience and meaning because of the struggle for power between the different tribal and regional interests in the national political arena.

The second main category of structural strain in the military comes from the special problems of setting up a new organisation – or what amounted to one when Nigerian personnel replaced expatriates in all command positions in the hierarchy within the space of only five years after Independence. For instance: (i) The simple absence of occupational or professional experience at all levels of command (Chapter III). (ii) An unbalanced and highly youthful age structure (Chapter VII), leaving only a narrow gap in experience between high level and junior officers; and NCOs who were often more experienced even than their middle-ranking officers; so that the experience and ability of commanders rarely matched up to the formal authority of their position. (iii) So much mobility from post to post, command to command, barracks to barracks that stable lines of command did not develop (Chapter VII). (iv) Very high rates of promotional mobility, also making it difficult to establish an integrated set of self-images around military careers, and tending to develop anomic or unreal expectations among officers about their functions, prospects and role (Chapter VII). (v) A haphazard and uneven pattern of recruitment as between different ethnic and regional groups (Chapter VIII). In some instances, these strains of newness were superimposed upon standard functional dilemmas of military organisation and thus tended to deepen and intensify them. For example, the high rates of mobility and the youthful age structure favoured heroism at the expense of the hierarchy (Chapter VI and VII) and made the balance between the two impossible to maintain; and the uneven pattern of regional recruitment (Chapter VIII) was the main reason it becomes possible to equate peer group and primordial cleavages.

We turn now to a more detailed analysis of the strains in the Nigerian military, beginning in Chapter III with an inventory of its simple structural characteristics.

THE NIGERIAN ARMY: COMPOSITION AND STRUCTURE

THE COLONIAL HERITAGE[1]

The Nigerian Army, like those of all sub-Saharan African states, was first created, organised and trained under colonial tutelage. It originated from the small mercenary forces that had been used to establish British rule. But after conquest had been achieved, its role had been mainly symbolic, to serve as a visible demonstration to the populace of the coercion (or the threat of coercion) which was the ultimate basis of colonial rule. External security was provided by the metropolitan power, except at moments of great crisis like the First and Second World Wars when the West African forces were expanded and troops despatched to fight on remote fronts, as in the Burma campaign in the Second World War. This image was carried over into the early Independence period: the army was there to provide support for the fledgling state, to help maintain law and order and provide the ritual marks of sovereignty with military parades, march pasts and guards of honour that gladden a politician's heart. Foreign policy was the ground of the statesman not the soldier, an area of diplomatic offensives by the great powers; and of the defence of the status quo by the African states, in respect both of their own internal politics and of the inherited colonial boundaries. Serious pressures for military expansion were felt only where boundary disputes exceeded the Organisation of African Unity's capacity to mediate as in Ethiopia/Somalia/Kenya or where there were civil war situations, as in the Congo (Kinshasha), the Sudan and Nigeria.

For these reasons most African armies, like the Nigerian Army before the civil war, have been small and have had minimal material, organisational and human resources at their disposal, even taking the relative poverty of the African continent into account. In general, African countries have mobilised proportionately less of their available manpower under arms than most other areas of the world, including most other Third World countries. They have devoted smaller economic resources in absolute terms to defence. And all the

---

[1] See the more detailed account of civil military relations in the colonial and early post-colonial period in Chapter X below.

ex-British countries plus Rwanda, Burundi and Liberia have spent proportionately less of their national budgets and national products on defence than anywhere else in the world. To illustrate these differences we tabulate data on the military resources of Nigeria for 1965–6 and compare these in Table 14 with the ten other largest African countries and ten developing nations in the Middle East and Asia of comparable population size.

TABLE 14. *Comparison of Nigeria's military resources (1966) with selected African and Asian countries*

	Popula-tion (mn) mid-1965	Armed forces (mn) 1966–7	Armed forces/ popula-tion ratio[a]	Defence expendi-ture ($mn) 1965–6[b]	Defence as % of budget	Defence as % of GNP	Total GNP ($mn) 1965	GNP per head ($) 1965
Sub-Saharan Africa								
Nigeria	57·5	10·5	0·018	22·0	4·5	0·7[c]	3840	67
Congo (Kinshasha)	15·6	32·0	0·205	(22·5)	(14·5)	—	—	—
Tanzania	10·5	2·1	0·020	(7·2)	(3·8)	(0·3)	668	64
Kenya	9·4	4·2	0·045	11·3	5·5	1·1[c]	840	90
Ghana	7·7	16·0	0·208	29·6	6·9	1·8	1941	251
Uganda	7·6	5·7	0·075	6·9	5·2	1·1	586	78
Cameroon	5·2	3·5	0·067	(15·8)	(19·5)	(4·2)	618	118
Upper Volta	4·9	1·5	0·031	(2·8)	(14·1)	(6·1)	202	43
Mali	4·6	3·5	0·076	(8·8)	(21·2)	—	—	—
Malawi	3·9	0·9	0·023	1·1	2·2	0·6	168	43
Ivory Coast	3·8	4·0	0·105	(8·8)	(6·9)	(2·4)	773	20
Middle East								
Turkey	31·1	372·0	1·196	330·8	20·8	4·4	7593	244
UAR	29·6	180·0	0·608	425·5	21·5	9·0	4777	161
Iran	23·4	175·0	0·748	226·6	23·0	4·5	5805	207
Iraq	8·3	80·0	0·964	159·2	29·3	6·5	1771	217
Syria	5·4	45·0	0·833	96·0	48·9	10·2	815	163
S and S E Asia								
Pakistan	102·9	283·0	0·275	264·1	20·97	2·7	9724	95
Japan	98·0	250·0	0·255	423·9	4·54	0·6	68014	694
Philippines	32·3	22·0	0·068	57·4	10·83	1·3	7163	221
Thailand	30·6	103·0	0·337	90·1	15·74	2·7	3339	109
S. Korea	82·4	560·0	1·972	121·0	28·2	—	—	—

Sources: UN Statistical Yearbook, 1966 and 1967 (New York: United Nations); *The military balance 1966/67* (London: Institute of Strategic Studies, 1966); D. Wood, *The armed forces of African states* (London: Institute of Strategic Studies, 1966).
Notes:
[a] Ratio of armed forces manpower over total population in per cents.
[b] Defence and budget expenditures for 1965 calendar year or 1965–6 financial year. Some divergence in estimates based on *UN Statistical Yearbook* and the Institute of Strategic Studies publications. The estimates are based on the former, except where the figures are bracketed, when they derive from the latter source, being obtainable from it alone. The figures for Nigeria are based on the actual budget expenditures for 1965–6 in the Federation of Nigeria *Digest of Statistics*.
[c] Per cent of GDP not GNP: per cent of GNP would be a little higher in most cases.

In addition, the armies of most independent African states have had to be re-created anew following the departure of the colonial power. This was either quite literally true – as with the armies of the ex-French countries, which were created from scratch within a very short space of time – though African soldiers were usually recruited from among those returning from service in the French Army, and military installations were handed over by the French. Or they were new in the sense that indigenous personnel were injected in very great haste into an existing military organisation, especially its officer corps, in order to replace the expatriates of the colonising power, as happened in almost all the ex-British countries. By whichever method the new armies have been created, however, the legacy of haste has tended to lead to deficiences in professional experience and organisational cohesion such that the army has been weak in structure and vulnerable to revolts against authority.

We will now examine some of the simple structural properties of the Nigerian Army which it inherited from the colonial period and during the transition to Independence – namely its small size, the distribution of skills, the character of its format and boundaries and the extent of its structural differentiation – in order to throw some light on the collapse of the army's authority and the fragmentation of its boundaries in 1966.

SMALLNESS IN SIZE

A key factor in the Nigerian Army's inability to maintain its organisational integrity in a changing and conflict-torn political environment was that it was small. In January 1966, it comprised about 10,500 men, and an officer corps of only 511 men, of whom 330 were of combat status.

These limitations of size were, as we now know, no constraint against its intervention in politics. Even the imposition of colonial rule had been achieved with a minimal display of force. Lord Lugard conquered all the powerful Emirates of Northern Nigeria in 1901–3 with a few hundred trained African soldiers commanded by a handful of European officers. The force under Colonel Morland which took the great city of Kano numbered only twenty-four officers and 780 men and defeated armies of several thousands. Moreover, this small force was very primitive in modern organisational and technical terms, relying heavily on the classic military square formation and having only minimal artillery support. In January 1966, as we have seen, it was also only a fragment of the army, numbering thirty officers and some 100 to 150 Other Ranks, which overthrew a civilian regime strongly dominated by the Emirate structures of the North with little more difficulty.

Limitation in size, on the other hand, greatly reduced the capacity of the army to rule after the seizure of power. The small size of the officer corps is perhaps the most crucial consideration here. After most army interventions there is a wastage of officers: sometimes there are deaths and almost always there are officers shuttled off into 'safe' diplomatic or honorary posts, or absorbed in government or administrative tasks. It takes fewer such losses to weaken the authority structure of a small army. This was especially striking in the Nigerian case, where the rate of attrition among senior military figures in the course of the events of 1966 was extremely high, as can be seen in Table 15, even though the absolute number removed was not very many. The coup of January 1966 swept away by death or transfer into political roles more than half the combat officers who had attained the rank of lieutenant colonel and above and two of the army's three brigadiers (the third, Ogundipe, was in Britain at the time of the coup). The July 1966 coup completed the decimation of the upper ranks with only thirty-six per cent of the officers who had held the rank of lieutenant colonel and none who had held a higher rank remaining in military postings.

TABLE 15. *Combat officers absented from military duties as a result of January and July 1966 coups*

Rank, January 1966[a]	Killed[b]	Im- prisoned	Member of Military Govern- ment[c]	Remaining in army	Total number	Per cent remaining in army
Colonel and above	5	0	2	0	7	0
Lt Colonel	4	1	4	5	14	36
Major	6	2	1	23	32	72
Captain	3	5	1	43	52	83
Lieutenant	7	5	0	46	58	79
2nd Lieutenant	13	9	0	145	167	87

Sources: Federation of Nigeria, *Official Gazettes* (1960–7); *Nigeria 1966; January 15th: before and after.*
Notes:
[a] Gazetted ranks only; a number of officers (especially those in gazetted ranks of captain and lieutenant) held higher temporary ranks in January 1966.
[b] Numbers killed include two who had been in the Military Government after January 1966 (Major General Ironsi and Lt Colonel Fajuyi) as well as two of the January conspirators who were assassinated in prison after the July coup (Majors Okafor and Anuforo).
[c] The Head of the Military Government and the Military Governors, the Military Administrator of Lagos; plus Brigadier Ogundipe and Lt Colonel Bassey, both given ambassadorial positions after the July 1966 coup.

In addition, those officers who were still militarily active began from July 1966 to make up the nucleus of two armies. All Ibo officers of Eastern origin and a few of the non-Ibo Easterners fled to the Eastern Region to build up what was to become the Biafran army. All but one or two of the Mid-Western Ibos sought security in the Mid-West until their defection to Biafra when

The Nigerian Army: composition and structure

Lt Colonel Ojukwu's forces invaded their region in August 1967. Of the 330 combat officers in the army early in 1966, the Federal army was thus able to muster no more than about 184 for the civil war and the Biafrans some ninety-three. The Federal army, moreover, was virtually bare of officers of any seniority or experience at anything above the company commander level, as Tables 16 and 17 indicate. At the beginning of the civil war in 1967 there were no officers in active military roles in the Federal army (as opposed to 'political' roles in the Military Government) who had held a rank above gazetted major prior to 1966; and only four of the militarily effective officers had gained their commissions before 1960. In the light of this shortage of experienced commanders, the shortcomings of both armies in discipline and military effectiveness during the civil war do not seem surprising, the more so given the enormous numerical expansion in the men under arms on both sides in 1967–9.

TABLE 16. *Disposition of officers surviving events of 1966 in August 1967 (approximate numbers)[a]*

Rank, January 1966	Military Government		Active military postings[c]	
	Federal[b]	Biafran	Federal	Biafran
Colonel and above	2	0	0	0
Lt Colonel	4	1	0	5
Major	1	0	9	16
Captain	5	0	28	15
Lieutenant	0	0	34	17
2nd Lieutenant	0	0	113	40

Notes:
[a] Exact numbers in rank of major upwards. A small margin of error must be allowed for estimates at lower ranks.
[b] Includes additional Military Governors appointed from the army in 1967, Lt Colonel Kurobo, who was appointed ambassador to Moscow after absconding from the East in mid-1967 and Lt Colonel (later Brigadier) Ejoor, whose status in August 1967 after the Mid-West invasion can be regarded as indeterminate, until his appointment to the Federal army as Director of Recruitment and Training, later in 1967.
[c] Includes officers released from prison.

Aside from increasing its vulnerability to internal violence, smallness was an important structural characteristic in other perhaps less obvious ways. First, it was one determinant of the cohesion of the military, particularly that of the officer corps. Although the Nigerian Army lacked vertical integration as a system of command and control, it did, as we suggest elsewhere,[1] have a certain amount of cohesion as a solidary group, a 'brotherhood' as its first

[1] In the discussion of peer groups in Chapter V below.

Nigerian Commander in Chief, Major General Ironsi, called it. This was clearly made easier by the fact that the officer corps was small enough for most officers to know each other and for the careers of a good proportion of them to have crossed at one time or another. This is a condition under which the military might be expected to follow a consistent and unified political course, whether accepting civilian control or moving into politics under the leadership of the top command.[1]

TABLE 17. *Militarily active officers in Federal and Biafran armies (August 1967) as a per cent of January 1966 officer corps*

Rank, January 1966	Total number, January 1966	Active Federal officers as per cent of total	Active Biafran officers as per cent of total
Colonel and above	7	0	0
Lt Colonel	14	0	36
Major	32	28	50
Captain	52	54	29
Lieutenant	58	59	29
2nd Lieutenant	167	68	24

Sources of Tables 16 and 17: as for Table 15.

But there are other aspects of small size which favoured the success of a fragmentary revolt by a tiny group of conspirators. For such a group could destroy or neutralise the command structure of a small military organisation – as they did so effectively in January 1966 – much more easily than that of a large army. Moreover, a small army would not normally have a highly specialised intelligence corps; and the lack of good political intelligence was (as we pointed out above in Chapter I) among the reasons for the January coup's success.

Finally, size tended to limit the Nigerian military elite's ability to govern on its own. Few officers could be spared for government duties, so that direct military administration of ministries or localities was never possible – save in exceptional circumstances, as in the Mid-West after July 1966 when there was a temporary surplus of officers who had fled from other regions. Military rule in Nigeria has for practical purposes been government by delegation to civil servants, with some overall supervision by the military leaders.

One may draw some interesting implications from this for the stabilisation of the military's role after the ending of the Nigerian civil war. For the war brought about a tremendous expansion, particularly in the Federal army,

[1] Janowitz, *The military in the political development of new nations*, pp. 67–74.

which was believed to contain at least 150,000 men at the end of the war in January 1970. The officer corps too was expanded rapidly. The expansion was met on the Federal side by large-scale promotion of NCOs from the ranks, and by three- to four-month crash courses at the Nigerian Military Academy, Kaduna, for cadets of suitable educational qualifications, who were given temporary commissions. It is undoubtedly true that this expansion diluted the professional quality of the officer corps. Yet one may well argue that a larger and more powerful army will be able to play a more consistent political role by developing more complex skills; and by being less vulnerable both to revolt from within and political pressures from without. This conclusion may seem a little paradoxical in consideration of theories of civil-military relations that suggest the army will only stay within its political boundaries if constrained by strong civilian institutions to do so.[1] Taking into account the prevailing weakness of political institutions in Africa, such theories might seem to indicate a need to *reduce* the power of the armed forces. But in the African context mere reduction in size will not in itself reduce the danger of militarism when civilian institutions themselves are so weak as to succumb to even the most minimal amount of organised violence.

THE SKILL STRUCTURE OF THE OFFICER CORPS

Two quite contradictory views on the skills and capacity of the military as an elite in new nations have been put forward by writers on the subject. On the one hand, it is asserted that the army is uniquely qualified for nation-building tasks.[2] It is a large and complex organisation by the standards of the new nations; it has a high concentration of 'modern' skills; it is broadly recruited from modern rising-class or new middle-class groups;[3] and has a high degree of identification with the nation. Others, to the contrary, suggest that the functional characteristics of military organisations – especially those inherited from a colonial regime – are not such as to produce appropriate skills in symbol-manipulation, bargaining and compromise; few new nation's armies are complex enough to possess career lines that will produce many officers with adaptive decision-making skills.[4]

[1] See Finer, *The man on horseback.*
[2] L. W. Pye, 'Armies in the process of political modernisation' in J. J. Johnson (ed.), *The role of the military in under-developed countries* (Princeton, N.J.: Princeton University Press, 1962), and D. Lerner and R. D. Robinson, 'Swords into ploughshares: the Turkish Army as a modernising force', *World Politics*, XIII (October 1960).
[3] J. J. Johnson, *The military and society in Latin America* (Stanford, Calif.: Stanford University Press, 1964) and Halpern, 'The Middle Eastern Armies and the New Middle Class' in Johnson (ed.), *The role of the military in under-developed countries.*
[4] Janowitz, *The military in the political development of new nations*, pp. 40–9, though Janowitz suggests that new nations' armies may vary in this respect, depending on the exact nature of their skill structure and career lines.

The data on the distribution of skills in the Nigerian Army seem to support the latter view. Three considerations are relevant here. First, there is the fact that the basic educational standard for entry into the officer corps has been somewhat lower than for entry into other comparable bureaucratic elites. Secondly, there was the very rapid indigenisation of the officer corps, resulting in a lack of individual and collective experience. And finally, the variety of occupational experience that could be acquired was very limited because the army was small and career lines simple.

The basic educational standard for entry to the officer corps with an ordinary combat commission is the West African School Certificate or equivalent, the acquisition of which signifies little more than a basic secondary schooling. Few officers have had the educational requirements for university entry (a Higher School Certificate or equivalent) and only five of the combat officers in 1966 (and sixty or more of the one hundred and eighty-three 'technical' or non-combat officers) had university degrees or similar professional qualifications. Table 18 compares the educational levels at entry of the officer corps with that of other comparable occupations. We divide each into three groups: (*a*) those who have received university degrees or undertaken professional courses of study for at least three years after Higher School Certificate or equivalent; (*b*) school-leavers entering the occupation directly from school, normally with a West African School Certificate or (much more rarely) a Higher School Certificate and receiving a short professional training[1] before actively pursuing their vocation; and (*c*) entrants rising from the ranks (NCOs in the army and police, clerks and the like in the civil service). It will be seen that the educational level of the officer corps is lower in aggregate than those of the other groups with which a relevant comparison can be made – with the sole exception of the police, the supervisory levels of which are recruited very largely from the ranks. The relative position of the military looks slightly better if the non–combat–trained officers in ancillary positions (the doctors, accountants, engineers, etc.) are included. But very few of these played either political or command roles at any level so that their relevance to this comparison is limited.

A small part of this educational deficiency is made up in training, especially among officers who attended the two–year Sandhurst courses, rather than the much briefer Mons and other short-service cadet courses. Nigerian officers coming out of Sandhurst, where their performance is about average,[2] emerge

---

[1] A maximum of two to two and a half years for any officers going to Sandhurst from NMTC. Officers doing short-service training at Mons from the NMTC took about a year; this was also about the same time as the police training for entry to the inspectorate grade at the Northern and Southern Police Colleges.

[2] Or perhaps very slightly below average. But the point is that the Nigerian Sandhurst graduate does not differ much in general terms from his English course-mates.

on the whole as well qualified as their British confreres. But this is not saying much, for the academic standard of Sandhurst and the equivalent academies in other countries where Nigerians are trained (Ethiopia, Pakistan and India) is below university level. An officer may emerge from Sandhurst with much social confidence and some skill as a tactical leader. But he is unlikely to have a high level of comprehension of the major political and social issues of the day. Still less the Mons-trained officers, whose training consists entirely of the skills of tactical leadership, with minimal educational content.[1]

TABLE 18. *Comparative educational levels of Nigerian elite groups* (*in percentages*)

Occupational group[a]	Degree or equivalent professional qualification	Secondary school entry	Entry from the ranks	Total N=
The military (officer corps – combat only)	2	84	14	332
The military (officer corps – combat and non-combat)[b]	13	66	21	514
The police (Asst Supt. and above)	3	26	71	474
Federal civil service (administrative class)	58	—	—	301
Legal profession (registered practitioners)	100	0	0	1,394[c]
Medical profession (registered practitioners – doctors only)	100	0	0	2,070
Political party leaders[d]	20–25	—	—	211

Notes:
[a] At 1 January 1966 or thereabouts, unless otherwise specified.
[b] Non-combat category includes quartermasters, paymasters, education corps, some of the engineers and the doctors and nurses. Classification by education more approximate than for combat officers. Nurses counted as secondary school not graduate (professional) entry.
[c] *The Nigerian Bar Journal*, VII (1966).
[d] National and federal leaders of the three major political parties, 1958. Data approximate, since inferred from occupational origin of party leaders set forth in Richard Sklar, *Nigerian political parties: power in an emergent African nation* (Princeton, N.J.: Princeton University Press, 1963), p. 486. See Sklar for definition of 'party leader'. Almost all of the party leaders with degree or professional qualification belonged to the two southern parties, the AG and the NCNC Only one to two per cent of the NPC leaders had such qualifications.

The military, however, is unique in the degree of continuing education it provides for its officers throughout their careers. In the earlier stages of a career such training is largely technical: before they were promoted to major almost all Nigerian combat officers had been abroad for additional courses, but mainly in subjects like signals, transport, tank and armoured car command, weapons, or platoon leadership. Only at the level of major and

[1] It should be pointed out that the proportion of Nigerian officers who got the full academy treatment rather than short-service training at Mons, etc. was rather less than that of British officers.

upwards did they attend courses which would include indoctrination in strategy, higher-level management techniques, international relations or political matters. But the number who had been on such courses was few. Only twenty-two officers in the entire army in January 1966 had had staff college training at the Staff College, Camberley, the Joint Services Staff College, Latimer or the Pakistan Staff College, Quetta; and only five of these had been on to receive indoctrination in high level strategic command at the Imperial Defence College, London. The events of 1966, moreover, quickly depleted this small group. Six of the staff college-trained officers were killed in January 1966, one (Major Nzeogwu) imprisoned and four absorbed in the Military Government. The July coup killed one more and led to the absorbtion of a further four in administrative or diplomatic tasks. At the outset of the civil war, therefore, the Federal army had only eight officers trained at the Staff College or the Joint Services Staff College, of whom only two were available to play military roles.[1] The Biafran army also had eight, all but one or two of whom were pushed aside in sundry political upheavals in the Biafran leadership in 1967–9.

The shortage of educationally derived skills was reinforced by an absence of experience in command at all levels. This was above all because of the urgency with which the Nigerian government replaced the British officers with Nigerians after political control over the army was handed over to it shortly before Independence. Though there were good political reasons for this decision,[2] its automatic consequence was a military elite that was exceedingly youthful and inexperienced. Tables 19 and 20 compare the age structure and length of professional careers up to 1966 of the officer corps with that of the administrative class of the civil service and the police. The contrast with the police is particularly striking. While over sixty per cent of combat officers in the army in January 1966 were under the age of twenty-five, over half of the police officers exceeded the age of forty and only twelve per cent were under thirty.[3] What the latter did not possess in educational

---

[1] These figures do not reconcile exactly with the number we gave of staff college-trained officers in 1966, because two additional Nigerian officers attended Staff College, Camberley in 1966, one subsequently joining Biafra and the other, Lt Colonel Bissalla, the Federal army.

[2] See Chapter X below.

[3] One reason for this is that almost all police officers come up to the 'senior service' ranks (assistant superintendant of police and above) from the inspectorate grade, which has no real equivalent in the army. An inspector may either be promoted from the ranks or he may enter direct with a West African School Certificate (the same as the basic entry qualification for the officer corps in the army). He receives a year of training (about the same as short-service officers at the Nigerian Military Training College and Mons together). But his pay, status and responsibilities are less than that of the army officer. Not until he reaches the rank of assistant superintendant and above does he get the equivalent pay and privileges to army officers and the administrative class of the civil service. Nevertheless, this accounts for only part of the difference which is also due to; (i) the higher percentage of policemen promoted from the ranks, (ii) the earlier indigenisation of the police force and (iii) the slower promotion rates obtaining in the police, compared with the army.

TABLE 19. *Age structure of Federal Government bureaucracies in January 1966 (percentage distribution)*

Age in January 1966	Nigerian Army: combat officers[a] N = 332	Nigeria Police: Asst. Supt. and above N = 474	Federal civil service (administrative class)[b] N = 301
45 and above	0·3	28	10
40–44	1	26	14
35–39	2	20	25
30–34	12	14	33
25–29	23	11	17
20–24	62	1	1

Notes:
[a] Ages of army officers estimated from dates of commission according to the following assumptions:
(i) NCOs commissioned at the average age of 26, assuming around six years' service in the ranks on average (in quite a few cases it was less);
(ii) Sandhurst graduates commissioned at the average age of 22;
(iii) Short-service-trained officers (whether trained at Mons, in Canada, India or Australia) commissioned at the age of 21.
[b] Ages of police and civil servants shown in the Federation of Nigeria, *Staff List* (August 1966).

TABLE 20. *Experience levels of Federal Government bureaucracies in January 1966 (percentage distribution)*

Years of experience to January 1966	Nigerian Army: combat officers[a] N = 332	Nigeria Police: Asst. Supt. and above (years of experience from appt. as Asst. Supt.)[b] N = 474	Nigeria Police: Asst. Supt. and above (years of experience from appt. as Inspector)[b] N = 474	Federal civil service (administrative class)[a] N = 301
0–5	80	53	11	40
5–10	15	36	50	41
10–15	3	7	23	11
15–20	1	3	12	5
20 or more	0·3	0·4	4	3

Notes:
[a] Years of experience from commissioning in officer corps (army) and in administrative class (civil service) only. Experience in the ranks (army) or the clerical and executive branches (civil service) not counted.
[b] Years of experience of police officers in assistant superintendant grade and above at January 1966, shown both from their first appointment as assistant superintendant and from first appointment as inspector (or as ASP, if never in inspectorate).

qualifications they made up for in slow and arduous progress up through the ranks.[1]

Finally, the career lines were much too short and the army's structure too simple to generate an elite nucleus with any more than the most rudimentary administrative skills. The vast majority of officers had little more than routine command responsibilities during the whole course of their short military careers. The number that had alternated between command and staff responsibilities in the manner customarily prescribed for entry into the elite nucleus in large modern armies[2] was very few. Table 21 shows the writer's estimates of the number of Nigerian officers who, by January 1966, would have moved through staff positions from the level of adjutant of a battalion upwards. The centre column of the table indicates the total number of Nigerian officers who had up to 1966 held staff positions at each level. Officers who at various stages of their career held posts at more than one level are, however, counted twice. The right-hand column allows for this by cumulating the numbers who held posts at each level and/or above. It is seen therefore that there were no more than sixty to sixty-five officers in January 1966 who had had staff experience as adjutants of battalions or staff captains and upwards; and no more than about thirty with middle and higher-level staff experience at the staff major level or above.

The left-hand column of Table 21 also shows the number of officers who had held top level tactical commander posts (Battalion CO and above) by January 1966. The figures in brackets set alongside the arrows in the table give the numbers of officers who had held posts in *both* of the types of post linked by the arrows. They show that the normal career experience of members of the top military elite at the level of lieutenant colonel and above had been the routine rotation between staff and command posts, at least nine officers of this seniority having alternated in high level staff positions and battalion commands.[3] Surprisingly few of these, however (no more than five) had held middle level staff positions at the brigade major or GSO II level, though they were staff captains and adjutants in their time. And it is notable that the army's four most senior commanders,[4] and in addition three or four of its commanders at battalion level, were promoted so quickly that they had

---

[1] Still more than suggested in Table 20, for this shows only experience in inspectorate and superintendant grades, while the majority of police officers also had a number of years' experience in ranks below inspector also.

[2] See M. Janowitz, *The professional soldier* (New York: Free Press, 1960), Chapter VIII, where this is discussed in relation to the American military.

[3] Colonels K. Mohammed and Adebayo and Lt Colonels Njoku, Ojukwu, Gowon, Ejoor, Unegbe and Pam. Nine, rather than ten, as might be suggested by adding up the figures in brackets under the appropriate arrows, because Colonel Adebayo had been chief of staff, a battalion commander *and* a top level staff officer (GSO I).

[4] Major General Ironsi, Brigadiers Ademulegun, Maimalari and Ogundipe.

TABLE 21. *Numbers of officers with experience in staff and top command posts, January 1966*

Rank	Command posts	Staff posts	Cumulation of officers who had held staff posts at each level and/or above
Major General, Brigadier	Strategic command[a]	Chief of Staff	
	6 ⟷ (1) ⟶ 2		2
	(6) (2) (0) (1)		
Lt Colonel	High tactical command[b]	Top HQ staff[c]	
	18 ⟷ (7) ⟶ 8		9
		↑ (4)	
Major		Middle-level staff[d] (major) 25 approx.	30
		↑	
Captain		Staff captain/adjutant 50 approx.	60–65

Notes:
[a] GOC, brigadiers and COs of the Nigerian Military Training College.
[b] Battalion or unit commander (excluding the Recce Squadrons).
[c] Staff Officer I, Adjutant General, Quartermaster General.
[d] Brigade Major, Staff Officer II, etc.

no staff experience beyond the staff captain/adjutant level at all. If the numbers of officers who had alternated between staff and command assignments was small, moreover, the number of officers in the army with unconventional careers giving them any experience in political or diplomatic matters was quite minimal.[1]

[1] The writer himself can only think of two such officers. First, the GOC, Major General Ironsi whose political experience included training at the Staff College, Camberley and the Imperial Defence College, being equerry to the Queen on her visit to Nigeria in 1956, military adviser in the Nigerian High Commission in London, commander of the UN Force in the Congo and finally commander of the Nigerian Army (though his ineptitude when Head of the Military

It is hard to know exactly how much can be inferred from these deficiencies in education, age and depth of experience in the officer corps. It would certainly seem that the latter would cause inadequacies in the military's collective 'memory', the sheer absence of past experience making it less likely that members of the elite would know how to respond in a flexible way to complex new situations, such as arose from the Nigerian Army's new political responsibilities and its organisational difficulties in the period under consideration.[1] The failure of Major General Ironsi's regime to take control of events in early 1966 and the tragic series of misunderstandings among the military leaders leading to the civil war would both seem to show the army did not produce skills of a type that were readily transferable to the management of public affairs. On the other hand, the breakdown of the civilian government before the military took power suggests we should be cautious how much we infer, since the politicians – the supposed specialists in bargaining and compromise – did little better than the soldiers, no doubt because of the intractable nature of the problems which both ruling groups had to face.

ORGANISATIONAL FORMAT AND BOUNDARIES

The army's structure was highly centralised. In January 1966, there were five infantry Battalions and a sixth in embryo form (to be established late in 1966), two Reconnaissance (or Recce) Squadrons equipped with armoured cars, a Field Battery and necessary supporting units like the engineers and medical corps. The army was thus equipped to do no more than act as guarantor of internal order, to maintain the external boundaries of the nation, and provide a mark of sovereignty. Until the civil War, it did not have the technology of violence at its disposal (in terms of tanks, artillery, and air support) to undertake large-scale military operations even of the Second World War type; except, as in the Congo, when part of an international operation in which the infrastructure was provided by others.

The control structure of the military was based on the Army HQ at Lagos

Government from January to July 1966 does not suggest he learned very much). The second is Lt Colonel (now Brigadier) Kurobo, who was trained at Sandhurst and the Pakistan Staff College, was ADC to President Azikiwe, the Governor-General, equerry to Princess Alexandra at the Nigerian Independence celebrations, a member of the Six-Nation Military Observer Team sent to New Guinea, special UN Liaison Officer to the Indonesian government and CO of the Air Force after the January 1966 coup. It is unfortunate that such a sophisticated officer should have found himself thrust into the sidelines by the events of 1966–7 as ambassador to the the USSR.

[1] See S. P. Huntington, 'Political development and political decay', *World Politics* (April 1965); J. G. March and H. A. Simon, *Organizations* (New York: Wiley, 1968), p. 119; and A. Downs, *Inside bureaucracy* (Boston: Little Brown, 1967), pp. 18, 122–6. Downs suggests increasing returns of decision-making flexibility and the reduction of uncertainty as organisations age and their 'memories' are built up. At a later stage the organisation will start to become too rigidly 'bureaucratised', a stage, however, the Nigerian Army was nowhere near reaching.

and the two Brigade Headquarters at Lagos and Kaduna. Besides the police, the army was the only organisation in Nigeria possessing a unified, Federation-wide communications system of its own; a technical factor of some weight in regard to its capacity for political intervention in a country which is otherwise heavily deficient in basic communications. In some respects, however, the army was overcentralised, being insufficiently adaptive to changes in circumstances. A highly centralised purchasing system modelled on that of the British Army, for instance, tended to land unit commanders in difficulties over essential supplies because of the problem of moving and controlling stock under Nigerian conditions.

In purely physical terms, there was a considerable dispersal of army units throughout the country. The heaviest concentration was at Kaduna, the Northern Region capital, which was the location of the 1st Brigade HQ, the Nigerian Military Training College, the Nigerian Defence Academy, together with one (until 1965 two) infantry Battalion (the 3rd) and a Recce Squadron, as well as being the base for the embryo air force. Other Battalions were posted to Kano (the 5th), Enugu (the 1st), Ibadan (the 4th), and Ikeja, near Lagos (the 2nd). The latter was the only operational unit to be stationed in the vicinity of the Army HQ at Lagos.

This dispersion of units was a factor of importance in determining the pattern of military intervention. It was easier for a group to gain control of one or two isolated but strategic units (as in January 1966) in hope of seizing power. But it also tended to fragment any attempt by such a group to establish effective control throughout the country. Thus in January 1966 Major Nzeogwu was faced with the choice of surrender or civil war between the units he controlled at Kaduna and the rest of the army. Similarly, the course of events after July 1966 would have been very different if the Northern officers had been able to gain control of all units, including that at Enugu.

Though physically dispersed, the army's unity of structure ensured that the boundaries between army units and their local social and political environment were relatively sharply defined. Each army unit was in many respects a 'total' institution. The barracks was a residential unit, with all officers and men – whether married or unmarried – living in segregated areas of the same compound. Both the officers and the NCOs had their messes, each with its distinctive traditions and each providing an effective integrative focus for the social life of the unit.

Until 1960–1, when this became impossible because of the Congo operation, the battalions were periodically transferred around from garrison town to garrison town to prevent them from developing local ties. Even when units ceased to rotate, individuals continued to do so. Postings and promotions of officers and men were made without reference to area of origin, so that most officers and men were more likely than not to spend the greater part of their career outside their home area. Although officers and men were likely to develop contacts with the immigrant communities from their home areas in most garrison towns, the soldiers' contacts tended to be less extensive than those of members of other occupations because of their very high rate of mobility from one posting to another. The rates of succession in military command posts were so high, indeed (as we argue in Chapter VII), that this undermined the creation of an effective integrative focus for the discipline of the army units themselves, still more so the creation of durable alliances with local non-military communities and elites.

The system of civilian control up to 1966 was such as to minimise political influence in the internal functioning of the army.[1] The army's official boundary roles[2] for purposes of political control (unlike the Nigeria Police Force) were concentrated at the very top of the hierarchy, in the person of the GOC and through him the Chief of Staff and the two brigade commanders. The circle of political and administrative figures with any effective responsibility for the military was much narrower than for any other branch of the government, being limited to all intents and purposes to the Prime Minister, the Minister of Defence, the Ministers of State for the Army and Navy and the Permanent Secretary, Ministry of Defence.

Most purely administrative matters were left to the military staff and the Ministry of Defence to sort out between them – with some exceptions, as in the regional quota for recruitment into the officer corps imposed under political pressure from the North in 1961.[3] But the recruitment, promotion and postings of individuals were in most cases free from such pressures. There is little evidence (as we will demonstrate in Chapter VIII) of any systematic bias in favour of particular ethnic groups or regions, despite fears among officers that they might be penalised on regional or political grounds in the future.

The regional premiers had no *direct* access to decisions regarding the military, although the regional premier of the North had a degree of indirect influence through the successive Ministers of Defence, Alhaji Ribadu and Alhaji Inuwa Wada. The regional premiers also maintained informal links with the commanders of the brigades and units operating in their regions, though these were of the loosest kind and in no sense implied political controls of the kind the regional governments exercised over the regional police commissioners.

As the British vacated the uppermost parts of the command structure, embryo alliances and patron–client relationships between senior and junior officers, and between officers and politicians began to appear. Yet there is

[1] See Chapter X below, for further details.
[2] For the concept of 'boundary role' see Blau and Scott, *Formal organizations*, pp. 197–8.
[3] See Chapter X below.

little evidence that these were more widespread than the kinds of inter-personal linkages that are known to prevail at the relevant points in the hierarchy of the British and American militaries.[1] Often it was a matter of a senior officer picking out a promising or congenial young officer for posting under him – such as Brigadier Maimalari's choice of Major Ifeajuna as his brigade major (for his intelligence and professional qualities) or Major General Ironsi his ADCs (for congeniality and ability to out-drink him). Sometimes it was a matter of a politician befriending officers with whom he had cause to deal in a professional role, such as the friendship between the Sardauna of Sokoto and Brigadier Ademulegun or the Prime Minister, Sir Abubakar Tafawa Balewa, and the commander of the Federal Guard, Major Okafor. And sometimes it was a matter of an officer or politician like President Azikiwe taking an interest in the careers of his former ADCs or subordinates. Such relationships were neither frequent enough nor strong enough to subvert the normal channels of command and control, nor to bring about the serious permeation of the army by political pressures. Occasionally, it is true, patronage relationships developed among officers or between officers and politicians of the same ethnicity or region,[2] though not necessarily because of any conscious desire to patronise compatriots. But very often they did not, as in the Maimalari/Ifeajuna, Sardauna/Ademulegun, Balewa/Okafor dyads mentioned above: Major General Ironsi, indeed, is said to have deliberately chosen ADCs from outside his own (Ibo) tribe in order to place himself above suspicion.

The development after 1964 of conspiratorial groups among army officers (though probably quite a small minority) with civilian contacts (which we described in Chapter I) began to fragment the military's boundaries. But it could not be said that the army as a whole was politicised until the circum-stances of the January coup and of military rule opened up the cleavages on regional and tribal lines that led to the Northern coup in July 1966.

The events of 1966 also brought changes in the formal structure of com-mand and control. In the early phase, however, from January to July, the army's organisation format remained unitary, despite the great weakening in its cohesion. Military matters ceased altogether to be within the purview of

[1] Janowitz, *The professional soldier*, Parts VI and VIII, and C. B. Otley, 'The origins and recruit-ment of the British army elite', unpublished Ph.D. thesis (University of Hull, 1966).

[2] When Brigadier Ademulegun first assumed command of the 1st Brigade, Kaduna, the two most important posts as his brigade staff (brigade major and DAQMG) were filled with majors from his own ethnic group, in place of Major Ifeajuna (an Ibo) and an Englishman. It is normal for an officer to choose subordinates who are congenial to him and with whom he knows he can work, so there is not necessarily anything sinister in the choice and Ademulegun replaced his Yoruba brigade major with Major Keshi (an Ibo) just before January 1966. The January coup may be another example of networks developing on ethnic lines, though again, as we have argued in Chapter I above, this was probably not a matter of conscious 'tribalism'.

the politicians or other civilians and the army became a self-regulating corporation under the Supreme Commander, the Chiefs of Staff (Supreme Headquarters and Army) and the Supreme Military Council, with the assistance of the Ministry of Defence. The Regional Military Governors were represented on the Supreme Military Council, although they were essentially political/administrative figures in their regions and had no formal military command responsibilities, even for the military units stationed in their vicinity.

Following the revolt of July 1966, however, there occurred a *de facto* decentralisation of the military control structure and a greater fusion of military and political roles at a regional level.[1] In differing degrees each region obtained a degree of independence from the Federal command, Military Governors acquired local military responsibilities and brigade and unit commanders in the regions a share in political decisions. This situation was partially formalised on the establishment in each region of separate Area Commands with their Area Commanders in April 1967.

These developments went further in the Eastern Region. Northern troops in Enugu were exchanged for Eastern troops elsewhere in the Federation in August 1967, after Lt Colonel Ojukwu had refused to accept Lt Colonel Gowon as the legitimate commander of the Armed Forces. This led to the creation of a wholly independent army organisation in the East, with purely formal ties with the Federal army, though even these were broken when the East seceded on 30 May 1967. Command relationships between Lagos HQ and Eastern units were thereby transformed into semi-diplomatic relations, as at the Aburi meetings in January 1967.

Most officers and men of Mid-Western origin returned to the Mid-West after July – partly because the greater number of them were Ibos and were as much the focus of the Northern officers' fury as their colleagues in the East. The Military Governor, Lt Colonel Ejoor (himself not an Ibo), gave qualified acceptance to Gowon's legitimacy, and persuaded his Ibo officers to do so too for the time being. Politically this implied the neutralisation of officers of Mid-Western origin – at least until the invasion of the region by the East in August 1967 – because there were no military installations of importance in the Mid-West and very few Other Ranks (some 200) to command. There was a considerable surplus of officers and civilian duties had to be found for six lieutenant colonels, four majors, and three captains, all of whom were militarily redundant. The Mid-West, therefore, was the only region where army personnel were used extensively for purely administrative purposes.

A different type of command relationship again was elaborated in the Western Region. The West was short of officers but still more so of men (it

[1] See Chapter XIII below for a more detailed account of political developments after July 1966, the bare essentials of which – in so far as they shaped the army's pattern of command and control – are summarised here.

had no more than 700 men in the army altogether). Yet its military installations at Ibadan and Abeokuta were of considerable strategic importance. Many of the officers and men of Western origin were posted to the 3rd Battalion at Ibadan or to the Abeokuta garrison, and were put under Yoruba commanders. These had to be heavily supplemented however with Northern troops, though between August 1966 and July 1967 there was continuous political pressure from the West for them to be removed. The West's Military Governor, Lt Colonel Adebayo, the Area Commander, and the two commanders of the 3rd Battalion of the period all developed extensive contact with former Action Group politicians, especially Chief Awolowo. Lines of military command tended to develop into political bargaining relationships and discipline to be undermined, with cleavages between the Yoruba and Northern troops still in Ibadan and Abeokuta always near to opening.

Relations between the Brigade (subsequently Area Command) HQ at Kaduna in the North and Army HQ, Lagos, were also problematic, though not to the same extent as the other regions because of the greater identity of interest between the North and the Federal Military Government. Yet, as one officer put it: 'we do what we like and then ask Lagos afterwards'. This was perhaps an exaggeration, though command relationships between Northern units and Headquarters at Lagos were certainly much looser than they ever were before 1966.

This change in organisational format – together with the great weakening of the army's administrative structure even before 1966 – tended to give other elites greater access to the decision-making procedures of the military, especially at regional level. In the Western Region it involved the virtual access to power of Chief Awolowo and other former Action Group men. In the North some of the politicians of the former radical opposition to the NPC, like Aminu Kano and Joseph Tarka, greatly increased their influence as did the Northern civil servants. In the East intellectuals from the University of Nigeria at Nsukka and civil servants were initially more influential, though former NCNC politicians like Dr Okpara assumed greater importance in the course of events leading to the civil conflict in 1967. And at a Federal level the civil servants gained influence from the power vacuum that had been created at the centre by the fragmentation of the military. They became perhaps the most important corporate source of support for the maintenance of an effective Federation during the period of constitutional negotiations which began in September 1966 and ended with the East's secession at the end of May 1967.

The advent of civil war in July however, began a reintegration of the boundaries and command structure of the Federal army in accordance with functional imperatives brought to the fore by the war. The Area Commands atrophied and were finally superseded entirely after the invasion of the Mid-West in August 1967, when two and later – after the invasion of Calabar – three Divisional Commands were brought into operation. The Divisional Commanders were able to ask for – and get – a considerable degree of autonomy from Headquarters control. But this autonomy was quite different from that of the Area Commands since it was exercised in respect of military functions or the interests of individual war-lords like Colonels Adekunle or Muritala Mohammed and not on behalf of regional political interests.

BOUNDARIES AND DISINTEGRATION

In order to conclude this chapter we may call attention to some of the possible latent consequences of the army's unitary format and the sharp differentiation of military life from civilian life which characterised it, at least, until 1966. It may be argued that the position of the army as a small, self-sufficient corporation in the post-colonial period contributed as much to its disintegration as to its integration, particularly as this unity in structure concealed organisational weaknesses. These latent dysfunctions were of two kinds, though we put them both forward as plausible explanations rather than as verified facts, because they are hypotheses of a type which could only be confirmed in a comparative study of military organisations, not by a single case, as presented here.

First, it may be suggested that isolation from civilian life fostered an absolutist political outlook among middle-ranking officers, predisposing them towards direct solutions for political problems and towards intervention against corrupt and 'dishonourable' governments.[1] The lack of political boundary roles in the army, except at the level of the high command may have rendered it (relatively speaking) impermeable to direct cooptation by outside political forces. But it also encouraged the development of a corporate ideology, unfavourable to the politics of the politicians. It is no coincidence that the higher-ranking officers who alone had day-to-day working contacts with the politicians in power were reluctant to join in the overthrow of the civilian regime at the time of the January 1966 coup, even though some of them – like Brigadiers Ademulegun and Maimalari – were known to hold political views that did not differ greatly in content from those of the Majors.

Secondly, as a 'total' institution the Nigerian Army was prone to high interpersonal antagonism tending to promote strikes, mutinies and rebellions against its leadership. It is an often-noted fact that formal organisations, industries and communities in which roles are segmented and work separated from private life are less prone to disruption by violent conflict than those

---

[1] See Chapter XII below.

where personal life and private affect spill into the occupational context.[1] The Nigerian Army – like other armies – deliberately fused personal with military life through the mess and the barracks in order to foster cohesion and 'brotherhood'. Such an organisation, however, requires a higher degree of goal consensus than those in which relationships are more segmentary. Brotherhood only creates genuine integration if officers and men show self-discipline and if the system of command and control is itself adequately institutionalised. Otherwise it may be disruptive. As Georg Simmel notes:

it is precisely the keen awareness of dissonance against the prevailing general harmony which at once warns the parties to remove the grounds of conflict lest conflict half-consciously creep in and endanger the basis of the relation itself. But where this fundamental intention to get along under all circumstances is lacking, the consciousness of antagonism, sensitised as this consciousness is by similarity in other respects, will sharpen the antagonism itself. People who have many common features often do one another worse, a 'wronger' wrong than complete strangers do.[2]

From this point of view the January 1966 and the July counter-coup follow a definite logic. In January, the ruthless assassination of military authority figures seems to have followed from the Majors' antagonism towards them (in addition to the strategic need to eliminate them to make the seizure of power easier). In July, revenge was admixed with the sentiment that brothers had become judases (as we saw in Chapter II), and suspicions of treachery and fratricide led to violence of a preemptive and uncontrolled kind.

Thus the corporate unity which had earlier insulated the military from politics and conflict on primordial lines only made these cleavages worse when they finally penetrated the army's boundaries. This point is underlined by comparison with the Nigeria Police, which was a much more permeable and decentralised structure than the army; and yet during 1966–7 the police proved to be much more capable of keeping tribal and regional conflict under control and of maintaining the overall authority of its command, a fact which was particularly evident during the disturbances and massacres in the North in September–October 1966, when the police were virtually the sole restraining force and most army units were so unreliable that they had to be kept in the barracks and not sent out to control the riots (in which indeed the soldiers themselves sometimes participated).

[1] C. Kerr and A. Siegel, 'The inter-industry propensity to strike' in W. Kornhauser *et al.* (eds.) *Industrial conflict* (New York: McGraw Hill, 1954); J. S. Coleman, *Community conflict* (Glencoe Ill.: The Free Press, 1957) and Downs, *Inside bureaucracy*, Chapter VI, who notes (on p. 57) that 'organisations that utilise mainly secondary or segmental relationships amongst their members require a different degree of goal consensus from those based on primary or total relationships.'
G. Simmel, *Conflict and the web of group affiliations*, K. Wolff and R. Bendix (eds.) (New York: The Free Press, 1964), p. 43.

CHAPTER IV

OFFICERS AND GENTLEMEN: THE IMAGE OF AN ELITE

In the last chapter, we showed on the one hand that Nigerian combat officers were younger, less experienced and less well educated than any comparable elite group; on the other that the basic training they received at Sandhurst, Mons or elsewhere did not differ from their British counterparts. We are unable to describe in any detail the patterns of social recruitment of the military or the process of socialisation[1] – the *manner* in which Nigerian officer cadets and officers were imbued with the rituals and skills of military life in foreign military schools and academies.[2] We can, however, give some account of the *effects* of recruitment and socialisation on the cultural and professional image of the officer corps, particularly those related to the notion that 'officers are gentlemen'. It will be shown that the poor educational qualifications of army officers and their consequent low prestige among their elite reference groups tended to reinforce the gentlemen ethic and not to dilute it, as one might have expected. Low prestige led them to search for their own differentiated sphere of military honour with which to protect and validate their position in society. The definition of the situation which developed so very rapidly around the new role of the army officer after Independence was therefore such as to encrust in a new setting (with certain saving graces) a style of life that was already itself encrusted with the relics of the British rural past.

THE 'GENTLEMAN' OFFICER

The style of life of a Nigerian staff officer at HQ in Lagos is described by Lt Colonel (then Major) Akahan, the late Chief of Staff, in the following way, with tongue only half in cheek:

[1] It was impracticable to include a study of the socialisation process in British training institutions in this writer's research programme. Some rather impressionistic data on social background (in this chapter) and on ethnic and regional backgrounds (in Chapter VIII below) are, however, included.

[2] Or more latterly, the Nigerian Defence Academy, the first graduates of which entered the army in 1967. The same comments would apply to it, as it was set up with the aid of a training mission from the Indian Army and run on virtually identical lines to all other British-style academies.

Officers and gentlemen: the image of an elite

All Officers and Officer Cadets are traditionally referred to as gentlemen, but one cannot mistake the 'gentleman' Staff Officer when one meets him he is the most 'gentleman' of them all.

He is often seen arriving at the office at 07.55 hours; early enough to have five minutes to spare. He invariably arrives by boat or as a non-paying passenger in some other officer's car, depending on which part of Lagos he resides. He leaves the office at 15.00 hours prompt which, of course, is the closing time. As all soldiers are paid to work twenty-four hours a day, he is certainly going to do some work at home.

On weekdays all Officers are dressed alike; a near-white looking green uniform (unless he has a Quartermaster friend) a pair of brown shoes which should have been resoled last year, and a face cap...Saturday is the only day you can tell which branch of the Army HQ he belongs to. If he is in a Moss Brothers smart-looking suit, he certainly is from 'A' Branch – where the dress regulations are written; he must set the pace.

Gentlemen in the 'G' Branch are very nationalistic and so the gentleman Staff Officer from this section would probably turn up for work in an 'Agbada'. 'What is all this fuss about dressing up on Saturdays for work?' This remark is more likely to be heard from the gentleman in 'Q' Branch, and true enough he would turn up in a terylene shirt and a pair of skin-tight slacks. What could be more appropriate garb for counting rusty tins and 'compo hats' than that?

Invariably the contents of a Staff Officer's briefcase are likely to be those files he took home but never had time to look at, a half filled flask of strong nescafe, a cheque-book he can only use on the first of every month, mess bills he should have paid last month, a 'Private and Confidential' letter from his Bank Manager about that overdraft, an equally 'Confidential' letter from the UDC Manager...[1]

In the office he is a busy man. He reads newspapers during the first hour in order to keep abreast with world affairs, thereafter comes coffee time. The GOC's Conference followed by the COS's Conference come immediately after the coffee break in quick succession. He is back at his desk after these conferences only to make a short telephone call to that girl he met last night, a quick rude letter to the Brigadier copy to all units, A.C. paper – no that's for homework. Another Conference and oh! it's closing time already. How time flies.

The 'gentleman' Staff Officer loves games, but the facilities are only available Wednesdays. He looks forward to Officer Games days and starts off from his house every Wednesday all dressed up for a good game of volley-ball, but never quite arrives at the pitch...

He believes in maximum enjoyment, accepts invitations to all parties as long as there is to be free booze. He prefers 'Star Beer' to all those cocktails – it is more satisfying! He ensures that there is one Alka Seltzer with which to tranquilise the evening's debauchery. When there is no private party forthcoming he can always be sure of an equally exciting time at that 'Magic Nite Spot' the KKD.[2]

[1] About his new car loan. A handsome automobile is an indispensable item of elite equipment in the Nigerian context.

[2] Major J. R. Akahan, 'The gentleman staff officer', *Nigerian Army Magazine* (Lagos), III (December 1963).

We quote this at length because it illustrates in a pithy way three divergent themes in the elite image of the army officer. First, that he is a member of a social elite based on newly acquired skills, the values of which – like its patterns of conspicuous consumption based on the images of the Western world – he shares. Secondly, that these are fused into more indigenous and behavioural and cultural traits – like the wearing of an agbada – which are reinforced by an officer's access to social influence from below in an open elite structure. Thirdly, however, that officers have refined and developed differentiated conceptions of military behaviour and collective honour, enshrined in the slogan that officers are gentlemen.

SOCIAL BACKGROUND AND THE OPEN CLASS STRUCTURE

Nigeria's elite is an aristocracy of skills, skills for the most part acquired through the process of formal education. It is a recently created elite and therefore has been relatively 'open'[1] in its pattern of recruitment from lower strata.[2] Unfortunately, there are no systematic and comprehensive data either on the recruitment and social background of the elite in general,[3] or the army in particular, on the basis of which one might generalise about patterns of occupational mobility, or compare the army with other elite groups. On the strength of an impressionistic acquaintance with the social backgrounds of officers, it is, however, possible to conjecture that the great majority of them have had relatively lowly origins. Farmer, clerk, catechist, trader, primary school teacher, lower paid employee of the government or one of the large public corporations (like the Nigerian Railway Corporation) or non-commissioned officers in the army, are all fairly typical of the occupations of their fathers.

There are, however, one or two instances of distinguished families with soldier sons. For example, one large family of high traditional position in the North, which has produced a distinguished civil servant (formerly Permanent Secretary to the Ministry of Defence) and also three army officer sons (two through the cadet entry and one promoted from the ranks during the civil war). Or an Arabic scholar in one of the Northern Emirates who has produced two high-ranking civil servants (one at ambassadorial level) and a younger son in the army. Or Lt Colonel Muritala Mohammed, who is related to a

---

[1] For an elegant analysis of a West African elite, which defines the respects in which it is 'open' and relates this to rates of mobility, second-generation recruitment, etc., see P. Foster, *Education and social change in Ghana* (Chicago: University of Chicago Press, 1965), especially Chapters VII–IX.
[2] This is not, however, to say that the second generation will not be more closed to the upwardly mobile. See Foster, *ibid.*
[3] H. H. and M. M. Smythe, *The new Nigerian elite* (Stanford, Calif.: Stanford University Press, 1960), deal almost entirely with the life style of the top or ruling elite, and provide no systematic data on recruitment and mobility.

powerful aristocratic family in Kano, a member of which (Alhaji Inuwa Wada) was a prominent NPC politician and Minister of Defence. Or the two officer sons of the Emir of Katsina, including the former Governor of the Northern Region and Chief of Staff, Brigadier Hassan Katsina. Or finally, Lt Colonel Ojukwu, son of a millionaire businessman, the late Sir Louis Ojukwu, who was connected closely by ties of friendship and political patronage with Dr Azikiwe, the former President, and his party, the NCNC. Such cases, however, are by no means typical. Good family connections have probably been an advantage, but not necessarily essential to a successful career, as is clear from the presence at the top of the hierarchy of many officers without such advantages, like Major General Ironsi (son of a railwayman), Major General Gowon (son of a mission catechist), Brigadier Adebayo (son of a railwayman), Brigadier Ademulegun (son of a tailor and farmer), Colonel Shodeinde (son of a tax clerk) and Colonel Fajuyi (son of a carpenter and farmer).

Indeed, it could be said that 'good' connections have been of less importance for career development in the Nigerian Army than in the British military elite.[1] One essential ingredient of patronage and clientage in the British Army that is only weakly developed in Nigeria is the element of kinship between aspiring officers and top members of the military elite. If an officer has relatives of the older generation in the army – grandfathers, fathers and uncles – they are unlikely to be of much use to him in matters of military preferment, because they would all be NCOs rather than members of the officer corps (even though such men may have provided models for his original decision to enter the army). The only kinship links through which desire for preferment may be articulated are those between relatives within the same generation; and it is doubtful whether these are yet widely spread through the army.

One result of the openness of recruitment is the high accessability of army officers (like other elites) to persons of non-elite background. On evenings and at the weekends, there is a constant stream of 'brothers', kinsmen, acquaintances from the same village or town-ward or the same ethnic group who come to pay their respects at an officer's house and to drink his beer and

---

[1] See C. B. Otley, 'The origins and recruitment of the British army elite', who suggests in respect of the British Army that: 'where bureaucratic procedures of assessment are imperfectly developed, it is inevitable that kinship factors obtrude into the process of assessment and selection, and that the intimacy of a senior officer with a junior candidate for a post would be considered reasonable grounds for the former recommending the latter for the post...The militarily well-connected individual would move more easily into his superior's view than an entrant without such connections. Thus it would be possible for meritorious but connectionless officers to miss preferment. Any army leader would be in a position to give information and advice which might be of great benefit to his young relative. He could tell him in what posts or sectors of the service one was most likely to be "noticed".'

Fanta orange. They may be there for advice on recruitment into the army, to raise a contribution for a funeral or some other common function, to bring messages from family and friends, to pay homage, to listen to the radiogram or watch television, or merely to seek company. They may include private soldiers and NCOs in their off duty hours, as well as civilians: for it is impracticable to impose status barriers – as in the British Army – which cut across the accepted norms of sociability. Ease of access does not, however, free the more humble visitors of the obligation to make the suitable gestures of deference toward their host. Similarly, an officer, because of his high social position, will feel strongly obliged to demonstrate the appropriate hospitality, to keep an ever-open fridge, or to send his servant scurrying over to the mess for drinks, and in appropriate instances to expect his wife or manservant to produce a large supply of food for visitors.

Again, if he goes out, he may well stop on his way to visit a clerk who was a school-mate of his early days, or to pay respects to an important representative of his community in the urban area in which he resides. If he goes for entertainment in a public place, like a bingo hall or a night spot, there will be a stream of acquaintances pausing by his table to pay respects or to join him for a drink. As most of those at the table will insist on buying drinks for the whole party, the table will be covered from end to end with bottles of beer by the end of the evening, even if not all of them are consumed.

A degree of accessibility has its functions, both facilitating the maintenance of discipline on a consensual basis[1] and making the military elite more responsive to changes in its social and political environment. On the other hand, the social linkages between NCOs and junior officers were used to exert pressure on the latter to revolt against authority in July 1966.

A high degree of access has also tended to make the officers corps more vulnerable to corruption and political pressure, though such pressures were not very strong in the period of civilian rule, and were on the whole success-fully contained by professional and organisational controls. It is notable that, in the whole period up to 1966, there was no major scandal in the officers corps, merely two small affairs of lieutenants being cashiered for theft, and a senior officer being courtmartialled and reprimanded for appropriating government furniture from his house.[2] On the other hand, the record of the military since it acquired power has not been as good. Corruption and political pressures have been severest perhaps in the Western Region where more than one Yoruba officer has been caught up in the powerful power-patronage networks of the former political parties. A high-ranking officer anywhere in Nigeria is now constantly visited by persons seeking small favours and his

[1] See Chapter VII below.
[2] Compare with the navy, where a couple of officers were arraigned for misappropriating a large proportion of the naval budget.

goodwill sought with unsolicited gifts. Up to the civil war, one had the impression that outright attempts to bribe an officer on a *quid pro quo* basis were comparatively rare, because few army figures were then receptive to open invitations to corruption. Some, indeed, were still very sensitive as to the implications of accepting unsolicited gifts, and officers would reject crates of beer or bottles proffered at a night club because of suspicion as to the motive of those offering them. Others, however, were not averse to taking part in various business deals which are not strictly speaking proscribed by regulations, in the conclusion of which a military status is an advantage.[1] The scope for such deals as well as for outright corruption was undoubtedly widened by the civil war and there were, it seems, instances of officers taking bribes, misappropriating stores and failing to declare casualties in order to collect the pay of the dead soldiers. Major General Gowon himself felt it necessary to call upon members of the armed forces to point out 'the bad eggs among you' in response to such accusations for 'honestly speaking, there is some justification in what these people say...some of us truly go below the level expected of good officers'.[2]

The pattern of accessibility, it should be explained, is one that is normal among *all* persons in elite positions (it is probably less well developed in the officer corps than among other elites). It is predicated by the norms of hospitality and reciprocity in social relations that are common to the majority of West African societies.[3] Even in the Hausa–Fulani Emirates the prominent members of the aristocracy keep up relatively little cultural differentiation from their inferiors and are normally very accessible to the latter at the appropriate times and places, in spite of the high degree of political and economic differentiation, a steep hierarchy of status and power and strongly marked patterns of deference between social superior and inferior. It would be a matter of surprise, indeed, if such traditions of access and sociability to kin and community were not preserved – outside, of course, the normal military lines of command and control and other such relationships which specifically exclude particularistic ties of friendship, clientage and kinship.[4]

---

[1] Such business relationships were not unknown before the January 1966 coup, for example the appointment of one high-ranking officer as part-time manager of a contracting firm which did business with a public corporation in which his brother held an important post.

[2] *West Africa* (London), 18 January 1969.

[3] For a broad overview of the argument that African stratification systems – even of the most hierarchical sort – are based on political (and economic) rather than cultural differentiation, see L. Fallers, 'Equality, modernity and democracy in the new states' in C. Geertz (ed.), *Old societies and new states* (New York: Free Press, 1963). The detailed studies of individual societies that are of relevance are too many to cite here. Among the many relevant studies in Nigeria alone are Smith, *Government in Zazzau*, and W. R. Bascom, 'Social status, wealth and individual differences among the Yoruba', *American Anthropologist*, LIII, 4 (October–December 1951).

[4] This is not to deny that such linkages do not sometimes obtrude into relationships of command and control. The assertion is merely that the latter produce constraints against the influence of

STYLE OF LIFE AND PATTERNS OF CULTURE

The officer's style of life contains a strong emphasis on material consumption and its symbols. A modern education and occupational role is sought after, mainly because it gives access to a high standard of living. In the occupational structure inherited from colonial rule, the 'plums' in terms of income and material perquisites go to the holders of 'senior service' posts formerly held by Europeans, like the lawyers, senior civil servants, business executives and army officers. Income differentials in favour of such posts are much greater than in the industrial nations and occupational aspirations influenced correspondingly. The flavour of these expectations is nicely conveyed by some lines from a beach prophet's prayer by a well-known Nigerian playwright:

Make you not forget those of us who dey struggle daily. Those who be clerk today, make them Chief Clerk tomorrow. Those who are Messenger today make them Senior Service tomorrow.

Those who are petty trader today, make them big contractor tomorrow. Those who dey sweep street today, give them their own bicycle tomorrow. Those who have bicycle today, they will ride their own car tomorrow.

I say those who dey push bicycle, give them big car tomorrow. Give them big car tomorrow. Give them big car tomorrow, give them big car tomorrow.[1]

Education and occupational choice are manipulated in a highly utilitarian fashion by the individual to maximise the material and prestige benefits accruing to him.[2] (And indirectly, therefore, to the kinsmen or community which financed his education.) When the military authorities sought to increase the numbers of Nigerians entering the officer corps rapidly in the late 1950s, they were forced to take these realities into account by raising officer salaries and introducing car allowances and car purchase loans comparable to those obtainable by civil servants.

Officers, unless they are exceedingly prudent, will normally buy the largest and most prestigious car their means and the financial limit on car purchase loans will allow. Most of them possess a large radiogram of German or Japanese manufacture, together with a stack of records for the entertainment of visitors, and usually one or two other conspicuous items of furniture,

particularist ties which are normally not operative in leisure hours, so that patterns of behaviour learned in home, village and community are freer to persist then. See the discussion of ethnicity in Chapter VIII below.

[1] W. Soyinka, *Five plays* (London: Oxford University Press, 1964), pp. 219–20.
[2] See, for instance, Foster's discussion of the manner in which Ghanaian students make their choice of schools, preferring the higher prestige schools which would increase the probability of passing School Certificate and university entrance, the greater cost of these schools being discounted against the greater flow of future benefit a successful education would generate. Foster, *Education and social change in Ghana*, Chapter VII.

such as a television or an ornate table lamp or cocktail trolley.[1] Their hospitality is generous, both at home and in the mess, where drinks are dispensed on a lavish scale.

Patterns of consumption and standards of taste are heavily influenced by those of the British bourgeoisie. A quick glance around a typical officer's bookshelves for instance might reveal the following: a handsome leather-bound encyclopaedia – perhaps two, the second being a medical encylo-paedia, a *Whitaker's Almanack*, a *Who's Who*, or a dictionary; one or two military histories acquired during training abroad; a couple more general history books, in all probability one of Winston Churchill's tomes; one or two law books, including one of the classics on British constitutional law; a couple of technical treatises (if the officer were in a technical branch), and perhaps an elementary text in economics; a book, possibly two, in the Samuel Smiles/Dale Carnegie self-improvement category, *How to win friends and influence people*, *Your personality and how to use it*, *Self-confidence, the passport to success*, etc.; and finally one or two fly-blown detective novels. A more sophisticated officer might show greater political and social awareness and have developed more radical political ideas; placing Marx, Lenin or Mao or a commentary and critique of one of them on his bookshelves, possibly a book on the army's political role in developing areas; and a couple of works on African politics.

Gramophone records may show a greater predilection for indigenous traditions and tastes, including several 'high lifes' as well as ballads by Jim Reeves or Ella Fitzgerald, some Motown soul and a few popular classical works by composers like Tchaikovsky. A photograph album is a treasured item of cultural equipment and will reveal a rich mixture of the continuities of cultural and family life in the officer's home area, ex-girlfriends, and a long string of school- and course-mates. Photographs, usually group photo-graphs from Sandhurst, or of a course, or of a shooting competition or mess party will also be on the walls. So too may be one or two *objets d'art* picked up from a trader – a mask, a spear, a carved wooden head perhaps – though these will probably be of the kind picked up by any foreign tourist.

Standards of dress are meticulous. In leisure hours, an officer may wear European dress – with the appropriately conservative tie for more formal occasions, an open-necked shirt informally – or the indigenous agbada or similar costume, being equally at home with the cultural symbols of both styles of dress. At work and on mess occasions there will be an immaculate uniform, bright with brass buttons and shiny shoes, a swagger stick, and hat with the appropriate racy curvature. Public manners are tailored to the

---

[1] Most of the items of 'heavy' furniture, fridge, beds, chairs, tables, etc., being provided in their army housing for them, as is the practice in nearly all 'senior service' housing.

smartness of the uniform, a jump to the feet when ladies enter the mess, a snap of the heels as the Commanding Officer comes in, a brisk salute and 'sah!' when given an order. Officers who have received their training outside of the academies and cadet schools of Britain, India and Pakistan are sometimes a little less brisk in their habits than the others. American- and Canadian-trained officers, for instance, are less inclined towards spit and polish, even though they may be just as good soldiers in a professional sense. One American-trained officer of the writer's acquaintance developed an amusing sense of role-distance from the martinet image, wore a somewhat down-at-heel uniform, played drunk at parties when really sober, and used to mimic the military salute with a lank gesture like wiping the sweat off his forehead.

These specifically military traits apart, the characteristics of the officers' cultural image that have been described are shared in common with the majority of the other professional, Western-educated elites in Nigeria. The emphasis upon acquired cultural standards is perhaps stronger, however, among the officers than among other elite groups. In at least two garrison towns the writer has visited, the officers of the local military unit made considerably more use of the former European 'club' than any other comparable group, and in one of them at least the officers mess by custom purchased group membership of the club on behalf of the members. The maintenance of standards is viewed as a collective enterprise. Lapses in dress or misdemeanours in social behaviour are rebuked by Commanding Officers or made the subject of ridicule in the mess. The mess itself is full of tokens of continuity with the colonial past – silverware presented by 'twin' British regiments, photographs of regimental functions on the wall, relics such as captured flags or weapons from past campaigns in Burma, the Cameroons and the Congo, and hunting trophies protruding from the wall. Mess dinner nights are held to which other members of the elite – local and expatriate – may be formally invited. There are also early afternoon drinks on Saturdays in the mess of a number of the units, which every officer is expected to attend, to which they can bring friends of suitable elite status. (In contrast to the informal context of his house, an officer would *not* normally bring a humble friend or relative into the mess for drinks.) On such occasions, officers may arrange to partake in suitable games and field sports with their friends, like tennis or a shooting party, or to go out riding. The mess normally maintains a number of sporting facilities itself – tennis and squash courts, a swimming pool and sometimes riding stables. One of the Nigerian officer's role-images quite patently is the country gentleman posture of British officers, and hence the continuing emphasis on field sports and the like.

On the other hand, only the isolated officer (whom one does however occasionally meet) will go the whole hog, with cavalry twills, tweed jacket, moustache, tweed cap, shooting stick, field sports, polo and all. For most, such traits are mixed with and diluted by other images. Those who knew the colonial days say that protocol and style of life are less rigidly enforced now than they were then. Some of the older NCOs complain that the rituals and group life of the mess have fallen into disrepair and that officers are not what they used to be. It is not clear how far this represents a sentimentalisation of the past, or how far the fact that practices have changed: for instance, it is now usual for officers to have meals sent over from the mess to their houses rather than eating there, as it was in the past. Nor are commanding officers as rigid on matters of social behaviour as were some of the British. One commander, for instance, pointed out that one of his British predecessors used to keep the hedges and bushes clipped so that he could watch the entries and exits of his subordinates from his veranda (or so the Nigerians thought), and stated that he would not dream of imposing that much control over his officers' private lives. That daunting figure of British and American barracks, the commanding officer's wife, no longer controls standards of etiquette and entertainment: the wives of Nigerian officers for the most part lack a high level of education, spend most of their time on purely domestic matters and do not play a vital role in the social life of the unit.

In sum, the officers' style of life is strongly influenced by an ethos of conspicuous consumption, blending imported with indigenous images. This ethos might seem to be at odds with the image of austerity and self-discipline found in Western professional armies.[1] The latter was for instance exemplified by the unwillingness of British military authorities to acquiesce in attempts to recruit Nigerian officer cadets by providing car allowances and increased salaries for them until the Nigerian forces were removed from control of the British War Office in 1958. Yet there is no evidence of any *necessary* inconsistency between a high consumption ethos and military values. Nigerian officers continue, as we will argue in the pages that follow, to subscribe to notions of collective military honour; and indeed, as we have already begun to suggest above, certain of their conspicuous consumption traits serve to call attention to their distinctive identity as 'officers and gentlemen'.

SELF-IMAGE AND EXTERNAL REFERENCE GROUPS

A feature that is much apparent from his style of life is that the Nigerian army officer is a provincial in terms of his reference groups and his intellectual and cultural conventions. He borrows from the creative centres of Western

[1] Janowitz, *The professional soldier*, Chapter XI.

culture, but has not himself a creative grasp of its traditions.[1] It would be surprising, indeed, if he were not provincial, for colonial society was always peripheral to the intellectual currents of the metropolitan country and the new inheriting elites are not any closer. Nor, with the exception of one or two small circles of artists and writers and perhaps of social scientists in the universities, are they drawn towards vital intellectual and cultural centres of their own. Still less the military than other elites, for the educational standards imposed for entry into the officer corps and the intellectual stimulus provided during the process of military training are undoubtedly lower than those of all other Nigerian professional groups (except the police). The British officers of the Nigerian cadet's role model are themselves also very parochial in outlook. An impressionistic comparison of material in *Owl Pie* and *The Wish Stream*, the journals of the Staff College, Camberley and the Royal Military Academy, Sandhurst, with that in the *Nigerian Army Magazine* suggests that the former are no broader in their interests than the latter, nor any more sophisticated in their approach to social, political and military problems. The former devote more space to the trivia of social life – the sports, amateur dramatics, and foxhounds – and the latter more to matters of political and military concern. Many of the articles in the *Nigerian Army Magazine* are digests of military history taken out of the standard books on the subject, or generalisations about morale, personnel training and the like, picked up at the latest staff course abroad. But others – like that of Lt Colonel Akahan above,[2] or the article by Lt Colonel Pam quoted below[3] – show a capacity for humorous detachment from their professional role that is certainly no more frequent in the magazines of the British professional soldier.

People whose intellectual and social prestige horizons are at the periphery of a culture are in danger of acquiring a low or negative self-image. The American officer corps has had less prestige than other professions in the past, this being at least in part due to its lack of vital intellectual centres which might create and sustain its values. The result has been anti-intellectualism and an emphasis on collective honour,[4] a retreat from the cultural standards by which it is evaluated so lowly. These reactions occur, too, in the British military, though they are somewhat muted by the fact that the British officer

---

[1] See the analysis of the sources and results of the intellectual provinciality of elites in new nations in E. A. Shils, *The intellectual between tradition and modernity: the Indian situation* (The Hague: Mouton, 1961). It is difficult, however, to talk about these matters without sounding condescending.

[2] See p. 110 above.   [3] See p. 152 below.

[4] A good discussion of the role of intellectual centres, such as universities and professional training schools, in creating and sustaining the values upon which professions (and their prestige) are based, can be found in T. Parsons, 'The Professions' in *The encyclopaedia of the social sciences*, XII (New York: Macmillan and Free Press, 1968). For those trends in the US Army, see Janowitz, *The professional soldier*, Part V, and in Britain, Otley, 'The origins and recruitment of the British Army elite'.

is more able to shore up his prestige by emphasising his social niche in the ranks of the minor gentry.

The Nigerian officer has no such refuge, and is furthermore at the periphery of an alien culture not his own: a culture which has very strong undertones of racialism and has frequently put forward stereotypes of Africans as primitives or worse. Many officers will have had to struggle with the conception that Europeans have a low opinion of Africans thoughout the whole period of formal education in English; and many still continue to believe that this is so.[1] Although some officers emphasise the multi-racial character of their training at Sandhurst, Mons and elsewhere, that they were treated as officers and gentlemen and not as members of particular nationalities and racial groups, others are more cagey about their experiences in England. At least one British ex-officer of the writer's acquaintance emphasises that although there was no *overt* discrimination against African officers as such, British cadets did not 'mix with the black chaps very much'. Relatively fewer African cadets were given responsible positions as platoon leaders in exercises or made under-officers; and the attitude towards them was often one of condescension.

The first few months at British training institutions and some of the hazing rituals (like the notorious kit parades[2] at Sandhurst) they went through were sometimes traumatic. One officer of the writer's acquaintance, for example, said that in his first term at Sandhurst he was 'too busy to look for friends', practical jokes were played on him and 'I didn't understand their sense of humour and they didn't understand mine. I was accused of having an "inferiority complex" but it wasn't that at all'. He was always one of the last in the kit parade because he was not used to high collars and his fingers were always cold, and he refused to go to an English family for his first Christmas holidays because he was afraid of the social humiliations he might risk. He said, however, that he got on much better in his later terms and now looked back to his time at Sandhurst 'with pride'. Conformity to the military image was acquired by many officers at a high price: indeed, one suspects that the worse the humiliations endured the greater the attachment to the life of the officer and gentleman that was ultimately flaunted.

Beliefs about the perceptions and evaluations of oneself by others are intimately linked, both to self-conceptions and to reactions towards those

[1] Not without justification, given the prevalence of racial discrimination in colonial society. Jahoda, in his study of racial stereotyping, found that no less than four-fifths of his adult Ghanaian informants thought whites had a poor opinion of Africans. What is even more interesting is that many appeared to have internalised this poor opinion themselves. G. Jahoda, *White man* (London: Oxford University Press, 1962), pp. 42–54.

[2] At these parades the new cadets were made to dash up several flights of stairs, change uniforms and come down again in three or four minutes, and if they were too long, being made to repeat the process to the satisfaction of the cadet under-officer in charge.

others,[1] in this case the white man. European friends may be made, or wives and girl friends acquired, but there is often an undercurrent of anxiety about their motivations, whether they approve of the Nigerian officer's behaviour, whether they are not ridiculing him behind his back, whether deep down they do not think him inferior. It is difficult to say other than in a highly impressionistic way how widespread such anxieties are or how deeply felt. The writer has friends who have shown no sign of them: and others who, while displaying stress and anxiety about their racial identities, seemed to have stable personalities in all other respects. It is possible that there are other aspects of Western education and professional socialisation which serve to integrate identities and nullify such anxieties. Yet disquiet about both national prestige and racial image seems overall to be a powerful theme in the officer's professional identity.

There are two kinds of reaction one might expect under these circumstances, both of which many Nigerian Army officers seem to succeed in sustaining without noticing the apparent contradiction. The first is to knuckle under to the white man, to conform to the Sandhurst way of life, the polo, shooting and tweeds complex or the ritualisation of spit and polish in the mess. On the other hand, there may be reaction-formation, one form of which may be a recourse to national, Pan–African or racial images. This appears, for instance, in the earlier quoted cry of the January 1966 conspirators, that having done away with the corrupt old regime that brought Nigeria into disrepute abroad, 'you no longer need be ashamed of being Nigerians'. Or in the rage that the subject of white mercenaries in the Nigerian civil war can evoke not only, it should be said, among the soldiers; and the sensitivity to any hint of non-African interference in the war, whether from the American or European governments, or from charity organisations, portrayed very explicitly in Colonel Adekunle's statement that 'this war has shown the African not to trust anyone who is white'.[2]

The themes of conformism and revolt are often combined, the conflict between them not resolved. The difficulties of reconciling the two are apparent in a retrospective article by Major Ifeajuna on 'The Nigerian Army after a hundred years' appearing in the issue of the *Nigerian Army Magazine* just before the January 1966 coup in which he took part. This suggests on the one hand that

[1] An empirical study that is of relevance here is F. O. Okedeji, 'Social adjustment of African students in two United States communities', *Nigerian Journal of Economic and Social Studies*, XVI, 3 (November 1964). Okedeji finds that students who were high in subjective national status (as measured by their ranking of their own country as compared to others) also thought that Americans evaluated their countries relatively highly and were high in their personal satisfaction and adjustment to the USA.

[2] The *Sunday Times* (London), 8 September 1968, with some caution as to the somewhat sensationalist tone of the article from which the statement was derived.

if it is claimed that the British bestowed worthy traditions on the Nigerian army, the Congo was the place where it became very obvious...The army exists in the shape which our former imperial masters left it.

On the other hand,

with the passage of time it will change (or is changing) to conform to the social pattern of our people

for, during the colonial period

first all officers were white. This was not the main problem (*sic*). But then too there was the British NCO – that colonial institution of terrorism in the Lines. Claimed to be a vital link in the chain of command the British NCO was a veritable beast; treated like an officer, but behaving like a maniac. And yet, they had all the support, even when drawn against the earlier Nigerian Officers.

Such frustrations may help to account for the power of nationalism as a cultural motif among officers. On the other hand, the themes of humiliation, identity and self-assertion are the common stuff of nationalism among *all* groups in ex-colonial territories; and we have as yet given no reasons to suppose that the military is any different in these respects from other elites. If one looks more closely at the political beliefs of the officer corps differences in emphasis begin, however, to appear. Though it is difficult to be precise, one can say with some confidence that nationalism, distaste for corruption and mistrust of politics was greater in the military than in most groups outside it; and that each of these three themes was linked to specific conceptions of military doctrine and honour in the way we shall later describe in chapter XII.

What has been the source of emphasis on military values? This can be sought in strains generated upon the officers' self-image by their lack (until 1966 at least) of social prestige relative to other elites and the search for collective honour this encouraged.

SOCIAL PRESTIGE AND COLLECTIVE HONOUR

The social prestige of the officers among other elites has been governed in the main by their level of educational attainment. And the dilemma that they have faced is that by such standards they are poorly qualified compared with most other elite reference groups. The extent of this educational deficiency is impressive, as we already saw in the review of their training and skills in Chapter III. The great majority of combat officers had not even the minimum educational qualification for entry to the degree or professional training courses of other professions,[1] as the minimum standard for entry to officer

---

[1] In contrast, the majority of the 121 *non*-combat officers on contract commissions, the army doctors, nurses, some of the educational and paymaster corps and some of the engineers, had degrees or similar professional qualifications. (There were also sixty-two engineers, teachers and administrators with quartermaster or executive commissions. But these were almost all promoted

cadet courses was set in terms of mere GCE 'Ordinary Levels' or the West African School Certificate; and in the period after Independence, the minimum level of performance[1] that was accepted even in these exams was reduced to accomodate poorly qualified Northern applicants.

Set against this was a calculus of the flow of material benefits which put entrants to the officer corps in an extremely advantageous position relative to other professions. Taken at its most favourable, an officer cadet in the early 1960s could anticipate receiving his commission within one and a half to two years of his West African School Certificate, after training at the Nigerian Military Training College and Mons Officer Cadet School in England. His peers at secondary school could anticipate another five and a half to six years of formal education, (including the two years obtaining a Higher School Certificate) before obtaining a university degree. Yet the starting salary and material perquisites of the former upon receiving his commission would be slightly higher than those of the latter upon entering the civil service or teaching profession.

Not surprisingly, the army attracted very large numbers of applicants – especially from the North – who had either failed to get entry to sixth forms or who were willing to sacrifice the greater status of a higher formal education for a better chance of material benefit in the officer corps. There were still, of course, a number of entrants with the standard 'military' motivations – a desire for honour or the example of relatives in the army, and the writer knows more than one officer who gave up a good sixth form or university place for such reasons. Such candidates were likely to be favoured by the army's selection procedure, which relied quite heavily on the assessment of motivation and leadership quality at interviews. Nevertheless they were a minority. The public image of the profession among secondary school leavers and among most of the officers themselves was that it was the 'short cut to senior service', the easy way to the status, salary and perquisites of the elite.[2]

NCOs of relatively little formal education.) But these played a peripheral role in the life of most officers messes and their systems of values. Members of the educational corps, for example, have adopted the military manner, ritualise spit and polish just as much as any combat officer, and aspire to combat commissions. The fact that they adopt military reference groups rather than *vice versa* testifies both to the power of the army messes and the other integrative foci of barracks life; and to the fact that many outside 'professionals' joining the army do so only because they did not get a good degree or other professional qualification, and cannot get better jobs elsewhere, the military value system permitting them to repair their self-image by devaluating their poor civilian qualifications.

[1] In terms of the number of subjects to be obtained at 'credit' and 'pass' level. This was well below the standard required to obtain entry to a sixth-form course at secondary school to proceed to the Higher School Certificate. Some Northerners were admitted with only three or four subjects at Ordinary Level. For the regional quota system which brought about this position, see Chapter VIII below.

[2] The question arises, in view of such advantages, why it was so difficult to Nigerianise the army during the years of internal self-government from 1954 onwards, compared with the other public

This had a clearly discernible impact on the prestige of the officer corps relative to other elite groups in the judgement of those groups at least, if not in that of lower status persons as well. In a study of occupational prestige ranking by economics and medical students at Nigerian universities in 1965, it was found that army officers were ranked thirteenth out of forty-one by the former and nineteenth by the latter. While this study raises a number of methodological problems, suggesting the difficulties of using this kind of occupation–rating scale in an African setting,[1] in general it seems to indicate that with two exceptions,[2] the status of the army officer among this sample is less than that of other professions; although the military's lack of prestige is no less great than in the USA where, according to Janowitz, similar status problems arise.[3]

Such poor prestige evaluations are difficult to escape. Like the blood on Lady Macbeth's hands or their own colour, they cannot be washed away. For they have thoroughly internalised the prestige of a Western education, since after all it is the means whereby they have themselves ascended. Small consolation then, that the prestige of the army among the masses has greatly increased since Independence, or that military parades evoke deep sighs from a Nigerian crowd at the demonstration of power provided by the crash of heels and weapons. For the really salient reference groups for the officers have been their educated peers whose evaluation has still been very grudging. Even with a civil war, students at the universities were prone to sneer at the military and to suggest that despite their material accoutrements (of which students are jealous) they are unintelligent, somewhat 'bush' people.

On the one hand, officers still feel compelled to emphasise the value of education. Any hint of particularistic limitations on the rights of the educated and the able to occupational advancement are strongly resisted. Such concerns have been most deeply evident in fears that army promotions and

services. This was primarily because: (i) the material perquisites of the officer corps were slightly lower until 1958–9 than those of the equivalent civil service groups; (ii) standards of entry were higher than in the 1960s; (iii) the risks of failure in officer training courses were high, being much reduced when the Nigerian Military Training College was opened and instructed by the Northern Ministers of Defence to pass a higher proportion of cadets in the initial stages of training at the college, in order to let more Northern entrants through; and (iv) the prestige of the army was low in the colonial period.

[1] The study was by R. W. Morgan, Jr, 'Occupational prestige rankings by Nigerian students', *Nigerian Journal of Economic and Social Studies*, VII, 3 (November 1965). Difficulties in an African setting arise, for example, from the lack of any measure of general agreement among different groups in the population concerning the relative status of particular occupations and even concerning the very criteria by which the occupations are ranked. See, for example, the sharp divergencies in ratings between the two groups of students in this study: one might expect *a fortiori* the evaluations of groups with less in common than the students to be even more different.

[2] Lawyers and secondary school teachers. The low prestige of the former can possibly be explained by the manner in which this scale dichotomised between the higher and lower ranks of the legal profession (High Court judge and ordinary lawyer).

[3] Janowitz, *The professional soldier*, Chapter XI.

appointments might be manipulated on ethnic/regional criteria. When Ahmadu Bello University, in the North, proposed in 1967 to establish concessionary entry conditions for 'mature' applicants,[1] causing a student strike, the majority of officers of the writer's acquaintance were strongly in favour of the students, though they did not like their methods. Prominent army officers are often highly self-conscious about their educational standing, their occupational status and their role in history at one and the same time. Colonel Adekunle, the Divisional Commander of the Third Division in the civil war, for instance, applied in 1964 to read for an external LLB degree at London University. Both Major Nzeogwu and Major Ifeajuna completed, or were in the process of completing[2] manuscripts concerning the January 1966 coup. More than one other officer in the army is known to have been attempting to piece together a book. Others like to talk of resuming full-time education, of earning a degree, and show strong interest in the prospect of undertaking 'external' or part-time courses at universities.[3]

On the other hand, there is ambivalence and disquiet at their own relative lack of educational performance, at their lack of prestige among elite reference groups. In these modern times when men have books for testicles,[4] officers are galled by the prowess of their secondary school peers who have reached university.[5] When they are not regaling the listener with their own educational achievements and ambitions, they are saying how impractical and unreliable the intellectuals are. At Independence (1960–1) attempts were made

---

[1] The scheme envisaged was no more than a slight reduction in entry qualification for a small number of 'mature' students, but the emotional reaction produced against the scheme was out of all proportion.

[2] The latter completed his and gave it to a publisher's representative, though it was never published nor did it reach the writer's hands.

[3] This might seem to contradict the contention that the lower prestige of the less educated cannot be washed away. It is not so, however, for whatever self-improvement an individual officer may achieve, this does not entirely detach him from the lack of prestige of the officer corps as a group. The difficulties of part-time education are considerable: Nigerian universities – except Lagos – do not have adequate facilities for it, and few officers actually have the time to do more than talk wistfully about it. They are also, to an extent, hoist by their own petard in opposing proposals for special university entry qualifications for 'mature' students.

[4] See the lines by Okot p'Bitek, *Song of Lawino* (Nairobi: East African Publishing House, 1966), p. 208:

> For all our young men
> Were finished in the forest
> Their manhood was finished
> In the class rooms
> Their testicles
> Were smashed
> With large books!

This is a traditional woman's view of things, though others might say that education confers a novel kind of potency, rather than impotence.

[5] Although there is jealousy of this kind, it should in all fairness be said that at an *individual level* officers maintain very good and friendly contacts with their school-mates at the university, even though they might denigrate students as a group.

to recruit university graduates for direct entry into combat positions in the army but these were soon abandoned, in part for lack of recruits and in part because the three or four graduates who were recruited proved hard to assimilate.[1] There is a tendency now for officers to suggest that the January 1966 coup occurred because the Majors who staged it 'were too clever by half', read too many books about politics and were too much influenced by the university graduates among them. Consequently, there is a pressure to stress types of occupational achievement other than educational and intellectual skills; to point to the value of the 'practical' approach to problems a military man supposedly acquires. Lt Colonel Hassan Katsina stressed, in 1966, the need to revaluate recruitment: 'but recruitment', he said, 'must be on the right basis. What the army needs is real soldiers and not book people.'[2]

This ambivalence concerning prestige is perhaps the key to the search in the officer corps for differentiated conceptions of military honour. One officer, after discussing the 'sarcastic and jeering remarks' suffered after joining the army, illustrates this feeling well by saying that if the new officer had remained a civilian 'there would be no inspection or parades, frequent punishment and unnecessary "bull"... Nobody would chase him around... There would be no rigid discipline and little opportunity to test his leadership qualities... *He would only be subject to civil law and the question of being a gentleman would be at his discretion.*'[3] For one very effective way of offsetting the dissonance[4] between their own self-image and that held of them by other elites is to emphasise the special virtues that they must exemplify to civilian society,[5] such as self-discipline, comradeship, purity from 'corruption and decadence', and nationalism.

This is why the idea that 'officers are gentlemen' is pivotal. The Nigerian Military Forces Act[6] gives legal force to this conception when it states that 'every officer subject to law under the Ordnance who behaves in a scandalous manner, unbecoming the character of an officer and a gentlemen, shall, on conviction of a court-martial, be cashiered'. To impugn the honour of an

---

[1] It is significant that four of the six graduates to obtain combat commissions were in on the January coup. The last graduate to be commissioned as a cadet officer was Major Ademoyega, in 1962 (recruited 1961). An additional cause for jealousy was that the graduates were given three years' seniority over the normal entry. A further reason for the ceasing of the flow of graduates into the army was the quota system introduced after 1961 in favour of Northern entrants. From 1961 all graduates recruited went into the educational corps or technical services.

[2] Interview with Lt Colonel Hassan Katsina by the editor of the *Daily Times* (Lagos), 4 October 1966.

[3] Major A. O. Eze, 'From civilian to army life', *Nigerian Army Magazine* (Lagos), I, 1 (October 1963), 12–13.

[4] The concept of cognitive dissonance which is of obvious relevance here is elucidated in L. Festinger, *A theory of cognitive dissonance* (Stanford, Calif.: Stanford University Press, 1957).

[5] Janowitz, *The professional soldier*, Chapter XI.

[6] Royal Nigerian Military Forces Act, no. 26 of 1960. The passages of the act relating to discipline are very largely based on the relevant British military law.

officer is also an offence, false statements and 'statements affecting the character of an officer' being punishable by imprisonment if considered serious enough. Nor is this just an anomaly, a hangover from colonial days or a ritualised execrescence of British military education. Officers are extremely sensitive to questions of honour, and there is a very strong reaction to any suggestion that they may not have acted as gentlemen in any given set of circumstances,[1] to a point where it is not unknown for an officer to have threatened action against a superior under the act if he felt dishonoured by the latter.

The style of life in the mess is geared to the promotion of this image, and points of proper conduct and protocol are hotly disputed within it. Both Northern and Eastern officers took a strongly emotional view of the supposedly dishonourable conduct of the conspirators in the January and July coups in doing to death their comrades-in-arms, precisely because of the violations of comradeship and honour they brought. Lt Colonel Ojukwu, for instance, stated to his military colleagues (on the subject of the July coup) that:

Mention a name, we know who killed him, mention someone we know who at least hounded him out of his barracks. So Gentlemen, for as long as that situation exists men from Eastern Nigeria would find it utterly impossible to stay in the same barracks, eat in the same mess, fight in the same trenches as men in the army from Northern Nigeria.[2]

Yet the notion that officers are gentlemen has a quite different function in the Nigerian military from that which it has in the British Army, in spite of the similarity in behaviour and style of life. Being a gentleman in England is a status that is independent of being an officer. The role and the patterns of action that go with it belong to a particular status niche in the structure of rural English society, even though they have also been adopted by a number of middle-class groups including the military. To emphasise that an officer is a gentleman, then, is to indicate that he has a particular place in the class structure. It dilutes the collective and corporate identity of the officer corps, and has served to secure its loyalty to the ruling political elite.[3] In contrast, in Nigeria the gentleman notion is a device of collective military honour, being in this respect not unlike the practice of duelling in the German officer

---

[1] As the writer knows from experience. They are also quite ready to express shame if their behaviour has not been up to their own standards.

[2] Lt Colonel Ojukwu to the *Meeting of the Nigerian military leaders held at Peduase Lodge, Aburi, Ghana, 4th and 5th January 1967*, p. 27.

[3] Otley, 'The origins and recruitment of the British military elite', shows that the officer corps since the early nineteenth century has been recruited from the minor country gentry rather than the aristocracy or the ruling political elites. Its subservience and loyalty to the latter is thus assured, without making the officer corps itself prey to the cleavage and conflicts that have riven the ruling elites themselves. See also W. Guttsman, *The British political elite* (London: Macgibbon and Kee, 1965).

corps.[1] It affirms the professional identity of the individual officer and the corporate identity of the officer corps as a differentiated status group with its own system of values. There is no clearly defined status of gentleman outside the army, and no other elites make it part of their self-image in quite the same way as the officers.

To be a gentleman is therefore an effective way for the officers to provide honour for themselves on their own terms, to sustain a system of values that protects them from the shame and self-doubt inherent in the education-based status system operating among the elites. It also blends in with one of the standard military motivations for the production of honour, namely desire to remove and alleviate self-doubt in the face of the risk of death. One of the major grievances of Northern officers and men against the Ironsi regime was that it failed to acknowledge the death of senior officers in the January 1966 coup and thus to give them the proper military burial. When Major Nzeogwu was killed by Federal troops in the early stages of the civil war, Major General Gowon ordered that he be given a burial with 'full military honour' in recognition of the fact that he was a good, though 'misguided' officer. At the same time, there were many Northern troops and officers who felt he did not deserve this treatment – 'did they bury Maimalari, did they bury Largema, did they bury Kuru Mohammed, did they bury Ademulegun?' was the cry – and it is said that Gowon's orders were carried out with reluctance,[2] such was the sentiment about Nzeogwu's dishonour.

Strain on prestige and insecurity about the prospect of death are not the only reasons for seeking to uphold military values. Some officers chose a military career because these values were sought as ends in themselves, saying, for instance, that the army offered an occupation that was free of the pressures for corruption in some civilian occupations, or because they 'would not have to worry about losing promotion from tribalism' as in other governmental structures, or simply that chivalric honour was sought after for its own sake. Lt Colonel Ejoor, for instance, claimed he joined up because he 'wanted to die honourably'.[3] When he was in his final year at school, he had read about the

---

[1] K. Demeter, *The German officer corps* (London: Weidenfeld and Nicholson, 1965), develops the distinction between the officer corps' collective honour and individual honour, and argues that the practice of duelling between officers in disputes of honour tended to develop the former as opposed to the latter by emphasising the idea of the military as a self-regulating corporation with its peculiar set of values. This kind of professionalism, as Huntington, *The soldier and the state*, argues, tends to lead officers to identify themselves with an abstract concept of 'the nation' and of national honour rather than existing governmental institutions; and may provide a rationale for political intervention when circumstances are appropriate.

[2] Stories were circulating among Northern soldiers at that time that Nzeogwu's eyes were removed by the NCOs before he was sent up from the front for burial and that a Roman Catholic priest turning up to consecrate the burial was told to 'Fuck off'.

[3] Interview with Lt Colonel Ejoor, in *Daily Times* (Lagos), 5 October 1966. He also had an uncle who had fought in the Burma campaign as an NCO.

impressive funeral given one of the first Nigerian officers, a Lieutenant Wellington, and decided he too would like such treatment when he died. Kinsmen who had served in the army gave many officers their first taste of chivalry. It is likely that the majority of Nigerian officers – and especially the Northerners – had relatives in the army. Many of them – including Ejoor and Gowon – mention the example of relatives as being one reason for enlisting. Some families, indeed, could definitely be called military families, like one Northern family with two brothers in the officer corps and a further three in the ranks as NCOs, and another containing three officer brothers; both families also contained relatives of the older generation who were NCOs during the period of colonial rule. And just as the system of collective honour is underpinned by role-models from the older generation, some officers seek also to project it into the future by wanting their sons to join the army, in order, as Colonel Adebayo put it, 'to retain my name in the army'.[1]

By way of contrast to this corporative identification with the profession, let us provide an extract from an interview by a Nigerian journalist, Sad Sam, with Lt Colonel Ojukwu who, it will be recalled, differed from almost all of his colleagues in that his position in the elite owed very little to his membership of the officer corps. He had a degree from Oxford University, his father was a millionaire with very influential political connections, and he joined the army for political reasons as much as anything else. We find him rejecting the whole idea of military professionalism and by implication the conception of collective military honour.

OJUKWU: I would not like my son to be a professional. Let's leave it at that. I have never been a professional.
SAD SAM: You? Aren't you a professional soldier?
OJUKWU: I maintain my amateur status in all my approach. When you talk about professions, you talk about the specialist professions like lawyer, doctor, engineer and so on. I studied up to a point and left to become a soldier.
SAD SAM: Why did you become a soldier?
OJUKWU: Sam, I do not expect that from you.[2]

To conclude, the latent consequence of the officer corps' low prestige, the insecurity of army officers in relation to their reference groups both in the ex-colonial metropolis and among the Nigerian elite, was a hardening and reinforcement of the corporate image and identity of the officer corps rather

[1] *Daily Times* (Lagos), 30 September 1966. Though such ambitions have been affected by the political events of 1966 and the climate of insecurity they created. See Lt Colonel Ejoor's terse comment in the *Daily Times*, 4 October 1966 interview, to the question whether he would like his children to join the army: 'My wife would not'. Lt Colonel Hassan Katsina, however, stated he would like 'two or three' of his offspring to join the army.
[2] Interview between Lt Colonel Ojukwu and Sad Sam of the *Daily Times* (Lagos), 17 September 1966.

than its opposite. Officers were all the more gentlemen for being newcomers to the club. On the other hand, the short length of military careers, the fact that officers had had little time to internalise fully the pattern of expectations governing their life style and role, meant that this corporate image and identity was likely to be unstable, as in fact turned out to be the case. Being partly held in position, so to speak, by the prevailing definition of the situation, it was liable to change when that situation itself altered, as when the political events of 1966 suddenly shifted the distribution of power and values towards the soldiers themselves.

CHAPTER V

PEER GROUPS: SOLIDARITY AND CLEAVAGE

In this chapter we will analyse cleavages arising within the organisational identities of army officers, namely those developing between military peer groups. For one of the most striking features of the two coups of 1966 was the marked age and rank-grading of the participants, the Majors of January and the junior officers of July. It is also interesting to note that a group of lieutenant colonels discussed but rejected the possibility of intervening during the Federal election of December 1964.[1] How have peer coups in the army been created and maintained? What has been their importance for cleavage and cohesion in the officer corps? And how have they been related to the authority system of the army?

Unfortunately, studies of other bureaucracies shed little light on these problems. Peer groups are found in the nooks and crannies of most formal organisations, but only those at the lowest levels of the hierarchy – the factory worker or the enlisted man – have been frequently and systematically studied.[2] This may be because they are a more pervasive phenomenon there than at the command or supervisory level of an administrative hierarchy, where the sociometric links are often not as strong.[3] Compared with many other types of bureaucracy, however, military organisations frequently generate peer groups at supervisory levels, that is within the officer corps itself, extending right up to the higher levels of military command. Nigeria, moreover, is not the only country where military peer groups have brought the army into politics: one has only to think, for example, of the Free Officers Group in Egypt, or the Eighth Graduating Class, which was prominent in the Korean military revolution of 1961.[4]

[1] See pp. 135 and 237–8 below.
[2] See, for example, some of the classics in the field, like E. A. Shils and M. Janowitz, 'Cohesion and disintegration in the Wehrmacht in World War II', *Public Opinion Quarterly* (1948), pp. 280–314, or F. J. Roethlisberger and W. J. Dickson, *Management and the worker* (Cambridge, Mass.: Harvard University Press, 1939).
[3] Blau and Scott, *Formal organizations*, pp. 148–161, for example, found that the supervisors in the city welfare agencies they studied were much less tightly integrated in peer networks than their subordinates.
[4] For the former, see P. J. Vatikiotis, *The Egyptian army in politics* (Bloomington, Ind.: Indiana University Press, 1961), and for the latter, C. I. E. Kim, 'The South Korean military

Peer groups: solidarity and cleavage

Peer groups, we will argue, are produced by two rather distinctive characteristics which are to be found in many modern military organisations. First, the great emphasis on internal solidarity within the officer corps; and in this they may be said to be the structural counterpart of the corporate officers and gentlemen image. Secondly, the military status system, with its strongly enforced rituals of deference and avoidance between officers of different rank, which tends to turn the officer corps into a set of vertically divided fraternities rather than a single solidary brotherhood.

COHESION: 'FRIENDS AND CLASS-MATES'

Despite its disciplinary problems, the officer corps formed, until 1966, a relatively well-integrated corporate group, more solidary than any other section of the Nigerian elite. As Major General Ironsi put it: 'the Army is a brotherhood and I cannot emphasise too strongly the need for corporate life among its members.'[1] This solidarity was sustained by the integration of peer groups of the same rank, as much as by any other single factor. The sharpest expression of the concept of brotherhood was found among 'course-mates' who trained together, during at least their preliminary training at the Nigerian Military Training College (or the West African Command School, Ghana, before 1960), if not at Sandhurst, Mons or other training institutions as well. They were usually promoted more or less together and their careers were likely to cross frequently, especially as the army was small. And they tended to be bound by numerous solidary networks of friendship.

The Sandhurst network was an especially powerful one. This was partly because the two-year training was longer and more intensive than elsewhere.[2] The links formed at Sandhurst extended backwards and forwards in time to members of other immediately contiguous courses. New courses began every six months and African entrants to the junior year were taken in hand by their compatriots already there. There is not usually a great deal of mixing between senior and junior years among British cadets. But the relative social isolation of the Africans made them stick together more. Most of the January 1966 Majors were recruited from the overlapping courses at Sandhurst which we set out in Table 22.

The bonds formed with course-mates have been a most persistent influence on behaviour, even under the most adverse circumstances. For example, the first Northern officer to die in the civil war in 1967 is said to

coup of May, 1961' in J. A. Van Doorn (ed.), *Armed forces and society* (The Hague: Mouton, 1968).

[1] Foreword by Major General Ironsi in *Nigerian Army Magazine* (Lagos), III (December 1965).

[2] In comparison with the short-service training obtained at Eaton Hall, Mons, and later in the USA, Canada and India. After 1962–3, however, cadets were sent to other military academies in Ethiopia, India, Pakistan, etc., where the training was just as long and intensive as at Sandhurst.

have been killed by an Ibo course-mate whom he took prisoner and advanced in too much haste to greet without seeing that he was properly disarmed. Another example is Brigadier Ejoor's failure to take adequate precautions against a coup by Ibo officers in the Mid-West in August 1967. He alleges that he accepted their word that they would remain neutral in the civil conflict because many of them were his 'friends and class-mates',[1] even if this might seem a little unrealistic in the circumstances.

TABLE 22. *Sandhurst years of January 1966 coup figures*

	1958	1959	1960	1961	1962	1963
Major Nzeogwu	Jan	Dec				
T/Maj. Chukuka[a]		Jan	Dec			
Major Anuforo		Sept		July		
T/Maj. Onwuatuegwu[a]		Sept		July		
Captain Udeaja		Jan	Dec			
Captain Gbulie				Jan	Dec	
Captain Nwobosi				Sept		July

Source: The Wish Stream: Journal of the Royal Military Academy, Sandhurst (1958–63).
Note:
[a] Temporary or effective rather than officially gazetted rank.

The different generations of officers entering the army, however, have each differed quite markedly from each other in the type of military training they have received, as can be seen in Tables 23 and 24. These compare the training, first of the different standardised seniority cohorts entering the officer corps and then of the different rank levels.[2]

Of the first generation of officer entrants – the twelve officers in the cohorts up to and including 1953[3] – nine were former NCOs trained at Eaton Hall or Mons, in England. In 1966, these included all seven of the officers in the rank of colonel and above; and five of the army's most senior lieutenant colonels. The first Sandhurst graduate of the army, Maimalari, did not enter until the 1951 cohort.[4]

But the Sandhurst contingent did not become substantial in numbers until the entry of seven of them in the 1955 cohort (all of them commissioned

[1] *New Nigerian* (Kaduna), 26 September 1967. It seems somewhat strange he should have been quite so naive about the loyalties of his Ibo class-mates in the conflict with Biafra. He was, however, in very much of a political cleft stick, with Ibo officers in a majority in the Mid-West. His statement that he trusted his 'class-mates' may thus have been a rationalisation of this position, though it is still interesting if he felt he could legitimate his position in such terms.
[2] The profile of the latter differs slightly from the former because some types of entrant, e.g. the Sandhurst-trained officers, were more successful in obtaining promotions than others.
[3] Receiving their commissions between 1944 (Lt Colonel Bassey) and 1955, though in cohorts with earlier dates according to the rules for standardising the cohorts given in Table 23.
[4] Maimalari received his commission in 1953.

in 1956). Sandhurst graduates then made up over forty per cent of all the entering cohorts up to 1960. These are the officers who took up the middle-level positions in the army, from senior captain up to junior lieutenant colonel, so that exactly half of the lieutenant colonels and the same proportion of the majors in the army, in January 1966, were Sandhurst graduates.

TABLE 23. *Military training of different generations of army officers* (*percentage distributions of types of training by cohort*)

Year of seniority cohorts[a]	No. in cohorts	Sandhurst	Short-service ex-NCOs	Mons/Eaton Hall — school entry	Mons/Eaton Hall — graduate entry	Non-British training[d] — academy	Non-British training[d] — short service	Not known
Up to 1952	7	14	86	—	—	—	—	—
52–4	10	40	50	—	10	—	—	—
55–6	16	56	38	—	6	—	—	—
57–8	17	41	47	—	12	—	—	—
59–60[b]	41	44	27	27	2	—	—	—
61–2[c]	76	22	7	54	—	—	17	—
63–4[c]	163	8	—	42	—	13	31	6

Sources: Federation of Nigeria, *Official Gazettes* (1960–5); *The Wish Stream* (1952–65).
Notes:
[a] Seniority cohorts are defined so as to standardise all the various categories of entry into the officer corps as if they were secondary-school entrants gaining short-service commissions in the year shown. The cohort of school/short-service entrants is thus given by their date of commission; and of the Sandhurst, ex-NCOs and university graduate entrants by subtracting twenty, twenty-four and thirty-six months respectively from their dates of commission (with some adjustment for shorter Sandhurst training up to 1956). This more or less approximates the extra promotional seniority of these categories, though the exact amount of seniority for promotion varies from year to year.
[b] Figure does not include the five officers of those two cohorts who were seconded to the air force between 1963 and 1965, of whom three were Sandhurst graduates.
[c] A small number of the cadets receiving short-service training outside of Britain were ex-NCOs; four (i.e. 5%) in the 1961–2 cohorts and four (i.e. 2%) in the 1963–4 cohorts.
[d] In India, Pakistan, Australia, Canada, Ethiopia and the USA.

Junior officers in the cohorts of 1961 and after – with ranks of captain and lower – were a much less homogeneous group. This reflects both the expansion in officer recruitment and the diversification in sources of military assistance after Independence. A large proportion of these intakes were sent to attend the short-service courses[1] at the Mons Officer Cadet School, rather than Sandhurst, which would have been unable to cope with such a large extra

[1] So called because designed to train British short-service officers. Most Nigerian officers with this training, however, were able to obtain regular long-service commissions.

flow of entrants.[1] But cadets were also sent to academies and training schools in countries other than Britain, to India, Pakistan, Australia, Canada, Ethiopia and the USA. Further diversity was provided by the regional quota system introduced after 1961, which broadened the ethnic composition of the officer corps.

TABLE 24. *Military training of officers of different ranks (percentage distribution of training by rank)*

| | | | | Mons/Eaton Hall | | Non-British | | |
Rank level	No. in ranks[a]	Sandhurst	Short-service ex-NCOs	school entry	graduate entry	academy	short service	Not known
Colonel and above	7	29	71	—	—	—	—	—
Lt Colonel	14	50	43	—	7	—	—	—
Major	32	50	31	9	9	—	—	—
Captain	52	35	29	35	1	—	—	—
Lieutenant	58	24	9	53	—	—	14[b]	—
2nd Lieutenant	167	7	—	41	—	13	34	5

Notes:
[a] Numbers in ranks at 1 January 1966.
[b] All of these (four trained in the USA, four in India) were ex-NCOs. None of the school entrants who were trained outside Britain had reached the rank of lieutenant by January 1966.

The creation of the Nigerian Defence Academy in 1964 furnished a fourth layer with yet another set of training experiences; though the Academy's first graduates did not enter the army until early 1967.

None of the above seniority cohorts or rank groups – even the more senior ones – were completely homogeneous. Though peer groups clustered to some degree around nodal groups of class-mates they also pulled in associates of diverse training and background. The focal figure behind discussions of military intervention in the 1964 Federal election crisis was Lt Colonel Ojukwu, a graduate (then Quartermaster General) and the friends he attempted to pull in were Sandhurst men working at Headquarters of about the same seniority as himself.[2] The January Majors, though recruited predominantly from Sandhurst, also included two graduate peers (Ifeajuna and Ademoyega) as well as a former NCO (Okafor). The officers who staged the

[1] Though the absolute numbers of officers passing every year through Sandhurst from Nigeria remained about the same.
[2] Lt Colonels Banjo, Ejoor and Gowon to begin with, and perhaps others as well; though they did not all share Ojukwu's views on intervention.

July 1966 coup were completely diverse in their training, bringing in the whole spectrum of Sandhurst, former NCOs, Mons, the USA, Canada and India; nevertheless, they fell into fairly well-defined peer groups, each with a distinctive role in the coup, and none of them dominated by the products of any single course. All this goes to suggest that we need to seek for factors other than common training which might generate solidarity among military equals; that the officer corps was held together by something more than the mere agglomeration of different brotherhoods of course-mates.

THE OFFICERS MESS AND THE MILITARY FRATERNITY

A primary focus of solidarity for any peacetime military unit is its officers mess. It is there that collective military honour is defined and enforced. It provides a continuing process of socialisation in the manners and values of the officer and gentleman. As important, however, as the style of life which the mess encourages are the patterns of conviviality and reciprocity that it creates. An example is the way Nigerian officers barter among each other for the privilege of buying the next round of drinks, regardless of the current state of their mess bill. Anyone too obviously holding back will be told that he is not a gentleman and asked how long it is since he bought a round. The Commanding Officer will perhaps complain on a mess occasion that he has not been allowed to buy a drink all round for a long time; or a passing military dignitary may say he will foot the bill, since the last two or three times he visited he was not able to do so.

Conviviality is very much a prescribed element of the military way of life. Officers first joining a Nigerian unit after their military training are normally made to live in the mess for their first few months, in order to initiate them into the habits of mess life, even if they are already married, before they can move out to other quarters. It is reckoned to be particularly important for the ex-NCOs to do this in order to break the associations and styles of behaviour they may have brought up from the ranks. Officers' quarters form a small enclave in the military barracks and are usually within walking distance of the mess.[1] Fewer officers take their meals in the mess than in colonial days, many of the bachelors having their food sent over by servant to their quarters; but they frequently gather in the bar at the start of an evening's drinking, during which they might end up together in a bar or a night club in the nearby town. Attendance at formal mess nights is normally obligatory; and officers who do not arrive for the weekly Saturday afternoon's drinking that is customary in many messes, or arrive late, usually have to have a good excuse to avoid rebuke from their Commanding Officer.

[1] Except the mess of GHQ and Brigade HQ organisations in the Lagos and Kaduna areas, where the pattern of officer housing is more dispersed.

Sociability is not only itself prescribed, but it also reinforces the prescribed patterns of behaviour and routines of military life. Smartness of dress and correctness of demeanour are an essential element of mess nights and Saturday afternoon drinks. One of the functions of these, indeed, is to provide set-piece occasions when such standards can be maintained; and an audience (military visitors, higher level local administrative and police dignitaries, the occasional expatriate friend) by whom the performance may be appreciated. Dress and behaviour are immaculate, by the highest of British Army standards, boots and buttons shiny. If there are still ladies present when the drink begins to flow and risque stories begin to be told, there are admonitions of 'not in front of the ladies' and 'Offsahs are gentlemen', which are usually effective in silencing the offenders until the womenfolk are out of the way.

The principle of hierarchy receives constant emphasis. The Commanding Officer is constantly being requested for 'permission to buy you [or everyone] a drink, sir!'...'permission to tell a story, sir!'...'permission to tell Lieutenant X to shut up, sir!'..'permission to defend the 4th Battalion, sir!' [when an officer's old unit is under attack in conversation]...'permission to leave, sir!' On such set-piece occasions, officers are expected to remain until the Commanding Officer and/or the senior visitor (if the latter is a high-ranking army officer, an emir or perhaps – depending on the time-period – an important politician) have left the mess. Only if they have a good excuse – a duty to perform, for instance, may they ask permission to go.

The convivial focus on authority is, of course, no more than a supplement to the routines and command-situations of the office, parade ground and battlefield. But it is important in making discipline an acceptable part of military life, in maintaining support for military authority norms among the collectivity of subordinates. Conviviality is thus a good deal more than self-indulgence. Even if officers go carousing together to the bars or in search of girls until the early hours of the morning, they will still be up at 6.00 a.m. for early morning physical exercise with brother officers. Conviviality does not negate self-discipline and indeed in some respects supports it.

The sociability of mess life is by no means wholly ritualised. Sometimes it provides a chance to assert a degree of role distance from military routines, not by cynical deprecation of mess life and routine as in the British Army, but by somewhat boisterous, joking behaviour focusing to a large extent on the problems of military status. If, for instance, there is a nurse of senior rank around, she will be saluted and called 'sah!' by all the junior officers, emphasising the status discrepancy inherent in her position, but bringing laughter all round.[1]

---

[1] All nursing sisters (i.e. nurses with State Registered Nurse or Nigerian Registered Nurse qualifications) receive commissions. By 1966, there were one or two of these who had reached the rank of major.

The style of cameraderie is often distinctively Nigerian. Pidgin English will frequently be heard, though kept out of the way on the more formal occasions. The agbada or other native costume is acceptable as a substitute for jacket and tie for informal evenings in the mess. Officers are not ashamed to go off together in pursuit of 'ashawo' (tarts), though compliant nurses or telephonists would usually be preferred. There are none of the British officer's middle-class inhibitions about sexual life. Laughs are belly laughs, and interpolations are peppered into a conversation with shouts and visible signs of excitement. Gestures of friendship are more open and – among men – more physical. All this may seem a little peripheral to the subject of military cohesion, but for the fact, it may be suggested, that the military role is made easier to play by fitting it into patterns of sociability that are well understood in a Nigerian context.

At the same time, however, the cameraderie of the officers serves to differentiate military from civilian spheres of action, to reinforce the role-segregation of the military brotherhood. In some messes, for instance, certain women become 'mess property'. When one officer has finished with one of them, she goes the rounds of his comrades in arms. A special terminology sometimes develops among officers about sexual affairs. When one of them is occupied with a woman, his friends for instance may be warned not to disturb him because 'I'll be reading'. At the more prescribed level, most of the mechanisms of sociability that have been described also serve to emphasise the distinctness of military contexts. The treatment accorded to ladies in the mess is quite distinctly at variance with the way that most Nigerian officers would treat their womenfolk at home.[1] Even though wives are usually left out of official sociability, officers will jump to their feet for them just as for any other woman guest on these occasions they do appear in the mess (although they would not do so in their house). While less privileged kinsmen and towns-people are made welcome in an officer's home, they are not brought to the mess – certainly not for prescribed occasions[2] – as it is reserved for elite guests only.

In sum, the mess and the sociability – prescribed and spontaneous – that is focused on it tend both to promote a high degree of social solidarity among the officers of any military unit, and to emphasise their corporate distinctive-ness as a fraternal and elite body.

The strength of these sentiments is illustrated by the developments in 1966 which dislocated the shared expectations on which they were based. We have already suggested[3] how the very intensity of interaction in the military

---

[1] Unless – as in a few cases one encounters – the wives are well educated and in a position to assert their rights as emancipated women.
[2] A very close relative (e.g. the officer's father) might be taken in for an informal drink, even if he were of low status, however.   [3] Chapter III above.

enclave made sentiments of fear and hostility all the stronger, once the basis for mutual trust was undermined. Military commanders sought to maintain informers in the barracks and the mess 'in order to know which days it would not be safe to come into the office'.[1] Acute suspicions arose of the activities of officers of other ethnic groups, of which the escalation of fears of fratricide preceding the July 1966 coup was not the only example.[2] Personal as well as collective antagonisms were at a high level. And there were officers whose insecurity led them in 1966 or 1967 to express openly their wish to be out of the army, like the one who stated: 'I wish I could get out of this damned army. I don't want to be killed in my bed.' Others were willing to stay, but morale was very low all the way through to the outset of the civil war in July 1967, and the general feeling was that it was 'no longer the same army as it was before'.

THE NETWORK OF CAREERS

The officers mess will tend to generate solidarity primarily around a single military unit and only secondarily to promote the values of the military organisation as a whole. How, then, does the notion of a brotherhood of *all* officers in the army arise? How is solidarity created and sustained at an organisation-wide level? In this, we shall argue that the system of career mobility is of great importance.

The effects of mobility may be illustrated by a little scene at a mess party after a passing out parade at a training unit, the officers of which originated from a variety of the army's different battalions. The guest of honour was a brigade commander. Also present were the training unit's commander and the commander of a battalion. The Brigadier had in his time served in three battalions, the ath, the bth of which he had been the commander and the cth in which he had served in the Congo. The commander of the training unit had served in both the ath and the cth Battalions. Conversation drifted around to which of the battalions was the best to serve in. A lively discussion ensued which gradually drew in all the junior officers in a circle around the main disputants. The younger officers each took up the cause of his own battalion, and attempted to persuade the Brigadier to express a choice in its favour. The Brigadier refused to commit himself. A cogent point in favour of the cth Battalion was that he had seen active service in it. But he had commanded the bth, and he had had the best time in the ath because it was located in the best

---

[1] The writer knows of at least two commanders of whom this was true in the 1966–7 period, including the one quoted.

[2] See the discussion of the growth of antagonism in the officer corps prior to the July 1966 coup in Chapter II above. Similarly, at various periods of crisis in 1967 when it looked as if the Western Region was about to pull out of the Federation, the Yoruba officers in Northern military units went in fear of their lives.

garrison town in Nigeria to live in. The commander of the training unit then took up the cudgels and said that he personally had enjoyed the *c*th the best because he had been to the Congo in it; besides he had to say he enjoyed it more than the *a*th, 'just to annoy the CO of the *a*th Battalion' who was present. The CO of the *a*th Battalion then proceeded to defend his command, with shouts of encouragement from one or two of the junior officers.

This incident illustrates two things: first, the effect of identification with particular military units in defining an officer's position and status in the military, in developing his organisational loyalties, but secondly, the importance of career mobility from unit to unit in diffusing loyalties, so that they spread over the army as a whole. As we point out elsewhere,[1] mobility in the Nigerian Army was unusually rapid. Though this was dysfunctional in many respects, it did foster the development of multiple organisational identifications at quite an early stage of a military career. By the time an officer reached the middle ranks, he was likely to have served in at least two military units, besides the customary staff or training appointments and attendance at courses abroad. And by the time he came to be a battalion commander or above, his points of contact throughout the army would be still wider.

What is more, the circle of an officer's close acquaintance is developed and maintained at the level of peer groups stretching across the whole organisation, rather than cliques based on particular military units (or indeed on particular courses). In a small officer corps, as in Nigeria, the careers of most officers are likely to intersect at one time or another, while many officers' paths may cross several times. Thus it is that peer groups articulated right across the army could provide an effective frame for common political action, as in the two coups of 1966. This is best illustrated by charting the careers of some of the main conspirators of 15 January 1966, as in Table 25, in which it can be seen that in addition to common Sandhurst origins, the Majors overlapped one another at different periods in units in Zaria, Kaduna and at Headquarters, Lagos, during the four or five years prior to the coup.

CLEAVAGE: THE DIFFERENTIATION OF PEER GROUPS

Why did officers fall into a layering of fraternities rather than a single corporate brotherhood? One possible argument would be that it was because of the differing training of officers of various generations, the ex-NCOs at the top, the Sandhurst generations in the middle and the mixed group at the bottom. But none of these generations was entirely homogeneous or distinct in training from the other layers, as already pointed out. Moreover, peer group

[1] In Chapter VII below.

TABLE 25.[a] *Military postings of January coup leaders,*[b] *1961–5*

	1961				1962				1963				1964				1965			
	1st qtr	2nd qtr	3rd qtr	4th qtr	1st qtr	2nd qtr	3rd qtr	4th qtr	1st qtr	2nd qtr	3rd qtr	4th qtr	1st qtr	2nd qtr	3rd qtr	4th qtr	1st qtr	2nd qtr	3rd qtr	4th qtr
Kaduna																				
Major C. K. Nzeogwu	5th Btn						5th Btn										– – –NMTC – –			
Major E. A. Ifeajuna			– – –			– 5th Btn				– – – – –			– 1st Bde HQ		– – – – –					
T/Major[c] T. C. Onwuatuegwu			– – –				– – –			– 5th Btn – –			NMTC – – –				NMTC – –			
T/Captain[c] E. N. Nwobosi											NMTC – – –			– – – –			– – – –	1st Fld Battery		
Zaria																				
Major C. K. Nzeogwu					– – – Depot – – –															
Major D. O. Okafor		– – – NMS – – – –			Depot – – NMS – –															
T/Major[c] I. U. Chukuka					– – Depot – – – –															
Lagos																				
Major C. K. Nzeogwu									– – – GHQ – – –											
Major E. A. Ifeajuna													– – – – Federal Guard – – – – – –					– – – – 2nd Bde HQ – –		
Major D. O. Okafor									– – – GHQ – – –											
T/Major[c] I. U. Chukuka																				

Notes:

[a] Sources for this table are office and telephone directories for Kaduna, Zaria and Lagos, with amendments and other details included from other sources where necessary. Allowances have to be made for the fact that the directories are neither wholly accurate nor complete in their coverage of military posts during the period.

[b] Table lists only those officers for whom adequate data are available.

[c] Designation for temporary (effective) rank as opposed to substantive (formally gazetted) rank.

distinctions tended to be sustained *within* the three broad generations of officers. This is made apparent, for instance, if we examine the way in which the main conspirators of January 1966 emerged from the group of middle-ranking Sandhurst officers. They were among the most junior members of this generation. Most of them received their commissions in 1959–61 and are classified in the 1957–9 seniority cohorts. They were all majors or senior captains. In comparison, the more senior Sandhurst officers, those commissioned in 1958 or earlier, were mostly lieutenant colonels though some were senior majors. There were one or two who may have had a degree of complicity in the coup,[1] yet it is significant that they did not take an overt part, either because their investment in their careers was greater or because of the status ambiguities inherent in a close association with their juniors.

We must seek other reasons therefore for the development of differentiation between peer groups. The simplest and best explanation is the hierarchical nature of the military status system. The patterns of deference and avoidance between officers of different ranks tend to make easy social intercourse possible only between officers who are similar in seniority to each other. This contention receives some support from the fact that feelings of solidarity are stronger among course-mates (who carry the same rank most of their career) than among officers from immediately contiguous courses (who would normally have shared the same rank only for part of their military career); and stronger among the latter than among officers who have never been in the same rank at the same time. The operation of the status system and its relation to discipline is discussed in detail in the next chapter, and there is no need to elaborate on it here. It is worth drawing out some general implications, however, for the development of cleavage and conflict within the army along inter-generational lines.

The importance of peer groups in the social geography of the army might have led one to predict that the lines and issues of conflict within the officer corps would be drawn primarily along inter-generational cleavages. Yet although peer groups provided a pattern or frame for cleavage, in the manner described in detail in the historical section, the conflict drew its dynamic from elsewhere and created new conflict groups which transcended the lines between the generations. The Majors of January did have their grievances against their seniors, but these were definitely secondary to their main political and ideological objectives. As soon as the military was in power the focus of the struggle shifted rapidly towards ethnic and regional issues. Despite a flavouring of radical populism among Northern junior officers and NCOs, the main objects of hostility in July 1966 were officers and men of

---

[1] See Chapter I above.

particular ethnic and regional origin, rather than senior officers or the military authority system as such.

How do we account for this? First, it should be pointed out that the relation of peer grouping to cohesion and cleavage is always a complex one It is frequently noted, indeed, that the cohesion of primary groups at various points of a bureaucratic structure may help to sustain rather than to undermine existing authority relations.[1] Whether or not primary groups of peers in fact help to integrate the organisation will depend on a number of other factors. Conflict is more likely to be endemic at the lower 'proletarian' reaches of the structure, at the level of the manual worker or enlisted man, where opportunities for promotion and responsibility are likely to be restricted; and primary groups are just as likely as not to provide the social support for resistance to authority.[2]

At higher echelons, peer groups more usually buttress authority since their members are normally included in a regulated system of upward mobility, and have greater responsiblity and access to organisational goals and are therefore provided with inducements of a kind which elicit fuller cooperation. Yet cohesion is not automatic. Lack of an adequate promotional system to regulate the flow of officers through the ranks may for instance exacerbate inter-generational cleavage.[3] In the Nigerian case, however, our review of the data on promotions (in Chapter VII above) suggests that a clear conflict of interest between generations over promotions had not yet arisen, mainly because advancement had been easy for everyone – though such a conflict was in prospect for the future, after all the top posts in the army had been filled by Nigerians by 1965.

Another factor that must be considered when we ask if peer groups lead to cleavages is that they are themselves the direct consequence of military norms of status and solidarity. This has provided an important built-in set of restraints against the emergence of *overt* cleavages on generational lines, restraints deriving from the 'organic solidarity' between peer groups in the chain of command and control. To make a direct attack on senior officers would have been to challenge the entire authority system of the army. In contrast, cleavages of other kinds, such as that between different ethnic groups, have not run up against the same kinds of constraints, and this may

---

[1] See, for example, Shils and Janowitz, 'Cohesion and disintegration in the Wehrmacht', for the manner in which primary groups sustained authority relations in the German Wehrmacht in the Second World War.

[2] See the summary of a number of studies of this kind by Blau and Scott, *Formal organizations*, pp. 89–96, who conclude that 'cohesiveness increases the controlling power of the group over its members but the direction in which this control is exercised – whether toward higher or lower productivity *or* support or subversion of authority – is determined by other factors such as the group's orientation toward the organisation'.

[3] Janowitz, *The military in the political development of new nations*, p. 71.

help to explain why the conflict in the army gravitated during 1966 towards ethnic and regional issues in so free-wheeling a manner. A direct and overt challenge against military authority was avoided by picturing the conflict in terms of the primordial identities of those being attacked, even if the mainspring for rebellion had been strains inherent in the hierarchy of command and control. Nowhere was the tenacity of authority norms illustrated so clearly as in the attempts made in both the coups to maintain the necessary fictions and continuity of command and the way in which the role of the various coup participants fell into a pattern that fitted with their level in the army hierarchy and their military peer group.

To sum up, it would be premature to conclude from the rather sharp rank-grading of participants in the 1966 coups that there was a simple conflict of interest between different military generations. If peer groups had any significance it probably lay in the conditions they provided of close informal interaction between officers of the same rank, within which discontents could be nurtured, developed and turned into conspiracy. In other words, they provided nodal points around which conflicts derived from a variety of sources could develop. This emerged with particular clarity during the January 1966 coup; and we have been able to demonstrate in some detail how the conspiratorial group developed around the interstices of Sandhurst, rank-grading and career patterns. Peer grouping and its place in the two coups of 1966 seems as much indicative of cohesion in the army as it does of cleavage.

CHAPTER VI

OF HEROISM AND HIERARCHY:
THE DILEMMAS OF DISCIPLINE

THE CHALLENGE TO AUTHORITY

We have just seen how the phenomenon of peer grouping in the Nigerian Army suggests the continuing power of authority norms. Yet in this chapter we hope to show how the revolts of 1966 arose from a conflict between the possessors of authoritative control in the army and their subordinates.[1] The notion of strain against authority seems to describe this kind of conflict better than that of simple cleavage between different ranks or peer groups. For power and authority are not values that can be allocated in quite the same manner as economic resources. Authority cannot exist if subordinates do not subscribe in some measure to norms and values which legitimise the exercise of power. Rebellion thus tends to be fraught with ambivalence, because it implies that previously accepted norms be cast aside. Hence, in the Nigerian Army, the way in which military status norms were maintained during the two coups; the way in which rituals of rebellion evolved around these norms; and the way the definition of the situation developed in terms of non-rational primordial or political imagery rather than openly avowed revolt against command.

We will try further to suggest how rebellion arose out of a central paradox of authority in organisations of the military type, that of the need to reconcile initiative and discipline, heroism and hierarchy.[2] The effectiveness of authority itself at each level of command hierarchy depends, it will be argued,

[1] For an interesting discussion of how the distribution of authority in organisations in and of itself (regardless of whether there is any cleavage of interest about other values, like wealth, associated with it or not) gives rise to conflict between the possessors of authoritative control and their subordinates, see R. Dahrendorf, *Class and class conflict in industrial society* (Stanford, Calif.: Stanford University Press, 1959).

[2] See Janowitz and Little, *Sociology and the military establishment*, p. 42: 'the military establishment with its hierarchical structure, with its exacting requirements of co-ordination, and with its apparently high centralisation of organisational power, must strive contrariwise to develop the broadest decentralisation of initiative at the point of contact with the enemy...The combat soldier is hardly the model of Max Weber's ideal bureaucrat following rigid rules and regulations. In certain respects he is the antithesis. The combat fighter is not routinised and self-contained. Rather, his role is one of constant improvisation, regardless of his service or weapon. Improvisation is the key note of the individual fighter or combat group.'

on the degree of initiative that can be sustained there. Any commander at an intermediate level in the hierarchy must be left enough room for manoeuvre by his superiors to develop sufficient charisma on his own account to dominate *his* subordinates; so that such an authority system will tend to contain the seeds of revolt against itself by the pocket heroes it nurtures.

One of the most striking features of military intervention in Nigeria, indeed, was the way in which heroism triumphed over hierarchy. This was particularly true of the decision by the Majors to wipe out the whole command structure of the army in January 1966 with a few platoons of men in army landrovers and staff cars: a feat which required both considerable qualities of initiative and a fine disregard of the restraints of military discipline. Much the same could be said of the counter-coup by the Northern Lieutenants in July, except that this took place in a situation in which discipline had already been undermined. The conspirators in both cases combined a good appreciation of the calculus of violence – of the logistics of small-scale operations, of the advantages of surprise and a speedy strike – with an apparent inability or unwillingness to plan or foresee the wider consequences for either the military or the political system. Even the Majors of January 1966, with their relative ideological and professional sophistication, had no very concrete ideas about how they would rule afterwards or an appreciation of the dangers of disrupting military discipline. Other examples come readily to mind, such as Lt Colonel Banjo's audacious plans to stage a coup within a coup against Lt Colonel Ojukwu after the invasion of the Mid-West in August 1967. The 'dare or die' spirit prevailing among many young officers was nicely expressed by one young Captain (a participant in the July coup) who said prior to the Eastern Region's secession in 1967 that if the Federal government did not invade the East, he personally would lead his company there and attempt to capture Ojukwu. He was probably joking, but it is sometimes rather difficult in such conditions to distinguish a joke from reality, witness the case of Lieutenant Arthur, the young Ghanaian officer who attempted a counter-coup against the Ghana military regime on 17 April 1967, killed Lt General Kotoka; and confessed afterwards that he had wished to become the first lieutenant ever to seize power[1] and that: 'on the formation of the new junta I counted all Colonels and above out. I knew in the coup I would eliminate all of them.'

This does not mean that the constraints of discipline, though frequently violated, were not in some senses real and important, as should be clear from the preceding chapter. The binding rope of authority was cut, but a few

---

[1] See *West Africa* (London), 6 May and 13 May 1967. Apart from his ambition to be the first lieutenant to stage a coup, he had no explicit aims apart from a vague dislike of the Ghana National Liberation Council and disappointment with promotions.

threads were always left, providing a continuity by which the normal relations of command and control could be restored after the coups had occurred. During the very uncertain period between the July 1966 coup and the civil war in 1967, discipline was, as it were, held together by such threads of string of a make-shift nature. It was only with difficulty that Major General Gowon was able to prevent the more adventurous of his subordinates from leading their units unilaterally against the Eastern Region as they threatened to do on more than one occasion. Yet the fact remains that he was able to generate sufficient consensus around his objectives and his person to maintain his authority as Commander in Chief and head off army moves in this direction. Patterns of discipline, though much weakened, were not entirely destroyed; although their effectiveness depended very much on the political and organisational context in which they were exercised.

THE DEBATE AT ABURI, GHANA, 1967:
TWO PRINCIPLES OF LEGITIMACY

The problem of authority was one of the main subjects of discussion between the Nigerian military leaders at Aburi in Ghana, in January 1967, when they were trying to resolve the situation that arose from the disruption of the hierarchy of command by the two military coups and the division of the army into two opposed fragments after July 1966. Both sets of protagonists sought to validate their own political positions by reference to two opposed principles of military legitimacy, and put themselves into a logical muddle as an inevitable result.

The first of these principles was that of precedence or hierarchy. The rationale given by Lt Colonel Ojukwu for not regarding Lt Colonel Gowon as the 'legitimate' successor to Major General Ironsi after the coup of July 1966, for instance, was that there were other officers senior to him who should have assumed power according to the 'correct' rules of precedence.[1] One may see this clearly in his account of Gowon's assumption of power on 29–31 July 1966:

When this affair of the 29th July occurred [he says], I remember, for certain, the first 24 hours nobody thought it necessary to contact the East from Lagos. I made the contact later and I know the advice I gave Brigadier Ogundipe at that time. I said to him, 'Sir, the situation is so confused that I feel that somebody must take control immediately. Also, I would suggest that you go on the air and tell the

[1] The emphasis by Ojukwu on seniority stemmed at least as much from the desire to legitimate his current political position in military terms as from genuine conviction. He himself had been preferred by Major General Ironsi for appointment as Military Governor of the Eastern Region over three Eastern officers of greater seniority. Two of these (Lt Colonels Bassey and Njoku) had, however, been appointed to military posts of comparable importance (as the two brigade commanders after January 1966) and the other (Lt Colonel Imo) was under an official cloud.

country what has happened and that you were taking control of the situation'. . . He told me that he thought it was a good idea but it did not seem likely that it would be accepted by the faction.

Very soon after, I had occasion to talk to you, Jack (Gowon). . .I said that any break at this time from our normal line would write something into the Nigerian Army which is bigger than all of us and that thing is indiscipline. How can you ride above people's heads and sit in Lagos purely because you are the head of a group who have their fingers poised upon the trigger? If you do it you remain forever a living example of the indiscipline which we want to get rid of because tomorrow a Corporal will think because he has his finger on the trigger he could just take over the Company from the Major commanding the Company and so on. I knew then that we were heading for something terrible. Despite that and by force of circumstance as we did talk on the telephone, I think twice, you brought up the question of supreme command and I made quite plain my objections, but despite those objections you announced yourself Supreme Commander.

. . .I would not recognise because as I said we have a Supreme Commander who is missing. I would not recognise and to underline the validity of that claim of mine you appointed another officer, be he senior to you, Acting Governor of the West. . .

From there I think we started parting our ways because it was clear that the hold on Lagos was by force of conquest. Now, these things do happen in the world, we are all military officers. If an officer is dead – Oh! he was a fine soldier – we drop the national flag on him, we give him due honours and that is all. The next person steps in. So the actual fact in itself is a small thing with military men, but hierarchy, order is very important, discipline are sine qua non for any organisation that prides itself for being called an Army.[1]

Stirring words, and no doubt if every soldier in the Nigerian Army took them absolutely seriously they would all be marching in straight lines under a civilian regime still. But every army officer is equally aware, if one is able to penetrate behind what he will actually say in public on the subjects of hierarchy and order, that discipline is not automatic, that command depends on *effective* control over subordinates, in the last resort on the latter's acceptance of authority: that rules of precedence are not always followed to the letter, and promotion depends on soldierly qualities as well as seniority dates. Going back to the discussion among the Nigerian military leaders, we find them all falling back on this second principle of legitimacy when challenged on the first, as when Commodore Wey pointed out that there was no alternative but for Lt Colonel Gowon to take command of the army after the July 1966 coup:

I must say one thing that it is impossible for any man to expect to command any units which he has not got control over. Bolaji (Major Johnson) would bear witness,

---

[1] *Meeting of the Nigerian military leaders held at Peduase Lodge, Aburi, Ghana, 4th and 5th January 1967*, pp. 10–11.

he was there, he started it. He was the one who went out first and came back to say that a Private refused to take orders from him; it all happened in the Police Head-quarters. The Inspector General complained, I went into it and I said that if they cannot take orders from an Army Officer like themselves, they will not take orders from a Naval Officer. I retired and called Brigadier Ogundipe. He went out and if an ordinary Sergeant can tell a Brigadier – 'I do not take orders from you until my Captain comes' – I think this was the limit and this is the truth about it. There-fore, it would have been unfair to Ogundipe, or any other person for that matter, to take command and there is no point accepting to command a unit over which you have no control.

It was after that negotiations started. I do not know what conversation went on between Ogundipe and Jack (Gowon)...but I want to repeat that if we did not have the opportunity of having Jack to accept we would all have been finished.

Ojukwu is then very quick to point out that the principle of effective command and control leaves him in charge of the East:

Lt Colonel Ojukwu: Indeed, on the very principle that you have enunciated here, it is a question of command and control. I like to know who will stand up and tell me here that he commands and controls the Eastern Army or the Army in the East.
Lt Colonel Hassan Katsina: You alone.
Commodore Wey: I can tell you also here and now that you are doing it illegally because when we had the first Government no Governor was supposed to have the command of any Army.
Lt Colonel Ojukwu: You have started on the basis of the principles of command and control. If you control a group who will take orders from you, everybody doffs his hat, well done. Right, that person you doff your hat to cannot command and control those under him and indeed those of the East. What do you do to that?[1]

And later on again, when his military colleagues suggest the army should be reorganised, but retaining an effective Commander in Chief, who, in Colonel Adebayo's words, 'can really command, go to the ground every time and see that the Officers and the troops are doing the right thing', Lt Colonel Ojukwu again objects:

Any attempt to put somebody and say he commands the entire Army is – eyewash – it does not work, not in the present circumstances. Therefore we must accept that the Army would be regionalised whether or not we like the name we all understand what we mean by that. I do not think what we need is a Commander-in-Chief who is just titular. So that people will take orders from people, at least, that they have confidence in. Whoever you put in Lagos, I say this, will not command the loyalty of the East if that person is not acceptable to the East, this is the fact of today. So many things have happened and we do no longer trust each other.[2]

[1] *Meeting of the Nigerian military leaders*, pp. 12–13.
[2] *Ibid*. p. 32.

Ojukwu thus wins the argument, but only by jettisoning the principle of hierarchy and legitimate continuity he had earlier enunciated in favour of the alternative principle of effective command and control. The key to effective command, however, is leadership, an officer's ability to win loyalty for himself by his own charismatic example. In a well-integrated army, the two principles of legitimacy may, indeed, support each other as well as conflicting: each commander's right to give orders to his men and to set himself up as their hero would be validated by his position in the hierarchy; and the leadership qualities possessed by the officers would serve to validate the hierarchy itself. But just as they were seen to be inconsistent in the political debate at Aburi when used to legitimise political interests of a conflicting nature, so, we shall now argue, they were a serious dilemma in a poorly established authority structure, like the Nigerian Army.

HEROISM AND AUTHORITY

We may now try to amplify the contention made earlier, that the effectiveness of authority at all levels of the command hierarchy in any army depends on the degree of initiative that can be sustained at those levels: that initiative is functionally related to authority. The point is best made by contrasting armies with the classic bureaucracies (a clerical agency and a tobacco monopoly in France) described by Michel Crozier in his book, *The bureaucratic phenomenon.*[1] The organisations described by him carry out routine tasks, have a highly formalised control structure and are very inflexible. What is more, Crozier is able to show, strict adherence to formal rules in such a bureaucracy actually limits the management's room for manoeuvre, and rules can often indeed be turned *against* the management by its subordinate personnel.[2] The only lacunae in the over-bureaucratised systems he describes were where particular groups were able to control uncertainty – such as the maintenance men on whom depended the smooth functioning of the machinery on which everyone else relied – and so could secure an informal power in the organisation that had little relation to their formal status.

But there must be relatively few armies that operate in the same manner as this kind of rigid Weberian bureaucracy, for if they did they would quickly disintegrate or cease to be effective in combat. There seem to be two possible reasons for this: first, the purely military requirement that combat units right down to the platoon – or nowadays to the individual soldier – must be able to maintain the appropriate level of initiative in the field; and secondly, the need to concentrate *power* in the military hierarchy, to ensure the most rapid and flexible response of subordinates to orders that can be obtained in

---

[1] Michel Crozier, *The bureaucratic phenomenon* (Chicago: University of Chicago Press, 1964).
[2] Equally, of course, the rules also take away the subordinates' scope for initiative.

the circumstances. This is possible only if the military commander is able to control a wide area of uncertainty for his subordinates, if he is not too much encumbered with formal rules that may circumscribe his authority.

The principle of hierarchy in military organisations thus tends to be expressed more in terms of the *powers of command inherent in certain persons* than in terms of rules prescribing the roles, functions and respective rights and obligations of commander and subordinate. Discipline means unconditional obedience to persons in defined statuses in the hierarchy – subject only to the obligation to give priority to the orders of persons even higher in the hierarchy – rather than adherence to known rules.[1] The disciplinary system thus tends to vest each commanding officer *ex officio* with the right (indeed the obligation) to develop his own charisma[2] to create and command values for his subordinates. In the Nigerian Army this is expressed in the catchword of 'flexibility' borrowed from the British Army, where it performs a similar function.[3] This turns out to be the expectation that a subordinate should always do what his superior officer orders at the drop of a hat, regardless of his own views as to its usefulness. When a senior officer has changed his orders for the third time, confusing his subordinates and embarrassing him in the eyes of outsiders, the latter will as likely as not turn round and say in a sheepish attempt to preserve dignity, 'ah, but that's flexibility'.[4] Of course only a poor officer would exploit his position to demoralise his underlings in this manner. But it does illustrate the subordinate's obligation to accept his superior officer's orders and show initiative in carrying them out. Unlike the classic Weberian bureaucracy, in sum, where tasks are routine and self-contained, the military commander has wide powers of discretion to determine what the men of his unit should or should not do, and therein lies his power.

The position is complicated, however, by the fact that there are many intermediate levels in a command hierarchy. Again, the tendency in military organisations is to seek to develop and maintain initiative at all of the lower levels of command as well as right at the top. Armies obviously differ in the extent to which initiative is thus diffused down the hierarchy, but the most

[1] Not that the latter are entirely absent – indeed they are even needed to define the persons and statuses to whom obedience is due – but it is the relative emphasis on personalised authority, as opposed to rules, that is in question.

[2] We use the word 'charisma' here, as elsewhere in the chapter, not to denote any specifically *sacred* characteristics of military values – although the analogy may be in some respects a useful one – but to suggest the innovative role of the military commander. There is some justification for this in the concept's logical position in Max Weber's typology of authority. Charismatic authority is contrasted with the known precepts of traditional authority, on the one hand, and the routine principles of bureaucratic authority through the charismatic leader's ability to *create* new sacred values adhering to his person and giving him legitimacy, on the other.

[3] See the joke definition in *Owl Pie: The Journal of the Staff College, Camberley* (1958): 'flexibility = a substitute for a properly thought out plan'.

[4] As actually happened to one officer of the writer's acquaintance.

successful modern armies seem to be those, like the Israeli Army, which have developed a tradition of high initiative at the platoon leadership level, have promoted their officers on the basis of efficiency rather than seniority and made sure that a substantial residue of the heroic element of platoon leadership was implanted at the top of the hierarchy.[1] For the effectiveness of a high military leader's orders, the despatch and efficiency with which they are carried out, depend on the powers of command of intermediate commanders in the field, on the grip they have on their subordinates and this then in turn on their scope for initiative, their ability to control uncertainty for their subordinates. There is a very real sense, therefore, in which the power of a military commander, his ability to get a quick and effective response to his orders depends on the initiative of his subordinates, their freedom from excessive controls imposed from above and the amount of charisma that is dispersed at the lower levels of the hierarchy.

But here now arises the central paradox and dilemma. For how is the initiative of subordinates to be reconciled with that of their superiors, with the requirement that the latter be able to control values for them in order to ensure their dominance? And how is the initiative of both to be reconciled with the formal controls that are still needed to achieve the necessary co-ordination in a military bureaucracy, notwithstanding the emphasis within the latter on heroic leadership? There is some evidence, indeed, that some of the Nigerian Army's more perceptive commanders were sensitive to such problems, like Lt Colonel Pam, the late Adjutant General, who put the commanding officer's dilemma in an article in the *Nigerian Army Magazine* as follows:

If he has just taken command, it will be some time before he gets to know the Unit.

If he has commanded the Unit for some time, it is time for a change.

If he is a 'five per center' he is too green to carry his rank.

If he has made his rank with his class, he is no genius.

If he tries to make the system work for him, he is not practical and does things the hard way.

If he cuts corners he will get his fingers burnt if he hasn't already.

If he supports his officers and NCOs they have him 'snowed'.

If he questions their judgment he undercuts their morale.

If he...well, whatever he does, it is wrong. It is a miracle that he has been retained in the army. He ought to retire while he is ahead.[2]

[1] See A. Perlmutter, *Military and politics in Israel* (London: Cass, 1969), Chapter III. Note particularly the importance of the Palmach, the elite Israeli defence group in British Palestine, in providing the Israeli Army with its heroic tradition, the system of intensive training at mem-mem (platoon leader) level and with a large proportion of its military elite.

[2] Lt Colonel J. Y. Pam, 'The Commanding Officer's dilemma', *Nigerian Army Magazine* (Lagos), II (October 1964), p. 12.

In practice, therefore, the maintenance of the right combination of initiative and authority within a system of command and control depends very much on how the discretion of individual commanders is used. If a commander orders his juniors about in a capricious or indecisive manner, keeps changing his orders, refuses to accept suggestions and the like, he may weaken their power over their subordinates in turn. The effectiveness of authority all along down the line, therefore, depends on each senior officer being prepared to recognise the need for self-restraint in his dealings with his immediate subordinates to ensure that they in turn have sufficient freedom of action. At the same time, he must be firm enough to keep the heroism of his juniors under control and to make sure the basic requirements of coordination are met. Such a balance of freedom and restraint is obviously very difficult to achieve even in the best established of armies, let alone one in which there were so few experienced commanders as in Nigeria.

CONTROL THROUGH THE HIERARCHY

We may now turn to the various efforts made through the hierarchy to resolve the paradox of initiative and discipline. What is the effect upon this dilemma of differing styles of command; or of the shape and structure of the military hierarchy itself?

In more complex military organisations, the military elite often seek to resolve the dilemma by placing emphasis on managerial methods of control, such as are to be found in business organisations, with their emphasis on morale and persuasion rather than on authoritarianism.[1] Echoes of this kind of approach were to be found among Nigerian officers, particularly those who had received the appropriate indoctrination on courses abroad. For instance a major who had recently attended an infantry course at Fort Benning, Georgia, in the USA, came back proclaiming the doctrine that the individual soldier 'is equipped with two powerful weapons, the RIFLE and the SELF'.[2] Or Lt Colonel (now Brigadier) Ejoor, who put forward the view that 'the bulk of us are military business managers' and 'an Army is necessarily a

---

[1] Indeed Janowitz and Little see the paradox of initiative and discipline as arising mainly out of the need to reconcile high initiative with the bureaucratic coordination required in a complex modern military organisation: the management of violence becomes so complex, they argue, 'that the coordination of a group of specialists cannot be guaranteed simply by authoritarian discipline. Members of a military group must recognise their greater mutual dependence on the technical proficiency of their team members than on the formal authority structure.' *Sociology and the military establishment*, p. 12. Our position differs from this, however, in that we argue that the increased complexity of modern military organisations merely adds an extra dimension to the discipline/initiative dilemma, which is already inherent in the authority structure of even the most primitive and simple military hierarchies.

[2] Major P. A. O. Anwuna, 'The individual soldier', *Nigerian Army Magazine* (Lagos), III (December 1965), pp. 26–7.

conservative organisation…the problem there is how are we as leaders to instill a creative atmosphere in the Army Services in spite of the lack of the spur of competition'; and then went on to discuss 'creative leadership' under headings such as 'the creative problem solving process', 'fact finding', 'problem definition', 'idea finding' and 'solution finding'.[1]

All of this, however, seemed a little out of place in the Nigerian Army as it was then constituted.[2] The infantry battalion plus armoured cars format could be simply controlled through the hierarchy and there was not much need for an elaborate *apparat* of lateral coordination. Conflict between staff and line could occur, but was minimised by the subordination of the former to the latter, both in theory and in practice.[3] The army's hierarchy had been built up from steep pyramidical segments, in much the same way as the operational commands of the Second World War British Army. In 1966, there was a direct line of command down from the GOC to the two Brigade Headquarters and from these to the battalions, as can be seen in Table 26; and parallel to this was a very sketchy staff organisation, also in the form of a steep hierarchy of control. The ratio of combatant to non-combatant personnel in the officer corps was about two to one,[4] a proportion that would more or less need to be reversed in a more complex military structure. A proportion of the combat officers carried out staff duties, but these were no more than some thirty to thirty-five officers at any one time. The subordination of staff to line was perhaps most clearly seen in the fact that the staff officers of a brigade, the brigade major and DAQMG, were normally hand-picked by the brigadier for the post from among the combat officers, were subject primarily to his orders and liaised on *his* behalf with the headquarters organisation.

The style of control of Nigerian officers and NCOs over their subordinates is accordingly authoritarian[5] rather than managerial, punitive rather than

[1] Lt Colonel D. A. Ejoor, 'Head with creative thinking', *Nigerian Army Magazine* (Lagos), II (October 1964), p. 12.

[2] Though things may have been changed by the civil war and the expansion of the army. It is interesting that by all accounts the Federal Nigerian war effort suffered from lack of adequate staffing and coordination between the Divisions.

[3] In contrast, the continued subordination of staff to line tends to intensify strain in armies which become more complex, without adjusting their hierarchy to accord with the change from the simpler military organisation of the past. See Janowitz and Little, *Sociology and the military establishment*, pp. 28–34. The British Army, from which the Nigerian military inherited its simple hierarchical format, has been beset by such problems and has only recently begun to make the necessary adjustments: see P. Abrams, 'The late profession of arms: ambiguous goals and deteriorating means in Britain', *Archives européenes de sociologie*, VI, 2 (1965), 238–61.

[4] Figures given in Ejoor, 'Head with creative thinking'. Compare with the figures for the US Army in Janowitz and Little, *Sociology and the military establishment*, p. 31, in which the ratio is roughly reversed.

[5] Not that we wish to say that the presence of authoritarian methods in a simple hierarchical structure is automatic. Both were, in the Nigerian Army, part of the British heritage. One can say, however, that the simplicity of the army's structure meant that there was not much incentive for the adoption of less authoritarian types of control than that taken over from the British.

TABLE 26. *Shape of command hierarchy, January 1966*

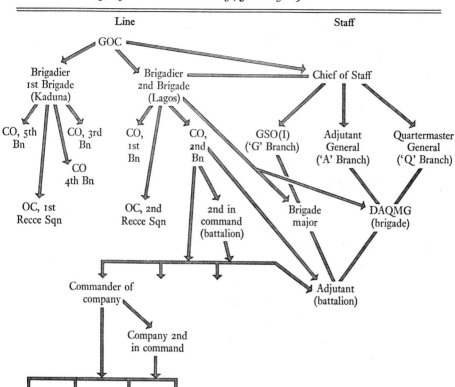

Note: Owing to expansion of size during the civil war, the present-day hierarchy differs from the above. The basic model is the same, however, with three divisional commands instead of two brigades; each of these divisions possessing a similar structure under its divisional GOC to that shown above, except that each has more brigades and battalions.

Arrowed lines indicate direct lines of command.

The Ibadan battalion (the 4th until September 1966, the 3rd after that) was transferred some time in the course of 1966 from the Kaduna (1st Brigade) command to the Apapa (2nd Brigade) command.

persuasive. This was in large measure a consequence of British training. At Sandhurst and other British cadet schools the emphasis has been[1] very much on three elements which reinforce the tradition of authoritarian leadership.

[1] At least until the recent reorganisations of the Royal Military Academy, Sandhurst, which were designed to make it more like a military university.

First, unreflective obedience to commands,[1] however arbitrary, as instilled for example at the notorious kit parades or at the four hundred and fifty three-quarter hour periods Sandhurst-trained officers boast of having spent on the drill-field. Secondly, the emphasis on battle-leadership at the platoon level, the fact that about half a cadet's graduation list evaluation was based on 'leadership' quality; and that much emphasis was placed on sports, which were also one element in the final evaluation of this leadership quality. Thirdly, the development of the special charismatic qualities of the military leader, partly through example, as in the heroic spectacle of legendary figures like RSM Lord putting hundreds of cadets through their paces on the drill square; and partly by imbibing the style of military life and the conceptions of the unique honour of the military commander that goes with it (described in more detail in Chapter IV above). These basic elements were also provided at the Nigerian Defence Academy when it was established, with Indian technical assistance, in 1964; all cadets learned horse riding, but few of them did any social science.[2]

The style of command that Nigerian officers adopt often seems harsh. Any attempt to answer back is dealt with curtly, and punishment is very quickly invoked for disobedience or indiscipline. The punitive approach even appears in their joking behaviour, for example, the officer who was overheard shouting at his girl friend, 'I'm the Commanding Officer round here, you damn well do what I tell you'. On occasion the manner of command seems to have been influenced by the British NCO as much as by the officer, which is perhaps not surprising because of the way that NCOs are put in day-to-day charge of the cadets at academies and cadet schools. They tend to break quickly into expletives – which British officers would tend to avoid – and it would be quite normal for an officer to shout at a soldier: 'Get moving, or I'll put you on a bloody fucking charge'.

To be sure, problems of morale are recognised. Whatever they or army regulations may say about discipline, most Nigerian officers are aware that it is not automatic and that it depends to some extent on the consent of their subordinates. When discussing colleagues it would be quite normal for an officer to say, 'Ah! X is a terrible (= terribly good) officer, he knows how to look after his men, Y is useless, he doesn't look after his troops properly at all'. And most commanders show willing to consult their subordinates, hold 'conferences' to 'put them in the picture',[3] and the like.

---

[1] See above, p. 120, for the description of the psychological impact of the kit parade on a young officer.

[2] Economics was an optional subject (to science) in the cadets' academic programme, but this was the only social science subject taught. To begin with the academy employed a lecturer to teach economics, but later decided that a full-time teacher was not necessary because there was not enough work for him. Horse riding was taught up to 1967, though the writer does not know if this luxury was discontinued because of the war.

[3] *The Owl Pie* (1958) definition of this is: 'being submerged in a mass of useless information'.

156

Yet problems of morale are always subordinate to the demands of discipline. Even if a commander neglects the morale of his men, his orders must always be carried out. There is no place in the military book for the soldier who does not obey even if he feels his orders are wrong, or that the person who is giving them to him is less skilled or experienced than himself. The writer recalls suggesting to a senior officer of the Nigerian Defence Academy that there might be a problem of maintaining discipline among NCOs whose equals or inferiors had been lucky enough to secure commissions in the field during the civil war. 'I don't see any problem', was the reply, 'they would obey orders.' This suggests the essentially prescriptive nature of the military view. Any hint that in fact discipline may sometimes fail is resisted, because it may show one does not have sufficient confidence in it. On the sub-ordinate's side, to obey orders is also comforting because it reduces ambiguity and absolves one of the responsibility of taking unpalatable decisions oneself. Even a soldier as experienced and high up in the hierarchy as Major General Ironsi used to say (before 1966) that he never wished to do anything except obey orders.

Nonetheless an authoritarian style of command does not necessarily curb initiative or discourage heroism in the lower ranks. Coercive controls may not suit the specialist in an army which relies on complex technical skills. But in a simple infantry command hierarchy, as in Nigeria, it is not coerciveness as such that reduces initiative so much as too much interference with what subordinates are doing. It is the officious rather than the authoritarian leader who paralyses initiative. The archetypical good commander in the Nigerian Army, such as the late Brigadier Maimalari, Colonel Mohammed Shuwa and perhaps Colonel Adekunle,[1] is the man who leaves subordinates to get on with the job themselves, but breathes fire on them when they make mistakes.

Such a system depends heavily, however, on the personal qualities of its leaders. If they are inexperienced and unable to delegate authority, things very quickly go wrong. In a badly articulated system of military command and control, heavy-handed authority from above tends to go along with junior officers and NCOs taking matters into their own hands from below. Such seems to have been the situation in the Nigerian Army. Junior officers often complained that their commanders would not delegate authority to them, kept them too long in the office and insisted on checking all the details them-selves. They, correspondingly, would tend to evade instructions, to talk about how their CO had 'misbehaved himself' or to stand rather defiantly on their rights. Similar relations existed between officers and NCOs, accentuated by

[1] There is little doubt of Adekunle's ability to inspire confidence in his men, at least until things went badly wrong for his 3rd Marine Commando Division in the civil war: the latter happened not because of any defect in his leadership quality, but because he did not obey orders and cooperate with other divisions.

the fact that the latter were on the whole more experienced. The NCOs were indeed the most critical judges of leadership quality in the whole army and there were very few commanders in their opinion who had true command ability. One telling symptom of the strain upon discipline was the occurrence of phantasies of aggression against constituted authority among the NCOs in the July coup already described, such as the pretence that they could assume the rank of officers they had killed.

The hostility between the ranks was also endemic in the steepness of the command hierarchy of the army and the narrowness of its span of control. The span of control varied (as can be seen in Table 26 on p. 155) from two or three at the narrowest to five or six at the widest. Such a close degree of supervision at each level of command could be expected to intensify the difficulty of reconciling authority and initiative. For a wide span of control limits the ability of the most domineering supervisor to reduce the freedom of action of his subordinates and also reduces the interpersonal antagonism which might build up around the hierarchy.[1] In contrast, a narrow span of control and intensive supervision such as prevailed in the Nigerian military makes hostility between subordinate and commander much more likely, unless the latter is capable of great restraint. Nigerian officers of the writer's acquaintance usually tended to express ambivalence at best, hostility at worst, towards their immediate commanders.[2] These feelings are perhaps most intense between a commanding officer and his personal staff with whom he works particularly closely, between, for instance, a brigadier and his brigade major or DAQMG, or a battalion commander and his second in command or adjutant. Even when they are from the same home area and have been on friendly personal terms, strong tensions inevitably arise.[3] This kind of antagonism seems to have underlaid at least one, and perhaps more, of the killings in the January 1966 coup: for Major Ifeajuna is said to have had such feelings of ambivalence about Brigadier Maimalari, whose brigade major he was. Maimalari had picked Ifeajuna for his post himself and is said to have been very friendly with him, though the inevitable antagonisms arose, and the Brigadier is said to have become suspicious towards the end.

Hostility to immediate commanders also tended to spill over to senior officers and the hierarchy as a whole. Imagine the following scene in an officers mess. A very senior officer is making a visit to explain some of the

---

[1] See J. C. Worthy's important analysis of the effects of widening the span of control in the Sears–Roebuck organisation; and his suggestions that a narrower span of control tends to make an organisation rely less on 'punitive' styles of management. 'Organisational structure and employee morale', *American Sociological Review*, XV (1950), 169–79.

[2] Based on impressions gathered from officers in conversation, antagonisms flaring up during drinks at the mess, etc., though few officers will admit such feelings in public, except to good friends.

[3] As between at least two pairs of officers of the writer's acquaintance.

high command's recent political actions and military reorganisations in early 1967. He holds a secret session with the officers first, at which it is said he receives a blasting from junior officers who are disappointed with the way things have been going of late. They all then emerge and join a party of guests who have been invited to meet the visitor. Talk revolves around the traditions of various messes. Boisterous laughter about how the 1st Battalion mess in Enugu initiates its new officers by rolling them down the steps in a barrel. Junior officers suggest that the visitor should be 'chaired' out of mess (carried out in an arm-chair). Visitor says no. Junior officers become insistent, an undercurrent of hostility arises. Visitor's ADC realises what is going on, takes his commander by the elbow and suggests they should be leaving. ADC and the commander of the unit steer the 'big man' quickly out of the door. Junior officers shrug shoulders and get back to their beer. Admittedly, this particular incident was observed in a period of great political stress in 1966–7. But similar things had apparently been known during the period prior to military rule. Visualise another incident,[1] when a senior military visitor at a mess dinner became garrulous and spun out the conversation at the end of the meal. Eventually, two junior officers pointedly got up, saluted and asked permission to leave, in defiance of the tradition that no junior officer can leave until the senior officer present himself makes a move. The senior officer, an ex-NCO and a stickler for protocol, blasted them and told them to stay. He then dragged out his drink, deliberately it seems, and the junior officers became angrier and angrier, the atmosphere more and more unpleasant, until the 'big brass' left the mess. Such examples are, of course, only illustrative. But taken together with the military revolts of 1966 they do seem to indicate that hostility between junior and senior officer, subordinate and commander had become a somewhat striking feature of military life.

ROUTINES AND REVOLT

All that has been said above – the functions of heroism, the importance of charismatic as opposed to bureaucratic authority, the theme of revolt against discipline – may seem to be at variance with many of one's common sense notions of what any army is, with the prominence of routine and procedure, of 'bull' and all the rituals of shining boots, jumping to attention, asking permission to go to the john or to get married.

These things are no less prominent in the Nigerian Army, however, than elsewhere. Much emphasis is given in training at the Nigerian Military Training College, Sandhurst, Mons and now the Nigerian Defence Academy, to the development of such routines and the inculcation of seemingly

---

[1] Occurring prior to 1966. Details supplied by an expatriate informant who attended the dinner concerned.

unreflective obedience to command: witness, for example, the high proportion of a cadet's time spent drilling on the barracks square at all of these institutions (the same would be true of cadets sent for training to India, Pakistan, Ethiopia and to a lesser extent Australia, Canada and the USA). Punctuality is valued highly and officers turning up late even at a social function will be bawled out severely and in public by their commanding officer. At least two Military Governors indeed attempted to instill the same sense of punctuality into their civil servants in early 1966 by rounding up latecomers and threatening punishment if they did not arrive at the office in time in the future.

Many of the routines of military life are designed to emphasise the fact of hierarchy. As in most armies, there are well-developed rituals of dominance and avoidance, both between senior and junior officers and between officers and NCOs. On duty, an officer holding the more senior command post is usually addressed as 'Sir' even by an officer of the same rank; the rule applies even if there is a status inconsistency between command level and rank, unless the inconsistency is a particularly serious one.[1] In the mess and on 'public' social occasions when there are other officers present, a commanding officer of a unit is always addressed as 'Sir' by his subordinates. Officers of superior rank normally also expect this form of address, except that the practice is often relaxed on informal occasions between officers of immediate contiguous ranks, who may either call each other by their name and rank ('Lieutenant X', 'Captain Y') or use christian names if particularly intimate. It is ironic indeed that at a time when the British Army is abandoning the attempt to 'carry on the aristocratic tradition in Britain without the aristocrats',[2] the Nigerian military should be maintaining a status system that borrows from some of the more traditional and ascriptive aspects of British military life. The phrase from the *Queen's Regulations*, 'an officer and a gentleman', which has become the subject of some controversy in Britain, is one of the most frequently heard expressions in the Nigerian Army, not only because it articulates differentiated conceptions of military status and honour (as pointed out above in Chapter IV), but also because it emphasises the importance of order, continuity, hierarchy and the special position of privilege and responsibility the officers have vis-a-vis the Other Ranks.

[1] Sharp status inconsistencies of this type were rare before 1966; but the disruptions and rapid mobility caused by the events of that year and by the civil war from 1967 onwards have made them crop up frequently. The rules of precedence are laid down in The Nigerian Military Forces Act no. 26 of 1960. This states that officers and men stand in precedence over each other by rank and as prescribed by regulations; officers of the same rank stand 'in order of precedence and command' in accordance with the date of appointment into their present rank, or according to orders 'which may be signified by the President' – which may alter the rules of precedence in particular instances, as when, for example, a higher temporary rank is given to a more junior officer.

[2] P. Abrams, 'Democracy, technology and the retired British officer' in S. P. Huntington, *Changing patterns of military politics* (New York: Free Press, 1962).

How then does heroism fit together with 'bull', charisma with routine? First of all, it should be made clear that the characterisation of the military in terms of its non-bureaucratic characteristics put forward above was designed to emphasise its differences from other bureaucracies of the rigid Weberian type. In reality, like all complex organisations, an army is coordinated by means of an array of routines and procedures. The difference is one of the relatively greater *emphasis* on charismatic rather than bureaucratic authority in military organisations, and is not one of kind.

Secondly, routines may actually have positive functions in relation to the balance between initiative and discipline. For instance, they may be a means of handling the hostility that tends to develop around the hierarchy. Precise rules of precedence reduce ambiguity, reduce the likelihood of jurisdictional conflict over authority. The rituals of deference and avoidance between officers and their juniors create social distance between them, turning, we may argue, ambivalent and potentially hostile interactions into relatively clear-cut patterns of action governed by known rules.

On the other hand, in a poorly integrated authority structure, like the Nigerian Army, the routines may actually be put to use to legitimise indiscipline, to justify revolt. Officers of the writer's acquaintance have been known to threaten to demand their rights under the Nigerian Military Forces Act against their commander when incensed by the latter's treatment of them.[1] There is the story told by NCOs of the ritualistic officer who insisted that Other Ranks salute him on absolutely every occasion they encountered him, however inconvenient this might be. They eventually decided they had had enough of this and lined up at intervals all along the road between his office and the mess, saluting him as he went by and putting him in the ludicrous position that he had to return so many salutes 'that he could hardly drive his car'. Finally, as we saw in the description of the January and July 1966 coups, the routines and military forms were used to dignify revolt, as when officers hid behind the claim that they 'had their orders' when arresting military leaders or when Northern NCOs forced their junior officers to give them orders to kill in the heat of the July coup.

The integrative problems of the Nigerian Army, to conclude, were those of a simple hierarchical structure, not of a complex bureaucratic military machine. The basic elements were heroic leadership balanced with authoritarian discipline, accentuated by a steep hierarchy, but made less arbitrary by military routines and rules of precedence. We have suggested how these elements could be functionally related so as to support each other – how

---

[1] This act, like the corresponding British legislation, gives junior officers rights to appeal against their commanders but only in extreme cases. A junior officer might thus *threaten* to appeal, though it is unlikely that he would often really mean it, because his case would have to be very clear-cut for him to get away with it.

heroism may create authority or routines reduce the antagonism between the ranks – and also how strains may arise out of them. In Nigeria, we have shown how initiative unbalanced discipline, how punitive controls in the hands of inexperienced officers led to hostility against the hierarchy, how routines were used as a weapon against authority: things which clearly developed out of the characteristic strains of an authoritarian command structure. But we are still left with the question why the standard controls that operate in such a structure were apparently insufficient to cope with these difficulties, why there was a lack of balance between functions and dysfunctions. In the next chapter, therefore, we shall look at the organisational disruption caused by the rapid indigenisation of the officer corps between Independence and 1966. We will hope to suggest how this accentuated the army's organisational dilemmas so as to be beyond the critical range within which the norms and routines of military life, which the Nigerian officers and men had internalised so well, would be able to cope with them.

CHAPTER VII

NIGERIANISATION: THE LEGACY OF HASTE

In 1958, control over recruitment and promotion in the army was transferred from the British Army Council to the Nigerian government. Because the army had been a colonial force, nearly all the officer corps and a substantial proportion of the NCOs were still British. The colonial government had already started to indigenise the officer corps in preparation for Independence, but the results were meagre – only twenty-nine Nigerian officers commissioned before January 1958[1] – and it was left to the Nigerian authorities to carry through the major part of the localisation programme.[2] It took some time to get things moving, so that the major part of Nigerianisation took place after Independence in 1960, when still little more than eighteen per cent of the officer corps was Nigerian, as can be seen in Table 27.

TABLE 27. *Indigenisation of the officer corps, 1960–6*

Date	Number of British officers	Number of Nigerian officers		Per cent of officer corps Nigerian
		Combat commissions	Non-combat	
1 Jan. 1960	228	48	2	18
1 Jan. 1962	156	107	50	50
1 Jan. 1964	47	240	132	89
1 Jan. 1966	0	336	181	100

Source: Federation of Nigeria, *Official Gazettes* (1960–6). The record of the arrivals and departures of British officers in the Gazettes is somewhat incomplete, necessitating a number of informed guesses which may result in a small margin of error. Similarly, the number of British NCOs in the army fell from over three hundred in 1956 to around eighty in 1960 and nil in 1965.

We shall now describe some of the organisational distortions that this rapid replacement of expatriate with African officers produced. We will suggest how these intensified the structural strains that have already been described, most especially the pressures against the disciplinary system set forth in the preceding chapter.

[1] Of whom one was soon discharged and two died in the Congo.
[2] The political background to this will be described in Chapter X below.

TABLE 28. *Age structure of the Nigerian officer corps, 1966 (combat officers only)*

Age group	Per cent distribution	Military background of age group	Approximate span of ranks of age group	
			ex-NCOs	School-leavers[a]
20–24	62	Predominantly short-service trained; a few academy-trained	—	2nd Lt and Lt
25–29	23	Half short-service; half Sandhurst; only one or two ex-NCOs	Lt to Captain	Captain to Major
30–34	12	Half ex-NCOs; half Sandhurst	Captain to Major	Major to Lt Col.
35–39	2	Almost all former NCOs	Lt Col. and above	Lt Col. and above
40 and above	1·3	All former NCOs	Lt Col. and above	—

Note:
[a] School-leavers with either academy or short-service training.

DISTORTION IN THE ARMY'S AGE STRUCTURE

One of the most obvious results of indigenisation was to throw the officer corps' age structure out of balance. The middle and lower levels of the officer corps (from subaltern to major) were filled, as may be seen in Table 28, with young officers within a very narrow age span of each other compared with that which is normal in the equivalent spread of ranks in other armies, like the British. This automatically implied a very narrow span in length of experience between upper and lower levels of command in the hierarchy. In Table 29, we show the approximate average difference between the dates at which officers in the higher command positions were commissioned from those at which officers in subordinate command posts entered the officer corps, for each command level in the hierarchy. It will be seen that the gap in experience is a very narrow one, there being a differential of no more than fourteen years between the GOC and his lowliest platoon commanders. From the time of Weber sociologists have suggested that strain builds up in organisations at points where formal status is disparate with the expertise of the possessors of that status.[1] This generalisation receives support from the lack of respect shown by Nigerian soldiers to their commanders except the very few whose experience matched up to their responsibilities.

[1] M. Weber, *From Max Weber: essays in sociology,* H. H. Gerth and C. Wright Mills (eds.) (London: Routledge and Kegan Paul, 1948), Chapter VIII; and A. W. Gouldner, 'Organisational analysis' in R. K. Merton (ed.), *Sociology Today* (New York: Basic Books, 1959), where Weber's theme is taken up in a review of contemporary literature.

TABLE 29. *Average seniority differentials at points in Nigerian Army hierarchy*

	Years of commission (average)	GOC	Brigade CO	Battalion CO	Battalion 2nd in Command	Company CO
GOC[a]	1946	—	—	—	—	—
Brigade COs[b]	1951	2 yrs. 3 mths.	—	—	—	—
Battalion COs[c]	1956	6 yrs. 11 mths.	4 yrs. 8 mths.	—	—	—
Battalion 2nd in Command[d]	1959	10 yrs. 3 mths.	8 yrs. 0 mths.	3 yrs. 4 mths.	—	—
Company OCs[e]	1961	11 yrs. 11 mths.	9 yrs. 8 mths.	5 yrs. 0 mths.	1 yr. 8 mths.	—
Platoon OCs[f]	1963	14 yrs. 2 mths.	11 yrs. 11 mths.	7 yrs. 3 mths.	3 yrs. 11 mths.	2 yrs. 3 mths.

Sources: Federation of Nigeria, *Official Gazettes* (1960–6) and office and telephone directories for Lagos, Enugu, Ibadan, Kaduna and Zaria. The data are incomplete, covering some 130 of the army's approximately 330 combat officers in 1965. The coverage of officers at the top three levels is, however, comprehensive. The number of cases in the lower three levels (nineteen, thirty-one and sixty-five respectively) is sufficient to give a fair degree of confidence in the figures.

Seniority is estimated from dates of commission (not the same as the seniority dates utilised by the army for promotions; or as the putative seniorities allocated to different officer cohorts elsewhere in this analysis).

If we were to include experience in the ranks in the table, the gap between top and bottom would appear somewhat wider because of the greater concentration of ex-NCOs right at the top of the hierarchy, though it is unlikely that this would add more than about five years to the span of experience overall (and less, of course, to the differences between the ranks).

Notes:

[a] General Officer Commanding; in rank of major general.

[b] Brigade commanders, Chief of Staff and Commandant, Nigerian Military Training College: modal ranks of brigadier and colonel.

[c] Battalion commanders, staff officers (I): modal rank lieutenant colonel.

[d] Battalion 2nd in command, staff officers (II) and small unit commanders (e.g. OC Recce Squadron): modal rank of major.

[e] Company commanders, battalion adjutants, staff captains, etc.: modal rank of captain.

[f] Platoon commanders and other junior officers: modal ranks of lieutenant and 2nd lieutenant.

The problem was aggravated by a further status discrepancy, which arose because the officers at the very top of the hierarchy, who clearly did have some edge over their juniors in age, experience and probably competence, were for the most part ex-NCOs, and therefore had had less formal education.[1] Five of the seven officers at the rank of colonel and above in January 1966 (including Major General Ironsi) and six of the fourteen lieutenant colonels were former NCOs. But the great majority of officers below these ranks had come to officer cadet training straight from secondary school. Although a number of the ex-NCOs, for example Brigadier Ademulegun, were known to be competent, they were not always greatly respected by their more educated subordinates. This was in part due to the very close link between status and education in West Africa; and it was in part because even those like Ademulegun whose competence in military matters was widely known about, were felt (especially by politically radical officers) to be too narrowly professional in their outlook.[2] Some of the arrogant contempt one or two of the more intellectual officers felt for their commanders was pungently expressed by one of these, who in being asked to 'listen to his General' at an army banquet presided over by Ironsi was overheard to mumble 'General Idiot' at him under his breath.

OFFICERS AND NCOS

There was also a serious discrepancy in age and experience between the junior officers and the NCOs underneath them. The non-commissioned officer posts had always been partly in Nigerian hands; and by 1958 the bulk of the NCOs, and by 1962–3 all of them, were Nigerian; the indigenisation of these ranks having been completed earlier and more slowly than that of the officer corps. As a consequence, there were large numbers of NCOs of considerable experience. Some, it is true, had been promoted into the officer corps, but the majority – especially in the crucial General Duties departments[3] – had not got the educational qualifications for advancement.

It is normal in British-type military organisations for there to be some discrepancy in status and expertise between junior officers and their NCOs. The strain this might put on the disciplinary system is reduced, however, by

[1] Though in fact they did normally have to meet the minimum educational qualifications for entry to the officer corps in terms of GCE 'Ordinary' levels or West African School Certificate. Normally they would have taken correspondence courses to obtain the former, which definitely carries less prestige than going to a good secondary school; nor would they have had the prestige of a Sandhurst training, which was the most frequent training among the middle-level officers of the January Majors' generation.

[2] See the discussion of differences in attitude towards the use of the military to quell the disturbances in the Western Region in 1965–6, in Chapter X below.

[3] General Duties NCOs are those with command responsibilities in combat units, as opposed to the specialists and tradesmen in other branches.

the informal power the latter are able in practice to wield. Much of the day-to-day running of the army is left in their hands; and officers are forced to exchange some of their authority in return for the NCO's advice and support

In the Nigerian Army, also, status barriers between officers and Other Ranks have been in theory rigidly enforced, British-style. But the pressures running against them have been greater than in Britain. The general youth-fulness and inexperience of the officers as of 1966 meant that there were relatively few officers (themselves mostly from the ranks) who had sufficient self-confidence and experience to command genuine respect from the NCOs; and most of these were eliminated in the 1966 coups. Thus the inherent tension between officers and NCOs was near the surface. Status barriers of the British type, moreover, seemingly did not fit with traditional ideas of status. Most African societies are egalitarian in their basic values.[1] Even societies as highly stratified in political or economic terms as the Hausa–Fulani or Kanuri Emirates in Northern Nigeria[2] lacked the kind of cultural differentiation between strata that would support the status barriers and differentiation in styles of life that are normal in European armies.

On the other hand, the localisation of the officer corps did away with the cleavage between white officers and black Other Ranks.[3] The exchange of the formal authority of the officers for the experience and power of command over the troops of the NCOs thus could be established along lines more consonant with indigenous conceptions of authority. Interestingly, in 1963, we find the *Nigerian Army Magazine*[4] advocating the adoption of terminology for officers addressing Other Ranks which would be more 'full of affectionate touch and...appealing to men's hearts' such as the Hausa 'Asalam Alaikum Jama'a', the Ibo 'Ibe Anyi' or the Yoruba 'Eyin Elegbe Mi', though for obvious reasons, the editor asks his readers to suggest an appropriate equiva-lent to these in the English language. Nigerian officers out on foray with their troops tended increasingly to be addressed as 'Mallam' or 'Oga' in addition to the military 'Sir'.[5]

There was also a tendency for Other Ranks to expect that their relations

---

[1] This argument is put forward at length in Fallers, 'Equality, modernity and democracy in new states'.

[2] See, for example, M. G. Smith, *The economy of Hausa communities in Zaria Province*, Colonial Research Series no. 16 (London: HMSO, 1955).

[3] Though prior to Independence there had also been British NCOs, these also were resented because of the special privileges given them in pay and privilege compared with the Nigerian Other Ranks.

[4] 'Approach-officers to the Other Ranks', *Nigerian Army Magazine* (Lagos), I (1963). The editor's own suggestions for new English terminology are 'Comrades-in-Arms' and 'Friends'.

[5] 'Mallam' for Northern officers, 'Oga' for southerners. NCOs are sometimes heard addressing officers in this way, and it seems on the whole acceptable to the latter. Witness the style of interaction recorded by Lt A. R. Alabi, 'The hippo men', *Royal Nigerian Army Magazine* (Lagos), XI, 3 (May 1962), when his troops called him to look at hippopotamuses with 'Oga, look-o!'

with their superiors should be governed by patterns of reciprocity similar to those which traditionally accompany difference in power and status in Nigerian societies.[1] Officers, for example, are expected to show suitable largesse in entertaining their subordinates. The writer was told by an NCO of a senior officer who invited only a couple of officers and a few of his most senior NCOs to his child's naming ceremony. Only three of the NCOs turned up (said the informant with a gesture of contempt); the officer produced three bottles of whiskey and asked them to drink up; but they stayed only for a couple of tots and then were off, not hiding their disapproval. Another officer of whom the writer has heard drew censure from his NCOs for returning on his holidays to the unit where he was previously posted to harvest the crop from a garden he had planted behind his quarters, instead of donating it to the troops. The guards of another very senior military man were said to have been compliant in his capture and death in one of the military coups because he 'would not even offer them a Fanta' (orange drink). The informal power a number of the older and more respected senior NCOs were able to wield was very considerable indeed, like the old Drum Major with thirty years' service in the army, of whom a Company Sergeant Major said, 'If he asks for a whiskey, no officer will dare refuse him'.

Expectations of reciprocity were especially well developed between Northern officers and NCOs, both because of their similarity in social background and because a good proportion of Northern officers were sons or relatives of NCOs. The price to be paid by junior officers was in a sense even higher because the deference traditionally due to age among kinsmen and compatriots tended to reinforce the NCOs' advantage of military experience. The latter were able to put this to most effective account when they brought pressure to bear on their junior officers to stage the July 1966 coup on their behalf.

SUCCESSION AND THE LINES OF COMMAND

A further distortion in the structure of the army came from the fact that Nigerian officers were rising rapidly in the hierarchy, and therefore moving very frequently from one command position to another. At the same time, the progressive withdrawal of British officers meant that the latter were spending

[1] Accounts of reciprocity between those in positions of power and authority and clients or subordinates in particular Nigerian societies are contained in R. Cohen, 'Some aspects of institutionalised exchange: a Kanuri example', *Anthropological Quarterly* (July 1965), pp. 117–31; Smith, *Government in Zazzau*, pp. 259–61; and Bascom, 'Social status, wealth and individual differences among the Yoruba'. For a most interesting analysis of the way in which traditional norms and concepts of reciprocity are carried over into modern political relationships in Sierra Leone, see M. Kilson, *Political change in a West African state* (Cambridge, Mass.: Harvard University Press, 1966), pp. 259–74.

TABLE 30. *Succession in selected military command posts, 1962–4 (average number of changes in tenure of posts at level shown in a year – minimum figures)*[a]

	1962	1963	1964	Total numbers
GHQ				
General Officer Commanding	1	0	0	
(Major General)	(n = 1)	(n = 1)	(n = 1)	N = 1
Staff officers (I)[b]	0·66	1	0·33	
(Lt Colonels)	(n = 3)	(n = 3)	(n = 3)	N = 3
Brigade HQ				
Brigade COs	2	1	1	
(Brigadiers)	(n = 1)	(n = 1)	(n = 1)	N = 2
Brigade staff	2·5	1	2	
(Majors)[c]	(n = 2)	(n = 2)	(n = 2)	N = 4
Battalions				
Battalion commanders	2	0·67	1	
(Lt Colonels)	(n = 2)	(n = 3)	(n = 2)	N = 5
Battalion 2nd in command	1·5	2·33	0·5	
(Majors)	(n = 2)	(n = 3)	(n = 2)	N = 5
Adjutants (Captains)	2	1·67	2	
	(n = 2)	(n = 3)	(n = 2)	N = 5
Company commanders	[d]	1·9	1·5	
		(n = 13)	(n = 14)	N = 20

Sources: Figures are based on the Lagos, Kaduna and Enugu office and telephone directories and cover GHQ, the 1st Brigade HQ and the 1st, 3rd, and 5th Battalions.

The data are incomplete because of gaps in the directories and because postings were not listed while each of the battalions served in the Congo. It was therefore necessary to note the number of posts on which the data are based in brackets (n = ...) in each cell of the table. The total number of posts in the army at each level is listed on the right-hand side (N = ...).

Notes:

[a] Minimum figures because details of changes occurring *within* each three-month period are not available for most of the posts.

[b] Chief of Staff not shown, as this post was not established until June 1964.

[c] Brigade Majors and DAQMGs.

[d] No data available.

less and less time in the army and in command posts within it. Expatriate officers seconded to Nigeria after 1960 were usually spending only between six months and two years there,[1] and contract officers slightly longer.[2] The

[1] Previous to Independence, the periods of service had been longer, though still rather too short to encourage organisational cohesion: regulars had spent a normal two tours of service in Nigeria of fifteen to eighteen months each: and 'national service' subalterns of around a year each.

[2] After 1958 a number of expatriate officers were recruited on 'contract' terms, usually upon retirement from the British Army. The last British GOC, Major General Welby-Everard, was such an officer. The secondment of British regulars was still, however, the biggest source of expatriate officers, except right at the end.

combined effect of these factors was to produce very high rates of succession in command posts all the way up the hierarchy, during the whole period from 1960 to 1965, as can be seen in Table 30. In some individual postings the rate of turnover was astonishing, as in the 5th Battalion in 1960–1, which had no less than four different commanders in the space of slightly over a year.

It is sometimes argued[1] that high rates of succession in command posts are a widely found characteristic of military organisations. A high turnover tends to homogenise the officer corps, to foster the development of military peer groups cutting right across the organisation. It thus tends to develop the authority of the total complex organisation, the total military establishment, at a cost to the authority of the individual commanders of particular organisational sub-units. The success of this transfer of authority to an organisation-wide level cannot be assured, however, unless the individual commanders still keep some effective control over their units. If their authority is undermined too badly by frequency transfers, then the effective authority of the hierarchy as a whole cannot be assured either, and one may hypothesise that this is what happened in the Nigerian case. For the rates of succession shown in Table 30 are very high indeed, much higher than is common in other peace-time military organisations.[2] Under such conditions, it would be very difficult for any commander to stabilise his lines of authority over his subordinates, to develop enough leverage over them to keep their initiative sufficiently in check.

MOBILITY AND ANOMIE

Not only was there high turnover from military posting to military posting, but there was an exceedingly high rate of mobility in terms of promotion up through the hierarchy. This can best be illustrated by referring to Table 31, which shows the median time of promotion of Nigerian officers from rank to rank, from the late colonial period in the 1950s onwards. It will be seen that during the colonial period, promotions were relatively slow, and were very roughly comparable to promotion rates in the British Army at the same time. But from 1959, promotion rates became suddenly faster after serious Nigerianisation began.[3] Median promotion times from lieutenant to captain

---

[1] See O. Grusky, 'The effects of succession: a comparative study of military and business organisation', in M. Janowitz (ed.), *The new military* (New York: Russell Sage Foundation, 1964). See also Chapter V above.

[2] See the data in *The new military*, p. 91. The data are for length of service of officers in posts at various levels of the hierarchy in a military unit, and so are difficult to compare with the above figures. It is clear from Grusky's data, however, that turnover rates must have been much less (perhaps once every two years) than in the Nigerian Army, though rather higher than the business organisations with which Grusky compared the military.

[3] With the exception of promotion from 2nd lieutenant to lieutenant. This was mainly because of the shift in emphasis in recruitment and training from ex-NCOs to Sandhurst to a short-service

and from captain to major were only two to three years; and the really successful officer could expect even faster advancement. These, moreover, are the gazetted rates of promotion. Promotion into acting or temporary ranks was even faster. Command positions were frequently held by officers more junior than the ranks at which the seniority of the post was theoretically established. The impact of this was most strongly felt in the middle-level tactical commands. Whereas in 1961 almost all the battalion second in command, company commander and battalion adjutant posts were held by majors, most of them British, by 1963 two-thirds and by 1964 nine-tenths of the company commands were held by captains and sometimes even lieutenants, while all of the adjutants were captains or lieutenants; and only the battalion second in commands remained predominantly majors.[1] By 1966, however, two-thirds to a half of the company commands were again in the hands of majors, owing mainly, it should be said, to the promotion of officers up to ranks which fitted the responsibilities held.

Neither these high rates of promotions, nor the high rates of mobility between military postings that were also common, could have favoured the development of stable expectations around military careers. Officers could not be expected to have realistic expectations either about what was possible and not possible in the way of occupational advancement or what objectives it was realistic to seek outside their professional sphere. In other words, such an extremely high rate of mobility tended to create a classic state of anomie, in much the same way as Durkheim suggested that an economic boom or sudden accession to wealth would disorient expectations, make it difficult to define limits of possible and the impossible and increase the occurrence of indicators of social disorganisation, such as suicides.[2]

entry with a shorter period of training: the former types of entry carried greater seniority for promotion than did the latter. From 1962 onwards, the filling of the higher posts in the officer corps with Nigerians also began to be reflected in a slowing in the promotion rate at the bottom of the hierarchy.

[1] Based on data from three of the five battalions from the office and telephone directories of Kaduna and Kano. The ranks in many cases are temporary rather than gazetted substantive ranks, so that the disparity between rank and post is even greater than that shown.

[2] See Emile Durkheim's discussion and definition of anomie in *Suicide*, trans. and ed. G. Simpson (Glencoe, Ill.: The Free Press, 1951), p. 253: 'So long as the social forces thus freed have not regained equilibrium, their respective values are unknown and so all regulation is lacking for a time. *The limits are unknown between the possible and the impossible, what is just and unjust, legitimate claims and hopes and those which are immoderate.* Consequently there is no restraint upon aspirations. If the disturbance is profound, it affects even the principles of distribution of men among various occupations...Some particular class especially favoured by the crisis is no longer resigned to its former lot, and, on the other hand, the example of its greater good fortune arouses all sorts of jealousy below and about it...With increased prosperity desires increase. At the very moment when traditional rules have lost their authority, the richer prize offered these appetites stimulates and makes them more exigent and impatient of control. The state of deregulation or anomy is thus further heightened by passions being less disciplined, precisely when they need more disciplining. But then their very demands make fulfillment impossible. Overwhelming

TABLE 31. *Median times of promotion from rank to rank in Nigerian officer corps, 1953–65[a] (in months)*

Year of commission	Median promotion time to Lieutenant	Year promoted to Lieutenant	Median promotion time to Captain	Year promoted to Captain	Median promotion time to Major
Before 1953	0	Before 1953	35	—	—
1953–4	12	1953–4	41	Before 1955	84
1955–6	10	1955–6	48	1955–6	83
1957–8	0	1957–8	48	1957–8	65
1959	1	1959	25	1959	39
1960	11	1960	27	1960	35
1961	13	1961	25	1961	23
1962	27	1962	25	1962	30
1963	39	1963	36 + [b]	1963	25 + [b]
1964	—	1964	—	1964	—
1965	—	1965	—	1965	—

Year promoted to Major	Median promotion time to Lt Col.	Year promoted to Lt Col.	Median promotion time to Colonel	Year promoted to Colonel	Median promotion time to Brigadier
Before 1962	48	—	—	—	—
1962	0	1962	19	1962	0
1963	25	1963	25	1963	—
1964	—	1964	—	1964	0
1965	—	1965	—	1965	—

Sources: Federation of Nigeria, *Official Gazettes* (1960–6), *British Army Lists* (1955–60).
Notes:
[a] Promotions after 1966 not included in reckonings of this table because of abnormal conditions created by Biafran secession and civil war.
[b] True medians likely to be greater than figures shown, as only half or slightly under half the officers in category had received promotion by 1966.

Talking of a similar early phase in the development of the Pakistan Army, General Ayub Kahn states that: 'there was considerable unrest among the officers caused by a spate of swift promotions from junior to senior ranks. This raised expectations to unwarranted heights. Every officer felt that unless ambition always exceeds the results obtained, since there is no warning to pause here. Nothing gives satisfaction and all this agitation is uninterruptedly maintained without appeasement. Above all since this race for an unattainable goal can give no other pleasure but that of the race itself, if it is one, once it is interrupted the participants are left empty-handed. At the same time the struggle grows more violent and painful, both from being less controlled and because competition is greater.' This is quoted at length because it provides more than one important clue as to how to interpret the crisis in the army and outside it in 1966 in sociological terms.

he was made C. in C. no one would believe he had done well in life. It was a curious phenomenon. Perfectly sensible people, Brigadiers and Generals, would go around bemoaning their lot. Each one of them was a Bonaparte, albeit an unhappy one...It was this sudden devaluation of the higher posts which produced fantastic ideas and ambitions in people.'[1]

Such an impression is certainly conveyed by the political actions of many of the Nigerian Army's officers. This also seems to bring more light on our earlier discussion[2] of how and why they were prepared both to cast aside the restraints of discipline in favour of initiative so lightly and to contemplate, like the Majors of January 1966, the junior officers in July 1966, Lt Colonel Banjo in August 1967 (and the inimitable Lt Arthur in Ghana in February 1967) actions of a most ruthless and irresponsible kind. Those British officers who served in the army between Independence and 1965, to whom the writer has been able to speak, certainly tend to confirm that many of their Nigerian confreres were restive. There was an overall feeling among the former that the Nigerians wanted jobs without the responsibilities going with them; that they were 'difficult to teach', especially after Independence; that promotions were too fast and instead of remaining 2nd lieutenants for a couple of years after Sandhurst to 'have the stuffing knocked out of them' like any British academy graduate, they quickly became company commanders; and as such were unwilling to accept advice. It is possible that this reflects some of the habitual gripes of retiring expatriates, though it is likely also to contain more than a grain of the truth.

If, as has been contended, the high rate of promotion and of other kinds of mobility tended to destabilise expectations, one would expect this *both* to undermine stable lines of authority and patterns of action in the officer corps as a whole; *and* to disorient those groups of officers who have had greater exposure to such processes more than the others. Which particular groups in the officer corps might one expect to be the most affected? There are two types of anomie-creating process that might seem to be at work.[3] First, the officers who have experienced the fastest promotion are *themselves* likely to develop unrealistic expectations, to be unable to discern the limits between the possible and the impossible. Secondly, the officers whose promotions have not been as rapid as those of their salient reference groups will probably experience feelings of frustration and relative deprivation.[4]

---

[1] Reflections on the Rawalpindi conspiracy by General Mohammed Ayub Khan in his book, *Friends not masters: a political autobiography* (London: Oxford University Press, 1967), pp. 37–8.

[2] In the preceding chapter, pp. 145–6.

[3] Both of these are implicit in Durkheim's discussion of anomie, although he does not seem to make a clear distinction between them, as can be seen in the long quotation from *Suicide* that we footnote above.

[4] This second aspect of Durkheim's theory of anomie is the one that has been developed most extensively in sociological literature, following upon R. K. Merton's celebrated essay on 'Social

The officer groups which had experienced the fastest sustained rates of promotion in the whole army were at the middle-ranking seniority levels. This can be seen most clearly if we divide the officer corps into seniority cohorts, which make some allowance for the fact that officers came into the officer corps after different lengths of training and with differing kinds of past experience and were allocated seniority for promotion accordingly.[1] In Table 32, we are able to show the effect of the changes in promotion rates given in Table 31 upon the median speed of promotion of each seniority group from lieutenant to captain, major and lieutenant colonel respectively.

It is interesting to note that the 1957–9 seniority years, from which the Majors leading the January 1966 coup were recruited, had enjoyed *faster* rates of promotion through to captain and major than any of the preceding cohorts in the officer corps.[2] They were thus the group most likely to suffer from inflated, unrealistic expectations concerning their military and political role. By the same token, however, they had little real basis for feeling relative deprivation in regard to their seniors, except perhaps in anticipation of future promotion. The fear of future deprivation arose because middle-ranking officers were only too well aware that – with the top positions in the army now indigenised – there was little prospect for further promotion, a fact that was made galling by the high expectations arising from their earlier advancement. Such anxieties made it difficult to settle an orderly pattern of ambition for military advancement; and made middle-ranking Eastern officers all the more likely to respond to the rumours circulating in 1965–6 that there would soon be compulsory retirements to make room for the promotion to the middle and upper ranks of junior Northern officers.[3]

It is less easy to make any positive statement about the sources of anomie among officers at other points of the structure. The junior officers of the cohorts from 1961 onwards were held at the rank of 2nd lieutenant longer than their predecessors; and faced the prospect of much slower promotion to captain and major respectively. Nevertheless, it is difficult to say how much

structure and anomie' in his *Social theory and social structure*. In this essay, however, the idea of anomie is not concretised in relation to reference groups (though for this see his essay on 'Reference group theory' in *ibid.*) but is developed in terms of the relation between cultural goals and the institutionalised means of achieving them.

[1] For the basis on which these allowances for seniority are made, in our assignation into seniority cohorts, see above, Table 23.

[2] Though in fact Chukuka, Ademoyega, Onwuategwu and Udeaja were among the members of the 1959 cohort whose promotions to major had not been gazetted by 1966. The first three of these were all Temporary Majors, however.

[3] See Chapters I and X. Another possible source of relative deprivation for individuals in the middle-level group would be if they were left behind when their peers received such rapid promotion. This did happen to one or two officers, including a couple of those in the January 1966 conspiracy; but the January 1966 group as a whole were distributed more or less evenly around the promotional medians for their peer groups.

TABLE 32. *Comparison of median speeds of promotion[a] of officer seniority cohorts[b]*

Year of cohort	Total no. of officers in cohorts	Total time (in months) from lieutenant to			January conspirators in cohorts	Other important military figures in cohort
		Captain	Major	Lt Col.		
Before 1951	4	35 (4)	110 (4)	157 (4)	—	Ironsi, Ademulegun, Shodeinde
1951–2	7	48 (7)	98 (7)	98 (7)	—	Maimalari, Ogundipe, Kuru Mohammed, Largema, Fajuyi, Adebayo
1953–4	6	45 (6)	71 (6)	85 (6)	—	Pam, Ojukwu, Kurobo, Effiong, Njoku
1955	8	48 (8)	66 (7)	92 (7)	—	Ejoor, Banjo, Gowon, Unegbe
1956	8	26 (8)	59 (8)	95[c] (5)	—	Ekpo, Akagha, Ogunewe, Okonweze
1957	8	22 (8)	61[c] (5)	—	Okafor	Hassan Katsina, Okoro
1958	9	19 (9)	46[c] (7)	—	Nzeogwu, Ifeajuna	Akahan
1959	27	24 (27)	57[d] (8)	—	Chukuka, Ademoyega, Anuforo, Onwuatuegwu	Adekunle, Muritala Mohammed, Mohammed Shuwa, Haruna, Obasanjo, Bissalla, Alao, Johnson
1960	19	25 (19)	—	—	Udeaja	—
1961	30	31 (16)	—	—	Gbulie, Nwobosi, Oji	Danjuma

Sources: as for Table 31.

Notes:

[a] Only the gazetted promotions up to July 1966 are included. Speeds of promotion are the median times of promotion in months from lieutenant to the rank shown. The actual numbers in each seniority cohort who reached each rank are indicated in brackets underneath the promotion figures.

[b] Basis for assignation into seniority cohorts as for Table 23 on page 134.

[c] Only the more senior members of cohorts had had their promotions. The median is based on the assumption that any officer in the cohort not yet promoted would be above the median when his promotion was eventually gazetted (though it is just conceivable that a late entrant into the cohort might fall below it).

[d] As less than half this cohort had had their promotion to major gazetted, the figure shown is the longest time any of the eight officers gazetted took to reach major from lieutenant. The majority of the officers in this cohort (including the January conspirators) had, however, been made acting majors and the gazetting of their appointments would have followed shortly. For this reason the figure given is probably more or less correct, and could even be too high.

the relative deprivation of the lieutenants contributed to the July 1966 revolt compared with other factors, such as the activities of the Northern NCOs or political pressures from outside the army.

By contrast with the majors, captains and lieutenants, the more senior officers of the army had had a more orderly and less frustrating introduction to military roles. They were all promoted relatively slowly through to major and (most of them) *only then* obtained accelerated advancement to lieutenant colonel. Nor were they especially likely to contrast their promotion to date (or further prospects thereof) with that of reference groups above them in the officer corps (if indeed they had them) in an unfavourable light; except perhaps the 1953–7 cohorts of lieutenant colonels, whose promotion had been relatively faster and some of whom had been restless enough to talk of army intervention late in 1964.

To conclude, military careers were too short and too broken up by rapid mobility to provide a binding thread by which aspirations and loyalties might be stabilised and directed to the maintenance of authority in the army. Indeed, mobility was so great as positively to destabilise aspirations, an explanation of the disorganisation of behaviour in the Nigerian military which is specially cogent because it allows us to predict differences between seniority groups on the basis of their respective promotion chances.

CHAPTER VIII

TRIBE AND REGION: THE ACTIVATION OF PRIMORDIAL[1] IDENTITIES

In this chapter we shall ask how cleavages based upon the primordial identities of Nigerian soldiers – their region and/or their tribe – penetrated the army. This raises issues at two levels of generality: first, how the growth of conflict in the military emerged from particular political disputes about the distribution of values between subnational groups; secondly, how such cleavages were related to cultural values and the social setting of Nigerian life.

Here we encounter a paradox. For if these questions had been asked before 1966, few people would have thought that ethnic or regional loyalties within the army would be strong enough to break through its boundaries, which were seemingly well protected by professional loyalties and the army's unity of structure. The focus of the Majors' hostility in the coup of January 1966 which set off the conflict was indeed a supposedly decadent *ancien régime*; their objective was to establish a puritanical order which would be free of the taint of corruption and tribalism; and the Ironsi regime they brought to power, though more conservative in approach, was in theory also committed to a seamless national unity in which ethnic and other primordial loyalties were to have no part. For both, the army was the exemplar for the nation to follow, being the only national institution in which tribalism and regionalism played no part. Yet once the army was in power its vaunted unity began to crumble, and by July 1966 its disciplinary system had been broken by the struggle for power between regional and ethnic groups. To complete the irony of the situation, the main actors in the events of January came to be accused of the very vices they preached against; and their protestations of

[1] The concept of 'primordialism' is borrowed from the essay by C. Geertz, 'The integrative revolution' in Geertz (ed.), *Old societies and new states*, although we make an attempt to refine it in certain respects in this chapter. We do not accept the implication that primordial ties are pre-modern or that they are necessarily any closer to the well-spring of emotion than other kinds of ties, though Geertz talks of the 'givens' of existence, 'gross actualities of blood, race, language, locality, religion or tradition' and compares 'these specific and familiar identifications' with the 'generalised commitment to an over-arching and somewhat alien civil order'. The reason we use the concept of primordialism here is that it calls attention to tribe, region and race, etc., as a single definable field of social investigation.

hostility towards tribalism came to be viewed as a Trojan horse which concealed the evil plans of Ibo domination.

Had ascriptive solidarities been salient within the army all along, being concealed from the casual outside observer only by a gloss of manifest military norms? Or had they been genuinely latent, to be activated and brought into focus only by the special matrix of organisational and political strains that prevailed in 1966?

In this chapter, we shall first ask how and to what extent social relations in the military were insulated from such parochial attachments, especially up to 1966. We shall then attempt to show how region as well as tribe could be a focus for primordial loyalties and cleavages. Thirdly, we shall examine the pattern of recruitment of the different ethnic and regional groups into the army. How did this depend on such factors as variation in achievement motivation between the ethnic groups, different opportunities for education or the recruitment policies of the colonial power and the independent Nigerian government? And to what extent did the concentration of different ethnic and regional groups at different points of the hierarchy intensify conflict by aggregating primordial with peer group cleavages? Finally, what was the real nature of ties of ethnicity and region in the military? Did they derive primarily from officers' links with their home communities, the distinct social values and deep-rooted feelings of identity connected with the latter? Or could one say that such identifications were brought into being primarily by the immediate definition of the situation, by the groping for categories and relationships in which to place the roles of self and other in unstructured new contexts, as might be suggested by the apparent fluidity of primordial loyalties, in changing social circumstances?

MILITARY BOUNDARIES AND THE WEB OF ETHNICITY

The army had always been entangled to some degree in the web of urban ethnicity. Officers and men have been able to participate in the associational life of their home communities, although posted away from them for most of their military life, through the immigrant 'stranger' communities which are a characteristic feature of Nigerian urban life.[1] It would not be unusual for an officer to attend meetings of his division or town union, to go to its feasts and to attend or contribute towards the funerals of its members – even though he would probably be less active in it than other members of the urban elite. This would also give community elders a degree of leverage over him, even

[1] See for example P. C. Lloyd *et al.* (eds.), *The city of Ibadan* (London: Cambridge University Press in association with the Institute of African Studies, University of Ibadan, 1967) and L. Plotnikov, *Strangers to the city: urban man in Jos, Nigeria* (Pittsburgh, Pa.: University of Pittsburgh Press, 1967).

if these might sometimes be his own NCOs. The writer recalls, for instance, a statement by a seasoned NCO at a divisional union feast, that an officer present whom he had known since when the officer was only a child, was 'a nice boy though a bit foolish'. Or the strong urging upon a Northern officer in 1966 by community elders and NCOs from his home town to get rid of his Ibo wife.

Nevertheless, we should be careful not to exaggerate the significance of ethnicity in creating solidary bonds among members of each of the tribes. One must not forget that other bases of differentiation within the army at times assumed as much importance as that between ethnic groups; for example, the cleavages between peer groups or the difference between the NCOs and cadets fresh from Sandhurst or Mons, which was a focus of some tension in the early 1960s. Even when one considers a group as apparently well defined in ethnic terms as the Ibo Majors of January 1966, one finds there were many other things than tribe which marked them out from their peers. For instance, their career experience tended to make them more articulate exponents of political and professional values than most other officers;[1] their aims were expressed in ideological terms which expressly condemned 'tribalism'; and they could in no sense be said to be acting for *explicit* ethnic group interest within the army in the way that had been characteristic of cliques in other Nigerian bureaucracies, such as the Railway Corporation or the University of Lagos.[2] There were, moreover, many Ibo officers – both within the rank of major and outside it – who were as socially and ideologically remote from Majors Nzeogwu and Ifeajuna and their associates as were any other group of officers.

One must also emphasise that the relevance of latent identities has varied from social context to social context; and that the military has its own integrative mechanisms at work in the mess and the barracks which differentiate military from non-military arenas of interaction so as to isolate purely military transactions from the outside influences of community and kin.

Military norms emphasise particularly strongly that discipline should not be contaminated by personal relations. One may take the following incident as an example to illustrate both the power of the norm and some of the fundamental difficulties in carrying it through. An officer is driving his car into the barracks after dark. The sentry fails to challenge him. Officer pitches into him: 'Why the bloody hell are you asleep, Corporal?' and so on. The NCO is of the same ethnic group as the officer and attempts to excuse himself in their native tongue by saying he recognised the car (rather difficult after dark). Officer yells 'shurrup!' and tells him to speak in English.

[1] See Chapter I above.
[2] See Chapter IX below.

One could not take it for granted that all officers would be equally capable of resisting such appeals. But many of them would be sensitive enough to avoid social situations where they could be made; or in which others might be able to raise the accusation of 'tribalism' against them. There are officers who have gone to great lengths to get out of postings which would have put them in close proximity to others from their home area – like one acquaintance of the writer who refused to accept a posting as second in command to a unit commander of his own tribe – because they have feared that this might lay them open to unwelcome accusations later.

Prescribed sociability and the bonds between class-mates and peers emphasise the brotherhood of all officers regardless of origin. When asked by an outsider what region or tribe they come from, officers will often dismiss the question, saying 'I am Nigerian', a reply that was still heard even after the events of 1966. The ideology of the nation spilled over, indeed, from prescribed contexts to those of everday life. There was a high rate of ethnic/regional exogamy in the officer corps, whether because of the ideology of Nigerianism or the frequency of postings outside home areas. Quite a number of Northern officers, for instance, have or had Ibo wives, including one of the present Military Governors, a divisional commander in the civil war and one of the senior Northerners killed in the January 1966 coup.

THE APPEALS OF REGION

Region as well as tribe was an important axis of cleavage in the army in 1966. Yet if one examines regional ties closely, it is difficult to see why they should have had any compelling force, since they were not directly linked like ethnicity to the day-to-day interaction of kin and community. All the regions except the West were ethnically and culturally heterogeneous, and so were the officers and men recruited from them. Even the apparent ethnic homogeneity of the West was deceptive, the different areas and towns of Yorubaland being set in conflict against each other under both civilian and military regimes.

What then was the main source of regional identity? How did narrower identifications based on tribe and community become linked to the cause of region? The most convenient way of approaching this is to examine the Northern officers: a group on whom we have some data, and who were seemingly mobilised consistently on regional lines in the July 1966 coup.

At first glance, the Northerners seem very diverse. It is possible to sub-divide them into four broad categories. First, there are those who originate from the Moslem Emirates of the 'dry' north. The distinctive characteristics of these are their shared culture and religion and their highly centralised political organisation – rather than their kinship structure or community organisation – so that the appellation 'tribe' seems still less appropriate to them than to other Nigerian groups. The Emirates subdivide on the basis of language and history into the Hausa–Fulani kingdoms in the far centre-north and north-west, and the Kanuri in the far north-east. Bornu (of which the Kanuri are the main inhabitants) and Sokoto have traditionally been among the heaviest areas of recruitment of Other Ranks since colonial days. The three most senior Northerners in the officer corps (Maimalari, Kuru Mohammed and Largema) were all Kanuris.

Secondly, there are the soldiers from the formerly pagan areas, which were conquered and to a greater or lesser extent culturally assimilated by the Emirates, mostly by the Hausa–Fulani. These we can call the Hausa–Fulani diaspora peoples. The main areas involved are in a belt to the south of the 'dry' north, ranging in an arc from Niger Province in the west, through southern Zaria to Bauchi and Adamawa in the east. These areas have a social structure of many culturally and linguistically diverse tribal groups on which a superstructure of centralised political institutions, Hausa as a lingua franca, and the Moslem religion, has been imposed. Mission schools penetrated these areas, however – unlike the 'core' Emirates – and many of the Northern diaspora officers (Major General Gowon for instance) were educated in them.

Thirdly, there are the soldiers of the 'Middle Belt' proper,[1] Benue and Plateau Provinces and the west of Kabba Province – all in the centre-south areas of the North. Again, there are variations in social and political organisation, from the large but acephalous Tiv to the many small tribes of the Plateau and to the more pyramidal kingdoms of the Igala, the Idoma and the Igbirra. What this area has in common is that assimilation with the Emirates was resisted (though some areas were temporarily under Emirate political control) and the autochthonous substructure of social, cultural and political institutions were preserved better. The most important external influence was that of the Christian missions, and more of the inhabitants acquired a Western education than in the other areas of the North (except the Yoruba regions). Some of these tribes – especially the Tiv and the Idoma – were areas of especially heavy recruitment of Other Ranks during the colonial period. This seems also to have encouraged officer recruitment,[2] especially among the Idoma, who were the third or fourth best represented ethnic group in the entire officer corps (behind the Ibo, the Yoruba and possibly the Hausa–Fulani).

Finally, there are the Northern Yorubas from Kabba and Ilorin Provinces in the south-westerly part of the North. These have strong cultural similarities and social ties with the Yorubas of the West, but historical links with the

---

[1] The political definition of the Middle Belt, used by the various political parties which advocated a political division of the North, usually included much of the Hausa–Fulani diaspora and Yoruba areas of the North, however, as well.

[2] See the account of military families and career motivations in Chapter IV above.

North dating from the Hausa–Fulani conquest of Ilorin in the nineteenth century. This was not a traditional area of recruitment for troops, though a few Northern Yorubas came into the officer corps as a result of the recruitment drive in the Northern secondary schools (in which they were very well represented) in the early 1960s.

Fortunately it has been possible to determine with a reasonable degree of confidence the origins of a majority of the Northern officers at January 1966, by combined use of (*a*) linguistic analysis of officer names,[1] (*b*) data on school origins, (*c*) biographical information, especially on the more senior officers and (*d*) personal acquaintance of the writer and other informed persons with officers. Nevertheless, there is a margin of error, both from the difficulty of identifying the boundaries of the four main areas described above with any precision; and from biases arising from the linguistic analysis of names. The latter arise from the fact that officers with *purely* Moslem or Hausa names could in principle have originated from any of our four areas. The majority of them are likely to have come from the 'dry' North Emirates and this will be our assumption – except in those cases where school origin, biographical data or personal acquaintance, etc., indicate otherwise. There is, therefore, a slight bias in our figures in favour of the Emirates and against the other areas, though the figures are almost wholly accurate for the more senior officers.

Another problem that arises is that Northern Yorubas are for all practicable purposes indistinguishable from their Western counterparts on a linguistic analysis of names. Eleven Yoruba officers can be positively identified as having come from Kabba and Ilorin, but it is thought that about twice this number of Yoruba combat officers originated from the North. For the moment, therefore, we exclude the Northern Yorubas, though it is worth bearing in mind that two or three Northern Yorubas took part in the July 1966 coup and that Lt Colonel Adekunle, the commander of the 3rd Division in the Nigerian civil war, is also from this area.

In spite of the great diversity of the Northerners, therefore, the data seem – on the surface at least – to indicate that the centre of gravity of the Northern officers was in the Emirates of the far North, together with the areas in the sphere of their political and cultural influence in the areas of Hausa–Fulani penetration. For even if one added in the numerical maximum of Northern Yorubas and made some allowance for an over-estimate of those recruited from the far North, well over half the Northerners in the officer corps would be made up of men from the Emirates together with their diaspora. Neverthe-

---

[1] For this the writer enrolled the assistance of two linguists specialising in Nigerian languages, who gave their informed guesses of the origins of the list of officer names; of four Nigerian students of different ethnic origins; and of two political scientists with Nigerian experience both of whom have a wide circle of acquaintances in the army, one among the Northerners and the other among the southerners.

less, the *percentage* of officers recruited from the Emirate areas is less than the proportion of these areas in the population of the North, reflecting the great deficiency in schooling in these areas more than anything else. Yet it is important to note that the far North and diaspora areas are better represented in the officer corps than in most other elite groups, both at national level and in the North itself (except, of course, in the Northern political class). The great majority of Ahmadu Bello University's intake from the Northern secondary schools, in comparison, has been from the Yoruba areas plus the Middle Belt (i.e. very largely from Ilorin, Kabba, Benue and Plateau Provinces).

TABLE 33. *Cultural origins of Northern combat officers*

	Percentage distribution of officers from each seniority cohort				
Cohort of seniority	Far North	Hausa–Fulani diaspora	Middle Belt	Total N =	*Plus* Northern Yorubas (numbers)
Before 1959	57	14	29	7	—
1959–61	37	37	26	19	5 to 6
1962–4	37	32	29	90	6 to 20
All cohorts	40	32	28	116	11 to 26
Per cent distribution of groups in Northern population (excluding Yoruba areas)	54	27	19	25·4 mn	1·9 mn

Source: Federation of Nigeria, *Official Gazettes*, plus analysis of names, as above.

The Hausa language, moreover, has become something of a lingua franca among Northern officers and men, from whatever part of the North they come, although there are a few Middle Belt officers who are still unable to communicate with their men in Hausa and – by contrast – a fair proportion of the southerners who are also Hausa-speakers.[1]

On the other hand, one could exaggerate the coherence of the Emirate/ diaspora group. One cannot *assume* a complete identity of interest between the Kanuri and the Hausa–Fulani in the far North, in spite of their cultural and organisational similarities – and, indeed, Bornu was one of the early centres of opposition to the NPC party in the North. Similarly, a large

---

[1] Major Nzeogwu, the leader of the January coup, indeed, was a fluent Hausa speaker (though an Ibo, he had been brought up in the North) and was popular with his Northern NCOs for this, among other reasons.

proportion of the diaspora officers are Christians, as a result of mission education, and did not always identify strongly with the Moslems of the Emirate North.

If one looks back at the figures for participation in the July 1966 coup, as presented in Table 13, it can be seen that both the Emirates and the diaspora were better represented among the active conspirators (or at least among those we were able to identify) than were the Middle Belt officers or the Northern Yorubas. Nevertheless, a substantial proportion of officers of Middle Belt origin took part; and there were many from the far North who, as far as we know, did not. It seems, therefore, that something else is required other than the cultural and political 'pull' of the Emirates to help account for the emergence of common interests and perspectives among the Northerners in 1966.

TABLE 34. *School origins of Northern combat officers*[a]

Seniority	Government College, Zaria Government College, Keffi	Other secondary schools		Total N =
		origins known[c]	not known	
To 1959	100	0	0	7
1959–61	38	29	33	21
1962–4	8	35	38	93

Per cent distribution of entrants from schools[b] in seniority cohorts

Sources: Federation of Nigeria, *Official Gazettes*, plus school lists for one or two secondary schools, including Government Colleges Zaria, Keffi, Kaduna, P.S.S. Okene and *The Wish Stream: Journal of the Royal Military Academy, Sandhurst*. Some help with school origins was also provided by Norman Miners.

Notes:

[a] Includes Yorubas known for definite to be of Northern origin (unlike Table 33).

[b] Excludes ex-NCOs, therefore.

[c] Including officers traced to sixteen different Northern secondary schools.

One line of enquiry is to look at the school origins of the Northern officers, on the theory that friendships formed at school might have provided some basis for common identification later. It is interesting to note that all the seven most senior Northern officers in the army went to one or other of the North's two leading secondary schools at the same time, six to Government College, Zaria and one to Government College, Keffi. But speculations as to the political importance of friendships formed at school do not lead anywhere, as four of the seven were killed in the January 1966 coup and the other three

(Gowon, Hassan Katsina and Akahan) were left on the sidelines in the July 1966 coup by the more junior Northern officers. Further down the seniority listings there is a diversification of school origins, as can be seen in Table 34, with only the Nigerian Military School (a dozen or more officers in the 1959–64 seniority cohorts), Government College, Keffi (eight officers), Government College, Zaria (seven officers) and the Niger Provincial Secondary School, Bida (seven officers) being remotely close to producing enough officer entrants for any kind of clique formation.

School origins however do allow us to speculate that regional identification and patterns of social mobility may have been related. For it is clear that there was a shift in recruitment from the North's one or two elite secondary schools towards a wider base of schools of lower prestige located all over the region, most of them without (at that time) sixth forms for preparation for university entrance, such as the Benue Provincial Secondary School, Katsina Ala, the Provincial Secondary School, Katsina, Niger Provincial Secondary School, Bida and the Provincial Secondary School, Sokoto. This corresponds in some degree to a shift in the area of recruitment from Bornu and the Middle Belt (both the heaviest areas of recruitment of Other Ranks in the army) towards the Hausa–Fulani areas[1] and diaspora areas, like Niger Province, southern Zaria and Bauchi; though it also brought in large numbers of officers at the less well-known schools of the Middle Belt. This was the result of three things. First, the opening up of a Northern university, Ahmadu Bello University, at Zaria, which drained off many of the graduates of elite secondary schools. Secondly, the operation of the officer recruitment quota after 1961 in favour of the North, opening up a big demand for officers of Northern origin; and the subsequent recruitment drive by Northern politicians, like the Sardauna of Sokoto. And thirdly, the lowering of the educational qualifications for entry.[2]

The general effect was to create a group of Northern officers who were rather deficient in educational qualifications compared with their peers and who owed their position in the officer corps largely to the operation of a regional quota in their favour. They were, moreover, somewhat provincial in social background and likely to be sensitive about their social prestige compared with other officers.[3] This could explain why it was that Northern officers felt so much threatened by Ibo promotions under the Ironsi regime in 1966; and by that regime's adoption of various measures that hinted that

---

[1] The prosperous Hausa–Fulani farming areas (e.g. Kano, Katsina, Northern Zaria) had not been good recruiting areas, though Sokoto and other poorer areas had. A number of the Northern officers pulled in by the quota were from Sokoto.

[2] For details of the quota system and the lowering of qualifications, see Chapter X below.

[3] Compare with Chapter IV above, where it is argued that similar status problems crop up for the officer corps *as a whole* vis-a-vis civilian elite groups.

the regional quota system and similar restrictions of a particularist nature operating under the civilian regime would come under review.[1]

Nonetheless, it cannot be said that this produced a stable focus of identification with the North, as it depended very much on the immediate socio-political context in which occupation aspirations and anxieties were placed. Shortly after the July coup, for example, many diaspora and Middle Belt soldiers who had earlier supported the secession of the North realigned their position. And, as we shall see,[2] they successfully brought pressure to bear on the Northern delegation at the September 1966 constitutional talks to alter its proposals from a loose confederation including an integrated North to a federation in which the North – like other regions – would be subdivided into new regions or states. Even if, to conclude, one can see a number of factors tending to create bonds among the Northerners over and above their social and political diversity, these bonds were still very elusive and contextual in character.

PRIMORDIALISM AND PEER GROUPS

What was the relation of ethnic and regional identities to other sources of cleavage? To what extent were they reinforced by other sources of differentiation? To answer this we must first look at changes in recruitment to the army and how these distributed the various sub-national groups in the hierarchy. Table 35 shows the numbers of officers of different ethnic/regional categories being commissioned into the officer corps with combat commission, both from the ranks and through direct entry from school to cadet courses at Sandhurst, Mons and the like. Unfortunately, it is impossible to build up a complete picture of both ethnic and regional origins and the best that can be done is to distinguish four groups. First, the Ibos, most of whom were from the Eastern Region, but with a substantial minority from the Mid-West; secondly, officers of Eastern and Mid-Western origin from tribes other than the Ibo (Edo, Ijaw, Efik, and so on); thirdly, the Yorubas, mostly from the West, but some from the North; and finally, the Northern officers.

Before Independence there were two main sources of recruitment. First – and going back the farthest[3] – the former NCOs. These had almost all been specialists – education officers, clerks, technicians – with a degree of formal education, rather than General Duties NCOs from the infantry. They were

[1] For example, Decree no. 34 and its unification of the administrative services; or the dismissal of air force cadets in April 1966, many of whom were removed because of their lack of formal educational qualifications. For a fuller discussion, see Chapter XI below.
[2] In Chapter XIII below.
[3] The first four officers commissioned were ex-NCOs, Bassey in 1944, Ironsi and Ademulegun in 1949 and Shodeinde in 1950.

all, therefore, from the south, initially mostly Yorubas but later on predominantly Ibos.

TABLE 35. *Numbers of officers of tribal/regional groups commissioned
1944–65 (combat officers only)*

Year of commission	Entry from the ranks (ex-NCOs)				School entry through cadet courses			
	Ibo	E/MW	Yoruba	North	Ibo	E/MW	Yoruba	North
Before 1956	3	1	6	0	0	1	0	5
1956–7	2	2	0	0	7	1	1	1
1958–9	9	2	0	0	6	0	3	1
1960–1	3	2	4	2	19	5	9	17
1962–3	1	1	4	3	34	12	25	55
1964–5	1	2	0	2	20	18	16	36

Sources: as for Tables 33 and 34. Table includes, however, all officers commissioned, including those
dying, cashiered or transferred to the air force, up to 1966.

Secondly, from 1953 onwards[1] increasing numbers of officers were commissioned from Sandhurst, all going directly into army training from secondary school. Most of these early recruits were drawn into the army through
contacts with one or two elite secondary schools, at which the army established
officer cadet units, offered scholarships and had recruiting campaigns. The
first school with which links were established was Government College,
Zaria, presumably because of its proximity to the training depot at Zaria.[2]
This school produced five of the six Sandhurst graduates commissioned
between 1953 and 1955, though recruitment from it fell off in the late 1950s,
most likely because of the opening up of more attractive opportunities in the
Northernisation of the regional public services and the opening of Ahmadu
Bello University. Meanwhile, army contacts were established with a number
of other secondary schools, including Government College, Keffi (also in the
North), Government College, Ughelli (in the Mid-West) and Government
College, Umuahia (in the East).

The two latter schools produced eight of the cadets commissioned between
1955 and 1959, six of them Ibos,[3] which was the main reason for the high
proportion of Ibos commissioned from Sandhurst between 1956 and 1959.
This coincided with an increase in the numbers of Ibos coming up from the
ranks, with the result that there was a concentration of Ibos in the middle

[1] When the first two officers were commissioned from Sandhurst – Maimalari and another
Northerner who was later cashiered.
[2] Though we could also conjecture that British colonial policy may have favoured recruitment of
Northerners.
[3] The Government Colleges at Zaria, Ughelli and Umuahia between them produced fifteen of the
twenty-six officers commissioned from Sandhurst between 1953 and 1959.

levels of the army hierarchy when indigenisation of the officer corps was complete in 1965.

One could suggest that this upsurge of Ibos into the officer corps resulted both from the Ibos' high aspirations for achievement in modern bureaucratic occupational settings;[1] and from the fact that due to the differential impact of modernisation, educated Ibo elites arrived on the scene later than the Yorubas and were driven to seek advancement in occupations like the army where the latter were not already entrenched.[2] But there is no conclusive way of verifying these contentions, especially as the numbers involved were small enough for this result to have been produced by purely accidental factors: for example, the particular secondary schools with which the army established contact in the 1950s.[3] The concentration of the Ibos as NCOs in trades and technical branches of the army from which they could be promoted is another mobility factor one would like to know more about.

The transfer of control over the armed forces to the Nigerian authorities in 1958 had two main effects on the pattern of recruitment. First, the expansion and diversification of recruitment from the secondary schools, away from the emphasis on one or two specially chosen schools. The consequences of this in the south were similar to those already discussed in the North, though the qualifications of entrants were on the whole higher (because of the wide educational base in the south) and the secondary schools from which they were recruited therefore less marginal.

Secondly, for the first time a conscious effort was made to balance the regional origins of officer recruits[4] – this being largely the result of the alarm of the Northern politicians in the Federal government at the small proportion of Northerners in the officer corps[5] – as in other Federal bureaucracies to which similar remedies were applied. Initially, from 1958 onwards, the policy was to give preference to Northerners for officer selection, where their qualifications were roughly equal to those of southern applicants. The results of this are seen in the increased numbers of Northerners commissioned in 1960 and 1961. But even this was not enough, and in 1961 Alhaji Ribadu,

---

[1] See the comparison of an achievement among Ibo, Yoruba and Hausa secondary school boys in R. LeVine, *Dreams and deeds* (Chicago: University of Chicago Press, 1966) and the discussion of the reasons for his finding that achievement was highest among the former.

[2] The Yorubas had the earliest and most intense contact with the West through trade, missions, education and conquest. For the implications of this in the development of Nigerian nationalism, see J. S. Coleman, *Nigeria: background to nationalism* (Berkeley, Calif.: University of California Press, 1958).

[3] Though it did establish contacts into schools in other areas (e.g. Government College, Ibadan or Kings' College, Lagos), from which the response in terms of recruitment was less enthusiastic than in Ibo areas.

[4] And also of Other Ranks – the latter, however, implied greater recruitment from the south – though mostly into 'trades' rather than the General Duties.

[5] For this and details of other Northernisation measures, see Chapter III above.

the Minister of Defence, introduced a quota and instructed that entry qualifications be reduced for Northerners (including sons of NCOs at the Nigerian Military School, Zaria, who now got in with two or three 'O levels'). The effect of this was a great increase in the Northerners commissioned from 1962 onwards.[1]

The sum effect was that there were three distinct layers in the officer corps. These can be picked out from Tables 36 and 37 which show the effects of the entry pattern on the ethnic/regional composition of both seniority cohorts and rank levels in the officer corps. First, one can identify a regionally mixed group at the top, mostly but not all ex-NCOs. Secondly, there was a middle layer of lieutenant colonels and majors recruited dominantly from the Ibos, and split more or less evenly between Sandhurst graduates and ex-NCOs. Thirdly, there was a lower layer, at the level of captain and below, dominated (especially at the very bottom) by the North and extremely heterogeneous both in ethnic origins and in training. Below the officers, in addition, some sixty to sixty-five per cent of the NCOs were Northern. The Northerners, moreover, were concentrated in the General Duties branches, where they constituted seventy-five per cent or so of the infantry, whereas the southerners were largely in the non-combatant branches.

TABLE 36. *Regional/ethnic origins of officer seniority cohorts*

Seniority cohort	(Per cent distribution of regional/ethnic groups in cohorts) Regional/ethnic origins				Total N =
	Ibo	E/MW	Yoruba	North	
Before 1952	14	14	57	14	7
1952–4	30	30	10	30	10
1955–6	63	19	13	6	16
1957–8	65	12	12	12	17
1959–60	34	15	27	24	41
1961–2	32	11	17	41	76
1963–4	20	16	20	44	163

Sources: as for Tables 33 to 35.

May one therefore suggest that it was the *combination* of ethnic and regional cleavages with those deriving from the rank and peer group structure that was important, on the lines of a hypothesis familiar in sociology[2] that cleavages

[1] The quotas were fifty per cent North and twenty-five per cent each, East and West. These were first applied on the group finishing preliminary training at the Nigerian Military Training College in mid-1961, so that the impact was felt in the officers commissioned from 1962 onwards. Our figures show slightly under half being commissioned from the North, partly because of the non-inclusion of the Northern Yorubas, partly because of the carry-over into 1962 and 1963 of commissionings of academy-trained officers, recruited before the quota was put into effect.

[2] For elaboration of the concepts of consistent and cross-cutting ties and the way in which such ties amplify and reduce social conflict respectively, see Simmel, *Conflict and the web of group affiliations,*

that are consistent with one another, rather than cross-cutting, tend to be additive and lead to the polarisation and intensification of conflict? Whether or not one accepts the assumption that the cleavages concerned are in fact additive, this attractive hypothesis must be treated with some caution.[1] The fit between ethnic/regional and generational boundaries is by no means as impressive as it might be. The only two levels with an appreciable degree of homogeneity are the middle-ranking officers and the NCOs; yet these are not positioned at the immediately contiguous levels of the hierarchy, where levels of inter-rank tension might be expected to be the highest. The imperfection in fit between the two types of cleavage might, on the contrary, be said to be a major factor in the fragmentation of the two coups of 1966. This is evidenced in the failure of the Majors to recruit from among their non-Ibo peers or to elicit genuine support from any of their Ibo seniors. Similarly, military status relations barred all but a few senior Northern officers from direct and overt participation in July; and this contributed to the breakdown in discipline which followed the coup.

TABLE 37. *Regional/ethnic origins of officers at different rank levels*

| | (Per cent distribution per rank level) | | | | |
| | Regional/ethnic origins | | | | Total |
Rank	Ibo	E/MW	Yoruba	North	N =
Colonel and above	14	0	57	29	7
Lt Colonel	36	29	14	21	14
Major	66	6	22	6	32
Captain	29	15	23	33	52
Lieutenant	34	10	17	38	58
2nd Lieutenant	25	14	19	42	167

Sources: as for Tables 33 to 35.

Nevertheless, it is probably true that the cumulation of differences in rank and generation with ethnic/regional differentiation sharpened the processes of discord without necessarily being their main source. This was especially true, as we pointed out in Chapter II above, after the elimination of most of the Northern and Western officers at the top in the January 1966 coup. After this, it will be recalled, Ibo officers advanced because of their seniority, from

L. Coser, *The functions of social conflict* (New York: The Free Press, 1956) and Coleman, *Community conflict.*

[1] It is interesting that the Belgians deliberately diversified recruitment of the Force Publique in the Congo along ethnic/regional lines, and attempted also to diversify the origins of all its military units. Nevertheless, the Congolese Army fragmented on regional lines after the 1960 mutiny. The latter, of course, had resulted from the fact that all officers were white and the ranks black. See C. Young, *Politics in the Congo* (Princeton, N.J.: Princeton University Press, 1965).

the middle ranks at lieutenant colonel and major, to positions of greater prominence in both the upper ranks and the main command posts. They thus became a much more conspicuous target for the hostility and suspicion of the junior officers and Other Ranks of other ethnic/regional origins.

PROMOTIONS: REALITY AND THE PERCEPTION OF BIAS

One possible source of tension between sub-national groups that requires examination at this point is the operation of the promotional system. Is there any evidence of systematic discrimination in favour of any particular group? In particular, did the Northerners benefit from accelerated promotion under the politicians, as a result of the ascendancy of the NPC and the Northern Ministers of Defence? Did the Ibos suffer from discrimination?[1]

Up to the rank of captain, it is clear that both in theory and in practice (judged by close scrutiny of the promotions up to that level) promotion was governed almost entirely by seniority rules, with the exception that officers were not advanced if they failed promotion exams or if they had black marks against them for disciplinary or efficiency reasons. Seniority also weighed heavily in promotion to major, though there was more scope for 'merit' or other considerations. An element of flexibility was more in evidence in the promotions to lieutenant colonel and above – although seniority principles still were powerful.[2]

The comparison is narrowed, therefore, to promotions to the rank of major and above. In theory, one might compare the advancement of the different sub-national groups in each seniority cohort, to see how it compares with that of their peers. In practice, however, a systematic comparison is not possible[3] (though the reader may consult lists of officers in the 1942 to 1961 cohorts in Appendix 1). One can, however, make one or two impressionistic statements on the subject.

To start with, there is little evidence of any systematic discrimination

---

[1] These two questions are in some measure independent of each other. Preferential treatment for Northerners in the middle of the hierarchy, for instance, would not necessarily have carried the implication of slower promotions for the Ibos, because the former were so few in number at this level.

[2] They accounted, for instance, for the promotion of Ironsi to GOC in 1965 against two or three rivals of slightly lesser seniority. See Chapter X below.

[3] First, the numbers in the seniority groups whose members got as far as major are small, and then the fact that there was a very high concentration of particular ethnic/regional categories in certain of the peer groups, makes it difficult to compare them with other groups (of whom there were in some cases only one or no representatives in the relevant cohort). Thirdly, the seniority allowances for ex-NCOs on the one hand and the Sandhurst graduates or graduates of short-service cadet courses on the other, differ and also have changed relative to each other from time to time. One could deal with this by standardising the officers by type of training for purposes of comparison. But this would reduce still further the number of cases from which one can make relevant comparison.

against the Ibos as a group. A number of the Ibo ex-NCOs were promoted rather slowly, but in this they were no different from other ex-NCOs. The promotions of Ibo Sandhurst graduates were usually about average, with some falling behind and others (notably Majors Anuforo and Obienu) who were definitely the 'fliers' of their Sandhurst years.

Moreover, it does not seem as if the Northerners received favoured treatment in promotions, except perhaps right at the very top. Two of the three most senior Northern officers in the army (Maimalari and Kuru Mohammed) did better than others at their seniority level, though this may be because they were the only Sandhurst graduates of their generation.[1] All of the three Northern officers commissioned between 1955 and 1959 (Pam, Gowon and Hassan Katsina) also did marginally better than their Sandhurst course-mates,[2] though the numbers are too small to attribute much significance to this fact. Below them, however, the Northerners, as far as one can tell, did no better and no worse than their peers and course-mates.

The facts about promotion certainly do not indicate any dramatic ethnic/regional bias. But they were uncertain enough for *perceptions* of bias to creep in. Such suspicions were encouraged by close proximity to peers with whom constant comparisons were made; and officers who fell behind their mates in promotion were prone to seek out insidious machinations by other groups and individuals as explanation for their failure. In addition, the high rates of promotion prevailing after Independence both raised aspirations and (because of frequent changes in seniority rules) created uncertain expectations as to the normal sequence of promotion. Hence, for example, the suspicions of the January 1966 conspirators that they had suffered or would suffer discrimination in promotion on grounds of their ethnic origin; and their fear and belief that they would eventually be forced out of the army to make room for Northerners beneath them who had been brought into the officer corps through the quota system. Hence also, perhaps, the rather intense reaction of Northern officers to the large numbers of Ibos promoted in April and May 1966, although a little reflection might have convinced them that this was to be expected on normal seniority principles alone.

PRIMORDIAL IMAGES OF SELF AND OTHERS

All of the above still tends to leave one in a state of puzzlement about tribe and region as a basis of common identification and of differentiation. What exactly was it about these two things that could lead to cleavage? For both

---

[1] And thus would have benefited from changes in seniority allowance in favour of Sandhurst men. It would, of course, be impossible to tell whether the alteration in seniority rules was deliberately adopted to favour Northerners, though Ibos could well have suspected this.

[2] Though, on the other hand, Pam did *worse* than his non-Sandhurst peers.

tribe and region, from the account given above, would appear somewhat threadbare as bases of self-identity, and officers seemed to spend much of their time denying such identities and, indeed, avoiding social situations where they could be pinned on them.

A clue is presented if we observe that the conflict-orientations focused around promotions or the distribution of the different sub-national groups in the hierarchy arise in large measure out of perception of bias in favour of *others* in promotion or the threatening position of *others* at higher levels of the command structure.

It is useful at this point to provide a little conceptual clarification about what one means when one talks of 'tribalism' or 'regionalism' in the African context. It is necessary to distinguish – for analytical purposes at least – between the assertion of common identity based on ties of race, blood, religion, region and the like, on the one hand, and the articulation of a posture – be it one of aggression or alliance – towards other groups on *their* supposedly shared characteristics, whether of race, tribe, religion, area or some other index, on the other. One might talk of a primordialism of identity for the former and of a primordialism of projection for the latter.[1]

Self-images, to be sure, are closely linked to others' images of oneself; and collective identities to the stereotypes used by other social groups and individuals to order their perceptions and regulate their interaction in encounters with strangers.[2] Therefore the two aspects of primordialism of which we speak are often so closely linked that it becomes all too easy to overlook the fact that there is a distinction.

In respect of the military, it can be argued that much of the tension that built up can be attributed to the development over time of projective tribal and regional antagonisms in the army. Under civilian rule, during the period immediately prior to 1966, resonances of conflict of this nature were roused in the military by the political struggle outside it. The accusations and counter-accusations of 'tribalism' in the Railway Corporation and the Universities of Ibadan and Lagos aroused a high degree of interest among all educated elites, especially those in public bureaucracies, such as the army. By 1965, it is clear that at least a few army officers were casting apprehensive eyes at their colleagues: for example, the senior officer who was attempting at this time to shift a number of Ibo officers away from his command, because he believed that they 'packed their own' into posts under them. Undertones of anti-Ibo

[1] The analysis in Geertz, 'The integrative revolution', in *Old societies and new states*, is primarily of the primordialism of identity.

[2] There is on this a long tradition in sociological analysis, going back to sociologists such as Cooley, G. H. Mead, W. I. Thomas, etc. For use of this kind of approach to account explicitly for inter-ethnic stereotyping in an African setting, see J. C. Mitchell, *The Kalela dance* (Manchester: Manchester University Press for Rhodes–Livingstone Institute, 1956).

feeling are said to have gone back to the British officers, a number of whom were prejudiced against them and in favour of the North. Yet before 1966 this was, it is believed, no more than an undercurrent of feeling, not very strong among the officers, not shared by all of them and counteracted by the brotherhood sentiment.

From the Majors' coup onwards, however, a heavily charged symbolic environment developed. Both sides of the conflict came to believe that the others were plotting against them, planning to restrict their promotions, to destroy them, drawing up lists of enemies to be eliminated and the like. Both developed myths around their own 'invulnerable' heroes. And both reinterpreted the struggle for power in the light of generalised beliefs defining it in terms of sin and retribution; guilt was extended by association to *all* of the members of the relevant ethnic/regional groups, all Ibos being held responsible for the January coup and all Northerners for the July killings in the army and the May and September–October massacres outside it. To be sure, there were a number of group interests at stake. But it is preferable to conceptualise the situation as a complex interaction between these differences in group interest; the particular social contexts in which they were brought forth; the acts or statements of hostility made against other groups; the assertions of group identity called forth by the hostility of others; and the symbolic meanings given to these alignments and events by all of the participants.

In this charged situation, even the primordialism of group identity was extremely fluid in character. This is evident in the way that identities developed, increased in salience and dissolved in response to changing definitions of the situation.[1] Major General Ironsi, for instance, might well have avoided the hostility of the Middle Belt officers and men, had he been prepared to talk with political intermediaries from that area and to create a Middle Belt Region, as will be argued in Chapter XI. The soldiers from this area thus temporarily threw in their lot with the North; but as soon as the supposed Ibo threat was removed by the July coup, they put their weight behind the dismemberment of the region again.

As an initial formulation, it might be argued that tribal or regional affiliations are sharpened when members of the group concerned are made the focus of hostility *as such*. But even this would seem over simple. The Ibo officers – who had undergone the most hostile attacks on their ethnic identity of any group in 1966 – still preferred to assert their regional rather than ethnic origin.

[1] This is the main reason for the reservations expressed in the footnote on the concept of primordialism at the beginning of this chapter (see p. 177). Geertz seems ambivalent on this point. For on the one hand he argues that primordial attachments have 'an ineffable and at times overpowering coerciveness in and of themselves' flowing '*more from a sense of natural...affinity than from social interaction*', and on the other hand he agrees that political modernisation 'tends initially not to quiet such sentiments but to quicken them'. See Geertz, 'The integrative revolution'.

Lt Colonel Ojukwu specifically denied on a number of occasions that he saw himself as in any sense an Ibo leader, and claimed – overtly at least – that he withdrew the Eastern Region from the Federation in the interest of the whole region, not just that of the Ibos in it. This was partly a matter of persuasive definition, tied to the political strategy of obtaining the support of the non-Ibo oil-bearing areas of the East. And partly, one might suggest, because fragmentation on regional lines was easier to legitimise in ways that were consonant with the secular nationalism prevailing in the officer corps' political ideas.[1] Lt Colonel Ejoor, the Military Governor of the ethnically heterogeneous Mid-West,[2] also came to think in regional rather than ethnic terms, for similar reasons.

On the other hand, other groups facing a different situation were led to emphasise common ethnicity over region. At various points in 1966–7 Colonel Adebayo, the Military Governor of the Western Region, explicitly adopted the language of tribal self-interest, as in his acclamation of Awolowo as 'Leader of the Yorubas', just after the July 1966 coup. There was a balance of advantage in adopting such a posture, both because the West was ethnically homogeneous and because it had territorial ambitions in other regions with Yoruba minority populations. Another example is the dilemma of the Mid-West Ibos who found refuge in their region after the July 1966 coup, as to whether they should stay neutral in the civil war in July 1967 or make common cause with their Ibo confreres in the East.

Finally, the response of other groups – and especially the smaller 'minorities' tribes of the North, Mid-West and East – to attacks on their identity was to de-emphasise or underplay that identity.[3] At various times between the July coup and the civil war, one or two Northern ethnic groups, like the Tiv and Idoma, which were disproportionately represented in the army, came under attack from officers and Other Ranks for their 'tribalism'. There was one battalion, for example, the commander of which, plus one or two of his more senior subordinates, came for accidental reasons from the same area. In the general climate of hostility and suspicion prevailing at that time, a number of brother officers came to formulate various accusations of favouritism against them. The response of the commander in question was to go into a rage, to say that his accusers were 'people with sawdust in their brains', who were merely disrupting army discipline and national unity by their behaviour, and to make a personal trip to Lagos GHQ to file a complaint on

[1] See Chapter XII below.
[2] Especially so as the region did not possess a 'core' ethnic group that was a majority of the population, like the Hausa in the North, the Yoruba in the West or the Ibo in the East.
[3] One clear-cut example of this was the attempt of many civilian Ika–Ibos from the Mid-West to abandon their associations with the other Ibos altogether – prior to the August 1967 coup in the Mid-West – by writing letters to the newspapers claiming that they were Ikas, not Ibos, and that they had entirely different historical traditions from the latter.

these lines. The efforts of officers, noted earlier in this chapter, to avoid postings in units that would put them in association with others from their home area fall into the same category. These soldiers were evidently as highly sensitive to the symbolic evocations of their ties with their home areas as anyone else. But being unable – unlike the big tribes – to stage a coup or a secession, they sought security in appeal to national and professional norms. Despite, therefore, the fragmentation of identities that had taken place in 1966–7 one still found officers – especially among the minority ethnic groups – who identified themselves primarily as Nigerians.

CONCLUSION: THE DYNAMICS OF CONFLICT

We are now in a better position to account for the dynamics of primordial conflict in the army, to explain how primordial ties became in 1966 so much more salient than before, and so powerful as to override the constraints provided by other organisational and social loyalties. For the ethnic and regional identities of others became explicit cues or stimuli for the projection of aggression against them. This was also related to another facet of the conflict that demands adequate explanation, namely the manner in which it developed as a hostile outburst, in which perceptions and expressions of antagonism were out of all proportion to the actual issues at stake. The sudden florescence of primordial animosity in 1966 occurred when tribal and regional ties became the symbolic outlet for the expression of a whole range of tensions, both within the military organisation itself and outside it in a wider political context. One major source of tension was political, namely that the army's newly acquired political role exposed it to unaccustomed political demands and pressures; and did so under circumstances which seemed to represent a transfer of political power from the North, resulting in the urban riots in May and September–October 1966 as well as the July coup itself. Secondly, there were the purely organisational sources of strain defined in the preceding chapters.

Why did social strain and unstable expectations have such an electric effect on ethnic and regional differences but leave alternative sources of cleavage almost unaffected? There are a number of reasons why tribe and region were highly appropriate objects for the projection of anxiety and hostility – among them political salience; the elaboration and diffusion of stereotypes in politicians' speeches and the news media during the period immediately preceding military rule; and the connection of such primordial ties with self-images and feelings of identity. The only other basis of differentiation within the military that might have been relevant was cleavage between different ranks and peer groups. The structure of the army and its authority norms did not allow for the open displacement of aggression against senior officers *as such*, as already argued. Ethnic scapegoating permitted aggression to be channelled against the men in power but not their offices, most notably during the July 1966 coup, when the Ibos who were attacked were in a very visible position in the upper echelons of both the Military Government and the officer corps itself. 'Tribalism' was the symbolic master key which unlocked pent-up organisational tensions, communal rivalries and political conflict all at the same time.

PART THREE

THE MILITARY AND POLITICS

INTRODUCTION

In the preceding chapters we concentrated on the internal structure and functioning of the army and argued that political conflict from the outside was able to penetrate it so rapidly because of its characteristic organisational weaknesses and strains. We must now, however, fit the military back into its political environment, in order to obtain a more balanced and complete picture of the interaction of organisational and political pressures.

In this part we shall therefore be dealing with five related questions. Firstly, what were the main characteristics of the political environment? In Chapter IX we sketch a brief history of political conflict in Nigeria from 1951 to 1966 and then try to extrapolate a few broad trends, some of which are as valid for the period of military rule after 1966 as for the civilian period. Secondly, what were the nature, origins and consequences of specific political pressures from the outside upon the army, a question that will crop up several times in Chapter X, on the civilian control of the military, as well as in Chapters XI and XIII on the different periods of military rule? Thirdly, what kind of political goals did the military leaders have, if any (Chapter XII), and of what relevance are these to understanding their political behaviour? Fourthly, what was the impact of the army on politics and, in particular, how did its intervention in the political arena from 1966 change the existing system of political allocation and conflict (Chapters XI to XIII)? Lastly, what kind of 'feedback' was created by the military's political role?[1] To what extent did the political pressures on the army's boundaries in 1966–7 result from the military elite's own policies and actions?

In describing the place of the army in politics, a number of propositions about civil–military relations will emerge, of which a few of the more important can be summarised in advance, to help guide the reader through the later discussion:

1. The conditions for military intervention in politics were provided by the weakness in civilian institutions and their decline in legitimacy between Independence in 1960 and 1966. The civilian regime's loss of support not only made it easier to overthrow, but also provided army officers with the

---

[1] The notion of feedback from transactions with the environment is central to any idea of system, such as outlined in the introduction to this book. Both Deutsch, *The nerves of government*, and D. Easton, *A system analysis of political life* (New York: Wiley, 1965), contain good discussions of the relation of feedback to the performance of political organisations.

motive and justification to intervene, in order to rescue the nation from politicians who were seen to be hopelessly venal and unable to keep conflict among themselves and between the regions within bounds.

2. Political pressures on the army and antagonism towards the political authorities within it grew in proportion to the redefinition of its role, in terms of internal security rather than external defence. Because of their client status in the international system, there are relatively few new nations where the military has a particularly important role to play in relation to external security; whereas in most of them, the army cannot avoid being drafted into performing internal security duties. Yet the training of army officers usually predisposes them to regard the former and not the latter as their legitimate function,[1] as was the case in Nigeria. Consequently, the use made of the army to provide a show of force for governmental authority, as in Tiv Division in 1960 and 1964 and the Western Region in 1965–6, increased the antagonism of the army to the political class – and contributed directly to the January 1966 coup.

3. The expansion of the political and internal security role of the army drew upon it political pressures from the outside to allocate values. This could be seen, for instance, in the anxiety of the Northern politicians to achieve a regional balance in the officer corps through the quota system, and in the contacts various politicians and members of the intelligentsia established, or attempted to establish within the military. The pressures became all the greater once the army had entered politics directly; for then politicians and others sought all the more to ally themselves with groups in the army, as the surest way of changing the allocation of values in the required direction; though such alliances for the most part did not emerge into the open until after the July 1966 coup (see Chapter XIII).

4. The ability of the military leadership to legitimise the army's own internal patterns of action and their own commands depended – to a varying extent in different periods – on the legitimacy secured for the military's role in the wider social and political context of Nigerian society.[2] More especially, any loss in legitimacy – as in early 1966 – undermined the authoritativeness of the command structure itself. The relation between legitimacy and military authority was probably much less direct in the period preceding the army's seizure of power than in that following it. In the former period the army stood aloof from civil society, creating and maintaining its own distinct values through which the authority of the command structure was upheld. Even though there were problems of the reconciliation of military roles with

---

[1] Janowitz, *The military in the political development of new nations*, pp. 37–8.
[2] Compare the effect of lack of public support for its role in Algeria on morale in the French Army, described in J. S. Ambler, *The French Army in politics, 1945–1962* (Ohio: Ohio State University Press, 1966).

latent social roles, such as age, kinship, tribe and patronage, etc., there was no obvious conflict between military role obligations and widely shared sentiments held by salient *political* groups. Nor, on the other hand, was there any very obvious social or political support for the military role. A certain amount of prestige, it is true, accrued to the army in the post-Independence period because of its identification with the symbols of newly acquired sovereignty and because of the role it played in the Congo; but this was hardly sufficient to provide perceptible support for the authority of leadership in the army. The army did, however, have a popular stereotype as a more impartial arbiter of civil conflict than the police and this clearly made its intervention of January 1966 more acceptable to the public.

But this diffuse prestige depended to an extent on the army's very aloofness. The acquisition of power made it more difficult for the military to keep its reputation for impartiality. It also meant that the cooperation of military subordinates with their commanders depended to some extent on the level of political support the latter were able to aggregate and maintain. When, for example, in the course of early 1966, military leaders became the object of popular hostility (in the North) of a kind from which their neutrality had previously protected them, hostility quickly spilled over into the army and made discipline much more difficult to secure.

5. The army's legitimacy problems were intensified by the military leaders' own lack of political acumen: the feedback of pressures upon the military elite was related to the quality of their political decisions. These in turn tended to be somewhat rigid and simplistic, less influenced by the political realities of the situation than by the search for conduct that fitted the soldiers' conceptions of an honourable way of life. This is a theme that emerges with some clarity from the detailed analysis of decision-making under the Ironsi regime from January to July 1966, given in Chapter XI. It was also present among the motives of the Majors who staged the January 1966 coup, analysed in Chapter I. The tendency to think about politics in simple and moralistic categories comes, it is suggested in Chapter XIII, both from the isolation of the military from civilian society, and from the officers' rather low status compared with other elites, motivating them to provide honour for themselves on their own terms through emphasis on the distinctive values of martial life, which were contrasted with the more complex and dubious morality of the politician.[1]

6. The political weakness of the military regime was accentuated – at least in its early stages – by its failure to recruit the talents and organisation of other groups, except the civil service, to help it either in policy-making or in developing sources of political support. The Ironsi regime relied heavily on

[1] See also Chapter III, pp. 107–8, and Chapter IV.

its permanent secretaries, and virtually all important decisions were taken by a narrow group of half a dozen military leaders, together with a handful of civil servant advisers.[1] Politicians were shut out altogether; there was no attempt to organise politically, whether for the purposes of creating political support or for the surveillance of possible sources of opposition; and the police, with its relatively sophisticated grass-roots organisation, played a less important role in the Military Government compared, for example, with the important position of the police in the National Liberation Council in Ghana. Not until the army leaders were forced by political pressures to do so after the July 1966 coup were other power groups brought in to butress the Military Government, culminating in Gowon's appointment of civilian commissioners after the secession of the former Eastern Region as Biafra.

7. Cleavages in the military establishment came to parallel and reproduce cleavages in civil society. Not only was this because 'tribalism and regionalism' could be made the idiom of organisational divisions, in the way explained in Chapter VIII, but also because there was an increase in the salience of tribal and regional antagonism in civilian society itself. This increase came from the competitive struggle for modernisation between the main ethnic nations, which was intensified by the shortage of resources to be distributed between them relative to aspirations. One of the most significant developments, as we will show in Chapter IX, was the cumulative emergence of ethnic differences and power struggles in the Federal bureaucracies and universities from 1964 onwards, of which the developments of 1966 in the army were a culmination.

8. The structural incoherence caused by cleavage in the army made it a most unreliable arbiter of political conflict. Though it intervened in politics to put an end to tribal and regional disputes in the name of national unity, it ended up itself divided on those very issues it purported to resolve. Indeed, it made conflict much more damaging, by introducing the use of violence to resolve it. The effect of the military's organisational weakness on political events outside it was most noticeable in the period between the July 1966 coup and the beginning of the civil war in July 1967. The army was so unreliable, as we will see in Chapter XIII, that it was difficult to use it to bring to an end the cycle of civilian violence which built up in the North in September–October 1966 (in which indeed individual soldiers actually participated). And the division of the army into two parts which resulted from the second coup, meant that the problem of military legitimacy – whether or not, to put it baldly, Lt Colonel Ojukwu in Enugu should take orders from Lt Colonel Gowon in Lagos – engulfed that of political legitimacy. For control of the legitimate means of violence being divided and both sides

[1] See the details of the structure of military government under Ironsi in Chapter XI below.

laying claims to sovereignty,[1] it became very difficult to find viable alternatives, either to outright political surrender by one of the two sides, on the one hand, or to a resort to arms by both, on the other. The fragmentation of the army, in sum, not only reproduced the nation's cleavages, but brought them to their logical conclusion, by making secession a realistic possibility for a region which had the force of arms at its disposal.

[1] The former Eastern Region to its independence from Lagos, whether *de jure* or *de facto* under some kind of paper confederation arrangement; and the Federal side, of course, to sovereignty over the East.

CHAPTER IX

THE POLITICAL BACKGROUND

THE COLONIAL INHERITANCE

Colonial rule imposed a complex of bureaucratic, legal and market institutions over several groups of different peoples in the area that is now called Nigeria.[1] The structure of society was thus dual, with the instruments of government power and the grand merchant companies at the centre and the indigenous peoples with their traditional culture, political institutions, cities and farms at the periphery.[2] The latter, however, were modified and in some cases completely transformed by the colonial impact. Political institutions – even those of the Emirates which were supposedly left intact by the policy of indirect rule – were changed by the mere fact that the ultimate say on important decisions was transferred elsewhere. Central institutions expanded: roads were built, the cash economy widened and the native inhabitants were recruited into schools and posts in the bureaucracy. And the periphery also pushed towards the centre: schools were built by voluntary effort to export young men to the urban areas; new cash crops were pioneered and more complex economic institutions like credit associations, new types of tenancy, or lineages which organised themselves to run their property along the lines of modern economic enterprises developed; clan, district, town and tribal unions and political parties were established to protect and enhance local interests. Many kinds of intermediaries emerged to act as brokers between centre and periphery: traders, lorry owners and all sorts of middlemen in the economic sphere; organisers and politicians in the political. These social changes increased the interdependence of centre and periphery, but the dualistic nature of Nigerian society, the dialectic between traditional and modern, between the nation and its complex substructure of kingdoms, tribes, clans

[1] For an interesting attempt to show that while there was no equivalent in the pre-colonial past to a single national or political unit called Nigeria, there were a variety of links between the different groups of peoples that make up that country, see T. Hodgkin's introduction to *Nigerian perspectives: an historical anthology* (London: Oxford University Press, 1960).

[2] The analysis of colonial and post-colonial societies in terms of their structural dualism or pluralism dates from Boeke and Furnivall: see J. S. Furnivall, *Colonial policy and practice* (London: Cambridge University Press, 1949). In contrast we emphasise here the increasing interplay of the dual institutions – see E. A. Shils, 'Centre and periphery' in *The logic of personal knowledge, essays presented to Michael Polanyi* (London: Routledge and Kegan Paul, 1961) – and the combination of structural dualism with ethnic pluralism at the social periphery.

and villages, was not destroyed. Indeed, there were many ways in which the periphery became more resilient, as in the emergence of associations to fight for local interests at the centre, or in the widening of primordial identifications to the level of large ethnic nations, like the Ibo or the Yoruba, made up of previously warring village-groups, towns or kingdoms.[1]

The political independence of Nigeria came because the political brokers, the nationalist politicians, succeeded in mobilising the indigenous periphery against the colonial power. Yet it brought about little fundamental structural change in Nigerian society. To put it at its most cynical, the colonial government handed over to the inheriting elite, the political class, the right to control the machinery of government in return for the protection of its economic interests. In practice, this meant the inheritors had the right to create and mobilise political resources without hindrance, to appropriate to themselves all patronage in government jobs and appointments, to create networks of political clientage and to use the bureaucracy and the means of coercion to maintain themselves in office, to make themselves secure in their enjoyment of the lucrative rewards of politics. In return, the departing British kept control of large-scale private economic enterprise and the profits extracted therefrom. Political pressures and changing economic forces might persuade some enterprises, like the United Africa Company, to change the direction of their activity and diversify towards manufacture rather than the export/import trade, but the dominance of expatriate enterprise in the economy was not seriously shaken. This pattern was reproduced even during the Nigerian civil war: one reason Britain sold arms and gave diplomatic support to Nigeria was to minimise the disturbance suffered by expatriate enterprise, mainly because it calculated that the Federal government would be a better bet than Biafra in this respect.[2]

Furthermore, the legal/constitutional arrangements for independent

[1] The best general introduction to Nigerian societies and the changes effected in them by colonial rule is still to be found in Coleman, *Nigeria: background to nationalism*. Ethnic politics, the complex of voluntary associations and their relations with the political parties are described quite fully in R. L. Sklar, *Nigerian political parties* (Princeton, N.J.: Princeton University Press, 1963). The classic treatment of the development of indigenous entrepreneurial activity is to be found in P. T. Bauer, *West African trade* (London: Routledge and Kegan Paul, 1963). The role and functions of credit associations in filling the interstices between modern and non-modern sectors in the economy of developing countries, with some examples from Nigeria, is described in C. Geertz, 'The Rotating Credit Association: a middle rung in development', *Economic Development and Cultural Change*, X, 3 (1962), 241–63. An interesting account of the adjustment of the Yoruba system of land tenure and corporate descent groups to modern economic conditions is to be found in P. C. Lloyd, *Yoruba land law* (London: Oxford University Press, published for the Nigerian Institute of Social and Economic Research, Ibadan, 1962).

[2] The USA gave diplomatic support (though more hesitant) for similar reasons. There were, of course, several other political considerations behind the alignment of the powers, for example the OAU's support of Nigeria and the USSR's involvement. But the protection of British enterprise seems to have been the basic consideration behind the British government's policy.

The political background

Nigeria, which had been agreed to in negotiations with Britain, built a pattern of political competition between the regions into the Independence settlement. The country became a federation of three (after 1963, four) regions. The balance of initiative tended to be with the latter rather than with the Federal government[1] and one of the regions, the Northern, was assured of a dominant position by mere virtue of the fact that it was larger in population and area than the others put together. The federal structure also reflected the wide cultural and political differences between the country's three largest ethnic groups, the Ibo, the Yoruba and the Hausa–Fulani, each of which constituted the majority of the population of the Eastern, Western and Northern Regions, respectively (see Table 38). One reason for this arrangement was that the British government believed it would protect its own future interests in Nigeria.[2] But the Nigerian politicians also played a major part in shaping the constitution, from the negotiations bringing the Macpherson Constitution into being in 1951 to Independence in 1960. The final document reflected the major disagreements between them; and Independence left undisturbed the belief that only a loose federation would ensure the kind of security within their own regions that they desired.[3]

TABLE 38. *Population size of regions and main tribes,[a] 1963*

North	29·8 mn	of whom 16 mn Hausa–Fulani
East	12·4 mn	of whom 10 mn Ibo, mostly in East
Mid-West	2·5 mn	
West	10·3 mn	of whom 9 mn Yoruba plus 1·5 mn Northern Yorubas
Lagos	0·7 mn	

Note:
[a] Rough estimate of size of tribes, because ethnic breakdown of 1963 census not yet available.

[1] See J. P. Mackintosh *et al.*, *Nigerian government and politics* (London: Allen and Unwin, 1966), Chapter II, for details of the constitutional structure. See also B. J. Dudley, 'Federalism and the balance of political power in Nigeria', *Journal of Commonwealth Political Studies*, IV, 1 (1966), 16–29.

[2] The influences on colonial policy were complex. There was a vogue in the Colonial Office at the time for federations, as a device for achieving stability in plural societies to which Britain transferred power. The existing regions were retained in spite of the disparity in size, partly because the colonial officials working in the North who foresaw the political advantage that would accrue to the region were a very effective lobby in Whitehall; and partly no doubt because the British government felt that a Nigerian government controlled by conservative Northern politicians would be more 'stable' and favourable to its interests.

[3] There is a good short summary of the reasons for the choice of these constitutional arrangements, together with an analysis of their effects right down to the coups of 1966, in Fr J. O'Connell, 'Political integration: the Nigerian case' in A. Hazelwood (ed.), *African integration and disintegration* (London: Oxford University Press, 1967). The constitution and its making are discussed in K. Ezera, *Constitutional developments in Nigeria* (London: Cambridge University Press, 1960) and O. I. Odumosu, *The Nigerian constitution: history and development* (London: Sweet and Maxwell, 1963).

POLITICAL COMPETITION, 1951–66

For most of the period between 1951 and 1966, therefore, each regional government was controlled by a political party which was built around the majority ethnic or nationality group of the region: the Northern People's Congress (NPC) around the Hausa–Fulani Emirates in the North, the Action Group (AG) around the Yoruba nation in the West and the National Council of Nigerian Citizens (NCNC) around the Ibo nation in the East. From this base, each party proceeded to try and eliminate independent sources of opposition,[1] whether within its ethnic core or outside it in minority group areas. Only in the Western Region after 1962 was this process reversed, because of dissension within the ruling party and outside intervention in the region's politics.

One object of the consolidation of power in the regions was to improve each group's bargaining position at the centre. National politics was characterised by competition for the Federation's resources, which was made all the more intense by the variations between the regions in culture, wealth and access to means of modernisation, like education. The objects of competition were of three kinds.

First, the country's scarce economic resources. This was most obvious in the struggle between the regions for the siting of Federal development projects, such as the iron and steel complex under the 1962–8 Nigerian National Development Plan, because of the lack of clear-cut and mutually agreed criteria for allocation (the iron and steel complex never succeeded because of the Northern premier's objections to an economic feasibility report, which said it should be located in the East). It also appeared in the periodic negotiations over revenue allocation between the regions, the extent to which the financial needs of the regions should take precedence over the derivation of the revenues in fixing the allocation or *vice versa* – though these disputes were relatively muted until the rapid expansion of oil rents and royalties in the mid-1960s.

Secondly, there was the distribution of the fruits of political office and patronage in political and administrative posts. Each regional government was, of course, able to create patronage at will in its own sphere of competence and all of them are known to have manipulated bureaucratic appointments, put political nominees on the boards of their public corporations and made loans to or channelled contracts towards their political supporters or those who would pay the required ten per cent bribe. But the regions were also in competition for control of the sizeable Federal bureaucracies and patronage apparatus. This was bitterly evident in the disputes between the Yoruba and

[1] Mackintosh, *Nigerian government and politics*, Chapter XII.

the Ibo over the ethnic composition of the Nigerian Railway Corporation and the Universities of Lagos and Ibadan, in 1964 and 1965. The composition of the army was also in dispute, as in the argument over the imposition of a regional quota on officer recruitment in 1961 and in the objection by Northerners in July 1966 to the dominant position of the Ibos in the military hierarchy.

Thirdly, there was the struggle for political power, for control of the machinery of government in the regions and in the Federation. For the political kingdom held the key to all other types of allocations. Until the army took power in 1966, the relative population sizes of their regions and their ability to control votes were the factors which determined the relative bargaining power of the political parties. That is why the disputed population censuses of 1962 and 1963 took on so much political importance; why each party was prepared to use all the means of coercion and patronage at its disposal to eliminate opposition in the region which was its home base; and why the parties of the United Progressive Grand Alliance (UPGA) took their defeat in the 1964 Federal general election so bitterly.

The competition between the regional elites at the centre took the form of an oligopolistic bargaining between the three main political parties. Usually, this meant a coalition of two parties in control of the Federal government, with the third temporarily in opposition. From the time that Nigerian politicians first came to share responsibility at the centre with the colonial government, under the Macpherson Constitution of 1951, there were periodic changes in the coalition structure, and one region after another was either excluded from power at the centre or came to believe that it might be.

In 1953, the North felt threatened after Action Group politicians had precipitated a crisis in the central legislature by pushing forward a motion in Chief Enahoro's name, calling for self-government in 1956, earlier than the Northerners were, by reason of their educational and economic backwardness, prepared for it. This led the NPC to prepare an Eight-Point Programme, which if implemented would have made Nigeria a confederation with only defence, external affairs and some basic services shared in common. And there were riots in Kano after delegations of southern politicians had come up to the Northern cities (that which prompted the riot in Kano was led by Chief Akintola) in order to campaign for early independence.

The colonial government, however, was able to get the dissenting politicians to the conference table round which they agreed to a new constitution in 1954, which made Nigeria a Federation, regionalised the civil service and the judiciary[1] and allowed those regions that wanted it to have full internal

---

[1] Both had been centrally controlled up to 1954. Now they became concurrent subjects, the Federal and regional governments both being entirely responsible for the staffing, organisation and control of their own civil services and judiciaries respectively (though the regional judiciaries were subject to appeal to the Supreme Court).

self-government by 1956. The constitution also provided for a central Executive Council, in which from 1954 to 1959 all regions were equally represented[1] and cooperated reasonably amicably throughout the constitutional negotiations which brought Nigeria to Independence.

This accommodation between the regions broke down in the 1959 general election. The AG contested a large number of parliamentary seats in other regions than its own in an attempt to win power for itself at national level, lost heavily in the North and East and found itself in opposition to a coalition of the NPC and the NCNC, which took over the national government in preparation for Independence in 1960.

The election was also important because it was the first to be fought on universal suffrage, the seats being distributed according to population.[2] From that point forward, political competition was shaped by the inequality in political resources between the regions which resulted from majoritarian electoral politics. For the allocation of seats by population gave the North a majority of seats in the House of Representatives. In 1959, the NPC still did not hold enough of the Northern Region seats to guarantee control in the House, but by 1964 its monopoly of Northern political life was so complete that it was able to command a simple majority of votes. This created a situation that was extremely frustrating for the other parties, because although they might go into coalition with the NPC, they would have to do so on the latter's terms, accept its somewhat conservative domestic and foreign policies and refrain from attacks on the legal–constitutional arrangements which enabled the North to perpetuate its dominance. The strategy followed by the Federal Prime Minister, Sir Abubakar Tafawa Balewa, was to play off the AG and NCNC against each other in the hope he could force them both to become political clients of the NPC: the security of the North's position was best maintained by ensuring that the NPC had compliant allies in the south rather than encouraging or even tolerating opposition within the other regions.[3]

Paradoxically, it was this strategy which drove the West into political alienation between 1962 and 1965. For in 1962 the Federal government used a dispute within the AG between the party's President and Leader in the

[1] Between 1954 and 1957 the NCNC insisted on nominating the Western as well as the Eastern representatives, having won the 1954 elections in the former region. Between 1957 and 1959, however, the government was an all-party coalition, and included the AG.

[2] The previous allocation of seats at the centre in the proportion of two:one:one for the North, East and West, respectively, putting the North even then in a dominant position; but it was not until after 1959 that the region really became aware of the political potentiality of its position. Voting in the North in the 1959 election was by universal manhood suffrage only, women not yet having the vote.

[3] Though the regional leadership of the NPC under the Sardauna of Sokoto was more inclined to dispense with allies in the south – which was a recurrent source of tension between the Sardauna and Sir Abubakar.

Federal parliament, Chief Awolowo, and the premier of the West, Chief Akintola, whose dismissal Awolowo had been able to secure, as an opportunity to destroy the AG or at least make sure it had leaders who could be trusted as allies.[1] A fracas created by Akintola's supporters in the first meeting of the Regional House of Assembly after his dismissal was made an excuse to declare a state of emergency in the region. The Coker Commission of Enquiry was set up to investigate allegations of corruption in the West's public corporations, and Chief Awolowo and Enahoro were tried and convicted for having plotted to overthrow the Federal government by force in September 1962. The procedure for the creation of a new Mid-West Region out of the non-Yoruba areas of the West was also set in motion. And when the emergency administration ended in 1963 the Federal government turned power back to Chief Akintola, rather than holding new regional elections (which would probably have returned the AG to office).

These measures were interpreted by most Yorubas as a calculated attempt by the NPC and NCNC to cut them off from the centres of national power and influence; or at least to permit access to the latter only on terms dictated by themselves. Chief Awolowo, in prison, became the symbol of their alienation, which persisted until the coup of January 1966.

Chief Akintola formed a new party, the Nigerian National Democratic Party, and led this into coalition with the NPC in the 1964 Federal election. The NNDP was able by a mixture of patronage and coercion to win a majority of the region's seats both in the Federal poll[2] and in the regional election of 1965. But it was popularly viewed as oppressive and was made all the more unpopular because its brief period of ascendancy coincided with declining cocoa prices and an economic recession in the region.

Meanwhile, however, the NCNC, which had been a more than willing accomplice in the assault on the AG, found to its alarm that its own position in the Federal coalition was increasingly insecure. Two things brought this home to the NCNC leaders: the disputes over the censuses of 1962 and 1963, and the emergence of new political alignments in the Western Region.

The census was an extremely delicate issue, because the apportionment of parliamentary seats and thus the political balance between the North and the southern regions depended upon it. The first returns from the census in May 1962 showed very substantial increases in the populations of the Western and Eastern Regions and a more moderate increase in the North, the sum effect

[1] The NCNC had its own reasons for going along with Sir Abubakar on this – namely that, hopefully, the destruction of the AG would enable it to re-establish itself in the West, or to detach from the West the non-Yoruba Mid-West, or both. For details of the crisis, see R. L. Sklar, 'Nigerian politics: the ordeal of Chief Awolowo 1960–65' in G. M. Carter (ed.), *Politics in Africa: seven cases* (New York: Harcourt, Brace and World, 1965).

[2] Very much helped of course by the boycott of voting by the UPGA parties (see below, p. 216).

of which would have been to put the North at a slight population and electoral disadvantage relative to the combined south. On information that the application of demographic checks was likely to reduce the Eastern total, Dr Okpara, the region's premier, announced the East's results and said he would not tolerate any revision of them. A major political dispute between the NPC and the NCNC followed; and in the end the Prime Minister decided to cancel the entire census and hold another in November 1963. This new enumeration was carried out under much less satisfactory conditions than in 1962, and it is clear that the figures were gerrymandered by the regional officials who administered it,[1] especially in the North. The results were announced in February 1964, and showed quite unrealistic increases from the previous 1952–3 census in all but one of the regions. The new figures restored the balance between the North and the rest of the country to more or less what it was before, the Eastern Region total being the only one to remain unaltered from 1962. Dr Okpara immediately rejected the result, accused the North in detail of a long list of irregularities and attempted (unsuccessfully) to challenge the census in the courts. Both the NPC and Chief Akintola's government in the West, however, stood by the result, and, protest as it might, the NCNC was quite powerless to prevent the apportionment of seats in the forthcoming Federal election on the basis of the census figures. This dispute also led to vitriolic exchanges between the North and the East in politicians' speeches and the regional government-controlled newspapers, the *Nigerian Citizen* and *Nigerian Outlook* respectively. In the North, the Ibos were already the focus of much hostility as a large and successful immigrant group and the open conflict between the regions at a national level was made the occasion for punitive measures against Easterners at a local level, such as expulsion from market stalls by the Native Authorities.

The census dispute also gave Chief Akintola the opportunity to destroy the Western Region wing of the NCNC and bring the majority of its membership under his party. For the 1963 count had given the West the biggest proportional population increase of all. By endorsing the census, therefore, Akintola

---

[1] Both censuses were carried out by the regional administrations, though with checks by outsiders in sample areas and other precautions. Nevertheless, ways were found round the latter, for instance, in the leakage to the regional governments in advance of which areas were to be sampled. The figures for the two censuses of 1962 and 1963 are as follows (in millions):

	1962	*1963*
North	22·0	29·8
East	12·3	12·4
Mid-West	2·4	2·5
West	8·1	10·3
Lagos	0·45	0·7

could both win friends in the North and put Yoruba members of the NCNC in a dilemma where they had to choose between Yoruba nationalism (as represented by accepting the 1963 figures) as against their party ties with the NCNC and alliance with the East in confrontation between North and south. The West NCNC split open and the larger group opted for the Yoruba cause and the fruits of office which Chief Akintola offered them.[1]

The NNDP then turned on the Ibos, the Yoruba's most important rival in the competitive struggle for modernisation. In March 1964, the Western Region government published an official 'White Paper'[2] which accused Ibo politicians, academics and administrators in a number of Federal bureaucracies of creating particularist empires for themselves by packing kinsmen and fellow Ibos into jobs in these institutions. The accusations also struck a resonance in the North and contributed to the particularisation of hostility against the south in general towards the Ibos by themselves[3] (though a great deal of ambivalence about all of the south remained, as when the *Nigerian Citizen* proposed to rename the Nigerian Railway Corporation the 'Southern Nigeria Railway Corporation'.[4]) These onslaughts contributed greatly to the growing sense of isolation of the Ibos and the conviction that they were being unjustly persecuted for their success in the competitive struggle for modernisation.

The disenchantment between the two partners in the Federal coalition over the census and the new alignments in the West, brought about the formation of two new alliances of political parties to contest the Federal elections to be held in late 1964. On one side was the Nigerian National Alliance (NNA) – the NPC, the NNDP and various minority group splinters in the East and Mid-West; on the other, the United Progressive Grand Alliance (UPGA) – the NCNC, the AG and two radical Northern parties, the Northern Elements Progressive Union (NEPU) and the United Middle Belt Congress (UMBC), themselves merging to form a Northern Progressive Front.

At about the same time as the NCNC and NPC began publicly to dissociate themselves the one from the other, there had occurred a general strike, starting on 1 June 1964, arising partly from demands for pay rises from government workers and partly from the unimaginative way in which the government handled these claims and the Report of the Morgan Commission

[1] It was at this point that the NNDP was officially formed out of the NCNC remnants and Chief Akintola's own following of the Action Group, which was then know as the United People's Party.

[2] Western Nigeria Official Document no. 1 of 1964: 'White Paper on the New Political Alignment in Western Nigeria' (Ibadan, 1964).

[3] A natural trend in the North because of the Ibos' special position as a large immigrant group there – compare the similar situation when anti-southern nationalist feeling was crystallised in anti-Ibo riots in Kano in 1953, with members of other southern groups being left alone.

[4] *Nigerian Citizen* (Zaria), 13 February 1965.

of Enquiry which it had appointed to review the minimum wage. This strike was organised by a temporarily improvised Joint Action Committee, which brought together all the various segments of the trade union movement. It was effective throughout the Federation (though the Northern unions defected half way through) and the government had to accede to most of the strikers' demands. The strike demonstrated the depth of public feeling against the conspicuous corruption of the politicians, with which the meagre minimum wage was contrasted. It showed for the first time, moreover, just how fragile the institutions of central government were, how easily they were disrupted by the temporary coordination of an otherwise fragmented trades union movement. The strike was among the issues which the UPGA built into the radical political posture it struck for the election, in which it put itself forward as the true representative of progress in the struggle against the conservatism and feudalism of the NPC. Nevertheless the unions themselves put their weight behind a newly formed Socialist Workers and Farmers Party (SWAFP) rather than UPGA (though SWAFP loosely coordinated its efforts with the latter in the election). For whatever their rhetoric, the UPGA politicians belonged in the main to the 'political class', which profited both materially and politically from the existing order. The real issues for them were the uncomfortable dominance of the North in the Federation and of the NPC in the former, the conflict of the major linguistic 'nations' for jobs and influence and the rise of the NNDP. Only the Northern progressives and the radical fringe of the AG represented in any genuine way the dispossessed of the political order.

The 1964 Federal election campaign was long and violent. There were riots and clashes between thugs employed by rival political parties. The machinery of local government was used to prevent meetings, to intimidate candidates and sometimes to incarcerate them. These things happened more often in the Northern and Western Regions. The Mid-West and East were relatively peaceful, mainly, it should be said, because of an electoral alliance between the main contestants in these regions.[1] The irregularities and, still more important, the realisation that the UPGA was unlikely to win the election, led a number of UPGA leaders together with the President, Dr Azikiwe, to contemplate what would have amounted to a constitutional *putsch*. It would have been premised upon the contention that the electoral malpractices gave the President the moral right to dismiss or replace the Prime Minister, nullify the election and order a new one; that the NNA was to all intents and purposes pulling off an electoral coup d'etat, so that it was the President's

[1] Intimidation had not been unknown in these regions in previous contests. The AG and NCNC, who were the only serious contenders in the East and Mid-West, reached an agreement among themselves as to which of them would contest each of the constituencies in the East, the Mid-West and the West.

duty to stage a counter-coup to prevent the *de facto* violation of due constitutional process.[1] The excuse or occasion for this was the announcement when nominations had closed that large numbers of seats – especially in the North – were uncontested, although the UPGA had fielded candidates in every one,[2] many of whom were fraudulently prevented from putting in their nominations. The UPGA leaders sought to obtain a postponement of the election, and then, failing this, resolved upon a boycott of the poll upon mistaken legal advice that an electoral boycott would permit the President to refuse to appoint a Prime Minister, assume executive powers and order a new ballot.[3] The election took place on 30 December 1964. The boycott was only effective in the Eastern Region, where the region's electoral officers did not turn up for the voting; it was called off at the last minute in the Mid-West; and went off half-cocked in the West and North, badly damaging the electoral chances of the AG and NPF respectively, without actually halting the election; so that victory was won by the NNA overall, with the NPC sweeping the North and the NNDP the West.

To begin with, the President refused to 'reappoint' Sir Abubakar Tafawa Balewa as Prime Minister, on the contention that the elections were not satisfactory; and a constitutional deadlock ensued. Nevertheless, he was forced in the end to capitulate; and he appointed the new government on 4 January 1965, after Sir Abubakar had promised to nominate a broadly based 'national' cabinet. During the crisis the President had been under pressure to endorse direct action by trades unions and a mob organised by the Joint Action Committee, as well as to call in the armed forces. The employment of the latter – short of a military coup – was, however, ruled out because the military authorities indicated to the President on legal advice that they would not accept his orders.[4] Dr Azikiwe, in the last analysis, was unwilling to step outside the existing constitutional framework, especially without the backing of legitimate organised force. Accordingly he deferred to the advice of the Federation's chief law officers[5] that his constitutional position was untenable

---

[1] For divergent views as to the rights and wrongs of the President's position, see Mackintosh, *Nigerian government and politics*, pp. 576–96 and R. L. Sklar, 'Nigerian politics in perspective' in *Government and Opposition*, II, 4 (July–October 1967). Whatever the political rights of the President's position – as argued for by Sklar – there is little doubt, however, that he would have been exceeding his constitutional power.

[2] Sixty-six NNA and fifteen UPGA candidates were returned unopposed. All but two of the unopposed NNA candidates were in the North.

[3] The advice came most notably from the Eastern Attorney General, Mr C. C. Mojekwu, and was all too attractive to Dr Azikiwe because of his hankering after a presidency with 'executive powers': see Mackintosh, *Nigerian government and politics*, p. 587.

[4] See the discussion below of the President's dealings with the military during this crisis, pp. 237–8.

[5] Especially the Attorney General and the Chief Justice of the Federation. It is significant that Dr Azikiwe also received similar advice from the Chief Justice and Solicitor General of the East, as well as from an Ibo Supreme Court judge.

rather than to the urgings of the Joint Action Committee and radical fringes of the AG and NCNC that he do something more drastic.

This amounted to a major tactical defeat for the President, for the UPGA alliance and for the radicals. Dr Azikiwe's decision to back down, the re-appointment of Sir Abubakar and the compromise formula for a national government were denounced by Dr Okpara, the National President of the NCNC as well as Eastern premier, in no uncertain terms. But in March 1965 after the election had been re-held in the East, East NCNC ministers crept back into the cabinet. Their position in the coalition was much weakened, however, and it was clear that the NPC looked towards its new ally in the south, the NNDP, now represented in the Federal government,[1] more than to the NCNC. There is little doubt that this was popularly perceived as a shift in community influence at a Federal level from the East and the Ibos on the one hand, towards the West and the Yorubas on the other, both by the mass electorate and by the various elite participants in the political process. And that the NCNC saw itself as being at least potentially in much the same position as the AG had been in 1962.

The most immediate consequence was a jockeying for power and patronage in various Federal public bureaucracies, along lines presaged by the Western Region 'White Paper on the new political alignment' in the region. In March 1965, it was announced that the Council of the University of Lagos had decided not to renew the appointment of the University's Vice-Chancellor, Dr Eni Njoku, an Ibo academic, and to replace him with Dr S. Biobaku, a Yoruba. There were no good academic grounds for the termination of Dr Njoku's appointment; and this step was actively opposed by the University Senate and the majority of both staff and students. The decision was quite clearly a political one, reflecting both the change in the balance of regional power, as well as competition between various factions within the university. There was an open schism between Senate and Council, both of which refused to recognise each other's jurisdiction; factional conflict among staff and students, ranging – with a few notable exceptions – Yoruba staff and students on the one side and the non-Yorubas and expatriates on the other, and featuring vituperative attacks against group identities, whether expatriate, Ibo or Yoruba; there followed the temporary closure of the university and the mass resignation of the non-Yoruba faculty, during which the Federal government through its newly appointed NNDP Minister of Education, Mr R. Akinjide, came down firmly on the side of the Council and the Yoruba faction.

Following closely upon this, in May 1965, the government dismissed the

[1] It had had a couple of minor cabinet posts, since when the alliance was concluded with the NPC (in 1964), but this was the first time it was represented as befitted a full partner in the coalition.

Ibo chairman of the Nigerian Railway Corporation, Dr Ikejiani, and replaced its board. The latter then set up a committee to 'determine the fitness and qualifications' of the holders of posts in the corporation and to review the existing system of training, recruitment and promotion.

While patronage networks sometimes – but not always – on tribal lines did undoubtedly exist in the Federal public bureaucracies, particularly the public corporations and the universities, the circumstances under which these steps were taken and the manner in which they followed upon the accusations of the Western Region 'White Paper' and the 1964 election indicate their cynical political origins. It is against this background that one must understand the growing insecurity of many southerners, but especially the Ibos, about the future of their careers in the public services, an insecurity penetrating even the more isolated bureaucracies, such as the army.

After the debacle of December 1964–January 1965, the hopes of the UPGA leaders for a restoration of their fortunes were pinned upon the Western Region elections, forthcoming later in 1965. It was hoped that the AG would win the region back from the NNDP on the strength of Awolowo's martyrdom, the oppressiveness of the Akintola government and the jealousies between the different areas of Yoruba country. The regional premier, on the other hand, was prepared to use all the weaponry of intimidation and coercion at his disposal – including the dismissal or non-payment of salaries of recalcitrant chiefs, local government councils and native court incumbents, control of local government police and bribery of Nigeria Police, the employment of party thugs under the protection of the local government police and native courts, and the banning of regional and national newspapers if hostile – to secure a result favourable to himself. The AG was disadvantaged by not having any 'legitimate' means of coercion at its disposal, although it did employ party thugs paid partly by UPGA funds, coming from sources outside the region. But its cause acquired strong populist undertones, because of the political radicalism of its leadership, the martyrdom of Awolowo and a very big cut-down in the cocoa producer price for the new season, to almost half its previous level.

The campaign was the most violent in Nigerian politics so far; and the election itself, which took place in October 1965, was openly rigged by the NNDP. Candidates were prevented from filing their nominations, local government police and thugs kept political opponents from the polls, ballot boxes were stuffed with extra ballot papers and when all else failed, NNDP candidates were declared elected by the regional radio station in contests that went against them.[1]

---

[1] A month after the election the chairman of the Western Nigeria Electoral Commission, Mr Esua, published a letter to the Governor of the Region in which he set out a long list of malpractices

The outcome was popularly regarded as unjust and illegitimate and the AG refused to recognise the result. Widespread rioting ensued, from October 1965 to January 1966, and the conditions of disorder permitted gangs of party thugs, or brigands purporting to be party members, to rob, loot, burn and kill. The official police toll of casualties was 153, though in reality considerably more are thought to have been killed. The army was called in to aid the Mobile Squad of Police in November 1965 – having stood by during the election – and (as we pointed out in Chapter I) the Federal government was considering a still heavier military commitment in the region when it was overthrown on 15 January 1966.

Put in this context, the January 1966 coup may be seen as simply one more episode in the periodic shifting of power between the regions – this time cutting the North off from the centres of political power in the Federation – though the method of transferring power was new. Similarly, the July 1966 coup, as we will show in Chapter XIII, redressed the balance in favour of the North and cut the East's links with the centre so thoroughly that its leaders attempted to take it into secession.

The events following the July 1966 coup and then the civil war likewise brought to the centre of the political stage the ethnic minorities of all the regions:[1] in the North, the peoples of the Middle Belt and diaspora areas,[2] in the East, the peoples of the Calabar, Ogoja and Rivers areas and in the West, the non-Yorubas of the Mid-West. Whereas the three dominant ethnic groups, the Ibo, the Yoruba and the Hausa–Fulani, each suffered no more than episodic exclusions from power, the minorities had been more or less permanently submerged in the three-region constitution under which Nigeria became independent.[3] The Mid-Westerners alone had been able to

which in his view invalidated the election. It was to no effect, because of the tardiness of the allegations and because he was supposedly in charge of the elections at the time, as his colleagues on the commission were not slow to point out in a rebuttal of his letter. Nonetheless, the Electoral Commission was powerless to maintain adequate checks, because of its dependence on regional government agents; and the chairman's allegations are well substantiated. See the *Daily Times* (Lagos), 20 and 23 November 1965 for Mr Esua's letter and his colleagues' reply.

[1] See the detailed account of politics in the July 1966 to August 1967 period in Chapter XIII below.
[2] See the discussion of the tribal composition of the region and the Northern soldiers in Chapter VIII above.
[3] A commission had been set up after the 1957 Constitutional Conference to look into the minorities question. See 'Nigeria: Report of the Commission Appointed to Enquire into the Fears of the Minorities and the Means of Allaying Them', Cmnd 505 (London: HMSO, 1958). The terms of reference of this commission were heavily weighted by the British government against the creation of more regions, because it was believed this would be administratively inconvenient. The commission was able to find little or no evidence of actual discrimination in terms of amenities provided by regional governments and the like. By and large, it made little of the political aspirations of the minorities, and was debarred by its terms of reference from considering the political implications for the Federation as a whole of a three-region set-up dominated by the North. Its practical recommendations were for safeguards within the existing framework, like a federally-controlled police system and a constitutionally guaranteed bill of rights.

obtain their own region in 1963, more because of the efforts of the NPC and NCNC to weaken the AG in the West, after the so-called 'Emergency' of 1962, than because of their own political exertions.

Elsewhere, the minorities had faced the alternative of being in permanent opposition to the ruling group in their region, or making the best of a weak position by seeking an alliance with that group. The few minorities which chose the former course found themselves locked in fierce conflict with the regional government. The Tiv in Northern Nigeria, for instance, were alienated by the attempts of the regional government to interfere with their local government system and to use the Tor Tiv, the clan heads and local court system, to acquire support for the NPC in the area; and twice, in 1960 and again in 1964, rioting, the burning of houses and killing swept through the Tiv Division, necessitating the calling in of the army to aid the police.[1]

For the most part, however, after a period of intensive agitation and political organisation before Independence, most of the smaller ethnic groups settled down into a position of clientage. In the North indeed the elites of many of the Middle Belt groups, like the Idomas, Igalas, Igbirras, the Nupe and Northern Yorubas, found there were positive incentives for so doing, because their educational advantages over the far North gave them favourable access to the large number of bureaucratic posts that became available when the public services in the regions were 'Northernised' to the exclusion of both expatriates and (still more so) southern Nigerians.[2] By 1966, however, these groups were coming again to feel insecure because – the bureaucracy now being almost completely full up and other patronage openings exhausted – the politicians of the NPC were under pressure from the far North to give preference to entrants from the Emirate areas to Ahmadu Bello University and the Northern and Federal public service, compared with other Northerners.

The exhaustion of the three major groups in the fratricidal political struggles of 1966, together with the strategic position of the Northern diaspora and Middle Belt and Eastern Rivers soldiers in the army after the July 1966 coup, gave the minorities their opportunity. As we shall see in Chapter XIII, the outcome of the political debate in 1966–7 was the sub-

---

[1] The background of the Tiv riots of 1960 and 1964 is discussed in detail both in the official document resulting from the regional government's commission of enquiry into the 1964 disturbances, 'A White Paper on the Government's Policy for the Rehabilitation of Tiv Native Authority' (Kaduna: Government Printer, 1965) and in M. J. Dent's chapter on 'A minority party, the UMBC' in Mackintosh, *Nigerian government and politics*, Chapter XI. Disturbances of this kind have also, however, been noted before in Tiv political life: see P. Bohannan, 'Extra-processual events in Tiv political institutions', *American Anthropologist*, 60 (1958). Up to 2,000 people are believed to have been killed in Tiv Division in 1964.

[2] And also access to the various posts that were opened up for Northerners in the Federal bureaucracies by regional quotas (as in the army) or preferential treatment in appointments and promotion as in the Federal civil service.

division by Lt Colonel Gowon in May 1967 of all the existing regions except the West into new states, in which the minority groups – or at least the larger ones – were able to play a more independent political role. The new twelve-state structure also increased the number of bargaining coalitions among the states, doing away with the rigid three-party oligopoly dominated by the North which led, as we have argued, to so much conflict and instability within the Federal structure up to 1967.

THE STRUCTURE OF CONFLICT

Having recounted the history of political conflict and its relation to the constitutional structure, we may now put forward a few tentative propositions about the sources from which it came, the processes it followed and the consequences it produced, in the hope that these will contribute not only to the understanding of events before the seizure of power by the army, but also of the problems the military faced when it was called on to rule.

1. Periodic exclusions from power have tended to engender a deep sense of alienation from the political process on the part of the different groups which take part in that process. Nigeria is a mass society,[1] in the sense that almost all its population, even in the villages, are aware however vaguely, whether through the newspapers, the radio, word of mouth or participation in the market economy, that there is a national society and a government or governments capable of affecting their conditions of life. Yet most people's understanding of the political process is very limited, and they feel the power of the centre to be vaguely threatening. They rely on intermediate groups with roots in their local society that they understand – whether these are traditional authorities, as in the far North or community interest groups such as clan, town or divisional unions, as in much of the rest of Nigeria – to mediate with government on their behalf; normally until 1966, this was through the political parties, which tended in certain respects to be agglomerations of such community groupings.[2] When the link between the community and the centre was believed to have been broken – whether because of a rupture between community leaders and a political party, or the exclusion of the political party from power at the centre or in the region or both, or because of the abolition of parties, or the appearance of a new ruling group, like the military, at the centre, which did not deal with the community's recognised intermediaries – then the sense of threat crystallised. This alienation has some-

---

[1] Indeed, W. Kornhauser's analysis of mass society in *The politics of mass society* (Glencoe, Ill.: Free Press, 1959), seems to bear more resemblance to the situation described here than it does to most fully industrialised societies, in which there is usually a plethora of secondary institutions to bridge the gap between the periphery and the political centre.

[2] See in particular the analysis in Sklar, *Nigerian political parties*, especially Chapter X.

times taken the form of projective fears and ethnic or regional stereotyping and persecution of others; sometimes it has led to violence directed against those others as in the North in the riots of May and September–October 1966; and sometimes to violence turned inwards on members of the group itself who were held responsible for its humiliation or subordination to outsiders, as in the Tiv riots of 1960 and 1964 and the Western Region outburst of 1965.

2. Most Nigerians – including members of the elite – have a strong sense of loyalty to their community of origin. The political importance of this may be seen in the plethora of voluntary associations attempting to secure amenities for their local areas,[1] the conflict over the location of development projects and the fact that Question Time in both Federal and Regional parliaments was usually largely taken up with requests from members for schools, electricity supply, roads and water for their own constituencies.

But this sense of community – what we have earlier called the 'primordial-ism of identity'[2] – can be articulated at many levels. As the leading counsel to the Tribunal of Enquiry into Lagos City Council put it in July 1966: 'almost all the people in the Council practise tribalism. And to them all tribalism is the greatest misery...It splits and re-splits again and again, first into Easterners and Westerners, then into Ibos and Yoruba and again into Ijebu, Ijesha, Egba, Ekiti and Oyo and still further into Lagosian, Lagos Muslims and Lagos aborigines.'[3] It might be more accurate to say that people carry round with them a whole bundle of different primordial identities, ranging from lineage group, village, clan, town and administrative division, through to ethnic group, region and finally nation.[4] Which level is evoked depends on the context and circumstances and may indeed be in conflict with loyalties at other levels.

It is usual to talk of 'tribalism' in terms of the maximal ethnic groups sharing common language and/or culture. The main so-called tribes in Nigeria are, however, very large and might more appropriately be called nations. Some contain considerable diversity within themselves. The Hausa–Fulani, for instance, are divided by the racial distinction (or traces thereof) between the conquering Fulani and their Habe subjects,[5] which

---

[1] See for instance the interesting discussion of ethnic unions among the Mbaise Ibo in M. C. Smock, 'The NCNC and ethnic unions in Biafra', *Journal of Modern African Studies*, VII, 1 (1969), 21–34. Smock argues that in certain respects the NCNC in the area could be regarded as a 'holding company for a gathering of clan unions', although there was also some specific loyalty to the party as such.

[2] See the preceding chapter.   [3] *West Africa* (London), 16 July 1966.

[4] Here we differ from Geertz, 'The integrative revolution', who, as we have seen, contrasts the over-arching civil order at a national level with tribe, religion, race etc.

[5] Though this was usually diluted by generations of intermarriage. For the social organisation of the Emirates, see the works of M. G. Smith already cited and B. J. Dudley, *Parties and politics in Northern Nigeria* (London: Cass, 1968).

222

corresponds to some extent with the class distinction between the *sarakuna* and the commoner *talakawa*; they are split between rival kingdoms, some (but not all) of them owing spiritual allegiance to Sokoto or Gwandu; they contain various subject peoples sharing their culture and Moslem religion to a greater or lesser degree; and they possess a language, Hausa, which is also spoken widely outside their own boundaries. Even groups like the Ibo or Tiv which are more homogeneous in culture and social organisation have in the past not acted as a single political unit.[1] For many such tribes the idea that they might have a common political identity and common interests at stake against the competition of other groups is a relatively new one. Tribes in the modern context are thus often little more than loose agglomerations of the primary communities of origin, whether these be towns, clans or villages. It is the more intensive contact with *other* groups in the modern situation which brings wider loyalties into focus. And even then internal cleavages often take precedence over pan-tribal loyalty, as in the recurring disputes between different areas of the West, which have plagued all attempts to achieve unity among the Yorubas.

3. Tribal, regional and communal images are given an extra sharpness because they are used by others to categorise and guide their interaction with the groups they mark out (this is what we earlier defined as the 'primordialism of projection'). Sometimes the identities of others may be used as a butt for extra-punitive hostility, anxiety and fear, as we have shown in our analysis of the July 1966 coup; sometimes to define the situation created by the arrival of new immigrant groups, like the Ibos in the North; sometimes as a short-hand for the conflict created by the competition for economic resources and jobs; and sometimes politicians have deliberately manipulated such images to widen their own support, as when Chief Akintola launched his onslaught on the Ibos in 1964. Whatever the precise function filled, such images have been a powerful influence on political conduct, as we emphasise at several places in this book, because of their simplicity and ability to touch the springs of non-rational motivation.

4. Region was also built into the political identities of Nigerians though, for the most part, less sharply than their narrower communal ties. The strongest assertion of regionalism before 1966 came from the North, where the Sardauna of Sokoto's slogan of 'One North, One People, irrespective of religion, race or tribe' was aimed at the Northern minorities, whose support the NPC was trying to secure but also expressed a kind of universalism which the Hausa–Fulani leaders, almost alone among Nigeria's communal patrons,

---

[1] Not, at least, in contacts with outsiders, even though one may in certain cases, like the Tiv, be able to talk of a common political system, in their case constructed out of opposed lineage segments and mythical common ancestors.

possessed.[1] Mutual distrust between the North and the south in Nigeria was associated with different attitudes to tradition and modernity. In terms of education and economic development, the North was, to be sure, far behind. It relied very heavily on the traditional Native Authorities for both its local government and courts system and for the organisation at local level of the NPC. The Sardauna of Sokoto, Sir Ahmadu Bello, was himself a member of the royal family of Sokoto and the majority of the other important NPC figures were aristocrats and traditional office-holders. So that the image of the North held by the southern intelligentsia (among them the officers who staged the January coup) was, in the words of the UPGA manifesto for the December 1964 elections, one of 'reaction, feudalism and neocolonialism'. This image did not, however, do justice to reality in the North: the traditional structures were only partly ascriptive and high political office was attained through intense competition between aristocratic eligibles; most of the NPC's leaders were among the small group of Northerners who first received a post-primary education at Katsina Training College in the 1930s; and Alhaji Sir Ahmadu Bello initiated a number of important administrative reforms in the North, which reflected his ideas about the obligation of the aristocrats, like the Tories of Britain, to earn by their reforms 'the right to go on ruling'.[2] The politicians and intelligentsia in the south perceived little of this, perhaps because of the difficulty of reconciling the North's feudal exterior with the symbolic trappings of modernity, and perhaps simply because it was humiliating for them to feel beholden to the rulers of the North, because of that region's dominant position in the Federation. The misunderstanding that lay behind these images, in sum, was responsible for much of the bitterness of the intelligentsia towards the North, as well as for the inward-looking policies of the Northern government itself.

5. Power under the politicians was used to divert resources for three purposes. First, for personal enrichment, whether by outright corruption, or by using political office to secure import licences, tariff protection and other advantages for industries in which they had a personal interest (a practice initiated by Chief Okotie-Eboh, the Federal Minister of Finance), or by

[1] Partly, it should be said, because ethnic particularism made little sense inside the Hausa–Fulani area itself because of its heterogeneity. This did not of course prevent Northern politicians, the Sardauna included, from making projective attacks on members of the southern tribes, particularly the Ibos, or from engaging in Moslem proselytisation.

[2] C. S. Whitaker, Jr, 'Three perspectives in hierarchy: political thought and leadership in Northern Nigeria', *Journal of Commonwealth Political Studies*, III (1965), 11. The reforms included the introduction of elected councils in the Native Authorities, the consolidation of Moslem and common law principles in the Penal Code of 1959 and Criminal Procedure Code of 1960 and an economic development programme that compared favourably with those of other regions. Politically, however, the NPC regime in the North remained oppressive and was not at all tolerant of dissent (see Dudley, *Parties and politics in Northern Nigeria*). Yet the politicians in the south were themselves no more tolerant.

purchases or leases of government land on unduly favourable terms, or by contracts from government departments, or loans from government development corporations and finance agencies. The politicians came increasingly to regard all of these things as their legitimate perquisites of office.[1] Secondly, to divert resources to the politicians' own communities and keep their own local patronage machines well-oiled. And, finally, to keep themselves and their party in power. Even a supposedly radical party like the Action Group was found by the 'Report of the Coker Commission of Enquiry' (set up by the Federal authorities to look into the Western Region public corporations after the declaration of emergency in the region in 1962) to have misappropriated funds on a very large scale, in order to improve the party's finances and electoral organisation.[2] The other parties never had their finances so thoroughly looked into, but there is no doubt that all of them diverted government monies, either directly into party funds or indirectly into party patronage networks.

6. Conflict has been increased by the unevenness in the distribution of resources between the different parts of the Federation and the uneven pace of modernisation. Thus the greater buoyancy of revenue sources, like oil, in some regions has tended to lead to conflict with the other regions and the Federation over revenue allocation. The energy and commercial success of immigrant groups in the more backward areas, like the Ibos in the North, has also brought resentment upon them. The collective efforts of groups like the Ibos, who were later in the field with education, to establish themselves in the Federal bureaucracies and universities, led to bitter conflict with those like the Yorubas who were already established in them. And the attempts of the North to use its dominant political position to catch up by applying political criteria to the location of development projects, promoting Northern civil servants above their southern contemporaries and applying a quota on recruitment to the army, all added to the bitterness of the south's politicians and intelligentsia against its 'conservative' leadership.

7. Another factor of conflict was that resources were diminishing overall through the last years of civilian rule, relative to the high aspirations of

---

[1] When there was a press scandal about the conduct of the Minister of Aviation, Dr K. O. Mbadiwe, in certain land deals in 1965, he was defended by Chief K. Balogun, the NCNC's legal advisor, with great frankness: 'to say that financial transactions in land and landed property by many leading citizens of Nigeria have not become a gainful pastime is to start deceiving ourselves. All top Nigerians, Ministers, Parliamentarians, top civil servants, journalists, hold positions of trust in one form or the other. They all indulge in these transactions. When it suits our purpose we quote conventions surrounding the British Parliamentary system. When it again suits our purpose we close our eyes to certain practices, all in the name of the Nigerian way of life. Our journalists must make up their minds which system they are going to uphold in Nigeria, the British Parliamentary conventions or the Nigerian way of life as it exists today, where everybody regards it as fair to make money.' *West Africa* (London), 6 March 1965.
[2] 'Report of the Coker Commission of Enquiry into the Affairs of Certain Statutory Corporations in Western Nigeria', 4 vols (Lagos: Ministry of Information, 1962).

Independence. The vast resources of the marketing boards in the regions were all squandered, and could not be replenished because of low world prices. Chief Akintola's government in the West was particularly hard hit, because the regional emergency and transfer of power from the AG to the NNDP coincided with the exhaustion of the region's reserves: so that his regime was doubly unpopular, because it could no longer maintain the lavish development and welfare expenditure of its predecessors and was forced, furthermore, to reduce cocoa producer price because of the exhaustion of reserves and falling world prices. The scope for patronage was also decreased, both because of worsened financial conditions and because the indigenisation of the public services came to an end. The filling up of the top posts in the civil service, the corporations and the universities with Nigerians meant that there were relatively few openings still to be occupied, and competition for them became fierce, all the more so because of the high aspirations raised by the rapid advancement of the earlier entrants and the expansion of the educational system.

8. Political resources also diminished after Independence. The popular legitimacy of both the Federal and the regional governments declined and the ruling parties had to rely more and more on coercion to keep themselves in power. One simple reason for this was the shortage of economic and patronage resources for the ruling class to distribute around. Another was that the conspicuous consumption and corruption of the politicians eventually made them disliked, this being among the main reasons for the wide support in urban areas for the general strike of 1964. And, finally, the increasing reliance on coercion itself brought unpopularity on the government: there was a spiral of unpopularity, force, illegitimacy and more force. Commercial privileges were withdrawn from political opponents[1] and the local courts and local government machinery used to intimidate them in all regions. Opposing candidates were prevented from putting in their nominations and, in a number of cases, imprisoned on flimsy charges, particularly in the North during the regional and Federal elections of 1961 and 1964, respectively.[2] Local government police forces were used in the West and the North to break up political meetings and intimidate those who attended; and in the West attempts were actually made to buy the support of the Nigeria Police.[3] Party thugs were

[1] See the Eastern Region examples given in Sklar, *Nigerian political parties*, p. 449.
[2] See the discussion of this in Dudley, 'Federalism and the balance of power in Nigeria', *Journal of Commonwealth Political Studies*, IV, 1 (1966), p. 25.
[3] See the strange case of Chief Odofin Bello, the Western Region Commissioner of Police, who was convicted by the Western Region High Court after the January 1966 coup of having received bribes from the NNDP to protect party supporters, but was acquitted on appeal by the Supreme Court. At the first trial the Treasurer of the Party, Chief Adeyi, and the Regional Minister of Finance, Oba Akran, admitted the party budgeted monies for 'police'. *Odofin Bello v. The State*: Supreme Court of Nigeria, 21 October 1966, see *Nigerian Monthly Law Reports* (January 1967).

employed by political parties, most notably by the NNDP and AG in the West, in 1965. And when protests against the political order led to violence or organised protest against it, the 'legitimate' means of violence, the army or the Mobile Squad of the Police, were brought in to restore order, as in the Tiv Division and Western Region disturbances, or to patrol the streets and run essential services, as during the general strike of 1964. The coups of 1966 may thus be seen in some respects as the culminating twists to a spiral of violence that had been building up for some time, and which reached a crescendo in the Western Region in late 1965 and January 1966.

9. There were few institutions in Nigerian society that had the strength or the autonomy to stand up to these processes. The political kingdom was supreme. Economic allocations were distorted to reflect the relative political power of the groups making them,[1] and most indigenous businessmen were clients or members of the political class. The judiciary was cowed.[2] The universities were riven with factional disputes. The civil service, police and army had been very much weakened both by the hasty indigenisation of their personnel and by the vastly greater demands that were placed upon them after self-government; and, in any case, they were committed by a code of political neutrality (at least in theory) to do what the politicians told them, even if to their own detriment.

Yet the political parties and other political organisations for their part also lacked autonomy. They were prone – particularly the southern parties – to internal disputes which arose from the difficulty of keeping all the communal interests they represented satisfied. And they had too few institutional roots, and too little genuine popular support, to stand up to a determined attempt to resist or overthrow them: as was demonstrated both in the capitulation of the government to the demands of the strikers in 1964 and in its quick collapse after the January 1966 coup. Even if the political kingdom was supreme, the political organisations which sought to mobilise, control and satisfy political demands were themselves also fragile in the extreme.

10. The intrusion of political conflict into some of the major bureaucracies, so that these split on communal and ethnic lines, is a special case of this institutional fragility, and is of interest here because of the comparison it affords with the army. There were four main factors in this process, though

---

[1] W.H. Warren, for instance, shows in 'Urban real wages and the Nigerian trades union movement', *Economic Development and Cultural Change*, xv, 1 (October 1966), that wage movements in Nigeria have borne little or no relation to economic conditions in the labour market, being mostly determined by the political strength of the unions vis-a-vis the government at different points of time.

[2] Though there was no actual confrontation with the judiciary, there were subtle ways of encroaching on its independence: see the examples given in Mackintosh, *Nigerian government and politics*, pp. 42–6, of how the Prime Minister, Sir Abubakar Tafawa Balewa, sought to bring the judiciary into line.

all were not necessarily present in every case. Firstly, a certain amount of favouritism in appointments, promotions and the like, based on nepotism, friendship and political intrigue, the sum effect (though not necessarily the overt intention) of which was a degree of preferment for certain ethnic or regional groups over others. This was often as much a matter of organisational weakness – as in the procedural confusion surrounding appointments and promotions in the Nigerian Railway Corporation[1] – as it was of design.

Secondly, there was the political context of the times and symbolic use made of ethnic arithmetic by the politicians and others to fit the bureaucracies into that context. The onslaught made by Chief Akintola's government in its notorious 'White Paper on the New Political Alignment in Western Nigeria' on the position of the Ibos in the University of Ibadan, Nigerian Airways, the Railway Corporation and the Ports Authority, was made all the more effective by the use of detailed but largely spurious tribal statistics.[2] A certain amount of tribal and regional preferment did indeed exist in these institutions, but it was greatly exaggerated by the suspicions and fears of all the groups concerned and the calculated use made of them by the politicians.

Thirdly, all of these organisations were beset by severe organisational cleavages and strains, especially the universities, where Nigerianisation had been almost as recent and as fast as in the army. This lack of cohesion made it difficult for them to withstand outside pressures. In addition, their own cleavages often came to be projected in primordial imagery. This was particularly noticeable in the Lagos University dispute, where the difficulties between the Registrar and the Vice-Chancellor, Dr Njoku, the tensions between the Medical School and the other faculties, the replacement of Dr Njoku with Dr Biobaku, the split between the Senate and the University Council, and the quarrels between different staff and student factions, were all interpreted, or came subsequently to be interpreted, in terms of machinations among varying combinations of Yorubas, Ibos and expatriates (the

---

[1] A very detailed account of the administrative confusion and irregularities in the appointment and promotion of staff is contained in the 'Report of the Nigerian Railway Corporation Tribunal of Enquiry' (Lagos: Ministry of Information, 1967), Part X. From the account contained in this report, it seems that preferment proceeded mainly on nepotistic lines – so that one finds several complaints against those responsible coming from their own ethnic group – although the *cumulative* effect may have been tribal.

[2] See the point-by-point refutation of the allegations in Nigerian Railway Corporation: 'A Rejoinder to the Western Nigeria Government White Paper No 1 of 1964 on "The New Political Alignment in Western Nigeria"' (Lagos, 1964) and University of Ibadan: *A statement on recent accusations of tribalism* (Ibadan, 1964). Of course, these documents clear up only the most obvious distortions of fact and are themselves as subject to political bias as the documents they purport to refute. The 'Report of the Nigerian Railway Corporation Tribunal of Enquiry', cited above, suggests there was some 'tribalism' in that institution, but by no means as much as the Yoruba politicians were trying to make out.

expatriates counted as a tribe in this context) or of *anti*-Yoruba, Ibo or expatriate intrigues.[1]

Finally, there was a cumulation of conflict throughout the Federal bureaucracies. As each of the groups saw their compatriots coming under attack in the other institutions, so their fears for their own position and suspicion of their colleagues from other areas increased. Even those organisations which were less vulnerable, because better institutionalised, like the Federal civil service itself, started to feel the impact. For example, there was a furore caused late in 1965 by the transfer into administrative class of a bloc of civil servants from the Northern public service, who were placed a grade above their southern university contemporaries. And it is against this ferment in the other bureaucracies that some of the anxieties of the Majors of January about the army must be placed.

[1] Witness the violent accusations made in the pamphlet war engaged in by both sides.

CHAPTER X

CIVILIAN CONTROL OF THE MILITARY, 1958–66

INTRODUCTION

In this chapter, we set the army's political role against the conflict-torn political environment after Independence. Two questions immediately suggest themselves. What features, if any, of civilian control of the military, of the way in which the politicians handled the army, led to the politicisation of various groups in the officer corps and encouraged them to intervene in politics? And conversely, in view of the high level of political conflict, why did the military not intervene *sooner* than January 1966?

To answer the second of these questions, it will be shown that the army emerged from colonial tutelage later than most other institutions in Nigerian society. The most obvious result of this was that most of the leading positions in the command hierarchy remained in British hands until 1964–5. Senior Nigerian officers who took over had also served for several years in the colonial period and were well-indoctrinated with British ideas of civilian control of the military, so that the impetus for intervention had to come from below them. In addition, it will be argued, the politicians in the Federal government were very careful not to bring the army into politics. On the one hand, the military leaders played little or no part in the making of the major policy decisions on foreign policy, security or indeed military expansion, except as the executants of policy. And on the other, the politicians and especially the Federal Prime Minister, were cautious about interfering in matters of the internal organisation of the armed forces, with the single notable exception of the regional recruitment quota.

The impetus to intervene came, we shall argue, from a number of largely unanticipated or latent consequences of civilian control. In the first place, the very isolation of the military establishment from policy-making made officers more prone to criticise. Their own hands were clean and there was therefore no contradiction in telling the politicians that theirs were dirty. The puritan political ethic of the military man (for which see Chapter XII below) was more clearly defined, however, in the middle ranks than at the top, because the senior officers alone had had a certain amount of political experience with which to dilute it. Secondly, the crisis of the civilian regime in certain respects *imposed* political choices on the military, as when the commanders of the armed forces and police decided not to take orders from the President during the crisis after the Federal general election of 1965. Thirdly, the efforts of the Northern People's Congress to achieve a regional balance in the officer corps through a quota in recruitment, was widely regarded by southern officers as undue political interference in the military corporation, and raised acute suspicions that similar principles might be applied to the appointments and promotions of officers already in the army. And fourthly, the use made by the civilian authorities of the army for internal security operations in the Tiv Division and the Western Region was resented by many officers, both as a challenge to their professional identity as soldiers rather than policemen, and because they objected to dealing with disorders which resulted from the actions of a government with which they disagreed and for which they were not responsible.

OUT OF TUTELAGE

In the first years of Independence, therefore, the Nigerian Army seemed to be isolated from the vigorous political conflict outside it. For it was decolonised later than other institutions, having evolved in a direct line of continuity from one of the instruments of violence of imperial rule, the Nigeria Regiment of the Royal West African Frontier Force. Because colonial rule was based in the last resort on the threat of coercion, control over the army, like the police, was devolved on Nigerian politicians later than the other instruments of power. Under colonial rule, indeed, the West African forces had been part of the *British* Army under the direct control of the British Army Council – in contrast to the colonial civil service and police force, which had been to a large extent self-regulating agencies. The West Africa Command was broken up in 1956, shortly before the Independence of Ghana in 1957. It was not until 1958, however, that the disposition and control of the Nigerian forces, together with their budget, was transferred to Nigeria, and even then the final authority for the operational control and use of the army remained with the colonial Governor General.[1]

Independence did not immediately end dependence on Britain, though steps were taken to seek assistance and equipment from other sources and to develop a broader-based foreign policy. At the 1958 Constitutional Conference, the Nigerian delegates had initialled a draft defence agreement with Britain, giving the latter over-flying facilities and the right to construct air-

---

[1] Advised by a Federal Defence Council, which included the Federal Prime Minister and the regional premiers. The Prime Minister himself took on the defence and internal security portfolios in 1960, shortly before Independence.

staging facilities at Kano airport, in exchange for British assistance in the training and equipment of the army.[1] In April 1960, before Independence, Chief Awolowo released details of the agreement (which he himself had initialled) and precipitated an acrimonious attack on it. The proposal for staging facilities were dropped. But the agreement was finally ratified after Independence, in November 1960, in a stormy debate in the House of Representatives. One year later, however, it was abrogated by mutual consent, in December 1961, in response to external diplomatic pressure from other African states,[2] rather than to domestic political pressure. The issues raised by the defence agreement and its rupture were, however, largely symbolic. The facilities granted to Britain had been relatively minor and some of them were continued by executive agreement after the abrogation of the pact. Britain continued to supply military equipment and provided strong support for the Nigerianisation of the officer corps by making increased numbers of officer cadet places available at Sandhurst and other officer cadet schools.

Nevertheless, from 1961 the government sought to diversify its sources of military assistance. In that year the first Nigerian officer was sent to a staff training course outside the UK.[3] By 1963, officer cadets and serving officers were undergoing training in Australia, Canada, Ethiopia, India, Pakistan and the USA, as well as in Britain. The Nigerian Defence Academy, which was opened in 1964, was staffed and organised by a military mission from India. Sources of arms procurement were also diversified to a number of different suppliers. A West German firm contracted to build an ordnance factory in Kaduna on a turnkey basis. And the German government also gave assistance in the establishment of an air force after 1964 by providing training and planes.

The most substantial change from imperial tutelage, however, was the indigenisation of the command structure. In 1958 nearly all the officer corps and a substantial proportion of the NCOs were British. The tardiness in Nigerianising the personnel of the army compared to other governmental structures may have been partly due to the special status of coercion in colonial rule. This was no excuse, however, for the unreasonable delay in finding Nigerian officers when Independence was in sight. An important factor in the delay was that control over recruitment and promotions, until 1958, had been with the British Army Council, which was relatively immune to political pressures on the spot. The British command had also found it difficult to attract qualified applicants for the cadet-school places it

[1] There are discussions of the Anglo–Nigeria Defence Agreement and its implications in C. S. Phillips, Jr, *The development of Nigerian foreign policy* (Evanston, Ill.: Northwestern University Press, 1964), Chapter III, and Mackintosh, *Nigerian government and politics*, Chapter VI.

[2] Mackintosh, *Nigerian government and politics*, p. 278. The agreement was probably dropped by Sir Abubakar in order to encourage the radical 'Casablanca bloc' African states to attend the Lagos Conference of 1962.

[3] Maimalari to the Pakistan Staff College, Quetta.

offered Nigerians, because it was unwilling to provide the material and symbolic inducements in terms of salary, car allowances and promotions that would make the army as attractive to potential officer recruits as other elite occupations.[1]

After the transfer of control in 1958 all this was changed. The government was subject to strong public and parliamentary pressure – both from the Select Committee on Nigerianisation and from the floor of the House – to replace the remaining expatriates with Nigerian officers and men. It was reluctant to be pinned down to a firm schedule, however, though in 1959 it suggested six years as the *minimum* length of time within which it would be possible to achieve the complete Nigerianisation of the officer corps[2] – a minimum that was eventually adhered to, despite demands that the process be still further accelerated. Yet it required drastic action to step up the recruitment and promotion of Nigerian officers. Qualifications for entry were reduced and salaries and car allowances raised. Promotions were stepped up, with the effect both of filling the top posts in the officer corps with Nigerians more quickly and of providing visible incentives for secondary-school leavers to join. As we noted in Table 27,[3] whereas only eighteen per cent of the officers were Nigerian on 1 January 1960, the entire officer corps was indigenous by the end of 1965.

The emergence of the army out of tutelage seems to have brought a perceptible improvement in the military's prestige and self-image. The unpopularity of the military as the instrument of colonial rule and the low pay of soldiers had meant that recruits came mainly from the more remote and less prosperous areas of the country. Morale had not been very good and there had been at least one attempt at mutiny[4] in the post-war period. There is some controversy over whether the British officers seconded to the army were of poor calibre – though what little hard evidence there is does not seem to support this contention.[5] What is important, however, is that their period of service in West Africa was very short, tending to reduce their commitment to the country and its army; and to make it difficult to establish stable lines of authority because of the rapid turnover in command posts.

Independence linked the army to the symbols of sovereignty, not depend-

---

[1] For a detailed discussion, see N. J. Miners, 'The Nigerian Army 1956–66', unpublished Ph.D. dissertation (University of Exeter, 1968). Miners covers the period prior to the 1966 coup in more detail than is given here. This chapter owes a certain amount to Miners' thorough description of the period, soon to be made available in book form by Methuen.

[2] 'Final Report of the Parliamentary Committee on the Nigerianisation of the Public Service', Sessional Paper no. 6 of 1959 (Lagos: Government Printer, 1959).

[3] See p. 163 above.

[4] By southern clerks, etc. at the Ordnance Department, Yaba, 1952.

[5] The data provided by Miner's, 'The Nigerian Army 1956–66' as to the subsequent careers of officers who had been seconded to the Royal West African Frontier Force do not, however, seem to support this contention.

ence, a transition that was marked by changes in uniform and the insignia of rank. The ceremonial dress of the troops, in particular, was no longer the red fez, monkey jacket and shorts, which made them look like figures in a colonial comic opera, but was changed to more distinguished and serviceable green and khaki uniforms. A Federal Guard unit was created for guard duties at important public buildings in the capital and for guards of honour on ceremonial occasions (though ironically the Guard figured significantly in both the January and July 1966 coups). Parades, military bands and marchpasts all served to associate the army in the public mind with the rituals of Independence. The successful role of the army in the United Nations contingent to the Congo from 1960 to 1964 served also to link its image to national pride, especially when Major General Ironsi was made the commander of the UN force in 1964. The improvements in pay and conditions introduced after 1958 also improved morale and increased the quality of recruitment into the ranks (though the same was not true of the officer corps because of the great expansion in the officer entry). The level of communication between officers and men may well have improved too, but to offset this was the organisational disruption created by the hasty indigenisation of the officer corps, discussed in Chapter VII.

MILITARY POWER AND MILITARY NEUTRALITY

To what extent did the army's role in providing symbolic and coercive backing for national power give it any political power itself? Not very much, it seems. On the one hand, it preserved its neutrality and organisational integrity, its lack of permeation by civilian values and interest – to such an extent, indeed, that its neutrality was a political resource of some value, which helped to legitimate its seizure of power in January 1966. On the other hand, the price for neutrality was political emasculation, the lack of any significant ability to influence specific government decisions in favour of itself or of policies it supported. On the surface at least, civil–military relations in the period 1960–6 followed the classic model of civilian control, on lines familiar from the British heritage of a non-political army, only more so.

The army's lack of day-to-day political influence was perhaps most evident when it came to the expansion of the armed forces. The military needs of an independent state exceeded those of the colonial government, which could rely in the last resort on the military power of the metropolitan country. By any standards (as we argued in Chapter III), the army was very small. Yet such expansion as took place between 1958 and 1966 was not at all impressive. The first meetings of the Federal Defence Council decided in principle, as early as 1958, to set up the Nigerian Military Training College to replace the

TABLE 39. *Trend of military expenditures, 1958–66*

Year	Army only (£mn)	Total defence costs (£mn)	Army costs as per cent of Federal re-current spending	Defence costs as per cent of Federal re-current spending	Year	Army only (£mn)	Total capital spending defence (£mn)	Army costs as per cent of Federal capital spending	Defence costs as per cent of Federal capital spending
		Recurrent expenditure					**Capital expenditure**		
1958–9	2·82	2·98	8·1	8·5	1958–9	0·86	0·89	3·1	3·2
1959–60	3·70	3·99	9·2	9·9	1959–60	0·35	0·55	1·0	1·5
1960–1	3·98	4·43	8·7	9·6	1960–1	0·83	1·27	1·7	2·6
1961–2	4·05	4·56	7·6	8·6	1961–2	1·26	1·62	3·9	5·1
1962–3	4·08	4·71	6·8	7·8	1962–3	2·00	3·82	4·9	9·4
1963–4	4·52	5·59	6·2	7·7	1963–4	2·82	4·10	6·3	9·2
1964–5	5·17	6·59	6·8	8·7	1964–5	2·69	5·26	5·2	10·3
1965–6	5·84	7·85	7·0	9·4	1965–6	2·13	6·75	3·8	12·1

Sources: Federation of Nigeria: *Annual Estimates, Annual Report of the Accountant General, Digest of Statistics.*

officer cadet facilities previously available in Ghana,[1] to create a Reconnaissance Squadron equipped with armoured cars and to raise a sixth Battalion. The first two objectives were achieved not long after Independence, but the 6th Battalion was not finally formed until 1966, eight years after the original decision to create it. Later in the period, it was also decided to create a Nigerian Defence Academy,[2] a second Reconnaissance Squadron and two artillery batteries, all of which were duly established by mid-1966. Numbers steadily increased – from around 7,500 in 1958 to 10,500 in 1965 – and so did the levels of military expenditure (see Table 39). But the expansion was by no means a rapid one – and it twice underwent serious cuts, once in 1962 and again in 1964. Looked at as a *proportion* of the budget, moreover, total spending on defence increased only very slightly more than other budgetary expenditure, whereas spending on the army actually decreased in proportional terms: total defence spending increased from 8·5 per cent of the Federal recurrent budget, or 3·2 per cent of the Federal and regional budgets combined, in the 1958–9 financial year, to 9·4 per cent and 4·5 per cent respectively, in 1965–6.

[1] The preliminary selection and training courses for officer cadets had been held at the West African Command Training School at Teshie in Ghana. Cadets passing out from this school (and later from the NMTC) were then sent to England for further training at Sandhurst, Eaton Hall or Mons.
[2] The Defence Academy established in 1964 provided a full three-year cadet training, unlike the NMTC, which only provided preliminary training prior to the sending of cadets to England.

235

Capital expenditures increased much faster, mainly because there was a heavy fixed cost component in creating military installations appropriate to an independent status (a new building for the Ministry of Defence, an ordnance factory in Kaduna, armoured cars for the Recce Squadrons and the creation of a navy and air force from scratch). The capital costs of the new navy and air force were especially burdensome, being, for instance, some £3·84 million out of the total defence capital outlay of £6·75 million in 1965–6. Whereas the capital spending on defence had been only 3·2 per cent of the Federal capital budget and 2·2 per cent of the combined Federal and regional outlay in 1958–9, it was 12·1 and 8·0 per cent respectively in 1965–6.

Nevertheless, the government still made *less* use of Nigeria's military potential in 1966 than did most other countries in Africa and, indeed, in the rest of the world. As we saw in Table 14,[1] Nigeria spent proportionately less of its budget and of its national product on defence and had proportionately fewer of its available manpower under arms than any other country of comparable size.

It is significant that much of the effective pressure for military enlargement, such as it was, came from the politicians, rather than the army itself. The guiding force behind the expansion was Alhaji Muhammadu Ribadu, Minister of Defence from Independence in October 1960 until his death in early 1965. Ribadu was a forceful personality and one of the leading politicians in the Northern People's Congress, with an influence that sometimes rivalled that of the Prime Minister. He was able to secure an allocation for his ministry of £30 million in the 1962–8 National Development Plan. And, as chairman of the Economic Policy Committee of the Federal Cabinet until 1964, he was able to maintain an effective grip on annual budgetary allocations to the military.[2] Opposition to an increase in military spending, such as it was, came mainly from other ministers, anxious not to sustain cuts in their own appropriations, and from the economists in the Ministry of Finance, the Ministry of Economic Development and the Economic Planning Unit of that ministry. But it cannot be said that there was much *public* criticism of expansion – indeed, the reverse was the case, as can be seen in any quick perusal of the press or parliamentary debates for the period. Since defence policy was virtually in a political vacuum, it is perhaps surprising that Ribadu did not do better.[3]

[1] See p. 89 above.

[2] It is said, for instance, that he used his position as chairman of this committee to get the other ministers to agree to his appropriations before allowing them to discuss the allocation of the remainder among their own ministries.

[3] In contrast, even in those nations like the USA, Britain or Sweden, where the military leadership is under a firm system of 'objective' civilian control, it usually plays an effective political role in shaping defence policies, calling attention to potential security threats, bargaining over weapons systems and evolving strategy. See Janowitz, *The professional soldier* and B. Abrahamsson, 'The

Nor did the army command play a leading part in policy-making on problems of national security.[1] In part, of course, this reflected the simple absence of an external military threat, a divorce between foreign policy (conducted largely in terms of overlapping memberships in international organisations, like the UN, the Organisation of African Unity and the Commonwealth) and problems of defence. The only foreign policy matters that had required the deployment of military force for ends of state had been Nigeria's participation in the peace-keeping operations in the Congo from 1960 to 1964, and the help given to Tanzania after the 1964 army mutiny there, when Nigeria was invited to send a small contingent to replace the British troops which had put down the rebellion. Yet this merely brought the army in as the executant of foreign policy, and the basic decisions about the Congo – like the decisions to take part in the UN venture in the first place, and then later to maintain the contingent in the Congo after the radical African states like Ghana had pulled theirs out – originated from the politicians alone.

The army was also brought in on a number of occasions to deal with threats real or supposed to internal security. It helped the police to quell riots in Tiv Division in 1960 and 1964, and in the Western Region in late 1965–January 1966. It paraded through the streets of Lagos, to 'show the flag', in the course of the crisis over the 1964 Federal election. It maintained essential services during the general strike of 1964. And it maintained an alert in the Western Region in 1962, both on the declaration of a state of emergency after rioting in the Regional Assembly and on the day of Chief Awolowo's alleged plot to overthrow the Federal government. Again, the army's role was a passive one: to carry out orders in the event of disturbance, rather than to assist the government to evolve consistent and effective policies on internal security matters.

Up to January 1966, there had been only one attempt by any of the politicians to pull the army into an overt political role. During the constitutional crisis after the 1964 general election, Dr Azikiwe, the President, tried to use his authority as Commander in Chief to obtain military and police backing when he proposed to suspend the government, annul the elections and appoint an interim government to conduct new elections. The GOC, Major General Welby-Everard, the Navy Commander, Commodore Wey, and the Inspector General of Police, Mr Edet, had, however, anticipated such

ideology of an elite: conservatism and national insecurity: some notes on the Swedish military' in van Doorn (ed.), *Armed forces and society.*

[1] This may be a measure of the increasing authority of the Prime Minister after Independence. One indicator of the waning of Ribadu's influence was that he was manoeuvred out of the chairmanship of the Economic Policy Committee in 1964, at about the same time as the second series of cutbacks in military spending.

a situation and had taken legal advice from the Chief Justice, which indicated that they were under the operational orders of the Prime Minister,[1] the President's powers being purely formal. Thus when summoned for an interview by Dr Azikiwe, they declined to take their instructions from him;[2] and Welby-Everard sent a circular to his officers on the constitutional issue, to make quite sure that the position was understood by them. A number of middle-ranking officers, however, Lt Colonels Ojukwu, Banjo and possibly Ejoor among them, seriously discussed whether the military should intervene to resolve the crisis.[3] There are suggestions that Ojukwu may have been in touch with the President. But it is not known how far any of these intrigues were taken. Major General Welby-Everard had the support of the more senior Nigerian officers in the army command, so that it is doubtful whether the army would have taken a different position from that which it did even if its commander was not an expatriate – except if there had been an outright coup by the lieutenant colonels or some other middle-ranking group.

One very good reason for the army's neutrality, its vacuity on policy matters within its competence, was the dominant position of British expatriates in the upper levels of the command structure, up to 1964–5. The first Nigerian GOC, Major General Ironsi, was not appointed until February 1965. Table 40 – though based on incomplete data – gives an indication how late Nigerian officers rose into the commanding heights of the hierarchy.

And even with the British gone, the top command still showed little sign of departing from a neutral posture. Major General Ironsi is said to have had difficulty coming to grips with his command, and did not evolve a political standpoint of his own. He and the other senior officers had spent the greater part of their careers in any army hierarchy dominated by the British. In Table 41, we tabulate the career origins of the seven most senior officers in the army in January 1966, those who had reached the rank of full colonel and above, and compare them with the main organisers of the January coup. It will be seen that five of the seven senior officers had been NCOs before officer-training. They had all served a relatively long apprenticeship in the junior ranks of the officer corps, comparable to the normal periods spent in

[1] Under the Royal Nigerian Army Act (no. 26 of 1960) and the Royal Nigerian Navy Act (no. 9 of 1960), the Army and Navy were respectively 'under the general authority' of the Defence Minister of matters of 'command, discipline and administration'. The Council of Ministers and Prime Minister, but *not* the President (despite his title as Commander in Chief) were vested with authority for the operational use and control of these forces.

[2] Mackintosh, *Nigerian government and politics*, pp. 589–92. Welby-Everard did not wish, as an expatriate, to appear partial and simply refused to comment to the President on his orders, leaving it to Commodore Wey, the head of the Navy, to make the refusal explicit.

[3] In a newspaper interview with the editor of the *New Nigerian*, Major General Gowon stated that he was sounded out on his views in a discussion with these officers, but advised against intervention: *New Nigerian* (Kaduna), 16 August 1967. He is also said to have warned Major General Welby-Everard about what was going on.

TABLE 40. *Nigerianisation of command posts, 1960–5*

	British	Nigerian	Details not known
General Officer Commanding			
Up to February 1965	1	0	—
After February 1965	0	1	—
Brigade Commanders*a*			
January 1962	3	0	—
January 1963	2	1	—
January 1964	1	2	—
January 1965	0	2	—
Key staff posts*b*			
January 1962	7	0	—
January 1963	6	1	—
January 1964	2	5	—
January 1965	0	8	—
Battalion Commanders			
January 1960	5	0	—
January 1961	4	1	—
January 1962	2	1	2
January 1963	2	1	2
January 1964	0	3	2
January 1965	0	5	—

Source: Office and telephone directories (where available) for Lagos, Kaduna, Enugu and Ibadan.
Notes:
a A third Brigade HQ operated in the Congo during the UN operation from 1960 to 1964 only. This brigade was commanded by an Englishman until Brigadier Ogundipe took over in January 1963.
b Chief of Staff, Commandant of the Nigerian Military Training College/Deputy Commandant of the Defence Academy, GSO (I), Adjutant General, QMG and staff/technical posts at similar seniority levels (DEME, DST, CNOS). No Chief of Staff appointed until 1964.

these ranks by British officers, rather than to the very brief periods spent at each level by the rapidly promoted officer-generations commissioned into the army around the time of Independence. And all of them had undergone intensive staff training in Britain to the level of the Staff College, Camberley, and above.

The top military elite, moreover, was divided by personal rivalries, as well as by the personal friendships between senior officers and members of the political class. It may indeed be that the divisions among them were as important in diverting them from any attempt to seize power from the politicians as was any idea of loyalty to civilian control. Major General Ironsi is said to have been on bad terms with both his brigade commanders, Brigadiers Ademulegun and Maimalari. The latter had quarrelled with Ironsi in the Congo, and is said to have been more inclined to favour military

TABLE 41. *Comparison of career origins of senior officers and January 1966 conspirators*

	Senior post(s) held	Ethnicity/ region	Year com- missioned	Professional origin
	A Senior officers			
Maj Gen Ironsi	Brigade CO, GOC	Ibo (East)	1949	ex-NCO
Brigadier Ademulegun	Brigade CO	Yoruba (West)	1949	ex-NCO
Brigadier Ogundipe	Brigade CO	Yoruba (West)	1953	ex-NCO
Brigadier Maimalari	Brigade CO	Kanuri (North)	1953	Sandhurst
Colonel Adebayo	Chief of Staff	Yoruba (West)	1953	ex-NCO
Colonel Kuru Mohammed	CO, NMTC Chief of Staff	Kanuri (North)	1954	Sandhurst
Colonel Shodeinde	CO, NMTC	Yoruba (West)	1950	ex-NCO
	B January Majors and Captains			
Major Nzeogwu	Chief Instruc- tor, NMTC	Ibo (Mid-West)	1959	Sandhurst
Major Ifeajuna	Brigade Major	Ibo	1961	University graduate
Major Okafor	OC, Federal Guard	Ibo	1959	ex-NCO
Major Anuforo	OC, Recce Squadron GSO (II) Training	Ibo	1961	Sandhurst
T/Major Chukuka[d]	Deputy Adjutant General (II)	Ibo	1960	Sandhurst
T/Major Onwuatuegwu[d]	Instructor, NMTC	Ibo	1961	Sandhurst
T/Major Ademoyega[d]	?	Yoruba (West)	1962	University graduate
T/Captain Oji[d]	—	Ibo	1961	Short-service (Mons)

intervention than many other senior officers. Ademulegun had been Ironsi's main rival for promotion to GOC, and in addition is said to have become worried about the issue of the ethnic composition of the officer corps.[1]

Thus the 'neutrality' of the Nigerian high command was not of the same order as that of the British. Nigerian commanders tended to be tied into the structures of political influence and control rather closer than British officers had ever been. Informal contacts between the local brigade and unit commands and regional governments – between the commander of the 1st

[1] At one stage he apparently became concerned about the prevalence of Ibo officers at his 1st Brigade HQ, and took active steps to make sure the necessary adjustments were made in postings in his brigade.

TABLE 41 *(cont.)*

	Rate of promotion (in months)			Years in officer corps before Independence	Staff training[a]
	Lt to Captain	Captain to Major	Major to Lt Col		
A Senior officers					
Maj Gen Ironsi	28	64	48[b]	11	psc 1957 idc 1963
Brigadier Ademulegun	24	64	46[b]	11	psc 1958 idc 1963
Brigadier Ogundipe	17	64	9	7	psc 1959 idc 1965
Brigadier Maimalari	48	39	0[c]	7	psc (p) 1961 idc 1964
Colonel Adebayo	48	58	0[c]	7	psc 1960 idc 1966
Colonel Kuru Mohammed	48	35	0[c]	6	psc 1962
Colonel Shodeinde	41	64	25	10	psc 1961
B January Majors and Captains					
Major Nzeogwu	19	31	—	1	psc (p)
Major Ifeajuna	24	20	—	– 1	—
Major Okafor	22	41	—	1	—
Major Anuforo	19	17	—	– 1	—
T/Major Chukuka[d]	19	—	—	– 1	—
T/Major Onwuatuegwu[d]	24	—	—	– 1	—
T/Major Ademoyega[d]	19	—	—	– 2	—
T/Captain Oji[d]	—	—	—	– 1	—

Sources: Federation of Nigeria, *Official Gazettes* (1960–6), *The Owl: Journal of the Staff College,* Camberley and *The Journal of the Imperial Defence College, London.*
Notes:
[a] psc = Staff College, Camberley; psc (p) = Pakistan Staff College (Quetta); idc = Imperial Defence College, London. Major Nzeogwu went to staff college either in India or Pakistan, though the writer has been unable to ascertain which.
[b] Both promoted direct from substantive major to substantive brigadier in 1962 (though both officers already held acting appointments as lieutenant colonel).
[c] Promoted direct from substantive captain to substantive lieutenant colonel in 1962 and 1963.
[d] Temporary or acting ranks, in January 1966.

Brigade, in Kaduna, and the Northern premier, the 4th and 1st Battalions and the Western and Eastern premiers respectively – became more important, and these officers were invited to regional security meetings more often than their British predecessors. Similarly the GOC, the Chief of Staff and the commander of the 2nd Brigade in Lagos associated more closely than before with the Prime Minister, the Minister of Defence and other members of the Federal government. Brigadier Ademulegun was a personal friend of the

241

Sardauna of Sokoto and inspired Major Nzeogwu's aprocryphal disgust for taking off his shoes as a matter of courtesy, whenever entering the Sardauna's residence.[1] Lieutenant Colonel Largema, the commander of the 4th Battalion at Ibadan, was reportedly chided (rather unfairly) by one of the January conspirators, not long before the coup, for being beholden to his 'Baba', Chief Akintola.

The link between the army and political structures was confined, nevertheless, to indirect liaison alone, and was in no sense comparable to the day-to-day control wielded by the premiers over their Regional Police Commissioners.[2] And even at Federal level, where ministers did possess formal powers over the army, there is little evidence of systematic use of these to politicise the military or to build up client networks within it. Yet the informal links between the military elite and the politicians, innocent though they may have been in practice, were enough to arouse suspicion among the more politically minded younger officers – the more so when some of them turned away the overtures of the Majors of January 1966 to endorse or support their proposed intervention.

The suspicions in the officer corps about the Federal government seem, nevertheless, somewhat misplaced, when one considers the considerable restraint that the latter actually showed in its dealings with the military, this despite the fact that the NPC as the dominant partner in the Federal coalition kept its hands firmly on the levers of political control of the army. Both Nigeria's post-Independence Ministers of Defence, Alhaji Muhammadu Ribadu (1960–5) and Alhaji Inuwa Wada (1965–6), were important figures within the NPC. The Ministers of State for the Army, Mr Jacob Obande (1960–2) and Alhaji Tako Galadima (1962–6), were lesser politicians in the same party. Though the civil servant with administrative responsibilities for defence, the Permanent Secretary, Ministry of Defence, is in theory politically neutral, it is also perhaps of significance that the post was held by Northerners from 1961 onwards, despite the shortage of Northerners in the Federal public service. Thus the NPC may have felt itself well-placed to exercise

---

[1] In the North, this might be considered a matter of common courtesy even if the younger southern officers might not deign to do it. Ademulegun's friendship with the Sardauna did not necessarily mean there were no circumstances in which he would consider intervening against the regime. As we point out in Chapter I, he had radical political views, and was distrusted enough in Kaduna for some people to suspect in the first confusion of January 15 1966 that he had had a hand in the coup.

[2] The constitution placed the Nigeria Police in each region and the Police Commissioner of the region under the day-to-day operational control of the regional premier. The commissioner could, however, refer any order he disagreed with to the Federal government. Matters of policy and of recruitment, promotion and discipline were, however, entirely in the hands of the Federal Police Council and Police Service Commission, respectively. There is a more detailed comparison of the role of the police with that of the military in the writer's doctoral thesis: A. R. Luckham, 'The Nigerian military: a case study in institutional breakdown', unpublished Ph.D. dissertation (University of Chicago, 1969), pp. 299–308.

political controls over the army and to interfere with matters of army organisation, had it so wished.

Yet the Federal Prime Minister and Alhaji Ribadu were evidently sensitive to the dangers of interfering in professional matters where the army was concerned. One clear example was the decision to promote Brigadier Aguiyi-Ironsi (an Ibo) to Major General and make him the first Nigerian GOC, in March 1964, against the professional advice of the retiring British GOC, Major General Welby-Everard. Welby-Everard had suggested that the Prime Minister choose between Brigadiers Ademulegun and Ogundipe (both Yorubas) in preference to Ironsi, both of them having more experience in command at the brigade level.[1] Ironsi, however, was senior to both these officers in promotional dates[2] and also exceeded Ogundipe in length of service as an officer. And his experience as the UN Force Commander in the Congo made up for his deficiency in brigade command. Nigeria had just passed through the general election crisis of 1964, during which the NCNC had been humiliated and the NNDP elevated to share the power at the centre. In this context, a decision to appoint a Yoruba above a more senior Ibo officer could only have been interpreted, both within the army and outside it, as a political decision reflecting the change in the balance of power between the Yorubas and the Ibos. It is a fair inference that Sir Abubakar saw that if he had accepted Welby-Everard's advice, the cohesion of the military would suffer, and it would be difficult to contain political and tribal pressures, the more so given the numerical importance of the Ibos in the middle and upper ranks of the officer corps. This may be a case, therefore, where a 'political' decision to reject professional advice may, on balance, have been necessary to protect the army from politics. It is significant that Sir Abubakar seems also to have resisted informal pressure from the Sardauna of Sokoto to appoint Brigadier Maimalari,[3] a Northerner who was junior to all three of the above, but was the first Nigerian to pass through Sandhurst. Ribadu, it seems, had also put forward Maimalari's name, but had not placed it above that of Ironsi, whom he felt it politically wise to support.

RECRUITMENT AND THE ETHNIC BALANCE

The Northerners, however, had been able to make their weight felt on the matter of officer recruitment. Concern was felt within the NPC over the fact

[1] See M. J. Dent, 'The military and politics: a study of the relation between the army and the political process in Nigeria 1966–67', unpublished seminar paper (London: Institute of Commonwealth Studies, 1967). These contentions are also confirmed by other reliable sources.
[2] Ironsi was promoted lieutenant six months before Ademulegun. After this he slightly antedated him in all promotions, except to brigadier, for which they both had the same promotion date.
[3] The Sardauna's second choice was Ademulegun. One factor that seems to have weighed in Ironsi's favour with the Prime Minister was that he is said to have warned Sir Abubakar about the talk of army intervention that was going on during the election crisis of December 1964.

that such a high percentage of the entry into the officer corps in the late 1950s was from the south[1] – and in particular from the East and the Mid-West (then part of the Western Region). At first the Federal government tried to use informal methods to recruit more Northerners. Army Selection Boards were instructed to give preference to them when their qualifications and aptitude were equal to those of southern applicants. This was made easier by the establishment of the Nigerian Military Training College in 1960, to give preliminary officer cadet training in Nigeria – before selection for training in academies and cadet school abroad – rather than at the West Africa Command Training school, in Ghana. Yet there were too few Northerners with academic qualifications comparable to their southern opposite numbers for these methods to be effective, mainly because of the shortage of secondary schooling in the North. Accordingly, the government established a regional quota for officer selection in mid-1961, to be applied both on entry into the NMTC and on selection from it for courses abroad, fifty per cent for the North and twenty-five per cent for each of the other two regions. The minimum academic standards for entry were lowered,[2] and even these were waived in one or two cases in favour of Northern entrants from the Nigerian Military School. The failure rate for selection from the preliminary course at the NMTC was reduced, on Alhaji Ribadu's instructions, to accommodate struggling Northern entrants. And the Sardauna of Sokoto personally undertook a recruitment campaign in Northern secondary schools, emphasising in his speeches the former martial glories of the Jihads, and calling on Northern boys to 'show that they were not women'.

It is arguable that recruitment policy is one matter on which it is hard to separate political and professional considerations: especially in Nigeria, where the reduction of ethnic imbalance might in the long run help to insulate the army from external societal pressures. As Alhaji Tako Galadima, the Minister of State for the Army, put it in a Senate debate in 1965: 'We introduced the quota system in the army, thus preventing the possible fear that the army would sometime become unreliable. If any part of the country is not represented in the army, we may harbour some fear that a particular section will begin to feel that it is being dominated. But now...the country's safety is assured.'[3] And – to be fair to the Northern politicians – it should be pointed out that a regional quota also operated from 1958 for recruitment into

[1] The regional distribution of the Federal civil service and of the Nigeria Police Force was also skewed, still more unfavourably, against the North – but did not cause the same level of concern because of their lesser strategic importance.
[2] The number of passes and credits required in West African Certificate and 'O' Level exams was reduced to a very low standard which would in many cases not even get an entrant into the sixth form of a secondary school.
[3] Federation of Nigeria, Senate Debates (Lagos: Government Printer, 1 May 1965).

the ranks, with a view to *reducing* the preponderance of Northerners among the ordinary soldiery.

TABLE 42. *Regional/ethnic distribution of officers commissioned up to 1961* (*combat officers only*)

Year of commission	North	Yoruba	Ibo	Others from south	Per cent Northern	Per cent Ibo
Before 1958	5	6	11	5	20·0	40·7
1958	1	0	6	1	12·5	75·0
1959	0	3	9	1	0·0	69·2
1960	4	3	8	4	21·0	42·1
1961	16	9	14	3	36·0	33·3

Sources: Federation of Nigeria, *Official Gazettes,* plus estimates of ethnic/regional distribution as given in Chapter VIII, subject to small margin of error.

Yet the fact remains that in the shorter run the quota for officer selection was a continued source of tension within the army, especially among the officers of Eastern and Ibo origin, including those who staged the January 1966 coup ('In the long run we are all dead' might have been an all too apt riposte to the arguments in favour of regional balancing of recruitment). Quotas introduced to meet the fear of one 'particular section...that it is being dominated' inevitably created fears on the part of the other sections that they would be pushed around in their turn. A fifty per cent quota would bring the North's representation in the officer corps in line with the rough parity of the North in the Federal parliament, which had permitted that region's leaders to dominate the politics of the post-Independence period. Northerners, moreover, still made up about sixty per cent of the Other Ranks in the army, the quota arrangements for recruitment into the ranks having been not very effective in the south, particularly among the Yorubas, who were notoriously unwilling to be recruited. The quota system also offended professional values and sensibilities. It was felt that it would lower the standards of entry – which indeed it did – and that it represented a particularist limitation on the right of the educated and able to occupational advancement.[1]

Many southern officers also feared that eventually promotion might be treated in the same manner. Up to 1966 the politicians had wisely limited control over the composition of the officer corps to the point of entry, and had not attempted in general to bend the promotion system and career structure in the Northern officers' favour. There were those who thought, nevertheless, that Northerners enjoyed better promotion chances. Our review of the facts

[1] See the discussion of the place of such ideas in the political beliefs of the officers in Chapter XII below.

on promotion in Chapter VIII did not provide any evidence of serious discrimination, though it is enough that this was believed to occur. Fuel to such suspicions was added because political interference occurred in one or two individual but isolated cases, as when Brigadier Maimalari was sent to the Imperial Defence College in 1964, a year ahead of Brigadier Ogundipe who was his senior, allegedly because of Alhaji Ribadu's intervention.[1]

Worry for the future was a more potent source of discontent than resentment about the past. All available command posts in the army from headquarters level down to the company commanders, had now been filled with Nigerians. The age structure of the officer corps was extremely youthful. None of the army commanders was near retiring age. Many officers were gloomy about their future promotions. One officer, when congratulated on his promotion to major in 1965, said thank-you, but he would probably be a major the rest of his life. Although the inflow of officers from courses abroad came almost to a halt in 1965, there was the prospect of up to fifty new subalterns graduating from the Nigerian Defence Academy annually, from early 1967. In these circumstances, it was believed that there would have been only two ways of accommodating the inflow of newly trained officers, let alone of assuring adequate career advancement for serving officers. Either the military could be expanded – for which the precedent of a one-battalion expansion in the space of eight years was hardly a good one – or some scheme of compulsory retirement would have to be worked out. There is little doubt that many southern officers believed that something of the kind was a possibility, and rumour had it that they would be axed earlier than their Northern confreres. Fears of this kind were especially common among the Ibo officers after the dispossession of Ibos during 1965 from controlling positions in Lagos University and the Nigerian Railway Corporation.

Nevertheless, these suspicions were too hypothetical to be a good reason for revolt against the army command. There had not been enough time since the post-Independence round of promotions – which did not end until 1964–5 – for frustrations about slow advancement to build up. The government had not made any public announcement on promotion and redundancy, or on any prospects of redundancy. If there were fears of political interference in these matters, it was not because of anything the government had done or said about them. Rather, it was because career expectations had been unsettled by rapid promotions (in the manner described in Chapter VII above), creating anxieties which were interpreted in the lights of current political trends. Promotions were not, however, among the explicitly stated directives of the makers of the January 1966 coup and they can have provided no more than a secondary motive for it.

[1] M. J. Dent's book manuscript, Chapter II, 'The roots in the history of the military prior to 1966'.

SECURITY AND THE STRAIN AGAINST AUTHORITY

The description given above of civil–military relations seems on the surface to indicate the development of a fairly stable pattern of control, even if subject at times to a certain amount of strain. Who, then, would have predicted the sudden destruction of the whole edifice of January 1966? The fact is that the pattern of civilian control was established in the shadow of colonial rule and maintained for a very short period after Independence. It resulted from the interaction of politicians (notably the Prime Minister), who understood something of the realities and constraints of power, and senior officers, who were either British or were Nigerians of enough seniority to have internalised the professional outlook of British officers. In other words, control was only institutionalised for one of the three levels of civil–military relations suggested by Huntington,[1] that of the highest military commanders and the civilian government leadership; but not necessarily at the level of the officer corps and other elite groups, or at the level of the military order as a whole and the society as a whole. This control was therefore automatically threatened by the organisational weakness of the military, especially by the absence of support among junior officers for the authority of their commanders.

Nor did it fit the facts of political life, in particular the government's loss of legitimacy, which impinged directly upon the military by drawing it into an internal security role in support of the established authorities when political order broke down. The effects of such a role on military organisation and cohesion were double-edged. On occasions when the army could be regarded as an impartial arbiter, it was extremely effective in restoring order and probably enhanced its own professional image in the process, as when the army was brought in to stop the Tiv from burning each others' houses in 1960 and from murdering each other in 1964. It may also have been true of the Congo operations of the UN, in which all five battalions were involved at one time or another between 1960 and 1964.[2] The contrast with the chaotic state of the Congo and the disorganisation of that country's army did much to polish the army's self-image. As Major Ifeajuna, one of the key conspirators of January 1966, put it in an article which appeared in the *Nigerian Army Magazine* of December 1965: 'If it is claimed that the British bestowed worthy traditions on the Nigerian Army, the Congo was the place where it became very obvious.'[3] The British officers who served in the Congo operation also noted the contrast between their own well-disciplined troops and the

---

[1] S. P. Huntington, 'Civilian control of the military: a theoretical statement' in H. Eulau *et al.*, *Political behaviour* (Glencoe, Ill.: The Free Press, 1956), p. 380. The pattern of control that we analyse in this chapter is what Huntington would call 'objective' control.
[2] Each battalion served two terms each in the Congo, each term lasting from six to twelve months.
[3] *Nigerian Army Magazine* (Lagos), III (December 1965).

poorly organised rabble of the various Congolese armies and the sense of pride this contrast created.[1] On the other hand, the Nigerian force in the Congo gained little relevant operational experience. It was mostly occupied in guard, riot-control and 'political' duties. There were only three major skirmishes in which Nigerian troops were involved – twice the result of ambushes and once when the Nigerian forces had to rescue an Austrian ambulance unit from hostile Congolese troops, at Bukavu, in 1961. The instructions from the UN headquarters were often ambiguous and confusing.[2] The deployment of Nigerian troops to rescue white ambulance teams at Bukavu evidently created problems, and was followed by a minor outbreak of indiscipline in the 5th Battalion, then under Lieutenant Colonel Aguiyi-Ironsi's command. And there was a degree of conflict between Nigerian and British officers,[3] though this disappeared as the Congo contingent was progressively Nigerianised.

Police-type operations, whether in Nigeria or in the Congo, tended to blur the line between professional and political matters and to strengthen the military's antipathy towards politicians in three ways. First, they gave direct experience of the seamier side of political life, which could be contrasted with the military image. For example, one unnamed officer's comment in the *Army Magazine* on some of his experiences in the Congo operation: 'the progress of Operation Union was retarded by the activities of various corrupt politicians; and the despicable actions by political elements of the Congolese Army', and 'the administrator [of a district] was found to be a sound and helpful man, but two subversive politicians were hampering his efforts'.[4] (It should be said that it is not known whether the author of this particular comment was Nigerian or British. This was perhaps immaterial, for the attitude to politics of the British officers, who were the Nigerians' role model, was not a favourable one either.) As one major political crisis in Nigeria followed another, the talk in officers messes became increasingly political. By 1964, at the latest, there were several groups of officers who thought military intervention 'to stop the political mess' was on the cards, though this is not to say they necessarily thought then of staging a coup themselves.

Secondly, the means of internal security operations are necessarily political

---

[1] See R. Lawson, *Strange soldiering* (London: Hodder and Stoughton, 1963), pp. 162–3.

[2] Lawson, *Strange soldiering* and C. Cruise O'Brien, *To Katanga and back* (New York: Simon and Schuster, 1962).

[3] Reflected two or three years later in some strong criticism of Lawson's book in the *Nigerian Army Magazine* (Lagos), III (December 1965), in which it is stated that Nigerians 'will not be happy to notice that no mention has been made of the Nigerian officers who served in this operation. The whole book looks like a subtle propaganda campaign to boost the very few British officers seconded to the Third Brigade...Nigerian troops spent as much time guarding British officers seconded to this Brigade as they did on operations.'

[4] *Royal Nigerian Army Magazine* (Lagos), II (May 1963), 47–9.

to some extent. This, again, was explicit in the Congo, especially in 'Operation Union' in the Kasai. The operation was aimed at pacifying Kasai and re-establishing internal trade in the wake of the Kalonjist movement in South Kasai and the breakdown of discipline of central government troops; and officers of the 3rd Brigade HQ and the 3rd Battalion undertook a programme of visits to outlying areas to secure the cooperation of local politicians, administrators, police and army units and explain the purposes of the UN operation. In the Western Region of Nigeria also in 1962 and 1963 military intelligence was also quite heavily involved in assessing the political situation. In 'Operation Banker' in the Western Region, in 1962, the 2nd Battalion operated a joint OPS room with the police; reconnaissance groups were sent to all the major towns in the West to 'sense the political climate' and the battalion commander, Lieutenant Colonel Maimalari, attended the rowdy session of the Western Region House of 25 May 1962, at which Chief Akintola's supporters rioted in order to bring about a closure.[1] During the Western Region disturbances of 1965, the 4th and 2nd Battalions again operated in close liaison with the police and Chief Akintola's regional government, especially in October–November 1965 during the regional election and its aftermath.

Thirdly, commitment to internal security destroyed the army's impartial public image. There was a considerable degree of press and public criticism of the government's support of the UN in the Congo (despite praise for the performance of Nigerian troops there). Such criticism was especially strong after the withdrawal of Ghana from the Congo operation, and it definitely contributed to the politicisation of some of the younger Nigerian officers. The use of the army for internal security also sustained the view that it was taking sides. It should be noted that in the Western Region crisis of 1962, the military, like the police, had already been alerted before the declaration of emergency and even before the notorious meeting of the House which was the pretext for it – tending to support the contention that the Federal government was privy to Akintola's plans. In 1964, the military was used to maintain essential services during the general strike of that year, a role which was not likely to be popular either with labour leaders or with officers of radical political persuasion.[2] During the Western Region elections of 1965, the pressures on the army to take sides were stronger than ever before. On more than one occasion army officers were seen with palm fronds – symbols of the Action Group (the opposition party in the West) – on their jeeps. Doubts as to the army's reliability could have been one reason why most of the

---

[1] *Nigerian Army Magazine* (Lagos), 1 (October 1963), 59.
[2] It was significant that the Other Ranks in the army had received substantial pay increases a few months *before* the strike took place.

army units were withdrawn from operations in the West by November 1965, leaving most of the work of controlling the continuing disturbances in the hands of the para-military Mobile Unit of the Nigeria Police. By January 1966 the situation in the West became so serious, however, that it looked as if violence would spiral out of control if there was not a political settlement of some kind. The Federal Prime Minister, however, was not prepared either to force Chief Akintola to make peace with the AG, or to lose the NPC's new ally by declaring a state of emergency in the West, even though the situation was far worse than that used to justify the 1962 emergency there. He was also under some pressure to stick to his guns from the Sardauna of Sokoto, who at first did not take reports of the Western disorders very seriously, and when he was finally convinced of the danger refused to contemplate letting his friend and ally Akintola down. The only alternative then was to sit tight and crush the disturbances by a much heavier show of military force than had been made before. There is some evidence that informal discussions as to whether and how this was to be done had already begun before the January 1966 coup.[1]

In the eyes of many officers, including the Majors participating in the coup, this would finally destroy the army's non-partisan reputation, in so far as this still existed. Yet it is interesting that not all officers took so despairing a view of the political situation or their internal security role. There was a sub-stantial difference of opinion in the military between the more politically engaged officers and those who were more organisation-minded. Most of the army's senior officers were in the latter category. Some of these – like Ademulegun and Maimalari – did not differ much in their purely political opinions from the January 1966 Majors, though they may have turned down the latters' overtures to them. Yet they still tended to accept the politicians' right to determine what political use could be made of the army; and thus had a higher flashpoint, beyond which they would perceive the army's integrity to be in danger. It is interesting to note that the issue of the *Nigerian Army Magazine* appearing just before the January coup contains an article by an army chaplain, suggesting that officers should receive training in the psychology of crowd behaviour; and an introduction by Major General Ironsi, stating that the army had been building up new traditions, 'traditions born in the peacekeeping operations in the Cameroons, Congo (Leopoldville) and Tanzania and maintained through the different internal security opera-tions it has been called upon to undertake'.[2]

In contrast, the most politically radical and engaged officers, such as the conspiratorial group of January 1966, did not take a sanguine view of the emergence of such traditions of peace-keeping. Most of these (as we attempted

[1] See Chapter I above.
[2] *Nigerian Army Magazine* (Lagos), III (December 1965).

to show in the tabulation[1] of the differences between the January Majors and the most senior officers) were in the middle ranks, had served shorter periods under British tutelage and had had faster promotions than members of the high command. In other words, it was paradoxically those who were *less* committed on the whole to organisational loyalties who were most likely to object to the use of the army for police operations in the West, on the pretext that it compromised its impartiality. The coup of January 1966 was staged by just such a group of radicals, and its immediate political purpose was to forestall the use of the military by the government to suppress its opponents (or those of the NPC and NNDP, which amounted to the same thing) in the Western Region.

[1] Table 41, p. 240.

CHAPTER XI

THE IRONSI REGIME: THE ARMY AS A GOVERNMENT, JANUARY TO JULY 1966

INTRODUCTION

In this chapter the central theme is the impact of the army on politics after Major General Ironsi's seizure of power following the Majors' coup of January 15 1966. How did the military operate as a ruling group when it first took office? Why did the first seven months of its rule see such a sharpening of conflict? Why was it that a military regime which took power amid scenes of rejoicing in most of Nigeria, even in the North, become so unpopular that it was so easily overthrown by the coup of July 28–29 1966? Was it because of how it governed, and if so, how did its style of government increase the pressure for allocation of values on the army itself, the feedback of demands on it which eventually broke it into fragments?

We shall argue that the Ironsi regime's difficulties as a government resulted from four things. First, there were the deficiencies of the military men as an elite group, the fact that they were few in number, lacked experience and did not have the political acumen to make use of the talents of other groups, like the radical politicians, to broaden their support base.

Secondly, there were the peculiar circumstances under which power was seized from the civilians, after a period of corrupt and unruly civilian rule, during which the politics of the politicians had been discredited. This encouraged the soldiers' own tendencies to reject politics as a form of organised activity that a government should engage in. Consequently, the Ironsi regime did not see the need to bargain and compromise with the growing forces of dissent in the North, it was unwilling either to deal with intermediaries or to build up its own political machine; and, indeed, it neglected to destroy the political networks of the old regime – such as that of the former NPC – because it underestimated their importance, to its own ultimate disadvantage.

Thirdly, there were the soldiers' own characteristic political beliefs (see the next chapter) which reinforced these anti-political tendencies and were responsible for the government's rather half-baked attempts at political reform. The outstanding characteristic of the Ironsi government's reforms, from the Decree on Indian Hemp to the notorious Decree no. 34, which purported to unify the country and occasioned the May riots in the North, was that they were mainly symbolic in intent. They *expressed* the military's commitment to certain types of political goal, without changing the distribution of power or anything else very much *in practice*, and thus they concealed the regime's inertness. By the same token they caused symbolic deprivations, especially among the Northerners, who felt themselves cut off from the centre of power; the consequences of which, however, were all too real.

Finally, there were Major General Ironsi's own personal defects. We shall not discuss these at length or separately below,[1] though his imprint will be seen at a number of different points in this chapter. He was a man of some ability, though of rather limited education, having risen from the ranks. He was an ordnance clerk during the Second World War and was sent for a short officer-conversion course at Eaton Hall, in England, in 1948. Although he had had both Staff College, Camberley, and Imperial Defence College staff training, he was not noted for his organisational ability, and had had a near mutiny on his hands shortly after his appointment as a battalion commander in the Congo in 1960; then quarrelled with some of his senior officers when sent back to command the brigade there. He had been Extra Equerry to the Queen on her visit to Nigeria, Defence Adviser to the High Commission in London and for a brief time UN Force Commander in the Congo, though he does not seem to have distilled much political tact from these experiences. Major General Welby-Everard (as already noted) advised against his appointment as GOC in 1965, and his doubts may have been justified, as it is said that Ironsi did not get a firm grip of his command in his short tenure of the post before the January coup and he acquired a reputation – whether justified or not – for hard drinking and intrigue. On the other hand, he does seem to have had a certain amount of bull courage and sincerity. His commitment to the army as a way of life and to a rather simplistic soldier's political code in which nationalism was the key element seems to have been quite genuine. It was his bravery in confronting rebelling troops – plus a certain amount of cunning – which had brought him through on top after the January coup. But military courage alone was no substitute for politics.

THE RULING GROUP: A NARROW ELITE

The officer corps (as we noted in Chapter III above) was small and on the whole younger, less well-educated and less experienced than most comparable elite groups. The inner elite nucleus of officers who had acquired some ability to handle large organisations and perhaps a few skills of a political

---

[1] There is a more detailed biography in *West Africa* (London), 20 March 1965, which rather glosses over his defects.

nature as well – those who had some staff training, some higher command or staff experience and relatively varied careers – was tiny and rapidly depleted as the events of 1966–7 unfolded.

Direct military administration, therefore, was out of the question and the problem was with which other elite groups the army would share power. The only groups the Ironsi regime thought worthy were the civilian bureaucracies and the police (though both were still given a somewhat subordinate position in the military administration). In this, Major General Ironsi did not differ from Major Nzeogwu who, after appointing his interim government of civil servants at Kaduna just after the coup, had said: 'after all we have now got experts to do the job rather than profiteers'.[1] The Supreme Military Council, the Federal Executive Council and all four Regional Executive Councils – though in different proportions – were a combination of military, civil service and police representatives.[2] Nigeria became in sum an administered rather than a political society.

The General allocated direct political responsibilities to only six of his senior officers: to himself as Head of the Military Government, a post fused with that of Supreme Commander of the Armed Forces; to Lt Colonels Ojukwu, Ejoor, Fajuyi and Hassan Katsina[3] as Military Governors of the East, Mid-West, West and North, respectively, and (from June 1966) to Major Mabolaji Johnson as Military Administrator of Lagos. In addition, the two Chiefs of Staff (or Armed Forces and Army), Brigadier Ogundipe and Lt Colonel Gowon, and the Commander of the Navy, Commodore Wey, took part in political decisions as members of the Supreme Military Council and Federal Executive Council.

Politicians, or for that matter all other non-bureaucratic persons, were kept out of formal government positions entirely (and did not reappear until Gowon's appointment of civilian commissioners to his government in 1967). Both the Supreme Military Council and the Federal Executive Council consisted entirely of military figures (see Table 43), plus the Attorney General (SMC and FEC) and the Inspector General of Police and his Deputy (FEC). Civil servants were brought in to meetings on an ad hoc basis, especially when

---

[1] The *Daily Times* (Lagos), 17 January 1966.
[2] The composition of the Federal bodies is given in Table 43. That of the Regional Executive Councils was as follows: the Northern Region: the Military Governor, the Secretary to the Governor and all the Permanent Secretaries of Ministries and the Regional Commissioner of Police. The Western Region: the Military Governor, the Commanding Officer of the 4th Battalion, the Commissioner of Police and eight civil servants. The Eastern Region: the Military Governor, the Commanding Officer of the 1st Battalion, the Commissioner of Police, the Solicitor General, the Chief Secretary, the Permanent Secretary, Ministry of Finance, and the other Permanent Secretaries coopted as necessary. The Mid-Western Region: the Military Governor, the Commissioner of Police, the Solicitor General, the Secretary to the Governor and the Permanent Secretaries of the Ministries of Finance, Economic Development and Establishments.
[3] Promoted from major in January 1966 for this purpose.

TABLE 43. *Organisation chart of the National Military Government at 31 March 1966*

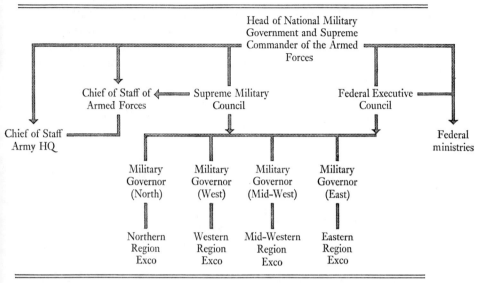

Notes:
[1] After 31 March 1966, when the Regional Military Governors were first included in the Federal Executive Council, this had virtually the same composition as the Supreme Military Council. The latter consisted of (*a*) the Head of the National Military Government and Supreme Commander, (*b*) the head of the Navy, (*c*) the Chief of Staff, Armed Forces, (*d*) the Chief of Staff, Army, (*e*) the four Military Governors, (*f*) the Attorney General. In addition to these the Federal Executive Council included the Inspector General of Police and his Deputy.

[2] This structure was essentially unchanged except in nomenclature by Decree no. 34 of May 1966, though the Executive Councils of the Regions became Executive Councils of Groups of Provinces instead.

decisions would have implications for matters within the responsibility of their ministries, but in an advisory capacity only.[1] At regional level, however, civil servants sat in the Executive Councils as of right, and probably had more influence on the decisions taken by their individual Military Governors than did the civil servants on the central government.

The circle of decision-makers under the regime was, therefore, an exceedingly narrow one. And neither the soldiers, nor the police, nor the civil servants – the three elite groups of which it was composed – were particularly

[1] The Secretary of the Military Government, Mr S. O. Wey, was the only official to sit in on all the meetings. Although the civil servants thus had no institutionalised role in the two councils themselves, the Head of the Military Government and the FEC could delegate executive powers and statutory powers to make subordinate legislation to the Permanent Secretaries, and in fact did so. See the discussion of the new constitutional arrangements in E. A. Keay, 'Legal and constitutional changes in Nigeria under the Military Government', *Journal of African Law*, x, 1 (Spring 1966), 92–105.

well connected in terms of the channels of political communication and control which had existed before. Small wonder that the military regime was neither responsive to the upward flow of political demands, nor able to reach downward for political support.[1] In this respect the comparison with Ghana is a pertinent one. In the first place, the important role played by the police in the NLC junta kept the latter more responsive to grass-roots political pressures. And secondly, the NLC of Ghana brought civilians in as advisors right from the very start in the Political and Economic Committees and the various advisory groups which succeeded them. This was made easier because there were a number of respected political figures, like Dr Busia, S. D. Dombo, E. Akufo Addo, W. E. A. Ofori Atta and Victor Owusu, of nationalist or opposition-to-Nkrumah vintage who could be coopted, whereas in Nigeria virtually the whole political class had been discredited. Ironsi might possibly, even so, have made use of some of the radical politicians. Instead, he failed to take the opportunity of releasing Chiefs Awolowo and Enahoro from jail and snubbed the advances after the coup of Northern radicals like J. S. Tarka and Aminu Kano.

It is sometimes observed by those associated with the Ironsi regime that there was a sense of decision-making vacuum at the top. In the whole of the General's seven months in office, the central government only produced two policy initiatives of any significance, namely Decree no. 34 on national unity in May 1966 and the rather tardy measures against corruption in public life that were embarked on in July 1966. It did not get round to taking a decision on the most important single dilemma faced by the regime, namely what to do with the Majors who had staged the coup of January 15. And the civil servants in charge of the ministries at the centre and in the regions acquired considerable powers to administer and determine policy in their spheres of competence as they wished by default of effective control by the soldiers.[2]

For a military regime with draconian powers at its disposal,[3] the government was surprisingly hesitant to show its teeth against potential opponents. There were no large-scale lockings up of members of the old regime, as in Ghana under the NLC, except in the Western Region under Lt Colonel Fajuyi. The

---

[1] Tending to confirm the contention of Janowitz, *The military in the political development of new nations*, that it is difficult for the military to keep support unless it develops mass organisations of a civilian type or works out viable relations with civilian political groups.

[2] At Federal level one crucial factor was that neither members of the SMC nor those of the FEC were allocated specific responsibilities with regard to ministries. This meant that the Permanent Secretaries could normally get on with the day-to-day business of their ministries without anything like the equivalent of ministerial control, as under the civilian regime. At regional level the position was similar, except that the civil servants' position was even stronger because they were in the Regional Executive Councils *ex officio* as well.

[3] Such as were provided by the Suppression of Disorder Decree no. 4 of 1966 or the various State Security (Detention of Persons) Decrees, from no. 3 of 1966 onwards, under which the Military Government ordered the detention of persons at its pleasure.

former NPC politicians in the North all remained at large to stir up trouble. And when there was widespread violence in May 1966 the government proceeded with such delicacy – locking up only a handful of suspected organisers, punishing nobody and appointing a tribunal of enquiry which was to have met for the first time more than two months after the uprising – that this was widely taken by the regime's detractors as a sign of weakness.

Ironsi leaned in practice rather heavily on a small circle of trusted officials and friends for advice, and this tended to bring about the closure of the regime, to make it less responsive to outside political pressures. For the men on whom he leaned[1] were also mostly bureaucrats, predominantly from his own ethnic group, who tended to share his own political predispositions and to provide moral support for, rather than effective criticism of, his policies and actions. The fact that many of them were Ibos also tended to lend support to the whisperings of 'tribalism' which arose around the regime.

Communications between the centre and the regions were particularly defective. The sole official channel by which 'regional' interests and points of view could be articulated were the Military Governors themselves, through their participation in the Supreme Military Council and Federal Executive Council, so that the main responsibility for circulating each region's demands at the centre belonged to only one man.[2] Moreover, meetings of the councils were held only once every two or three weeks, even less towards the end. As cleavages appeared in the military elite, moreover, Ironsi seems to have relied more and more for communications on his unit commanders in the North, rather than on Lt Colonel Hassan Katsina, the Military Governor. This reproduced at a wider level the same sort of informational 'closure' as was generated at the centre by his informal reliance on a small circle of key advisors. His unit commanders (especially Lt Colonel Okoro of the 3rd Battalion, Kaduna, and Lt Colonel Akagha of the Depot, Zaria) shared the same kind of political outlook as the Supreme Commander and are known to have provided him with political information of a kind that would tend to make him less, rather than more, responsive to regional pressures.[3]

All this contrasts with the political arrangements under the civilian regime, when regional interests had been so well represented at the centre that the

---

[1] They included Lt Colonel Njoku, the CO, 2nd Brigade, Pius Okigbo, the Federal government's Economic Advisor, A. A. Ayida, the Permanent Secretary, Ministry of Economic Development, G. C. M. Onyiuke, the Attorney General, Mr F. C. Nwokedi and S. O. Wey, the Secretary to the National Military Government. All these except Ayida and Wey were Ibos.

[2] And his advisors. Each Military Governor usually took his Chief Secretary and Solicitor or Attorney General to Lagos with him for meetings.

[3] For instance, some of the communications between Lt Colonel Akagha of the Depot, Zaria and Ironsi about Ahmadu Bello University staff and students at the time, the former tending to suggest on the basis of little more than fear and suspicion that there was a 'subversive' anti-Ibo movement among staff and students, and that they had 'planned' the May uprising.

major problem of government had indeed been to define and maintain national interests that transcended the adjustment and aggregation of regional claims. A good indicator of the difference is the sheer number of representatives of region-based political parties that had held decision-making posts at the centre. There had been twenty-one Federal ministers with portfolios in the second half of 1965,[1] of whom nine were NPC members, three were from the NCNC (Eastern Region), one from the NCNC (Mid-Western Region), one from the NCNC (Lagos), five from the NNDP (Western Region) and two non-partisan members. In addition, there had been thirty-three ministers of state[2] and twenty-six parliamentary secretaries, divided between the regions in similar proportions. If interests were not brought forward at cabinet level, they could always be raised by members of the House of Representatives or senators through informal political contacts or on the floor of the House. All of these numerous political actors, moreover, had been enmeshed in a complex network[3] of links with the regional leadership of their parties, the regional governments, community interest groups and local government bodies. They constituted a very much better elaborated system of political communication than that available to the military regime.

Adequate communications at all levels of military rule were also made difficult by the tendency of the Military Governors themselves to conceive of their relations with Major General Ironsi in terms of the normal military chain of command and control. Former members of Ironsi's Supreme Military Council testify that the General encouraged full and free discussion at meetings,[4] but it seems clear that the atmosphere was that of a military briefing, in which information is exchanged and orders given, rather than the political caucus in which bargains are struck and compromises achieved. The governors were there to provide information, take orders and obtain clarification of these orders.[5] They were entrapped, moreover, inside the military

---

[1] *Nigeria Year Book 1966* (Lagos: Daily Times Press, 1966).

[2] Eleven of these were in the cabinet, in addition to the twenty-one ministers.

[3] Best described in Sklar, *Nigerian political parties*.

[4] See, for example, Major Johnson's comment that 'General Ironsi, all of us will remember, used to say, "Look, it is easy to be a dictator, but it is not easy to try to not be one." There were several occasions when he would say, "look, we all take these decisions" – even at Council meetings and putting his hand down he would say "any comments?"' *Meeting of the Nigerian military leaders held at Peduase Lodge, Aburi, Ghana, 4th and 5th January 1967*, p. 31. See also Lt Colonel Ojukwu's comment: 'After all, we were all there when Decree No. 34 was made. The point was amongst the Governors and Senior Officers we knew and we saw it and left it. The people did not, they felt it and reacted, so we are told.' *Ibid.* pp. 21–2.

[5] In fact, this emphasis on the hierarchical rather than the conciliar principle in military government corresponded fairly accurately with the legal position. All legislative and executive powers derived from the Head of the Military Government, under Decree no. 1 establishing the regime. Neither the SMC nor the FEC possessed in themselves legislative or executive authority as such (the SMC's only statutory powers related to such matters as the appointment of judges and the prerogative of mercy), even though in fact Major General Ironsi took most major decisions in council.

image. Major General Ironsi's policies were formulated in accordance with principles on which most officers were agreed, so that it was difficult to legitimate overt disagreement. In the first few months of military rule, for example, Lt Colonel Hassan Katsina had consistently proclaimed his support for national unification. In March 1966,[1] he had gone so far as to claim that he did not recognise 'Northernisation' and that he would ensure that anyone from any part of Nigeria would be able to obtain jobs in the North. This made it difficult for him to articulate at the centre the growing dissent in the North, even though he himself was to become increasingly aware of its seriousness.

When political pressures did start to manifest themselves in the officer corps, they tended to by-pass the normal channels of communication and command. The various antagonistic cliques that formed from May 1966 onwards restricted the information flow, in order to protect themselves from the military hierarchy. This is reflected in the fact that, for example, Northern officers with important positions, such as Lt Colonels Hassan Katsina, Gowon and Akahan, tended to be omitted from the conspiratorial network of the Northern officers who effected the July coup. And Major General Ironsi, too, as pointed out later, also found it convenient to develop his own sources of intelligence, by relying on ethnic ties with informants at lower levels of command.

To conclude, both the very narrowly based structure of the military regime and difficulties in integrating military and political roles tended to restrict the free flow of communications. One reasonable inference would be that such restrictions on the feedback of political information and demands would inhibit a rational assessment of the political consequences of policy and reduce the political effectiveness of the government. On the other hand, it is more difficult to reach an assessment of the *actual* effect on decision-making processes. Ironsi, for example, clearly failed to make use of political information when it *was* provided, as when he stepped up the unification programme after the May 1966 riots. A cynical view might be that information that was dissonant with the military image simply called forth a stronger reassertion of military values rather than adaptive responses, so that even with a more effective system of political communication, the result would have been the same.

THE REJECTION OF POLITICS

For a long time instead of settling down to minister unto the people's needs, the politicians were busy performing a series of seven day wonders as if the art of government was some circus show. John Citizen was not amused, but he was powerless; he was helpless. Indeed at one period it seemed as if the country had

---

[1] *West Africa* (London), 26 March 1966.

reached the famous last days about which Paul wrote to Timothus – the days when men became lovers of selves; covetous, proud, without natural affection, truce-breakers, false accusers, fierce, despisers of those that are good, heady, highminded. Still we groped along as John Citizen watched politicans scorn the base by which they did ascend. We groped from one trouble to another; from one calamity to another. It was too much, it was enough but none there was to bell the cat. Until the last straw that broke the camel's back. Today there is a new regime in the Federal Republic of Nigeria, a military regime. About time too![1]

With this stirring mixture of cliches, a leading newspaper summarised the sense of disillusion with civilian politics, which was as deep outside the military establishment as it was inside it.

It is often said that the main problem of military regimes is their lack of legitimacy.[2] Yet the military came to power in Nigeria in circumstances which initially gave it a wide degree of support. The politicians had been discredited. They had shown little capacity for resolving the basic conflicts in Nigerian political life; and those crises they had succeeded in dissolving, such as that over the general election of December 1964 or the general strike of June 1964, they had done so in a manner which brought little or no credit to them. The Western Region situation had clearly become out of hand. In these circumstances, it was with relief that the military rulers were welcomed, though this welcome varied from the very evident enthusiasm in the south to a rather grudging acceptance by the political leaders of the far North.

Messages of political support were received from all four major political parties, including the Northern People's Congress, from the three parts of the split trades union movement, the National Union of Nigerian Students and most other groups of political importance. All the major newspapers ran editorials welcoming the new regime, only the *New Nigerian* introducing a note of warning against sycophantic support from those who had acquiesced in the old.[3]

The general sense of euphoria also extended to the intellectual community, and was well expressed by *Nigerian Opinion*, a monthly journal of political comment produced by a group of young social science teachers at the University of Ibadan: 'there can be few places where the military, far from acting as a conservative interest group, have expressed a radical popular will so coherently and efficaciously in driving elected possessors from power and putting forward schemes for reform'.[4]

---

[1] *Daily Times* (Lagos), 18 January 1966.
[2] See particularly, Finer, *The man on horseback*, pp. 17–22, 179–80; Janowitz, *The military in the political development of new nations*, pp 83–100, also sees legitimacy as a crucial variable but argues that military organisations may be more or less able to develop it, depending upon their political skills and/or ability to evolve mass political organisation.
[3] *New Nigerian* (Kaduna), 23 January 1966.
[4] *Nigerian Opinion* (Ibadan), February 1966.

It is important to bear this context in mind when analysing the difficulties of the military in comprehending the political pressures for which it became the focus when it was in power. It came to power with a political *carte blanche*, which permitted it to engage on a programme of reforms – albeit a hastily improvised and piecemeal one – the general drift of which was the creation of a cohesive and disciplined society in the military's own image. It was seemingly unaware or unconcerned that these reforms might also constitute a very important shift in the allocation of values between political groups or between the regions. One reason it could proceed in this way was that there was no one who would or could spell out the dangers to it.

It is clear for instance that the military rulers completely failed to anticipate the adverse reaction in the North to Decree no. 34 of 24 May 1966 which unified the country; and were therefore thoroughly traumatised by the rioting at the end of May. The same is true, it appears, for informed public opinion as a whole in the south.

Probably the first serious recognition in a Lagos newspaper of the growing current of dissatisfaction in the North, was a feature by the editor of the *Daily Times* which stated that 'the impression one gets in the North is that the intelligentsia is slowly rising in hostility'.[1] Yet, instead of concluding that the regime should bargain with, or attempt to conciliate the North, the editor advocated a stiffening of the military vision of society, a quickening of 'the revolution' – including the posting of Military Governors away from their areas of ethnic origin, a decree against tribalism and greater reliance by the army on its own decision-making resources in order to reduce its 'dependence on civil servants'.

The military's own built-in tendency to disregard political pressures, to refuse to 'play politics' received much support, therefore, from other elites, such as the journalists, university teachers and civil servants. For the failure of the politicians had led to a widespread devaluation of the skills of the politician and had accentuated the alienation from the political class of virtually all intellectual elites, and not only the military.

THE PROGRAMME OF REFORM

In piecemeal fashion the military rulers set out to build an image as a reforming government. There were three main planks in their programme. First, the restoration of basic conditions of law and order. This was made necessary by the conditions of lawlessness that prevailed in the Western Region and Tiv Division on the military's assumption of power. At his first press conference, Lt Colonel Fajuyi had said he wanted 'Peace first, and

---

[1] Quoted in *West Africa* (London), 7 May 1966. The editor in question is Peter Enahoro of the *Daily Times* (Lagos).

other good things will follow. We have got to stop people being burnt alive.'[1]
This also fitted in with the military's predilection for an orderly society,
which had been one of its reasons for intervention in the first place. Powers
were assumed under a Suppression of Disorder Decree and several State
Security (Detention of Persons) Decrees to imprison persons without trial,
to impose death sentences or long terms of imprisonment for offences against
public order, to proclaim martial law in disturbed areas and to hold trials
by military tribunals. In practice, however, the maintenance of conditions
of law and order depended but little on these formal powers or on the
very limited coercive resources at the military regime's disposal. The government was able to pacify the Western Region in a few weeks with minimal
show of force and without proclaiming martial law, because, above all, of the
basic legitimacy it then enjoyed. On the other hand, it was to be no more
capable of keeping order than the civilian government had been once it had
lost that legitimacy in the North a few months later.

Secondly, the army set out, though a little haphazardly, to destroy the
apparatus of political patronage and control. At one stroke, the state was to be
rid of both corruption and politics. The emphasis, however, was on changes
in the personnel of government institutions, rather than on structural reforms.
Political appointees were removed from the boards of all the Federal and
Regional public corporations; the Councils of the University of Nigeria,
Nsukka, the University of Ife and the University of Lagos were reconstituted;
and Lt Colonel Ojukwu announced that the law establishing the University
of Nigeria was to be reviewed, 'to ensure that matters academic are left
entirely in the hands of academicians subject to the overall direction of the
country's manpower needs'.[2]

Some effort was made to strike at the grass-roots of graft and political
influence in local government. In the three southern regions all local government councils and management committees were replaced by the regional
government's own officials as Sole Administrators: the colonial tradition of
rule by District Officer being thus re-emphasised.[3] Such reforms went
farthest in the Western Region, where the government revoked the appointments of virtually all local committees, such as the Advisory Boards of
Education and the Tax Assessment Committees. It also temporarily revoked
the appointments of the three most important grades of customary courts –
which had been an instrument of political coercion at a local level – and
removed their jurisdiction over criminal cases.

[1] *West Africa* (London), 29 January 1966.
[2] *Ibid.* 5 February 1966.
[3] A process which had already begun under the civilian regime: in the Western Region, for instance,
virtually all elected councils had been replaced by the end of 1965, whether because of their administrative shortcomings or for reasons of politics.

In the North, however, the overall approach was more cautious, for the identity of local government with traditional political systems presented a much more intractable and delicate problem. The Native Authorities remained intact for the time being and many former NPC ministers and politicians were reabsorbed into them. A beginning, nevertheless, was made on structural reforms of a quite fundamental kind. In February 1966 the Military Governor, Lt Colonel Hassan Katsina, made a policy statement that the Native Authority police were to be placed under the operational control of the Nigeria Police, as a prelude to integration with the latter; the Federal prisons service was to take over the Native Authority prisons; and the Native Authority courts were to be merged with the judiciary. Because of the complexity of the changes to be made and of political events, the government was rather tardy in putting these reforms into effect. The first stage in the reorganisation of the courts, for example, did not take place until April 1967. The reforms were to mean, however, a significant alteration in the distribution of political power in the Northern communities. For the Native Authority courts and police had played a key role in the system of political coercion and control operated by the Northern traditional elite and the NPC. The changes were thus, in many ways, more fundamental than the Military Government's reforms in the south, which were essentially temporary and corrective in nature and did not bring much long-run structural adjustment.

The attack on politics also took the form of direct harassment of the political parties and politicians themselves. Warnings were issued to the parties to desist from activity. The NPC headquarters in Kaduna was closed down by the government. The trades unions and tribal associations were warned to stay out of politics. Finally, by Decree no. 33 in May, the political parties (eighty-one of them according to a compendious list published by the government) and twenty-six of the more important pan-tribal and cultural associations were abolished.[1] On the other hand, few politicians were arrested, except in the Western Region, where Lt Colonel Fajuyi had put fifteen major figures of the former NNDP government in custody. Former NPC leaders were allowed to resume positions in the Native Authorities in the North, in which they could make trouble for the regime later.[2] There was no attempt by the military leaders to impose a system of authoritarian political controls from above: in practice, there was no drastic curtailment of freedoms of expression, movement or assembly.

Some effort was made to arraign a few of the politicians for the official corruption of the first Republic. But the approach to this was slow and piece-

---

[1] Announced at the same time as Decree no. 34 on national unity.
[2] Though thirty-eight persons in the North were detained after the May riots in June 1966, including three important office-holders in Zaria Native Authority, under the State Security (Detention of Persons) (no. 9) Decree no. 47 of 1966.

meal. To start with the initiative was taken up by the regional governments alone. In the East, Mid-West and West, they limited themselves to the investigation and prosecution of politicians and officials who could be prosecuted for indictable offences under existing legislation, for stealing, fraud or conspiracy. Lt Colonel Hassan Katsina set up Commissions of Enquiry into the Affairs of the Northern Region Development Corporation and the Marketing Board, but was too fearful of stirring up political controversy to proceed against individuals criticised in their Reports. The Federal government was slower to move. It was not until June that it appointed Tribunals to enquire into the Nigerian Railway Corporation, the Electricity Corporation of Nigeria and the Lagos City Council, and introduced comprehensive legislation empowering it to investigate assets and to seize wealth that had been acquired by corruption in public office.[1] Its dilatoriness was widely criticised and unfavourable comparisons were made with Ghana, where one of the first things the military regime of that country did was to appoint tribunals to carry out a truly comprehensive series of enquiries into bribery and corruption in official life.

ADMINISTRATIVE AND POLITICAL UNIFICATION

The military's third main political commitment on coming to power was to the unification of the country, and thus (it was believed) to the elimination of all the divisive social conflicts which had seemed on the verge of tearing it apart. It is important to emphasise that it was committed to this goal – albeit in vague and general terms – well before the final decision in May 1966. In his first broadcast statement on his political programme, in late January, Major General Ironsi stated in emotional terms that 'all Nigerians want an end to Regionalism. Tribal loyalties and activities which promote tribal consciousness and sectional interests must give way to the urgent task of national reconstruction.'[2] Two weeks later, he established the former Permanent Secretary in the Ministry of Foreign Affairs, Mr F. C. Nwokedi, as a one-man commissioner to study and report on the unification of Nigeria's administrative machinery and public and judicial services. At the end of February, he also appointed three more broadly based study groups to consider the future shape of the polity, a group on National Unity, one on Constitutional Review and a National Planning Advisory Group. The Constitutional Review Study Group did not meet until 24 March and then its terms

---

[1] The Tribunal of Enquiry Decree no. 41 of 1966, and Public Offices (Investigation of Assets) Decree no. 51 of 1966. It had previously assumed somewhat more limited powers to investigate the bank accounts of persons suspected of corruption and abuse of office under the Banking Amendment Decree no. 5 of 16 January 1966.

[2] Broadcast of 28 January. Reported in *West Africa* (London), 5 February 1966.

of reference were heavily weighted by Ironsi in favour of a unitary solution. It was to 'identify those faults in the former Constitution of Nigeria which militated against national unity and against the emergence of a strong Central Government; to ascertain how far the powers of the former Regional governments fostered regionalism and weakened the Central Government' and only then 'to consider the merits and demerits of (a) a Unitary form of Government, (b) a Federal form of Government, as a system of Government best suited to Nigeria'.[1] Despite assurances to the contrary, therefore, it did seem as if the basic political decision had been taken.

From this, it was a short step for Major General Ironsi to decide that it was not necessary to wait for the reports of these Study Groups before abandoning the Federal set-up for the duration of the Military Government, at least on paper. At a meeting of the Supreme Military Council on 22–23 May, he was able to secure the agreement of his colleagues, and in a broadcast the next day he promulgated Decree no. 34. In theory, this abolished the four regions, though the Military Governors were still assigned to groups of provinces corresponding exactly to the former regions. All legislative and executive power was vested in the National Military Government, though powers could be delegated to the Military Governors, who also kept for the interim all the powers they had formerly exercised as Military Governors of the Regions. And the public services were in theory to be unified under a single Public Service Commission, though as a first step this applied to the top few civil servants in super-scale posts only.

This decision was a major political miscalculation, bringing the political discontent in the North to a head in the riots in Northern cities at the end of May. The timing of the decree had been most inept, since it gave currency to the fear that existing procedures of consultation were a facade, and created an impression of arbitrary rule. Although Ironsi stated specifically that the decree was without prejudice to the report of the Constitutional Review Study Group, his assurance was regarded wth cynicism by his critics.

It can indeed be argued that the decree was a clumsy venture in impression-management and not a realistic attempt to redistribute power. It was a gesture of the Ironsi government's commitment to national unity, but did not strengthen central control in any important respect. Under Decree no. 1, establishing the military regime, the Head of the then Federal Military Government had already been vested with all the legislative and executive authority of the previous federal and regional parliaments and governments.[2] Though the Military Governors were delegated the powers of the

---

[1] Terms of reference of Constitutional Review Study Group, as laid down by Major General Ironsi at the inaugural meeting in March, *West Africa* (London), 2 April 1966.
[2] This is a bald summary of the constitutional position, which was more complex than this. See Keay, 'Legal and constitutional changes in Nigeria under the Military Government', for details.

former regions, Ironsi, as Head, had thus *already* possessed plenary powers to legislate in regional fields and to override the Military Governors' edicts and executive acts at will, if he so wished. The idea of a military government limiting its own powers or having them restricted by judicial review was a contradiction in terms. Lt Colonels Hassan Katsina and Gowon had been prevailed upon to accept Decree no. 34, because it was a purely paper measure and they themselves did not foresee at the time the symbolic impact it would have on the North. The unification decree could, in sum, be said to have overextended the central government's accountability, making it the legitimate repository of a wider range of expectations and demands from the regions, without increasing in any way its effective power to handle them. It might have seemed natural to the soldiers, as a subsequent meeting of the Supreme Military Council put it in its communique, 'to run the government as a military government under a unified command',[1] but to many civilians it looked positively foreboding.

THE ALIENATION OF THE NORTH

The unification of the country, implicit in military rule itself and explicit in Decree no. 34, entailed a transfer of power at more than one level. There was a re-allocation of values between political elites on the one hand and military and bureaucratic elites on the other; between the regions and the centre; among the regions themselves; and between the major ethnic groups. These re-allocations were distinct. The Northern civil service, for example, gained an influence in policy-making in the North it had never enjoyed before,[2] and at the same time was threatened by the pending dismantlement of the apparatus of regional government. Yet, at the same time, these levels of action were interrelated. The unification of the public service may not have been consciously intended to further the interests of particular groups or regions over those of others, but it was certainly feared that it would.

Initially, however, the reaction of the Northern elites to the seizure of power by the army in January had not been openly hostile. Many Northern officers and civil servants supported the regime, though some may now prefer to believe that they did so under duress. For example, both Majors Hassan Katsina and Alhaji Ali Akilu, the then Officer Commanding the 1st Recce Squadron and Secretary to the former premier, respectively, had been recruited by Major Nzeogwu at pistol-point, the latter to form an interim government of civil servants in the North; but once Ironsi had

[1] Communique of the meeting of the Supreme Military Council, 7–8 June, reprinted in the *Morn ng Post* (Lagos), 10 June 1966.
[2] It can claim much of the responsibility, for example, for the important structural reforms of the Native Authorities, which were initiated under military rule.

taken over, there was little doubt as to their willingness to cooperate with the regime, the former as Military Governor of the North and the latter as his Secretary and head of the region's civil service. The leaders of the two former opposition parties in the North, the NEPU and UMBC, were initially favourable.[1] The NPC was prepared to wait upon events, this being typified by the comment at a press conference just after the coup of the former Minister of Transport, Alhaji Zannar Bukar Dipcharima, that 'it's better to survive'.[2]

As information trickled through about the manner in which the coup of January 15 had been carried out and as the regime continued to temporise about the punishment of the conspirators, these evaluations began to shift. The deaths of the Federal Prime Minister, and the Northern and Western premiers were all confirmed within a few days of the coup. But there was total official silence about deaths in the army, which did not prevent the news of the killing of senior Northern and Western officers from beginning to percolate. Official silence only exacerbated the situation and tended to encourage the assumption of the complicity of Major General Ironsi. Rumours began to circulate, for example, that ten, or in some versions up to thirty or forty, Northern officers had been ordered to be shot by the Military Government two days after the coup, when Ironsi had assumed power. Varied stories were propagated about the death and/or miraculous survival of the Sardauna of Sokoto, Chief Akintola and Brigadier Maimalari – though stories about the former were easier to scotch because of the very detailed coverage of his death in the *New Nigerian*[3] – and there were lurid accounts of the alleged mutilation of Sir Abubakar Tafawa Balewa and Chief Okotie-Eboh. The government did not take steps to provide more adequate information concerning the circumstances of the coup or to settle the fate of the conspirators. The treatment of the whole affair as a purely internal administrative problem of the army that would be dealt with in its own good time, rather than as a political priority, inevitably allowed the development of suspicions in the North that the government was at one with the conspirators; that Ibo blood was thicker than water between Ironsi and the Majors; and that the North had been unduly and improperly deprived of power.

[1] Joseph Tarka, the UMBC leader, appealed to the army not to hand over to the politicians until 'nepotism, bribery and regional consciousness' were wiped out. His party would watch events 'with sealed lips'. *West Africa* (London), 26 February 1966.
[2] *West Africa* (London), 29 January 1966.
[3] The *New Nigerian* (Kaduna) actually carried pictures of the Sardauna's burnt house and of the bloodstains on the wall where he was shot. There was disbelief in some of the more remote areas of the North about his death, however, and rumours that he had gone to Mecca. For the importance of rumours in motivating the July 1966 revolt among Northerners in the army, see Chapter II above. The rumours about Akintola's death were almost as lurid as those described for Maimalari in that chapter. One version, for example, tells how he caught bullets and was only put to death when he could be held down and the bullets pumped through his mouth.

At the same time, suspicion that military government was a cover for southerners and, in particular, for Ibos to assume dominance in the occupational and political structures both in the North and at Federal level, began to grow. There is no evidence that this was in fact a conscious goal of government policy, except in so far, perhaps, as it flowed as a latent consequence from the military's distaste for restrictions on mobility and achievement. Yet a number of Ironsi's official appointments were sufficient, under conditions of uncertainty, to generate such an impression, such as those of F. C. Nwokedi as Commissioner on Administrative Unification and G. C. M. Onyiuke to replace Dr T. O. Elias as Attorney General.[1]

The high proportion of the new army promotions who were Ibos (for details see Chapter II) gave rise to alarm, despite the fact that it arose from their numerical dominance in the middle layers of the officer corps. And it diverted attention from the government's real attempts to redraw the balance in favour of the Northerners (for the army was coy about publicising any such efforts at regional balancing). In April, the air force dismissed over thirty cadets, mostly Northerners, who had been admitted with low educational qualifications under the civilian regime, but had already gone through up to two years' training. This clumsy gesture gave rise to fears that criteria of formal educational advancement might be more stringently applied against Northerners elsewhere in the occupational structure. There were fears that attempts would be made to control admissions to Ahmadu Bello University in the North, a fear given salience by the struggle for control of the universities by regional elites in the south.[2] The appointment of a young Northern medical professor to replace the retiring expatriate vice chancellor was hurried through, in order (it was believed) to forestall the appointment of an Ibo academic from the University of Ibadan. There is no conclusive proof in these events of premeditated Ibo expansionism, but to many in the North they seemed to fit into such a pattern.

The composition of the three study groups appointed to look into Nigeria's political and economic future was taken as a further slight to Northern opinion. The North, with only five of the total membership of twenty-four, was not even given parity with each of the other regions on the groups, let

[1] Both of these men were Ibos and Ironsi seems to have appointed them because he knew them personally and trusted them, and to have been rather naively unaware of ulterior motives that others might attribute to him. Nwokedi was the most senior public servant apart from S. O. Wey, the Secretary to the Military Government. He had also worked with Ironsi during the Congo operation, and may thus have seemed an obvious choice. On the other hand, in Northern eyes, some episodes in his past, including his role as the first Commissioner for the Nigerianisation of the Federal Public Services in promoting and staffing Federal institutions with southerners (for lack of qualified Northerners) in the late 1950s, did not seem auspicious.

[2] See the account of the Lagos University crisis in Chapter IX above. Fears for the North's university were raised by the shake-up of the universities in the south carried out by the government during these months, especially the appointment of a new Council for Lagos University.

alone the larger representation in accordance with its greater size and population that had been normal under the previous regime. None of the study group chairmen, moreover, were Northerners. And the region's five members[1] – the North's Solicitor General, the Governor of the Central Bank, two civil servants and a university teacher – could hardly be said to have been widely representative of opinion. The publicity given to the establishment of the study groups, moreover, tended to obscure the fact that Ironsi had been more generous to the North in several of his other public appointments; and that there was certainly not much evidence of his deliberately packing Easterners or Ibos into jobs.[2]

Another unfortunate feature was that the General chose to deal with the wrong intermediaries in the region, because he was misled by southern stereotypes of the North as being monolithic, traditional and static. Thus he attached undue importance to his good personal relations with the Sultan of Sokoto.[3] He was to attempt to use the meetings of emirs and chiefs, held after the May uprising, to re-establish order, though the control of these rulers over their own communities was limited. He had appointed Lt Colonel Hassan Katsina as Military Governor of the Region in preference to Lt Colonel Gowon, mainly because the former was the son of the powerful Emir of Katsina. Although Hassan was indeed probably the best choice for the job, Ironsi undoubtedly overestimated the influence he had in the North. The Military Governor, moreover, was personally in a bad position to convey to Ironsi the seriousness of the growing unrest in the North: for he shared the regime's overall goals concerning national unity and the like, he lacked a politician's sensitivity to the currents of public opinion, and found it difficult to bargain rather than take orders from his Supreme Commander.

The initial overtures of politicians of the former radical opposition in the North, like the Tiv politician, J. S. Tarka of the UMBC, or Aminu Kano

[1] The North's representatives in the study groups were as follows: on the National Unity Study Group (seven members), Yusufu Gobir (a Northern Permanent Secretary); Constitutional Review Study Group (nine members), Alhaji M. Buba Ardo (Solicitor General of the North), plus one Northern civil servant; National Planning Advisory Group (eight members), Alhaji Aliyu Mai Bornu (Governor, Central Bank), Dr Iya Abubakar (lecturer in Mathematics, Ahmadu Bello University).

[2] *January 15th: before and after* points out that of the regime's appointments of managers, chairmen and secretaries of the Federal public corporations, twelve were Westerners, six were Northerners, one a Mid-Westerner and only three Easterners. The Tribunals of Enquiry into the Nigerian Railway Corporation, the Electricity Corporation of Nigeria and Lagos City Council were headed, respectively, by a Westerner, a Northerner and an expatriate. Of the Federal Permanent Secretaries, eight were Northerners, seven Mid-Westerners, five Westerners and only three Easterners (though this was, of course, a position inherited from the previous regime). Lt Colonel Ojukwu had also made some effort to keep on good terms with the Northerners and appointed his friend, the Emir of Kano, to be the Chancellor of the University of Nigeria, Nsukka, in place of Dr Azikiwe.

[3] For example, he brought the Sultan to Lagos for consultation with him almost immediately after his assumption of power. From January to July, the Sultan acted as the recognised spokesman for the Northern chiefs and spoke for the meetings of emirs and chiefs held after the May uprising.

of the NEPU, were disregarded. Tarka, in particular, had two interviews at his own request with Ironsi, was completely unsuccessful in his attempts to persuade the latter that this was the moment to create a Middle Belt or to release Tiv political prisoners, and was sent away under rather humiliating circumstances.[1] By April 1966, these men were meeting with their former opponents in the NPC. This decision to ignore the minorities politicians of the North was particularly unfortunate for Ironsi, as he thus missed an opportunity to drive a wedge between the Middle Belt and the far North; and it was (as we saw in Chapter II) the impressive unity of Middle Belt, diaspora and far-North officers and men in July which was his ultimate downfall.

This, then, is the background to the rising disquiet among elites in the North. By early April 1966, these concerns were beginning to come out in public. At this time, the *New Nigerian* and the Hausa-language newspaper, the *Gaskiya Ta Fi Kwabo*, began to print letters and features criticising the regime and voicing support for the federal system of government. One of these went as far as to point out for the first time in the English-language media that officers and politicians from only one section of the country had been killed; that the appointment of Nwokedi commission seemed to indicate a commitment to unitary government; and that there had been a 'mad rush of application letters passing into the North from other parts of the country'.[2] Both these newspapers were owned by the regional government, and – though independent in regard to editorial policy – can be taken as authentic (if slightly muted) voices of informed opinion among the small Northern bureaucratic elite at Kaduna.[3] It is especially significant that one of the *New Nigerian*'s features at this time – a lengthy and well-argued case for a federal constitution[4] – was written by a former radical opponent of the NPC, Alhaji Ibrahim Imam. The Northerners' earlier heterogeneity of response to military rule was disappearing, as common interest seemed to override both political and cultural differences.

---

[1] Details from M. J. Dent, 'Tarka: Tiv background and the dynamics of Nigerian leadership', unpublished seminar paper (London: Institute of Commonwealth Studies, 1968). Some of the advisors around Ironsi apparently tried to buy Tarka off by offering to set him up in business. Ironsi did not apparently agree that the 500 or so Tiv in prison after the 1964 disturbances were *political* prisoners.

[2] Article by Alhaji Suleiman-Takuma of the Nigeria Broadcasting Corporation in *New Nigerian* (Kaduna), 19 April 1966.

[3] In an editorial on 23 May 1966 the *New Nigerian* replies to a charge of 'incitement' against it, made by a southern newspaper, that it was under fire in the North for being too moderate in its expression of federalist views.

[4] A series of four articles in the *New Nigerian* (Kaduna), 16–19 May 1966.

THE REVOLT OF THE MASSES

These strains were also felt in a more unreflective manner by the various sub-elites, particularly among the urban population[1] of the North. For the January coup severed the link between traditional allegiances, as crystallised around the Emirates and the NPC, and national political authority, thereby depriving the Northern masses of any means by which they could identify with the latter, so that they became an 'available non elite'.[2]

These tensions were initially expressed in rather inchoate rumours, some of which we have already described. The Sardauna of Sokoto and Brigadier Maimalari were rumoured to be alive. The Sardauna, it was said, had been seen in Mecca, though this rumour started to lose currency by the end of January. In early February, it was put about that the Military Government would stop the Hajj to Mecca, a rumour which became so strong that Lt Colonel Hassan had to make a specific denial on the radio.[3] The vernacular press began to play a key role in developing fears and suspicions that the North would be dominated by the south. *Gaskiya Ta Fi Kwabo*, published in Zaria, carried reports of Northern politicians being mobbed and insulted on their way up to the North after the coup.[4] As information concerning the killings of Northerners in the coup trickled through, rumours and fears began to focus on the Ibos, whose role in urban trade and employment also laid them open for attack.

It is interesting that the Ibos themselves seem to have shared in and played a role in generating popular perceptions concerning the new distribution of power.[5] In some Northern cities, for example, it was possible to obtain picture postcards showing a dead Sardauna of Sokoto with a cock (a symbol of the NCNC and thus signifying Ibo power) upon his chest. A gramophone record was on sale which began with a speech by the late Sir Abubakar which was drowned out by machine-gun fire. Ibo students at Ahmadu Bello University began to voice in public some of the comments about the North's backwardness they had hitherto kept muted. An Ibo

[1] In general, the rural population was below the threshold of political awareness at which it might be mobilised for effective mass political action. On the other hand, inhabitants of the larger villages in the immediate vicinity of the Northern cities could be and were mobilised during the May and September–October uprisings.
[2] Kornhauser, *The politics of mass society*.
[3] *New Nigerian* (Kaduna), 9 February 1966.
[4] See *Government statement on the current Nigerian situation* (Lagos: Ministry of Information, 1966). It is interesting that reports of this kind were one of the precipitating factors of the Kano riot of 1953.
[5] They were not alone in this. In the West, for instance, the coup was believed to have restored the fortunes of the Action Group and, indeed, Lt Colonel Fajuyi was believed to be an Action Group man. Within two weeks of the coup, there were postcards selling in Lagos and the West of Awolowo standing over Akintola's corpse, captioned 'Awo on top'.

lecturer at the university went so far as to criticise the appointment of the new Northern vice chancellor publicly at an official reception in the latter's honour and to suggest that better candidates could have been found in the south.

Major General Ironsi's broadcast announcement on 24 May, concerning the unification of the country and the banning of political parties under Decree no. 34, brought tensions to a head. Serious rioting broke out in a number of Northern cities on 28 and 29 May, directed mainly against the Ibos and their property, ninety-two persons being killed, according to the official figures,[1] and over 500 wounded. Further outbreaks followed, the next weekend, in more remote Northern centres.

Although higher-level Northern bureaucratic and intellectual elites may have played a role in articulating and diffusing discontent about the programme of unification, there is little evidence that many of them had a direct hand in this uprising. Some Northern provincial and district administrators, alongside the Nigeria Police and the military, played an active role in containing the disturbances, though there were others who let it ride. Nor does it seem that most of the emirs were involved: the Sultan of Sokoto and the Emir of Kano, indeed, actively tried to halt rioting in their cities.

What then was the link, if any, between elite fears and mass protest? How were the urban populations mobilised? What was the role of the different sub-elites in urban areas? The available sources of information are inadequate; and it is difficult to identify the relevant channels of political communication. There was clearly some degree of coordination, in that the riots took place in a number of different cities at the same time and attracted participants from the surrounding hinterlands. Federal government publications[2] identify four main groups as in different ways responsible: the university students; the ex-politicians; the lower-grade civil servants who felt threatened by the impending unification of the administrative services; and the local merchants, petty contractors and former party organisers.

The students played an important role in articulating discontent and were responsible for much of the newspaper correspondence on the issue of federation. They also staged a protest march in the streets of Zaria, with banners proclaiming 'Araba' (let us part or secede) shortly before the riots began there. But such evidence as we have – for example the protection they afforded to the Ibo students at the university during the riots – suggests that there was no direct coordination between their demonstration and the outbreak of violence.

---

[1] Which underestimate the number killed. This may have been in fact nearer to 400–500.
[2] See particularly *Nigeria 1966*. The lower grade civil servants were not immediately affected by Decree no. 34, which unified only the topmost grades of the public service, but the important point is that they *believed* their own positions would be affected sooner or later too.

It seems clear that the key groups were the local merchants, contractors and party men. These sub-elites had established symbiotic relationships both with the Native Authorities and the NPC party.[1] Many had become indebted by political patronage to the Northern Nigeria Marketing Board or the Northern Nigeria Development Corporation, and were likely to be under pressure from the Military Government to pay arrears accumulated under the civilian regime. They were in intense competition with the Ibos and other southern groups for the control of petty contracting and merchandising. Through the NPC, the Northern Contractors Union and the Northern Amalgamated Merchants Union, they had pressed the civilian regional government, with a degree of success, for 'Northernisation', or government restrictions on competitors from the other regions. They were close to the ordinary people, from whom they were able to mobilise a great deal of support through ties of patronage, trade, politics and gossip. They were also well connected with functionaries in the Native Authorities, and were able to profit from internal dynastic and political rivalries in the Native Authorities, to mobilise support in the traditional Hausa–Fulani towns even if not supported by the emirs.

It is significant that the cities where the disorders were most widespread were those where NPC support had been strongest, mostly in the Hausa–Fulani Emirates. Among these, however, the worst rioting took place in those towns with a more modern social and economic base, like Kaduna, Zaria, Kano, Bauchi, Funtua and Gusau, rather than in the more static traditional cities such as Sokoto, Katsina and Daura.[2] This reflects the greater intensity in the former of competitive modernisation in trade and employment and the presence of larger 'stranger' immigrant groups. It may also demonstrate the greater effectiveness of social controls in the latter, where law and order still rested more on traditional authority.

In the absence of such controls, the coercive resources even of a military regime were not enough to keep order. There were at most 4,000 troops, 4,500 members of the Nigeria Police Force and some 7,000 Native Authority Police in the whole of the North, only a limited number of whom could be mobilised to handle disturbances. This represents a population ratio of approximately one policeman per 2,700 and one soldier per 7,400 in the North (the equivalent ratios for the whole of Nigeria are one to 2,300 and one

---

[1] See Sklar, *Nigerian political parties*, especially Chapter VII, and Dudley, *Parties and politics in Northern Nigeria.*

[2] The difference between the 'traditional' and the 'modern' towns in the North is defined in terms of both difference in demographic patterns (length of residence; age and sex structure of the population, etc.) and the existence in the 'traditional' towns of an effective traditional political structure. Towns like Zaria and Kano are composed of both an old traditional city and of distinct areas of recent immigrant settlement, usually including one for Hausa 'strangers' and a separate one for all the non-Hausa immigrant groups.

to 6,200 respectively) – ratios of armed forces and police to population that are extremely low by world standards.[1] In such conditions it is clear that the government depended heavily on legitimacy rather than coercion for the maintenance of order. Its problems were compounded by the fact that the troops that had to be used to end the disturbances were mainly Northerners and could not be fully relied on. Soldiers were deployed as a *cordon-sanitaire* around the immigrant areas, but for the most part did not enter them to actually stop the rioting.

THE DISINTEGRATION OF UNITY, MAY TO JULY 1966

The May disorders marked a turning point, a challenge to which the government did not know how to respond. In the first instance, the riots were (rightly) diagnosed as a failure in public relations. Lt Colonel Hassan Katsina broadcast appeals for calm and called an emergency meeting of the emirs and chiefs, at which he agreed to transmit a memorandum on their grievances, and the latter accordingly agreed to appeal for peace. A meeting of the Supreme Military Council was held in early June and issued a public communique reiterating the Military Government's former statements that the constitutional changes were temporary; and that a permanent constitution would only come into effect after an elaborate process of consultation through the Constitutional Review Study Group, a constituent assembly and a referendum.[2] But it failed to make any tangible concessions which would satisfy the emirs and chiefs.[3] Peace committees were established in a number of Northern towns. Ministry of Information loudspeaker vans were sent on tour of the Northern provinces to provide reassurance that the constitutional changes were not intended to interfere with traditional institutions. Measures were taken to prevent the spreading of popular political and ethnic stereotypes; and in early June the singing of songs and publication of any display of photographs deemed likely to provoke any section of the community were made illegal.[4]

[1] See above, pp. 88–9.
[2] Major General Ironsi had already outlined this procedure of consultation in a press conference on 22 February. See *West Africa* (London), 4 March 1966.
[3] Lt Colonel Hassan Katsina transmitted the Military Council's reply to the chiefs at a later meeting with them. Although they thanked the Military Government (publicly) for the reply, it is understood that their feeling was that they had received little genuine satisfaction and they voiced strong criticism in private at the meeting.
[4] An official recognition of the role played by itinerant singers and informally distributed broadsheets and postcards in sharpening inter-ethnic stereotypes and causing antagonism. Shortly after this, the editor of the *West Africa Pilot* was detained because a cartoon in his newspaper depicted the Military Government as a cockerel crowing 'one country, one nationalism', thus providing a symbolic linkage between the nation, the military and the dissolved NCNC party and the Ibos. See *West Africa* (London), 18 June 1966.

On the other hand, the government took no clear-cut steps to punish those responsible for the killings or to demonstrate it had the authority to deal with them if disorders broke out again. A tribunal was established to examine the causes of the riots, to frame a scheme of compensation for loss and damage to property and to suggest means of promoting inter-communal harmony, though its first sitting (nullified by the July coup) was not scheduled until 2 August. It was in theory non-partisan – being composed of a British High Court judge as chairman, a former Attorney General as leading counsel and four representatives, one from each region – though in practice its composition gave some offence in the North.[1] Care was taken to allay fears that the tribunal might be punitive in intent, by provision of an assurance that evidence given before it would not be used in judicial proceedings against persons involved in the riots.[2]

In spite of all this, however, there were in practice no concessions on the important political issues. The assumption was that once the regime's case had been explained properly to the public, opposition would vanish and reason prevail. With singular lack of political realism, the programme of political unification was accelerated. In mid-July Major General Ironsi announced a number of important measures, designed both to lead to greater national unity and to implement the military vision of society. After their first six months in office the Military Governors were to be transferred to other groups of provinces (regions) and henceforth would rotate every six months. Sections of the Nigeria Police, notably of the Mobile Unit (the riot-squads), would also rotate. Men of the 4th Battalion at Ibadan were told[3] that they would change places with the 1st Battalion at Enugu, indicating a similar policy in regard to the military. 'Prefects' from the armed forces were to be responsible for government policy at a local level, presumably as heads of the provincial or district administrations. Military tribunals of unspecified jurisdiction were also to be established at a local level.

These measures were announced in a precipitate, off-the-cuff manner: those concerning the rotation of the governors and the appointment of prefects, for example, were part of an address to a parade of the Nigeria Police Force, two weeks before the July coup.[4] They evidently lacked adequate preparation: it was not clear, for example, at what levels and with what jurisdiction the military prefects and tribunals would operate. There had

[1] Northerners thought that a tribunal of enquiry into the internal affairs of the North should contain more than the one Northern representative (Dr R. A. B. Dikko). Moreover, the Eastern representative was Dr Eni Njoku, who was too closely associated with the conflict in 1965 over ethnic control of the University of Lagos to be viewed as likely to be non-partisan.
[2] *New Nigerian* (Kaduna), 28 July 1966.
[3] This was announced by Ironsi in an address to the 4th Battalion at Ibadan on 28 July, the day before the coup.
[4] On 14 July. See *New Nigerian* (Kaduna), 14 July 1966, for details.

been little consultation about these decisions between Ironsi and the Military Governors, especially Lt Colonel Hassan Katsina.[1] Above all, as with Decree no. 34, Ironsi seems to have been quite blind to the political impact of his actions.

What was the rationale for all this? Why did the Military Government feel unable to compromise with the political forces that had been loosened in the May uprising? It seems in part to have been an expressive reaction by the military leaders themselves to the stresses which they faced. They felt all the more strongly the need to reassert the military values they knew and understood. This was perhaps as true of the Northerners as of the others, though it became increasingly difficult for the former to reconcile this need with the political and organisational pressures to rebel, to which they were exposed throughout the period May to July 1966. In his first broadcast after the May riots, for example, Lt Colonel Hassan Katsina asserted that:

no soldier wants to rule. Our normal function is not to govern but to protect the integrity and safety of the nation. We should be much happier doing that than governing...We in the Armed Forces believe in discipline. We believe that Nigerian society cannot be brought together, so that every member of it irrespective of tribe or religion respects one another, without discipline. The Armed Forces also believe in fair play. You cannot manage a society in which some members dominate...It was for this reason that the Unification Decree was introduced. The Unification Decree is not intended to give advantage to any section of the community. Its aim is to treat all Nigerians alike. But we do realise that it is difficult to treat everyone alike.[2]

The expressive function[3] of the regime's attitudes and policy proposals is seen particularly clearly in the personal conduct of Major General Ironsi during the two months before his death. National unity remained a great emotional concern to him. And on the model of a good military commander, he seems to have thought he could propagate his beliefs and standards of conduct by personal example. The week before his death he undertook a tour of the nation, visiting Kano, Zaria, Kaduna and Jos in the North, at some risk to himself. At the end of this tour on 28 July, he addressed a conference of

---

[1] It does not seem from all accounts as if the Supreme Military Council had been called to ratify this decision; and it is thought that Lt Colonel Hassan Katsina was opposed to it. Decree no. 34 had, in contrast, been approved by a full meeting of the Supreme Military Council, and announced by Ironsi in a broadcast immediately following that meeting. Ironsi had, of course, full powers to do what he liked, without the Supreme Military Council's knowledge or approval, though this was not at all wise in the circumstances.

[2] He went on to attempt to resolve the apparent contradiction of the last two sentences by pointing out that Decree no. 34 was to be seen in the context of (unspecified) government plans for special measures to accelerate the development of 'backward' areas, especially in the North. Speech reprinted in *New Nigerian* (Kaduna), 30 May 1966.

[3] D. Katz, 'The functional approach to the study of attitudes', *Public Opinion Quarterly*, XXIV, 2 (1960), pp. 163–204.

natural rulers from all parts of Nigeria, which he had assembled at Ibadan, and asked them all to join with him in singing the national anthem, a few hours before he was arrested and killed by Northern troops.

It is also to be noted that Ironsi was under pressure all this time from the more radical southern officers in the army, many but not all of whom, were Ibos.[1] There was a widespread feeling that the revolutionary image of January had been lost, and should be recovered; and there were demands that the Majors of January should be released and that the government should take some more positive action against the sources of opposition in the North.[2] In fairness to Ironsi, therefore, the moves towards national unity must be seen as part of a wider response to demands of this nature. During June and July, the government committed itself to a number of other important reforming initiatives. It was at this time, for example, that it finally established tribunals of enquiry into Federal public corporations and the Lagos City Council, and legislated to investigate and seize assets corruptly obtained under the old regime. A new National Orientation Committee with vague responsibilities to correct inefficiency, corruption and other laxities in the public services and national life, was set up and Lt Colonel Anwuna was made its head (though this appointment looked ominous to the Northerners).

All these reforms were of no avail. There was an increasing breakdown in patterns of communications and control within both the military and the administration during the weeks before Ironsi's overthrow. A symptom of this is that the General himself came to rely increasingly on a small circle of trusted civilian and military advisors in Lagos and on a network of informants in other cities, formal channels of consultation being ignored. Lt Colonel Hassan Katsina and Alhaji Ali Akilu were consulted less fully and less frequently, and on one or two occasions, to the writer's knowledge, important decisions affecting the North were taken without them being consulted. The coup of July 29, as set forth in Chapter II, was the culmination of a similar breakdown of the pattern of controls within the military organisation itself.

Disintegration was not confined to the army and the administration, nor just to the North. There was a widening cycle of mistrust in most of the

[1] There were several officers at the lieutenant colonel level who are believed to have thought this way, including men like Lt Colonel Anwuna, the GSO (I), Lt Colonel Okoro, the CO, 3rd Battalion, Lt Colonel Akagha, the commander of the Zaria Depot and Lt Colonel Okwechime of the Engineers and Lt Colonels Ejoor and Ojukwu, Military Governors of the Mid-West and East. Some officers may have been content merely to criticise Ironsi for not going fast enough. Others may have considered (in a tentative way) attempting to replace him, probably by Lt Colonel Ojukwu. It is impossible to tell how significant or well-coordinated such moves were, because sources are fragmentary and inaccurate.

[2] A number of highly placed Northerners and expatriates report that there were lists circulating among the officers of Northerners and expatriate sympathisers, who were to be 'purged' from their positions and imprisoned or killed (the former) or deported (the latter).

important institutions of society. Ibo staff and students at the University of Ibadan, for example, felt increasingly insecure about their lives and property, from the time of the May riots onwards. These tensions called forth a bitter speech by Dr Kenneth Dike, the Vice Chancellor, at a university degree-giving ceremony in July, repudiating allegations of tribalism and corruption in the university but accusing the educated Nigerian of being 'the worst peddler of tribalism in Nigeria'.[1]

The coup of July 28 was not merely, therefore, a revolt against authority by Northern junior officers and NCOs. It was also the culmination of growing social forces inherent in the Nigerian political system, but sharpened by the Military Government's inability to take decisions which were either clear in their intentions or flexible in their application.

[1] *West Africa* (London), 9 July 1966.

CHAPTER XII

MILITARY IMAGE AND POLITICAL BELIEFS

> To govern, my dear Bishop, one must treat truth as the mariner treats
> the Pole Star: never let it out of your sight, but do not head straight for it.
> The Prime Minister (Winston Churchill)
> in Rolf Hochuth's *Soldiers*.[1]

THE MAP OF POLITICS

The soldiers' inability or unwillingness to adopt a complex or devious morality, like that of Winston Churchill in Hochuth's play, provides a key to the central paradox of military rule in Nigeria. When they took power, the soldiers marched out on a straight path towards their vision of a good society. But the vision became more elusive the closer they came towards it. In this chapter, it will be argued, first, that this was in some measure because of the content and character of the vision itself, and secondly, that the soldiers' political code was strongly influenced both in its content and in their own high degree of emotional commitment to it, by the conceptions of honour and good conduct, discussed in Chapter IV above. In that chapter, we looked at collectively generated and collectively enforced standards of *personal* conduct. It is now suggested that the same image was also turned outwards. The military was held to be the exemplar of values that should be copied by civilian institutions; and ideas of honour were generalised from the collectivity of the army to that of the nation. When the military took part in politics, it did so on a vaguely articulated premise that it was desirable for it to attempt to reconstruct government and society in its own image, in accordance with the values of which it was believed to be the unique standard-bearer.

Nevertheless, when we start looking closely at what the soldiers suppose their political values to be, we see that they are far from constituting a coherent system of political ideas – in other words, an ideology.[2] The political

---

[1] R. Hochuth, *Soldiers* (London: Andre Deutsch, 1968).

[2] Janowitz, *The military in the political development of new nations*, pp. 63–7, makes a similar point, though continuing to talk of a set of 'ideological themes' common to the military, as opposed to a fully consistent ideology.

beliefs of military men arise in a rather inchoate manner from the group experience of the officer corps, from their vaguely articulated ideas of personal and collective honour and from the need to legitimate their actions in a manner satisfactory to themselves, in the particular circumstances in which they play a political role. They constitute a cultural map[1] of politics and society, albeit a very crude one. This map, however, sometimes bears a somewhat tenuous relation both to the social and political realities it is supposed to depict and to the political behaviour of which, in theory, it is the guide. One very often gets the feeling that the map remains the same, with the familiar configurations of line and colour – soldiers are not politicians, politicians are corrupt and divide the nation, only soldiers are capable of expressing and discerning the national interest, and so forth. But the realities represented by each line and shading of the map keep changing; moreover, the lines and colours may come to mean different things to different people at the same time.

Nonetheless, the map has had some quite specific political consequences, both in motivating the Nigerian soldiers to take power, and in shaping the decisions they took while ruling. They took over office on the assumption that the politicians in power had been violating certain definable principles of good government; and that they were uniquely qualified by the level of their commitment to the national interest to judge when these were being violated. What were these principles? How did the officers think they had been transgressed? And in what way did they propose to establish their vision of the good social order?

It is possible to piece together the essentials of the military view, both from the pronouncements of the leaders of the January coup who took the military into the political arena, and from the statements and actions of the army leaders who took power from the hands of the January Majors during the first seven months of military rule. There is no essential difference in *content* between the statements of these two groups of military figures, although Major Nzeogwu tended to adorn his views with a few bits of Marxist jargon that the senior officers did not use. While Major General Ironsi, it is true, staged a counter-coup against the Majors, his regime tried to carry through the political vision and programme of the latter. The military view was indeed defined especially sharply during the seven-month period of his rule, because officers were forced both to reevaluate their role in relation to politics, and to legitimate their political activity in terms of their common stock of political ideas. At the same time, political events had not yet turned their world upside down, as after the July 1966 coup, so that the military

[1] C. Geertz, 'Ideology as a cultural system' in D. Apter (ed.), *Ideology and discontent* (New York: The Free Press, 1964).

image still seemed a relatively coherent one. Major Nzeogwu was later to castigate Ironsi's regime in no uncertain terms for its timidity.[1] Yet the difference remained essentially one of approach, of the urgency with which the vision should be implemented, of the way in which power should be used, rather than of the content of the vision itself.

The military view of the proper conduct of government can be summarised in the form of five antinomies: discipline versus disorder; honour versus decadence and corruption; achievement versus ascription; administered consensus versus politics; and the nation versus regionalism and tribalism.

DISCIPLINE VERSUS DISORDER

The army seized power after a period of civil disorder in the Western Region, which was the pretext at least for the seizure of power by the Majors. The restoration of order was the first task to which the Military Government turned. A disorderly society was an undisciplined one. It was also a shameful one. For the ideas of discipline and honour (or conversely disorder and dishonour) tend to be linked in the military imagination. It is impossible to seek for or to gain honour unless one has self-discipline; and discipline itself is made more attractive by ceremony, pomp and circumstance, by all the symbolic trappings of honour that make routine bearable. Nevertheless, discipline can only be acquired through an arduous period of socialisation, in which seasoned military men who are well-initiated in the arts of the control of self and others (the Regimental Sergeant Major?) play a crucial role.

The army's role in government was interpreted accordingly. Thus it was asserted in a communique of the Supreme Military Council that: 'The military Government is not an elected government and must not be treated as such. It is a *corrective* government designed to remove the abuses of the old regime and to create a healthy community for a return to civilian government.'[2] The interpretation given to this need for discipline was sometimes rather literal. Both Lt Colonel Ejoor in the Mid-West and Lt Colonel

---

[1] See his interview with D. Ejindu in *Africa and the World*, III, 31 (May 1967), 14–16:

EJINDU: It has been said that General Ironsi set out to complete your job for you. Was there anything you did not like in his administration?

NZEOGWU: Yes, everything. First, he chose the wrong advisers for the work he half-heartedly set out to do. Secondly, he was tribalistic in his appointment of his governors. Thirdly, the Decree no. 34 was unnecessary, even silly. In fact...

EJINDU: But you wanted a unitary form of government?

NZEOGWU: No, not a unitary government as such. We wanted to see a strong centre. We wanted to cut the country to small pieces, making the centre inevitably strong. We did not want to toy with power, which is what he did.

[2] *New Nigerian* (Kaduna), 10 June 1966, reporting a communique of the Supreme Military Council's meeting of 7–8 June after the May uprising in the North.

Ojukwu in the East, for example, surprised civil servants by throwing cordons of soldiers round their offices and detaining those civil servants who were late to work, in order that they might receive a schoolmasterly ticking-off from the Military Governor. In early July 1966, Lt Colonel Anwuna, chairman of a newly established Committee for National Reorientation, revealed plans to extend military spot-checks on the administration at a national level: officers would make surprise visits to government offices to detect 'inefficiency, lateness of office, absenteeism, closing early and the filling of football coupons'.[1]

HONOUR VERSUS DECADENCE AND CORRUPTION

The civilian regime had been notoriously venal, a venality which was both the subject of much widespread political gossip as well as open public enquiry, as in the Coker Commission of Enquiry into the public corporations in the Western Region. Corruption, therefore, figures prominently among the Majors' justifications for intervening. As Major Nzeogwu put it in his first broadcast:

Our enemies are the political profiteers, the swindlers, the men in high and low places that seek bribes and demand 10 per cent; those that seek to keep the country divided permanently so that they can remain in office as Ministers or VIPs at least; the tribalists, the nepotists, those that make the country look big for nothing before international circles; those that have corrupted our society and put the Nigerian political calendar back by their words and deeds.[2]

The theme was also taken up by Ironsi's regime which launched vigorous verbal tirades against corruption in official life, though – as pointed out in the previous chapter – it was a little tardy in taking legal action against those who had profited from corruption under the old regime. Lt Colonel Ojukwu, in one of his first broadcasts, spoke of the 'ten wasted years of planlessness, incompetence, inefficiency, gross abuse of office, corruption, avarice and gross disregard of the interests of the common men' of civilian rule.[3] This was in part a simple reaction to very evident abuse, a reaction that was widely shared in Nigerian society, being pungently expressed in the headlines of the *Morning Post* in an editorial after the coup: 'Bribe? "E Done Die; Chop-chop?" E No Dey'.[4] But in addition the soldiers were prone to a deep-rooted puritanism, an emotional reaction against all kind of supposed degeneracy and dishonourable conduct. This comes out clearly in Major Nzeogwu's Extraordinary Orders of the Day making

---

[1] *Daily Times* (Lagos), 13 July 1966.
[2] Panter-Brick (ed.), *Nigerian politics and military rule*, p. 185.
[3] *West Africa* (London), 5 February 1966.
[4] *Morning Post* (Lagos), 27 January 1966.

homosexuality, bribery, rape, looting etc., punishable by death, during the period of his temporary rule at Kaduna. It also appears in Lt Colonel Hassan Katsina's later speech in which he lumped together corruption, indiscipline and Indian hemp:

the machinery of government (under the civilian regime) was not functioning as well as it should. There was corruption. In some cases schools did not work as hard as they should. The standard of discipline was lax. For example, there was widespread indulgence in the smoking of Indian hemp, even among school-children.[1]

Indeed, one of the National Military Government's earlier pieces of legislation was a harsh decree providing minimum sentences of death or twenty-one years of imprisonment for persons growing or dealing in Indian hemp.[2]

Corruption was believed to be undermining efficiency. The latter also tied in with the military's political beliefs through the emphasis placed on education and occupational achievement.

ACHIEVEMENT VERSUS ASCRIPTION

Entry to the officer corps was based on educational achievement. Promotion – to the extent that it deviated from seniority rules – also depended on personal effort, as indicated by passing promotional exams and coming to the notice of superiors as efficient or 'promising' officers. In spite, or perhaps even because of their deep-rooted ambivalence concerning educational status, described in Chapter IV, officers evinced strong support for the notion that expertise derives from a formal education, and that advancement based on any criteria other than merit was wrong. Hence the strong reactions (particularly among southern officers) against the regional quota system operated by the politicians, described in Chapters VIII and X. Or the annoyance with which Lt Colonel Hassan Katsina dismissed the suggestion that his behaviour might be influenced by the fact that he is the son of the Emir of Katsina:

There has been an attempt, particularly by the foreign press, to give the impression that my birth or what they have chosen to call my aristocratic connections will influence my actions...I will like to be clear that as long as I bear the responsibility for the day-to-day affairs of this part of the country, birth, whether high or low, will not shelter anyone who misbehaves or commits an offence from the full weight of the law.[3]

Or as Major General Ironsi announced when explaining the objectives of his regime, soon after attaining office: 'efficiency and merit will be the

[1] *New Nigerian* (Kaduna), 7 February 1966.   [2] Indian Hemp Decree, no. 19 of 1966.
[3] *West Africa* (London), 16 April 1966.

criterion for advancement', and the barriers to achievement set up by tribalism, regionalism and corruption would be removed.[1]

Such considerations lay behind the unification of the public services in Decree no. 34, which – though temporarily confined to the upper levels alone – indicated a longer-run commitment towards occupational mobility between the regions. For 'regionalism and tribalism' were in their nature opposed to merit and were matters of strong emotional concern. As Ironsi once again expressed it: 'anyone who peddles tribalism is a sick man and there is no room for him in this society'.[2] Not surprisingly, the strongest manifestation of such feeling was among the Ibo officers who felt their own prospects of occupational advancement most threatened under the civilian regime. Lt Colonel Ojukwu, for example, felt so strongly about it during his first months in office that he directed that all reference to tribe should be expunged from Eastern Region government documents, forms and publications. Such sentiments were also, however, to be found among officers of most other origins, for instance, in the ambivalence of Lt Colonel Hassan Katsina towards the separatist pressures gathering in the North prior to the May 1966 riots and July 1966 coup.[3]

CONSENSUS VERSUS POLITICS

The attack on tribalism and regionalism also had roots in the hankering of the military for a disciplined cohesive society. The high value placed on 'brotherhood' in the officer corps tended to be generalised into a belief in the value of consensus at a societal level. Cleavages in the social fabric were in principle undesirable; and organisations, like political parties, ethnic unions or trades unions, which gave expression to differentiation in society were also regarded with suspicion – the parties and tribal unions so much so that they were banned under Decree no. 33 of 1966.

Linked to this emphasis on consensus was a strong distrust of politics. Politicians were a race apart, they were not to be trusted for one minute, even if sometimes one was prepared to cooperate with them temporarily. This comes out very clearly in a dialogue between Major Nzeogwu and a well-known writer and journalist, Tai Solarin, on the Majors' plans for the establishment of a government after the January coup (if Nzeogwu is to be believed):

NZEOGWU: Neither myself nor any of the other lads was in the least interested in governing the country. We were soldiers and not politicians. We had

[1] *West Africa* (London), 5 February 1966.
[2] *Ibid.* 23 July 1966.
[3] See the preceding chapter.

earmarked from the list known to every soldier in this operation who would be what. Chief Obafemi Awolowo was, for example, to be released from jail immediately and to be made the Executive Provisional President of Nigeria. We were going to make civilians of proven honesty and efficiency who would be thoroughly handpicked do all the governing.

SOLARIN: What would you be doing?

NZEOGWU: We would stand behind them with our fingers on the trigger.[1]

This last statement suggests an inescapable dilemma. On the one hand, the military feels compelled to intervene because of its dislike of the style and consequences of the politics of the politicians. On the other hand, it does not wish to become enmeshed in politics itself. One possible solution is indirect rule, as proposed by Nzeogwu, though this does not always work smoothly nor protect the military from political entanglements in practice. Another is for the military rulers to attempt to persuade themselves that their role is an *administrative* rather than a political one, so as to render what they are doing more consistent with their self-image. For example, Lt Colonel Ejoor, the former Military Governor of the Mid-West, said in an interview: 'One should not quote me because I am now an administrator. I am not a politician.'[2] Administrators have a tendency to see their function as attempting to secure a managed consensus around the goals of the structures they are administering, rather than as articulating cleavage or adjusting conflicting interests.[3] Independent social groups can only be tolerated if they fit in with a managerial view of society. A good example is Major General Ironsi's attempts to persuade the trades unions not to go on strike while the army was in power:

It is well within the power of the Trades Unions to help in the maintenance of industrial peace, and I should like your assurances that you and all your affiliates in the labour movement will take steps to avoid strikes which will disturb the prevailing peaceful and orderly atmosphere...All workers' organisations must from now on work as a team in the national interest.[4]

[1] Interview between Major Nzeogwu and Tai Solarin, reprinted in the *Nigerian Tribune* (Ibadan), 2 July 1967.

[2] Lt Colonel D. Ejoor, in an interview with D. Omoronyi of the *Daily Times* (Lagos), 5 October 1966.

[3] March and Simon, *Organisations*, pp. 129–31, suggest that it is a fairly general tendency of managerial elites to view bargaining or 'political' problems as 'analytic' problems, of a kind that can be got around by problem-solving techniques or persuasion designed to produce a 'managed' consensus.

[4] *West Africa* (London), 12 February 1966. An interesting footnote to this is that during the civil war there was a series of measures of increasing severity designed to curb the power of unions and prevent strikes culminating in the Decree no. 53 of 1969, which made it an offence to organise, threaten, encourage or prepare for a strike, punishable by up to five years' imprisonment (a proviso which was on a twelve-monthly basis) and set up an Industrial Arbitration Tribunal to replace the existing labour/management bargaining machinery.

285

The argument against politics thus became one of national interest, linking up with the final theme of the Nigerian officer corps' political beliefs, the identification of the military with the nation.

THE NATION VERSUS REGIONALISM AND TRIBALISM

The roots of nationalism in the officer corps lie in two things. First, in the desire – like other western-educated groups – to improve racial and national images and remove the self-doubt inherited from the colonial situation, as we described in Chapter IV. These images were threatened by the corruption and inefficiency of the politicians. They were also very much put in doubt by the existence of civil disorder of the kind that might suggest to outsiders that Africans were incapable of governing themselves. When Nigerian officers first encountered a serious breakdown of law and order, in the Congo in 1960–4, they were placed in a position of ambivalence. For at one and the same time, as Major Ifeajuna said,[1] they were able to contrast their own discipline with that of the Congolese Army, the civil order of their own country with that of the Congo; yet they also felt that the whole Congolese disaster impaired their African self-image. The Western Region disturbances in Nigeria, however, threatened both national and racial self-images at the same time. When the January 1966 conspirators staged their coup they did so, therefore, in the name of national honour, hence the slogan of their broadcast from Lagos, that 'We shall no longer be ashamed to be Nigerians'.[2] These views were not confined to the narrow group of radical conspirators. Lt Colonel Hassan Katsina relates national pride to international reference groups quite explicitly in his statement (when Military Governor of the North) that, 'From the international point of view, I would personally like to see a strong and virile centre. For only by such an arrangement can we as a nation continue to make an appreciable impact on the world scene.'[3]

This linked up also with the view that the army was uniquely qualified to speak for the nation, being identified with the latter more than any other group, as in Major Nzeogwu's contention that in the January coup 'it was a truly Nigerian gathering. Only in the army do you get true Nigerianism.'[4] Such was the January group's degree of confidence that they represented the true interests of the nation in destroying the civil power, that they found it difficult to conceive why anyone in the army could be in disagreement with them, even if this disagreement was confined – as was Major General Ironsi's

[1] See Chapter X above. [2] See Chapter I above.
[3] Interview with Lt Colonel Hassan Katsina in *Daily Times* (Lagos), 4 October 1966. This statement was made after the Northern counter-coup, though he also made similar statements before it.
[4] See Chapter I above.

286

– to their methods. Thus, when the latter took power after their own failure to consolidate their coup, Major Nzeogwu complained: 'We have pledged alliance to General Ironsi on behalf of all the men who *for some unknown reasons* are referred to as rebels.'[1]

Nevertheless, Major General Ironsi's regime carried forward the Majors' vision of a disciplined, united nation, linking this, as we suggested earlier, with an attempt to strike at the sources of 'regionalism and tribalism'. Nationalism was all too readily confused with national unity. The soldiers' conception of the national interest produced Decree no. 34, the proposal to rotate Military Governors and other measures of administrative and political unification. Yet it was precisely these proposals that the Northern officers and men came to find unacceptable, notwithstanding their *theoretical* commitment to the identical goals of national identity. For, as we shall see below, the good of the nation – like most of the soldiers' political ideas – could become a very slippery notion indeed, when exposed to the test of specific political bargaining situations.

FROM BELIEF TO DECISION

In the preceding pages, we have discussed the content of the military elite's beliefs. We now ask: how did these affect its political performance? Did the soldiers indeed try to do what they said they would do? If so, why did they fail, so that after no more than a few months of their rule the nation was more divided and disorderly than ever before? Was this because of the way they governed, the way they sought to put their principles into practice?

Before trying to answer these questions, however, we should add two cautions. First, that it is rather hazardous to predict patterns of political action from the beliefs that officers subscribe to. Deeds have a nasty habit of departing from words, the more so when the beliefs are so general – like those of the military – as to be of limited value as a day-to-day operative code for political conduct.[2] Secondly, it is not at all clear how much better the politicians – the supposed specialists in bargaining and the creation of legitimacy symbols – were at politics than were the soldiers, the specialists in violence.[3] How would one set about verifying whether or not the soldiers handled their conflicts less skilfully than the politicians, under whose rule, after all, Nigeria had also been prone to conflict and violence? On an impressionistic basis, one can say that serious conflict arose more rapidly

[1] *New Nigerian* (Kaduna), 18 January 1966.
[2] For further discussion of the way that ideology is usually re-specified in lower-level operative codes before it can be effective for day-to-day conduct, see P. Selznick, *TVA and the grass roots* (Berkeley, Calif.: University of California Press, 1949).
[3] H. Lasswell, 'The garrison state', *American Journal of Sociology*, XLVI (June 1941).

under military than under civilian government and the violence that ensued was worse. The politicians had shown some ability to compromise – sometimes to the despair of the soldiers and other intelligentsia[1] – and had been able to survive through its crises up to 1966. Whereas the government of Sir Abubakar Tafawa Balewa had survived for six years, that of Major General Ironsi lasted little more than six months. But are the two really comparable? To what extent was the army's failure due to the military elite's lack of skill, or to social and political processes outside its control, or to changes in the political process brought about by the use of violence to make and break regimes?[2] It is difficult enough to produce any clear-cut criteria to assess how much the Military Government's particular decisions worsened the particular crises it faced, still more to decide how far its own general lack of skill contributed to its political effectiveness or ineffectiveness as a whole.

Despite these cautions, however, it is perhaps possible to suggest a number of ways in which the military way of thinking tended to make it difficult for soldiers to assimilate political roles, to make them insensitive to political demands and to make them less capable of taking realistic policy decisions.

The first and most obvious stumbling block to the assimilation of political roles was the hostility of the military men to politics itself as an activity and a way of doing things, of which we have already discussed above the ideological (as opposed to the practical) implications. Frequently this meant that the political information and advice of politicians was not sought – and when it was offered, it was spurned, as when Ironsi refused to have dealings with the politicians of the former radical opposition to the civilian regime. Up to July 1966, moreover, the refusal to play politics was so marked that the Military Governors would not conceive their role in terms of anything else but the normal military relations of command and control. They were

[1] See Lt Colonel Ojukwu's comments in retrospect on the period of civilian rule (though also on Ironsi's regime as well): 'I hope we do not have any more compromises. Sincerely I hope we can tell each other the truth, because if we make this mistake again and start seeking compromises – just to be gentlemen – you will find well – I don't know what. Have you noticed that in recent years all the crises we have been having in Nigeria have been getting worse each time? I shudder to think what the next one will be like. I hope there will be no compromises in this.' *Daily Times* (Lagos), 17 September 1966.

[2] Violence could be said to have speeded up and sharpened existing processes of conflict, whereas previously conflicting groups could hold their fire (metaphorically speaking only) during a crisis until an acceptable compromise had been hammered out, as in the general election crisis of 1964–5. Violence provides a built-in advantage to the person who uses it first. Military cliques who controlled the means of violence were thus under a standing temptation to use it to settle disputes in their own favour; and under constant pressure to use force preemptively against opponents who might use it first. This seems to be the argument used by Dent in 'The military and politics: a study of the relation between the army and the political process in Nigeria'. The argument does, of course, *assume* that the army is sufficiently non-cohesive to give rise to armed cliques in the first place.

there to take orders from the supreme command, not to express regional interests or to bargain among each other or with the supreme command on behalf of those interests. As Lt Colonel Hassan Katsina put it: 'We have got a unified command and it is the method we are used to.'[1] Or the similar sentiments of the late Lt Colonel Fajuyi on his role as Governor: 'I am not a Regional soldier. I belong to the Nigerian Army. I am here on an assignment given by the Supreme Commander. Don't call this my government. It is the Supreme Commander's government.'[2] When pressures of a regional nature did begin to arise, therefore, the Governors, and especially Hassan Katsina, were unable, or felt unable in terms of their role as they conceived it, to insist strongly at the meetings of the Supreme Military Council that political pressures from the regions be taken into account.

After the July 1966 coup and the fragmentation of military authority, the Military Governors each began to go their own way. The politicians too were increasingly coopted into the processes of decision-making at both a formal and an informal level, culminating in the appointment of civilian commissioners in the Military Government at both federal and state levels in 1967. This was in part because the soldiers were (belatedly) learning to play the politician themselves, but mostly because, the army being fragmented and out of control of events, the politicians and the political forces they represented could no longer be ignored.

Nonetheless, the members of the military elite still persisted in the dangerous illusion that if only they could get together to hammer things out among themselves, away from the divisive pressures placed on them by the politicians, they would be able to settle all their differences. This is nowhere more clearly expressed than in the last meeting of all the military leaders, including Gowon and Ojukwu, at Aburi in Ghana in January 1967,[3] even though the agreement reached at this meeting turned out to be an illusion, being fraught with misunderstandings which led later to bitter mutual recrimination. The following extracts from the verbatim report will give an idea of both the search for solidarity amongst fellow officers and the mistrust felt towards the politicians. General Ankrah of Ghana, the host, starts off the discussions:

I will not like to dwell rigidly on any point whatsoever because I feel this is a domestic affair of Nigeria and, as I have always said, it is not difficult for military people to understand each other. It is a saying that if Generals were to meet and discuss frontiers, wars, or even go into the details to forestall war, there will never be any

[1] *West Africa* (London), 4 June 1966.
[2] Quoted from a press conference given by Fajuyi, in *Fajuyi, the Great* (Western Nigeria: Information Division of the Ministry of Home Affairs and Information, June 1967).
[3] *Meeting of the Nigerian military leaders held at Peduase Lodge, Aburi, Ghana, January 4th and 5th 1967.*

discrepancies, but unity and understanding. There will be no war because the two old boys will meet at the frontier and tell each other – 'Old boy, we are not going to commit our boys to die, come on, let us keep the politicians out' – and that is the end. I am quite confident that having met here today, you will continue and achieve what you are here for.[1]

The meeting then meanders on and the subject of politicians crops up in a disconnected way from time to time. For instance, Commodore Wey, the Commander of the Navy:

One thing I would like to repeat, I am a sailor and want to remain a sailor. I do not see why you soldiers should not remain soldiers. We were not trained to be politicians, let us run the Government, draw up a Constitution, hand over to the politicians and we get back into our uniforms.[2]

Finally, the issue comes to a head over the resumption of talks – on the constitutional issues raised by the July 1966 coup – by the civilian Ad Hoc Constitutional Committee which had suspended its sittings at the end of September 1966 owing to the Northern massacres.[3] Some officers maintain their hostility towards allowing the politicians to take part in these discussions. Others, like Lt. Colonel Ejoor, take the point of view that much as they might dislike the politicians, it would now be unrealistic to keep them out.

MAJOR JOHNSON: Gentlemen, if I can start talking on this one, please do not think I am taking undue advantage. Quite honestly, I think we all know what brought this country to where we are today, and while talking yesterday Emeka (Ojukwu) touched on a point of how, due to the situation, the politicians got what they have been waiting for to come in...While I know that definitely we are not going to be in Government for ever, I will like to say that, please for the next few months, let us leave everything that will bring the politicians back into the limelight out of the question. Let us go on all these things we have been discussing since yesterday, because this is the basis at which we can get the country back on its feet. Once we get the papers on these things out and we see them working, then we can call the Ad Hoc Constitutional Committee to come and discuss, but for now they are just going to confuse the issues more if you bring them out to come and talk anything again. I will say, let the Military Government continue for now and after working for six months, and we see how far we can go before we start thinking of calling these people back.

COMMODORE WEY: I hundred per cent support what you have just said. Candidly, if there had ever been a time in my life when I thought somebody had hurt me sufficiently for me to wish to kill him, it was when one of those fellows opened his mouth too wide...

LT COLONEL OJUKWU: On this statement, Gentlemen, a lot depends on what the Ad Hoc Constitutional Committee is. I agree that regarding other Regions it

---

[1] *Meeting of the Nigerian military leaders*, p. 2.
[2] *Ibid.* p. 13.　　　　　　　　　　　　　　　[3] See above, pp. 312–16.

was indeed a platform for politicians, in the East it was not. I did not send politicians to it, but be it as it may, if we say we are going to continue then we must obviously get quite satisfied the terms for running this thing properly. We have got to be able to meet, and I said it outside, and I repeat it here, as the Military Governor of the East, I cannot meet anywhere in Nigeria where there are Northern troops...[1]

The talks drift away from the subject of the Ad Hoc Committee but are brought back to it by Lt Colonel Hassan Katsina:

I do not think we have taken a decision on Item 4...There are two suggestions on this. Bolaji (Johnson) says we leave it for six months but there is a suggestion from Emeka that we can have it but not with politicians.

LT COLONEL OJUKWU: If I can modify that, I believe that the answer is for us to get together and give directions quickly, once this thing has started, for the Ad Hoc Committee to start meeting...

COLONEL ADEBAYO: I think we should agree that we carry on with the reorganisation and reconstruction and the Ad Hoc Committee should meet as soon as we find our feet.

LT COLONEL HASSAN KATSINA: But there is still one school of thought about the politicians. We know we cannot do away with some of them but Bolaji wants us to add that if there is any way out for them not to meddle in our affairs, let us try and do that.

LT COLONEL EJOOR: I think when you are deciding the future of the country, you are deciding for the people and you cannot exclude any particular person from taking part in deciding his future, politicians or technicians.

LT COLONEL GOWON: I think, as I said in my speech of 30th November, we all accept that they started very well until they ran into this difficulty of not being able to meet again. One of the things Emeka would like us to agree to is the question of where they are going to meet. I think that when we have been able to meet in the country without fear, probably the Ad Hoc Committee at a suitable time can be asked to resume.[2]

This distrust for politics as a form of organised activity goes together with a preference for direct and simple solutions, or, as Major General Ironsi said of one of his decrees: 'I want to leave no doubt in the mind of anybody that the provisions of the Decree will be enforced. This is a military regime and soldiers do not allow themselves to be diverted or obstructed in the fulfilment of their objectives.'[3] This exemplifies what we may call the *declamatory style* of military leadership, the emphasis on exhortation rather than truth, action rather than analysis. For there are certain things an officer must take for granted, lest his own morale and that of his men, who must be spurred by his conviction and example, are to suffer. In Chapter VI, we showed how

[1] *Meeting of the Nigerian military leaders*, p. 40.
[2] *Ibid.* pp. 44–5.
[3] *Africa Research Bulletin* (Exeter), May 1966.

officers will shy off discussion of the causes of indiscipline because the possibility of soldiers refusing orders is not supposed to exist in an army. Similarly, in the next chapter, it will be suggested how Lt Colonel Gowon's unwillingness to admit that there was a real problem of indiscipline in the army after July 1966 may have meant that he was not decisive enough in dealing with the Northern soldiers, whose unruly and uncontrolled behaviour was one factor leading to the massacres of September–October 1966.

The gap between principle and practice for a soldier is a small one, for he must act without lengthy reflection and put his plans or orders into effect by the most direct and effective means at his disposal. An extreme example is the way in which the Majors of January, having decided to overthrow the civilian regime, set about it with a truly hair-raising directness by assassinating all the leading army officers and politicians whom they thought might stand in their way; nor would they countenance any ambiguity or wavering in support for their revolution once it had been made, for, as Nzeogwu's Extraordinary Orders of the Day decreed:

Spying, harmful or injurious publications and broadcasts of troop movements or action will be punished by any suitable sentence deemed fit by the military commander. Shouting of slogans, loitering and rowdy behaviour will be rectified by any sentence of incarceration or any more severe sentence...Wavering or sitting on the fence and failing to declare open loyalty with the Revolution will be regarded as an act of hostility punishable by any sentence deemed suitable by the local military commander. Tearing down an Order of the Day or proclamation or other authorised notices will be penalised by death.[1]

Similar (though less extreme) statements can be found in many of the public pronouncements by the military figures who ruled Nigeria after January 1966, for instance Lt Colonel Ojukwu:

The Military government will regard disloyalty, inefficiency, bribery, corruption, nepotism, abuse of public office, and squandering of public funds as acts of sabotage against the regime and will not hesitate to invoke summary measures against any offenders in any position.[2]

Major General Ironsi too believed – to his own disadvantage – that a nation, like a platoon, could be led with snappy decisions, exhortation and inspired personal example. As shown in the preceding chapter, he went straight ahead with decisions, like Decree no. 34, to give an immediate earnest of his intentions to unite the nation, even though most of the practical steps to this end would have to come later; and he bound principle up with personal example, as when he had the emirs, obas and chiefs sing the national anthem with him at Ibadan on the day before he died.

[1] Quoted in Panter-Brick, *Nigerian politics and military rule*, p. 185.
[2] C. O. Ojukwu, *Selected speeches of C. Odumegwu Ojukwu*, 1 (New York: Harper and Row, 1969), 15.

Much of the legislation that has been passed by the various military administrations of the federation or of the regions and states to the present day bears the declamatory imprint very clearly. In the first place, there is the habit of legislation by radio, of announcing decrees or edicts through the media and only promulgating them in the official form in the *Gazettes* as an after-thought.[1] Secondly, many of the penalties or punishments provided for have a military flavour. There is the angry rhetoric of minimum and mandatory penalties of death or specified terms of imprisonment which have been introduced in many pieces of military legislation, from the Suppression of Disorder Decree no. 4 of 1966 and the Indian Hemp Decree onwards: a feature that was entirely absent from the legislation of the civilian period.[2] There are many more offences which have been made punishable by the death penalty, some of them by the firing squad.[3] Mandatory or non-mandatory canings and whippings have been introduced for several others, such as armed robbery or the hemp offences. And both the Federal government and those of the states or regions have introduced legislation allowing the preventive detention of persons at the government's discretion. Draconian punishment and instant government by broadcast, in sum, have allowed the military governments to feel that they have been dealing swiftly and directly with the country's social and political problems, whether or not such drastic methods have in fact been either just or appropriate to the problems in hand.

Declamation of their belief in general goals like national unity, efficiency and discipline has not made it any easier to define in terms of these goals where straightforward solutions are to be found. For most of these beliefs have in practice been too general and too poorly defined to provide a useful operational code of political conduct. And the collective practical and professional experience of members of the military elite has been too short for them to have elaborated a political grammar to sort out important from unimportant problems. There has been a tendency, particularly evident in the first months of military rule, to leap straight from first principles to decisions of a rather specific and sometimes trivial kind, as in the introduction of severe penalties for indian hemp, the sporadic spot-checks on administrative efficiency in the civil service, and the rounding up of civil servants late for work.

Many decisions have thus been made because they seemed broadly con-

---

[1] Indeed Keay, 'Legal and constitutional changes in Nigeria under Military Government', suggests that 'government by broadcast has made it difficult to determine at any one time what the law is', for 'a Decree or Edict may be made known by radio or television broadcast, in writing or in any other way, although if the written version clashes with the broadcast version the former prevails. Indeed the broadcast version does not always represent a formal legal document.'

[2] Except mandatory death sentences for murder.

[3] For example in the Public Security Decree of 1967.

sonant with the military world view and because they satisfied the soldiers' feelings that they were doing something, rather than because the consequence of the decisions in political, social and economic terms were rationally calculated. Thus, for example, the idea of economic planning was taken up with enthusiasm, in part at least because it was generally consonant with the officer corps' managerial view of a consensual and centrally articulated society. The Supreme Military Council meeting which endorsed Decree no. 34 in May 1966 also approved outline proposals or 'guideposts' for a new five-year plan (together with a twenty-year perspective plan).[1] This would have meant much tighter control by the central government over the planning and investment process than hitherto. Although a draft proposal of the Ministry of Economic Development on similar lines had been under discussion during the last months of the civilian regime, it seems clear that the military rulers were prepared to give the proposals a much stronger degree of endorsement than the politicians. The planning proposals, indeed, took precedence in Major General Ironsi's broadcast announcement of the decisions of the meeting held on the decree on political unification, in May 1966; for the former constituted one of the government's major rationales[2] for the abolition of federation.

On the other hand, planning did not derive in any meaningful sense from concern with socialist doctrine.[3] On the contrary, the Military Government issued all the usual assurances after the January takeover that it had no plans at all for nationalising industry or breaking outstanding financial agreements; and that it would encourage foreign private investment.[4] Nor did the enthusiasm for planning derive from any knowledge of economics, or adherence to a specific set of planning techniques. Planning was primarily an attitude of mind. This comes out quite clearly in the Ironsi government's attempts to control rents, in the Rent Control Decree no. 15 of 1966, by simply declaring a ten per cent reduction of all rents and providing for the establishment of rent tribunals (which were never in fact set up, so that the reduction in rents was never enforced).

Not that the direct approach was in all cases a disadvantage. As Lt Colonel Hassan Katsina put it, about a proposal for administrative reform in the

---

[1] *Guideposts for the Second National Development Plan* (Lagos: Ministry of Economic Development, 1967).

[2] Or rationalisation, depending on which way you look at it. There was, however, some pressure from the Ministry of Economic Development and the Economic Planning Unit for administrative unification. Dr Pius Okigbo, the Government Economic Adviser, was a very strong exponent of this point of view.

[3] Except perhaps in the mind of some of the January 1966 Majors, like Nzeogwu and Ifeajuna.

[4] This attitude has been maintained fairly consistently by the military rulers since 1966, although a new company law introduced in 1968, designed to get foreign enterprises to incorporate themselves more thoroughly in Nigeria, caused some alarm among foreign investors.

North which had been sitting on the politicians' desks for eleven years, 'I am not a politician and that is why I want to do something about it.'[1] There is little doubt that the greater freedom of the military from political pressures – at least in the early phases of army rule – did enable it to undertake a certain amount of fundamental change, especially in the North, where the civil servants were given a free hand to set in motion the well-worked-out programme of reforms which was embarked upon.

Another result of the soldiers' lack of a political grammar for their beliefs was a tendency to legitimise divergent points of view by the same first principles. The political beliefs of the officer corps, as we have described them, were too general and poorly articulated to provide specific enough normative constraints against the development of conflicting sub-goals in the officer corps.[2] The cleavages emerging within the officer corps in the period January to July 1966 reflect this lack of clarity of goals. Both Major General Ironsi and his associates on the one hand, and the more radical sympathisers of the January conspiracy on the other, shared the same anti-corruption sentiments, but this did not mean that the former were able to escape criticism from the latter for not conducting a thorough enough purge. Similarly, there is little doubt that Ironsi viewed the promotions and appointments he made in the military and civil administration as meeting all the criteria of impartiality and merit. But – for lack of adequate shared criteria of what impartiality might mean – he was considered by Northern officers (and other Northern elites) to be favouring his own tribe in the appointments he made. 'Tribalism', as we point out elsewhere,[3] is especially fraught with this kind of ambiguity. Because it is something one can predicate of others with the implication that it is something one is not oneself guilty of, it has become a surrogate means of articulating cleavage on ethnic and regional lines, while at the same time purporting to preserve one's own 'non-tribal' image unblemished. In the July coup, therefore, we have the spectacle of two opposed groups of officers accusing each other of tribalism and regionalism, while each themselves purporting to be committed to the national interest alone.

The political changes brought about by that coup, however, especially the increase in regional autonomy, were so great that they could scarcely be

---

[1] *Daily Times* (Lagos), 4 October 1966. Lt Colonel Hassan was talking about the Hudson Report on provincial administration and the Native Authorities which was shelved by the politicians as being politically too dangerous. Although he did set up a committee to advise on putting this report into practice, this was overtaken by events when the North was divided into new states in 1967. A number of other successful reforms were, however, embarked upon under his administration. See pp. 326–9 below.

[2] As March and Simon suggest, in *Organisations*, pp. 125–6, the less the 'subjective operationality' of organisational goals, the greater the potential differentiation of individuals' goals within the organisation.

[3] See Chapters VIII and IX above.

ignored. Regional interests were avowed in a more explicit manner, although each group was wont to suggest that it had in some sense been *compelled* to look after itself because of the hostility of the others. This theme was most explicit in the various speeches and interviews of Lt Colonel Ojukwu, who took the line that the East had been forced into its position of *de facto* secession because of the rejection of the Easterners – in particular, the Ibos – by the remainder of Nigeria. Although none of the Military Governors had entirely abandoned the anti-political image, as we saw in the extract from the Aburi discussions,[1] they began to conceive of themselves as administrators and leaders concerned with the interests of their regions as a whole, in much the same way that they had previously identified with the national interest. Colonel Adebayo's first speeches on appointment as Military Governor of the West in July 1966 keep reiterating the theme of the need for unity among the Yorubas. In August 1966, he chose Chief Awolowo after his release from prison as 'Leader of the Yorubas' because he wanted 'one man to talk instead of 10·5 million'[2] and he thus started to think in terms of Yoruba irridentism.[3] We begin to find Lt Colonel Ejoor, the Governor of the Mid-West, complaining that his region had been 'neglected by the Federal Government in the establishment of industries to absorb some of the unemployment. Yet the Region has contributed her full share to the building up of the country.'[4] And Lt Colonel Ojukwu leading his region into a *de facto* secession, saying that, 'If I am leader at all, it would be the leader of the East. But I am certainly not the new leader of the Ibos.'[5] And, further, suggesting that if any settlement were reached between the regions, it should be based on the principle that: 'each group should get its own patronage within its own group area, and wherever we meet each should come as representative of his own group...so that at no point are political patronages directly in competition'.

On the other hand, the ideal of loyalty to the nation never entirely lost its appeal. The Military Governors, whose words and actions we have discussed above, were, of course, under much greater political pressure than most serving officers, among whom the standard military themes of holding the nation together and the like kept their appeal better: hence, the rather hostile reaction of many Federal officers to the agreements reached at Aburi by their leaders, who were believed to have conceded too much autonomy to the regions in their attempt to effect a compromise with

---

[1] On pp. 289–91 above.   [2] *Daily Times* (Lagos), 30 September 1966.
[3] *Ibid.* He says, 'My salvation army is growing well. I have already got over 8 million and I will get more shortly. I am sure I shall get the remaining people.' Presumably he is talking of the proposals to incorporate Lagos (and also the Yoruba areas of the North?) into the Western Region.
[4] *Daily Times* (Lagos), 5 October 1966.
[5] *Ibid.* 17 September 1966.

Lt Colonel Ojukwu.[1] One reason for the popularity of the civil war was that it allowed the military men to slip back once more into the comforting cliches of a united army and nation.

The military image, to conclude, seems to have made it more difficult for the military elite to arrive at flexible political decisions that were responsive to the political demands with which it was faced. But that image became itself fragmented by these pressures after serious and irresoluble cleavages had cut across nation and army in May, July and September 1966. Yet how was it possible for political beliefs to be at one and the same time inflexible and yet capable of legitimising such distortions in the military vision? To come back to the analogy used at the beginning of the chapter, it was as if there was a map which depicted only a proportion of the roads in existence and left out many of the others, including some of the main ones. It was possible for officers to be sent scurrying down minor blind alleys in the pursuit of direct answers and objectives on the one hand, and for other parts of their cultural map to be so vague as to permit or legitimate a major cleavage within the military vision. An officer who believes that tribalism and regionalism must be opposed is in a similar position to the traveller set down in a large strange city, who knows only that he has to proceed North to get to where he wants to go.

[1] See the next chapter, pp. 316–21.

CHAPTER XIII

THE WAY TO SECESSION

THE MEANS OF VIOLENCE AND CONTROL OF VALUES

We begin this chapter with Lt Colonel Ojukwu's statement of the political dilemma which arose from the July 1966 coup and the September–October 1966 massacres in the North:

> May I respectfully submit that the Army problem, no matter what we like to say about it, is mixed up very closely with the political problem, the question of Government. It depends really on what form of Government you have for you to decide what sort of Army should serve that Government. If you do it otherwise, it becomes putting the cart before the horse or in military terms ass before teeth.[1]

There is no need to quarrel with the view that the military and political problems had by the middle of 1966 become inextricable the one from the other. It is submitted, however, that it is as misleading to assert the primacy of the political problem over the military one as to postulate the primacy of the latter over the former. The integration of the nation depended in the last resort upon the cohesion of the army: when the latter was lost the nation also was on the verge of disintegration. For the military situation influenced the course of political events in at least two important respects.

First, there was the crucial fact – which Ojukwu himself pointed out at the conference of military leaders at Aburi in January 1967 – that, from August 1966 onwards, he and he alone had effective command and control of the troops in the Eastern Region.[2] So long as he refused to recognise Lt Colonel Gowon as Supreme Commander or to treat his own command and control of the troops in the East as a negotiable element in a possible political settlement, in the last analysis the East could only be fitted back into the Federation by force.

One reason – though as we shall see by no means the only one – for Ojukwu's refusal to come to terms was the problem of military legitimacy. Gowon had come to power as a result of a coup in which military authority had been cast aside. Nor had the problem of succession to Ironsi been resolved satisfactorily, except as far as the Northerners were concerned, for

---

[1] *Meeting of the Nigerian military leaders*, p. 17.
[2] *Ibid.* p. 13.

there were still officers senior to Gowon in the army.[1] Ojukwu himself considered he took precedence over him, so that he could say that 'militarily Gowon is not my superior. Acknowledging him as Supreme Commander does not arise at this stage.'[2] (Though, as suggested earlier in Chapter VII, he espoused this argument as much for political convenience as for its intrinsic merits.) It is said also, that one reason for Colonel Adebayo's somewhat equivocal dealings with the Federal government in 1966–7 was that he considered himself senior to Gowon.[3]

Secondly, there was the role of the armed forces as guarantors of political order. As Hobbes might have said, order was dependent in the last resort on coercion by the armed forces and police – when used – being swift and effective, on the threat of violence being clear-cut, limited and credible. This in turn could only be assured if the legitimacy of authority and patterns of action *within* the forces were maintained. When the army lost its cohesion and its commanders their authority, then it became prone to sporadic, uncontrolled violence and itself was a further factor in public instability and disorder. There can be no doubt that this was the situation in Nigeria between July and October or November of 1966. Instability was, it is true, inherent in the political circumstances of the time; and the riots in the North of September and October 1966 would have occurred, army or no army. But indiscipline in the military severely restricted the use that could be made of it in controlling civilian rioting; and acts of terror by individual private soldiers themselves materially worsened the situation.

Equally, however, the political alignments and sentiments that arose out of this period of disturbance fed back into the military problem. In the first place, there was the legacy of animosity created in the army itself by the two military coups, of January and July 1966. In Ojukwu's words again:

In the Army our officers and men serving elsewhere in the country have been killed, again in cold blood...Instances abound where they were given assurance; based on the assurance they took in good faith, they moved to their work and got mowed down by machine-gun fire. They did try to stay but it became impossible for them to stay other than to stay in the graves there...

It is possible, I suppose, to find a solution, but in finding the solution we must recognise the fact that here it is not a matter of warfare where you fight today, some politicians make an agreement and then you embrace each other the next day. No! The essential difference in this is that...in war your enemy is essentially

---

[1] Ogundipe, Adebayo, Imo and Njoku. Ojukwu and Ejoor may be considered his exact peers, though the former's promotion to lieutenant colonel dates a day before Gowon's, so that formally he took precedence. Gowon owed his position as Supreme Commander, as we point out above in Chapter II, to the fact that he was the most senior Northerner.

[2] *Daily Times* (Lagos), 20 October 1967.

[3] Though his seniority, it is said, was itself the main reason Gowon selected him for the post of Military Governor of the West over his main rival for the post, Lt Colonel Olutoye.

a faceless enemy. You do not know him, he is not Jack, he is not John, he is not Bill...When that happens and you settle...you can then move in and become friends and individuals. In this case unfortunately officers and men of Eastern origin...know the names, the faces of individuals who perpetrated these atrocities.[1]

There were also the widespread popular sentiments of anger and fear created by the massacres of Ibos and other Easterners in the North in May and September–October 1966. At Aburi Lt Colonel Ojukwu was led to claim that were it not for his 'personality in the crisis the East would have thrown itself completely into a revenge. I halted it because I foresaw that anybody who started an inter-tribal war would never be able to control it.' Accordingly, he claimed, he had had to expel all non-Easterners 'to avoid bloodshed in the East. I knew what security forces I had and I knew that once a large-scale rioting broke out in the East it would be extremely difficult to control and rather than face that I decided to prevent the source of such necessity.'[2] The events of 1966 were indeed sufficient to make the people of the East, most especially the Ibos, turn in on themselves; and there is no doubt that there was widespread popular support there for withdrawal from Nigeria.

Nonetheless, Lt Colonel Ojukwu was being somewhat disingenuous in claiming that he had no choice in the matter. The bitter fruits of massacres of a scale and intensity as great or greater than those which took place in Nigeria have been suppressed, sublimated and eventually forgotten on other occasions, in other parts of the world.[3] The distinguishing factor in Nigeria, as in India/Pakistan after the disturbances and partition of 1947, was that the suppressed group had some control over the means of coercion and the means of communication with which to dramatise its plight. After the July 1966 coup, therefore, there was an intensive and sustained flow of officially sponsored imagery from the Eastern Region – in Lt Colonel Ojukwu's speeches and press conferences, on Radio Enugu, from the Ministry of Information and in the *Nigerian Outlook* – the sum effect of which was to create and sustain the legitimacy of withdrawal from Nigeria. As warned earlier, it is important to distinguish the rhetoric of the East's position – and also that of the Federal government – from the reality of events; and at the same time to be sensitive to the political stratagems and psychological functions that govern the choice and use of imagery.

One may see a number of themes coming up again and again in the

[1] *Meeting of the Nigerian Military leaders*, p. 27.
[2] *Ibid.* pp. 26–7.
[3] For instance, the anti-Communist and anti-Chinese riots in Indonesia, the revolt of the Southern Sudan, the White Russian revolt against the Communists after the Russian Revolution of 1917 or, indeed, the American Civil War. Of course some legacy remains from all these events – but not enough any more to legitimise the rebellion or secession of the groups concerned.

Eastern publicity media. First, the celebration of their wounds, real and symbolic. The reality of these was horrific enough and could be portrayed in words and pictures to great effect, as in the booklet *Pogrom*.[1] Nonetheless, the wounds were sometimes opened even more by the invention of details, as in the allegations against the Emir of Katsina set out below, or in the repeated inflation of the numbers killed in the massacres.[2] Secondly, there was the dehumanisation of the Ibos' assailants in the coups and massacres of 1966, with an implicit tendency to reject political and sociological explanation of these events in favour of an emphasis on the atavistic and primitive characteristics of the Northerners themselves. This may be illustrated by extracts from an article in the *Nigeria Outlook* by the East's Director of Information, the novelist Cyprian Ekwensi, which are typical of the kind of thing being put out by the East's media throughout the period:

Any anthropologist looking for material must get hold of a Northern brain and try to find the ingredient in it which has now become so atrophied that the megalocephalitic apes are two million years ahead of its owner...

It was lepers like the stubborn one who touched the bodies of beautiful Eastern Nigerian girls with their infectious hands and raped them while the girls were held down by intoxicated Northerners. Rape, murder, arson, infanticide, homicide, all the most fantastic crimes in the world suddenly became award-winning performances because they were being carried out against the Inyamiri, Kafiris, the unbelievers.

Any southerner who ever believed that a Muslim was his brother, suddenly finds himself alone. Islam in Nigeria is such an intolerant religion, such an obstacle in the way of clear thinking and progressive action that anyone who is not for it is not regarded by believers as possessing a soul...

The Government in Lagos is said to be headed by a man whose parents read the bible daily, who is himself supposed to be Christian, and who is by now distributing Christmas cards, wishing Easterners a 'Merry Christmas'. What an irony! At the same time a Tiv soldier is sitting at Lagos Airport slapping his cartridge belt and saying 'Dis na my matriculation'...

On Sunday June 5, some of the most horrible atrocities took place in the town of Katsina, ruled by the father of the Military Governor of the North, Lt Colonel Hassan Usman Katsina. Indeed, some of the eye witness accounts have it that one, at least, of the most gruesome murders (when an Easterner was held down and his throat slashed from ear to ear) took place at a Katsina police station and before the very eyes of the Muslim Emir of Katsina...[3]

[1] *Nigerian pogrom: the organised massacre of Eastern Nigerians. Crisis 1966*, vol. 3 (Enugu; Ministry of Information, 1966).
[2] In October 1966, the *Nigerian Outlook* was citing the police figure of 3,300 killed; at Aburi in January 1967 and after, Lt Colonel Ojukwu put it at 10,000; after a few months of civil war, the figure was inflated to 30,000 (see the estimates of the size of the massacre from other sources on page 309). The massacres themselves are reprehensible whatever the true number killed, but the exaggeration of the figures indicates both psychological and propaganda needs.
[3] Review of *Pogrom* by Ekwensi in *Nigerian Outlook* (Enugu), 8 December 1966.

The last paragraph (the accusation in which is certainly groundless) illustrates a second theme, namely the emphasis on conspiracy, on the central organisation of the killings by the North's military and political leaders. In other chapters,[1] we have noted the way in which each of the sides to the conflict built up their own cabalistic pictures of the January and July coups. Lt Colonel Ojukwu himself is on record as saying that:

In May thousands of people of Eastern Nigeria origin were premeditatedly slaughtered like rats...In July officers and men of Eastern Nigeria origin were systematically and calculatedly eliminated...[The September–October killings] were indeed a planned operation.'[2]

And the *Nigerian Outlook* was at pains to point out that the events were 'part of a cruel conspiracy of robbery, murder and extermination, the egg of which was layed in Kaduna *long before* the January incident'.[3]

Closely related to the image of events as a plot, is the tendency – to be seen in the quotation above – to generalise responsibility to all Northerners and to make all southerners or all Easterners the symbolic victims of the conspiracy, not just the Ibos alone. As Lt Colonel Ojukwu again put it: 'the crime of genocide was committed jointly by all sections of the North against all sections of the East.'[4] This generalisation of the symbolic wounds and of the responsibility for them can be linked to the political strategies of holding the support of Eastern non-Ibo minority groups and trying to develop a southern front against the North, both of which are discussed below. It may also have been connected with an ideological preference by Eastern army officers and civil servants for an image of secular Eastern nationalism, rather than parochial Ibo tribalism.

At the same time, the Federal government created its own myths to create and control values, though the emphasis tended to be different. For the official images of the latter were designed to play down the lives of cleavage, to put the case for the reintegration of the East. The undercurrents of popular feeling against the Ibos received little or no emphasis in Gowon's speeches or in Federal publications, like *Nigeria 1966*, which stressed the unplanned, almost accidental nature of historical events, like the July coup and the Northern massacres, and the Federal government's attempts to bring them under control. Even in the first phase of the civil war, up to the Mid-West invasion of August 1967, the conflict was presented as a 'police action' rather than a war against a hostile power, and a Code of Conduct was issued to the troops (and the foreign press) which emphasised the need for

[1] See particularly Chapters II, VIII and XI above.
[2] The first two sentences are from a speech to British and American diplomats *before* the big September massacres, reprinted in *Nigerian Outlook* (Enugu), 23 September 1966, the last from a press conference to foreign journalists to be found in *Nigerian Outlook*, 20 October 1966.
[3] *Nigerian Outlook*, 15 October 1966.   [4] Speech quoted in *Nigerian Outlook*, 20 October 1966.

restraint because the hostilities were against 'misguided' compatriots with whom Federal troops would have to live afterwards. Nonetheless, Federal imagery tended increasingly to objectify feelings of aggression by introducing a disjunction between the Ibos and 'Ojukwu' or 'Ojukwu and his Nnewi clique', by whom the former were supposedly being misled. And war posters, put out after the secession of the East, showed Ojukwu's head being ground by an army boot (captioned 'Crush rebellion') or affixed to a snake which was being sliced in two by a Northern farmer with his hoe. Symbolic humiliations of this kind against *Ibos* as a group, however, never became part of the governmentally manipulated image, although they were always a part of the popular folklore.

It is true that officially sponsored symbols may be undermined or pushed aside by popular and officially deprecated sentiments, such as the primordial imagery that legitimised the civil disorders of May and September–October 1966 and the July coup. Nonetheless, such popular imagery tends to be unstable and relatively easily forgotten or diverted in new directions unless solidified and communicated by myths and symbols sustained by a political elite with whom they identify. Many persons from the non-Ibo East and the Mid-West suffered as badly at the hands of the Northerners as did the Ibos. But their bitterness was not sanctioned by legitimate political symbols; in a word, it did not become institutionalised.

In retrospect, there was more than one occasion – particularly in August and September 1966 and then again after the conference of military leaders at Aburi in January 1967 – when Lt Colonel Ojukwu and other members of the Eastern military and political elite could have made substantial concessions of both sovereignty and of command and control of the army in the East, in return for suitable guarantees of security and participation by the East in the government of the Federation. Instead, as we hope to demonstrate below, the only options that were ever seriously considered were, on the one hand, a confederation in which the centre was deprived of all effective authority and of day-to-day command of the armed forces; and, failing that, outright secession. This limitation of the political options is understandable in view of the legacy of bitterness among Eastern elites, including Ojukwu himself, whose sincerity in this respect is not to be doubted; especially as the relinquishment of any effective sovereignty could have carried the risk of the political extinction, and possibly worse, of the particular Eastern leaders concerned. That they were able to close the first option, however, depended in the final analysis on their control over the nucleus of an army and governmental machinery in Enugu, and their freedom to create images that at the same time provided them with legitimacy and sharpened the existing lines of conflict.

THINGS FALL APART: VIOLENCE, JULY TO OCTOBER 1966

It is interesting to reflect, in retrospect upon its momentous political consequences, how narrowly Lt Colonel Ojukwu and the other Eastern officers
in Enugu had been able to maintain control of the 1st Battalion there in the
July 29 coup.[1] The negotiations which ensued continued until 9 August,
when representatives of the National Military Government met with those
of the Regional Military Governors. They provisionally agreed that, as far
as possible, all troops should be withdrawn to their regions of origin, except
that the security of Lagos should still remain in the hands of the Supreme
Commander[2] and thus, presumably, under a nucleus of federally controlled
troops; that the legislation establishing a unitary constitution should
be repealed; and that political representatives of the regions should meet
to discuss the country's future. The East's military autonomy was finally
assured on 13 August, when in accordance with the recommendations of the
9th, all non-Eastern officers and men were put on a train to the North.

In the remainder of the country, the position remained one of extreme
uncertainty. Although Lt Colonel Gowon had been formally established in
office as Supreme Commander, his authority was at first tenuous. Lt Colonel
Muritala Mohammed retained a considerable amount of charisma as the
putative leader of the coup. In the first three or four days, when Lt Colonel
Gowon wished to give guarantees of safety to surviving Eastern officers, he
found it necessary to ask the latter to confirm them with Mohammed.[3]
Even then the guarantees were not effective because not even Mohammed
had any real control over events. Lt Colonel Eze was machine-gunned and
almost killed when he attempted to return to work at the Lagos Garrison
Organisation, Yaba, after assurances for his safety had been given. During
the whole of the time that Lt Colonel Gowon was negotiating with the
East for an interim settlement and the return of troops, Lt Colonel Mohammed was sending his signals to the Northern soldiers in Enugu to take over.
And even after their return to the North he continually agitated for an
invasion of the East – on the contention, which seems quite cogent in the
light of later events,[4] that the longer the East was outside central control the

---

[1] See the account above, p. 75.

[2] To be exercised in consultation with the Military Governors of the Regions.

[3] Such guarantees were given to Lt Colonel Eze and another Ibo lieutenant colonel by Gowon and
Mohammed just after the former assumed power. After Lt Colonel Gowon had found that his
guarantees were in fact ineffective, his advice to them, passed through Lt Colonel Ojukwu, was to
get back to the East. See Peter Enahoro's account, 'Why I left Nigeria' in *Transition*, VII, 6
(1968), 28–9.

[4] It is probable that at any time during the first five or six months after the July coup, the Federal
army could have rapidly overrun the East, but Gowon apparently did not wish to risk incurring
the heavy civilian casualties that would have resulted from sending in undisciplined Northern
troops, particularly while there was still some prospect of a negotiated settlement.

more time it would have to organise its own army and the more likely it was that it would secede. The junior officers and men of the 4th Battalion, Ibadan and 2nd Battalion, Ikeja, were also apparently all set to invade the East during the first two or three weeks after the coup until dissuaded by Gowon and the commander of the 4th Battalion, Lt Colonel Akahan.

Lt Colonel Gowon's position was nevertheless slowly routinised. When a rift with Lt Colonel Mohammed temporarily opened up after a meeting of the Supreme Military Council in mid-October 1966 – when the latter insisted without success that the East be invaded forthwith – Gowon emerged from the confrontation with his authority unshaken. In November Mohammed was sent up to the North.[1] He made an informal tour of military units trying to win support, but failed, being nevertheless allowed to come back to his old post as Inspector of Signals at Army Headquarters.

All through the period from July to October, there was a strong undercurrent of indiscipline. It is difficult to determine precisely how far authority in the army had been undermined – or, for that matter, how soon and to what extent it was restored. Often the hierarchy was simply ignored as when groups of Northern soldiers abducted January conspirators including Majors Okafor and Anuforo from prisons in the Mid-West and tortured them to death. There were relatively few acts of *overt* disobedience, except the mutiny of a platoon of troops at Kano on 2 October. Many individual acts of brigandage by private soldiers occurred – beatings of civilians, robbery, looting and participation in civilian-led violence against the Ibos – but there was no consistent pattern of revolt against command. The weakness of authority remained to a large extent implicit. The most telling indicator was probably the inability of the military authorities to use the army – except in isolated instances – to keep order during the massacres in Northern cities in late September and early October, for fear that the soldiers themselves would become still more embroiled.

In addition, the authorities consistently repressed or underplayed information about lawlessness in the army, both at the time and in subsequent pronouncements. In a press conference soon after his assumption of office, Lt Colonel Gowon specifically denied reports of killings of Eastern army officers and men in the North.[2] There was complete official silence on the kidnapping of Ibo participants in the January coup from Benin prison on 22 August and their subsequent murder, in spite of the representations of the Mid-West's Military Governor, Lt Colonel Ejoor. Many of the official statements of the time were elliptical in the extreme. In the months of August

[1] Because he had apparently made a nuisance of himself, turning up at Supreme Military Council meetings uninvited and sending incendiary messages to Ojukwu.
[2] In a press conference on 6 August. See *West Africa* (London), 13 August 1966.

and September the newspapers carried several stories of persons impersonating soldiers engaging in acts of violence, together with official warnings to beware of 'fake' soldiers and an announcement that a decree was to be promulgated carrying severe penalties for the impersonation of army personnel.[1] By mid-September the government had openly to admit lawlessness by soldiers themselves; and on 13 September the Northern Military Governor announced the introduction of military/police patrols to deal with the problem. The 4th Battalion, still rebellious after July, had been transferred to Kaduna in late August because it had run riot in Ibadan; and had been split up, platoons being sent on duties in a number of Northern centres. But this merely spread disorder and violence still wider. Nothing the authorities could do prevented soldiers from taking part – alongside Northern civilians – in the terrorisation of Eastern civilians that began in September. And it was the mutiny of troops of the 5th Battalion at Kano which brought the massacres in that city to a head. Yet despite officially deploring the killings, the army authorities could still be heard to assert, like Lt Colonel Gowon, that reports of a breakdown in discipline in the army were 'not true. I am in a better position than anyone else to know.'[2]

There are a number of possible explanations for the official silence. The essentially prescriptive nature of military authority may have made difficult any open admission of breaches in discipline; indeed, many of the statements made by army leaders at this time ring true only if one understands that they were statements of how the soldiers ought to have been, rather than how they in fact were, behaving.[3] The simple fact was that the high command was so much out of control that it often did not know what was happening. Or if it did, it could not stop it, so that it was best not to call too much attention to its failings. As Lt Colonel Ojukwu put it at one of his press conferences:

I have got on the telephone to Gowon and informed him of the situation and I must say this for him that once he knows these things have happened, he does take action to see that they are stopped. The only trouble is that they happen so often and that he does not know about them quick enough. Indeed, at a certain stage I said to him that his men were not telling him the truth about the situation.[4]

There was little that the high command could do to prevent the assassinations of Easterners in the army in July and August or, indeed, to punish

---

[1] Skimming through some of the papers the writer noted reports of this kind in the *Daily Times* (Lagos) of 12 and 17 August and the *New Nigerian* (Kaduna), 17, 22, 24 and 27 August, and 12 September. The *New Nigerian*, 27 August, announces, for example, a ban on demonstrations and dances and the early closing of cinemas in Kaduna 'in order to prevent the present wave of armed robbery by persons impersonating the military'.

[2] In reply to questions at a news conference, *Daily Times* (Lagos), 9 October 1966.

[3] See the discussion of related points in Chapters VI and XII.

[4] *Daily Times* (Lagos), 20 October 1966.

the perpetrators of these killings. The effectiveness of measures to prevent the harassment of civilians depended very much on individual commanders in the field. There were instances where officers were forced to threaten to shoot (and in at least one or two cases to actually shoot) marauding soldiers, though not all officers were brave enough to do so. The constraints of discipline were in general accepted only where there was a consensus around them, as when the members of the platoon which went on the rampage in Kano gave themselves up, weeping in shame at what they had done, and were rebuked by their comrades in arms; so that the disciplinary action which was later taken against them caused no repercussions.

These fundamental internal weaknesses in the army severely undermined any attempts to bring under control the spreading cycle of violence that was building up in the civilian arena. The aftermath of the July coup was a severe sense of insecurity in all parts of the country, but especially in the North. The underlying social conditions were similar to those which had produced the outbreaks of May 1966 – namely the structural transformations taking place in Northern society, the decline in the power of the traditional authorities, the changes of the position of the North in relation to the centre and the special position of the Ibos as a pariah entrepreneur group at the interstices of Northern society. In addition to this, moreover, there was a widely shared sense that the outcome of the July coup was still uncertain until the terms of the new political contract were settled – whether or not the respective regions would each go their own way and secede or whether the country was to be held together, whether the North was to remain one region or to be divided to satisfy the demand of the minorities.

The large-scale emigration from the North of Easterners, most especially Ibos, that began again in August,[1] well before the massacres that brought the exodus to a head at the end of September, was a crucial element in the definition of the situation. It added to the feeling of panic, and it was widely believed, even by the sophisticated, that the migrations indicated a lack of confidence in the North and subversion defined at varying levels of explicitness. Just before the main outbursts started in late September, the *New Nigerian*'s front-page comment was attributing the exodus to:

Well placed personalities [presumably Ojukwu and the political leadership in the East] who abuse their office by whipping up hysteria and indulging in a war of psychosis...

The historic exodus of the Ibos from some parts of the Federation has been misinterpreted to mean that this pre-planned exercise is confined only to Northern Nigeria. This is untrue and wicked. Why should we not summon the courage to

[1] Easterners had started to move out of the North after the May killings, but the Military Government's assurances successfully checked the outflow until the Northern coup.

admit the fact that those so-called refugees have decided to migrate home out of their own volition and that the North as well as the West, Mid-West and Lagos have witnessed this abnormal social phenomenon. No-one can deceive all the people all the time.[1]

There were many rumours of actual or planned acts of sabotage by departing Ibos. There were one or two isolated incidents – the blowing up of a bridge on the road from Lagos to the Mid-West, an Ibo engineer who exploded a part of the Federal Palace Hotel in Lagos and then finally exploded himself, caches of explosives or arms reported in Kano (subsequently announced in the papers to be industrial waste and harmless), Jos and Kaduna – though they were too trivial and isolated to substantiate a genuine conspiracy. As in May and July, however, such events were woven into a texture of myth legitimising preemptive violence to remove the symbolic threats to the Northern community.

Another aspect of the emigration was that it showed that the Ibos were vulnerable, an easy target for attack. The social density of the immigrant community in the *sabon garis* of the Northern cities – real or perceived – was reduced, and when the riots came the destruction penetrated all the way through to the centre of the areas of Ibo settlement – unlike the May uprising and still more so the Kano riot of 1953, when the marauders had generally been held to the fringes.

Accordingly, the first forays in early September took place mainly on the roads and railway line leading south, where Eastern civilians were pulled off their transports, robbed, sometimes killed or otherwise harassed by groups of civilians and, in a number of instances, by Northern troops. By the middle of the month the atmosphere in the North was one of siege. Police patrols, restrictions on public assembly and in some cases curfews were imposed in the main towns. On 24 September, passenger train services to the East were discontinued until further notice. A rumour that the East was going to secede on Republic Day, 1 October, took root and was not dispelled by well-publicised denials by Lt Colonel Ojukwu. The final touch was added by an unfortunate broadcast by Radio Kaduna on 28 and 29 September of reports of massacres of Northerners in the East.[2] From the 28th to the 30th, rioting and killing on a large scale began in most of the major urban centres in the North, especially Kaduna, Zaria and Jos. In Kano things were relatively calm until the evening of 30 September when troops on guard at Kano airport

[1] Front-page comment in *New Nigerian* (Kaduna), 28 September, under the heading 'The genesis of the exodus'. This newspaper gave vent to anti-Ibo feeling on a number of occasions in August and September, though it moderated its tone after the massacres, when its editor was replaced.

[2] A small number of killings had in fact taken place in the East, in response to stories filtering through of the maltreatment and killing of Ibo refugees on their way out of the North. Reports of the Eastern riots were broadcast by Radio Cotonou in Dahomey and monitored in Kaduna.

killed a number of Eastern refugees there. This was followed by a large-scale massacre by the civilian populace. Events went completely out of control on 2 October when a platoon of the 5th Battalion mutinied, killed an officer and their Regimental Sergeant Major, forced the Battalion's commanding officer to flee for his life, and went on the rampage in the town.

Following these events, the Northern government, voluntary agencies, and the large firms undertook a large-scale evacuation of Eastern refugees from the North, though the greater proportion of the refugees made their own way out by lorry or on foot. By mid-October there were practically no Ibos left in the North and not many non-Ibo Easterners either. The number massacred is estimated variously as up to 10,000.[1] But these numbers in themselves are no measure of the trauma and suffering caused both by the killings and by the wholesale migration of up to one and a half million persons.[2]

It is difficult to make a clear-cut attribution of responsibility for these massacres, especially as they took the form of a collective outburst that was outside the control of any one person, group or set of institutions. It has been alleged[3] that they were set off by the former NPC politicians of the 'far North' in response to constitutional changes – including the proposed sub-division of the North into a number of new regions – then under discussion at the Ad Hoc Conference in session at Lagos. Eastern Nigerian sources generally emphasise that the killings were planned in advance, with responsibility being imputed with varying degrees of directness to the NPC, the emirs and the army leaders.[4] Others have speculated about the linkages between the NPC old guard and certain groups within the army.[5]

None of this, however, is conclusive. The killings, it is clear, had already begun *before* the weekend of 16 to 20 September during which the crucial

[1] The first police estimates were around 3,300. Other figures the writer has heard quoted are 4,700 (a Federal government source) and 6,000–8,000 (contemporary mission estimates). By the time of the Aburi conference in January 1967 Lt Colonel Ojukwu was claiming 10,000 dead.

[2] It is difficult to determine exactly how large a population movement was involved because no accurate ethnic breakdown of the Nigerian population has been available since the 1952–3 census. One informed guess is that of Dr S. A. Aluko of 1,580,000 persons leaving the North for the East: see *West Africa* (London), 15 April 1967, although the writer is inclined to feel that this figure may be somewhat on the high side.

[3] See, for instance, Fr J. O'Connell, in his 'Political integration: the Nigerian case' in A. Hazlewood (ed.), *African integration and disintegration* (London: Oxford University Press, 1967), pp. 177–8.

[4] No actual evidence has been produced by Eastern sources to substantiate allegations about any of the three. The insinuations against the army leaders themselves have always been indirect, e.g. the *Nigerian Outlook*'s editorial of 20 October 1966, which doubts the sincerity of Lt Colonel Hassan Katsina's statement that soldiers responsible for the October mutiny at Kano would be courtmartialled: 'it is not always easy to understand the workings of the mind of a boss who waits and winks while his subjects engage in atrocious acts, but he turns round to pour denunciations after the acts have been completed'.

[5] For instance, M. J. Dent in 'The military and the politicians'.

realignments at the Ad Hoc Conference had taken place, though they did gather pace afterwards. Unlike the May massacres, they were as bad in the non-Hausa areas of the Middle Belt as in the dry North strongholds of the NPC; and immigrants from the Middle Belt were also active in the disorders in the Hausa cities. Yet it is hard to discern any intelligible political motivation for the participation of the Northern minorities in the killings beyond the vague desire for revenge and the anomic circumstances of the time. Such evidence as there is about the complicity of the army relates only to the isolated participation of groups of indisciplined troops, and does not suggest that there was a well-organised pattern of cooperation between former NPC politicians and the soldiers.[1]

The military leaders – especially Lt Colonels Gowon and Hassan Katsina – did what they could to stop the massacres and to ensure an orderly evacuation of refugees. They may be blamed for being slow to realise the seriousness of the situation and for indecisiveness in their handling of it,[2] but certainly not for condoning or assisting in the disorders. Their predicament was not made any easier by the indiscipline of the army rank and file – and most of the work of bringing the rioters under control in fact fell to the Nigeria Police, with the army confined mainly to patrolling the perimeters of the affected areas. However, the lack of frank information from the government or the news media about what was going on, and the absence of a clear lead until Lt Colonel Gowon's broadcast appeal for peace on 1 October, undoubtedly contributed to the rumour and uncertainty that prevailed.

NEGOTIATIONS AND SECESSION, AUGUST 1966 TO JULY 1967

These events were a dire background to the sporadic negotiations for some kind of modus vivendi between the East and the remainder of the country which carried on through to the final secession of the former on 30 May 1967. The course and outcome of these negotiations were affected on the one hand

[1] Politicians may have been able to get the ear or fill the purse of the odd soldiers, particularly the Other Ranks, but there are few signs of system. Indeed Inuwa Wada, a leading NPC figure in Kano, was bamboozled by a civilian into giving him money and beer on the supposition that he was an army officer who had taken part in the July coup (*New Nigerian* (Kaduna), 12 October 1966). Such gullibility seems incredible in a former Minister of Defence and supposed link-man between the NPC and Lt Colonel Mohammed at this period.

[2] As late as 24 September (see the *Sunday Times* (Lagos), 25 September), Lt Colonel Gowon was threatening all public employees fleeing their jobs with dismissal if they did not return to their posts by 15 October, presumably on the theory that the problem could still be handled by the usual military exhortations to avoid panic. This was his last word until his broadcast appeal for peace on 1 October. It was not until 29 September that Lt Colonel Hassan Katsina issued an appeal to the North to 'keep calm' after the Radio Cotonou broadcast and stating somewhat unwisely that the Military Government 'is attempting to confirm whether or not the reports (of massacres in the East) are true', *New Nigerian* (Kaduna), 30 September 1966 – though later on he showed much personal bravery in going himself to confront the mutineers at Kano.

by the particular interests and bargaining strategies of the four regions; and on the other by the interests and organisational requirements of the major Federal bureaucracies, in particular the army and the Federal civil service. The disarray of the military leaders allowed a variety of political groupings to emerge. An important role in the discussions on the country's political and constitutional future was played by gatherings of so-called regional 'Leaders of Thought', which met regularly from August 1966 onwards, sometimes on their own and sometimes jointly with emirs, chiefs or other traditional dignitaries, as the 'Chiefs and Leaders of Thought' (or similar designations).[1] A prominent role was played in these meetings and in the constitutional negotiations by former politicians, like Chief Awolowo in the West, Aminu Kano and J. S. Tarka in the North, Chief Anthony Enahoro in the Mid-West and Dr Okpara in the East (though in the latter region the politicians were less important in the consultative gatherings and tended to take second place to intellectuals or members of the bureaucracy). Nevertheless as conditions became (relatively speaking) more stable and alignments hardened, it was again the military leaders and their civil service advisers who came to take the final decisions which led up to the civil war. It was generally accepted by all parties that a unitary system of government was no longer workable after the July coup, so that one of the first legislative enactments of Lt Colonel Gowon's regime was the restoration for the interim of a Federal framework by the repeal on 1 September of Decree no. 34. The choice, then, was effectively confined to three alternatives: a federation with an effective central government; a confederal solution maintaining the paper integrity of the country, but ceding all real power to the regions; or an outright break-up.

For the moment we may leave aside for later consideration the bargaining positions of the regions and focus on the survival of a 'Federalist' position through the course of the political bargaining in 1966 and 1967. What, during a period when it seemed as if there was little or nothing to hold Nigeria together, were the main structural and political sources of support for the centre, as against the concession of all power to the regions? One may identify at least three factors which explain the resilience of the Federal cause.

[1] The titles and process of selection of these assemblies varied from region to region and time to time. The term 'Leaders of Thought' was favoured by all the regions except the East which preferred to establish an 'Eastern Nigerian Consultative Assembly', which was the most important of the numerous consultative bodies set up by Ojukwu. The meetings were normally convened by the Military Governors of the Regions and the Administrator of Lagos. But they did not always control the composition of the assemblies closely; and this sometimes depended on who turned up at the meetings and was accepted by the others as having the right to be heard, and sometimes on the choice of particular politicians, like Chief Awolowo in the West, as to who was to be invited and who excluded.

First, there was the North (and its soldiers), which following a brief flirtation with the ideas of secession and confederation in the first month or so after the July coup, was fairly consistently behind the Federation.[1] The next – and most constant – buttresses were the remnants of the army, the Federal civil service and the Nigeria Police. The Federal public service was a bureaucratic estate with a certain amount of vested interest in effective central government. In this there was a continuity both from the days of civilian rule and from the Ironsi regime,[2] and under Gowon the civil servants were probably the most consistent advocates of a Federal position. The army was less stable in its commitment because of its internal problems. But, we shall see, the gradual restoration of discipline brought with it a crystallisation of organisational interest around a strong centre and against plans to subdivide command and control of the army on regional lines.

The final element of elasticity in the Federal position was Lt Colonel Gowon's own leadership. It is clear that he himself was all along in favour of a Federalist position and of the creation of more regions. At the same time, we find him fumbling for a consensus among the regions which would hold the country together, and balancing this against the need to maintain initiative in the centre. At times, therefore, his leadership looked – and indeed was – indecisive, as in the military and political vacuum immediately following the July coup, during the violence of September and October 1966 or in the two or three weeks following the Aburi negotiations in January 1967. He could only work within the limits set by the fragmentation of the army and the division of interest, resources and military power opened up between the Federation and the East – and it was these in the final analysis that were responsible for his failure to keep the latter in Nigeria on terms that could realistically be accepted. His most significant achievement was, as we shall see, to grasp the political initiative in May and June 1967 in a way that caught the consensus of the other regions – something that was constantly in balance right up to the start of the civil war – and prevented the disintegration of the remainder of Nigeria when the final break with the East came.

To begin with, however, the responsibility for negotiating the country's future political shape after the July 1966 coup was entrusted to an Ad Hoc

[1] See the discussion on pp. 326–8.
[2] Namely, the role of the civil servants in the economic ministries in insisting on some minimal use of economic criteria in the allocation of resources between the regions under the civilians; of certain prominent Federal civil servants in planning Ironsi's unification of the country under Decree no. 34; and of others in persuading Northern soldiers not to secede in the crucial days of 29 July–1 August 1966. As usual, Ojukwu was highly caustic about their role: according to him they were: 'men without roots, men who cannot fit into their own regional societies...people with vested interest in the continuance of a sort of domination in Lagos, people like Ogbu, Permanent Secretary, External Affairs; people like Attah, Permanent Secretary, Finance, who has never felt happy in his own region ever'. *Nigerian Outlook* (Enugu), 21 March 1967.

Committee of civilian representatives of the regions, selected by the respective Military Governors and 'Leaders of Thought', which began meetings in early September 1966. Though the meetings of the Ad Hoc Committee in the end came to nothing, its deliberations were of importance for a number of reasons.

Firstly, the delegations of the North, West and Mid-West and their advisers included the most prominent leaders of the opposition to the last civilian government, notably Chiefs Awolowo and Enahoro, Joseph Tarka and Aminu Kano,[1] indicating an important realignment of political forces.

A second – and related – feature was the resurgence of minorities demands for the subdivision of the North and East into new regions or states. When the conference met on 12 September, proposals of this kind were initially put forward by the West, Mid-West and Lagos delegations[2] and were lobbied for by prominent leaders of the Eastern and Northern minorities outside the conference hall. The minorities' position also commanded considerable support in the army, both among officers and men from the Middle Belt proper; among those of the partially assimilated Hausa–Fulani diaspora, many of whom were equally desirous of escaping the control of the dry North;[3] and among the Eastern minorities officers still with the Federal army, like the Military Secretary, Lt Colonel Ekpo. The Northern delegation had initially come to the conference with a proposal for a loose confederal arrangement among the existing regions, styled on the East African Common Services Organisation. But its members were subjected to intense lobbying by junior officers and men and also, it is understood, to pressures of a more discreet kind from Lt Colonel Gowon, to abandon this. Lt Colonel Muritala Mohammed is also said to have lobbied strongly against confederation, because it would have allowed the East to get away with *de facto* secession, even though he was not a noted supporter of the creation of new regions or states for the minorities.

During the adjournment of 16–20 September there were hurried consultations among members of the Northern delegation and with military figures and civil servants in the North. When the conference reassembled the

---

[1] The principals in the respective delegations were as follows: North, Sir Kashim Ibrahim, J. S. Tarka and Alhaji Buba Ardo; West, Chief Awolowo, Dr Oluwusanmi and O. Akinfosile; Mid-West, Chief Enahoro, Chief J. I. G. Onyia and Dr M. N. Odie; East, Dr Eni Njoku, Mr C. C. Mojekwu and Mr E. A. Edem; Lagos, Dr T. O. Elias and L. Jakande. Aminu Kano was adviser to the Northern delegation.

[2] Later on, however, the West changed its position, indicating it would no longer insist on new regions if Lagos were made part of the Western Region.

[3] See the discussion of ethnicity and region in Chapter VIII above. Note that the Middle Belt and diaspora officers were a strong majority among the Northerners in the officer corps, and the same is believed to be true of the NCOs.

representatives of the region announced a *volte-face* in their position. They came out in favour of federation rather than confederation; and for the creation of new regions or states, subject to the proviso that they be created simultaneously in the other existing regions (notably the East) and not just the North. This was strongly opposed by the official Eastern delegation,[1] which argued that what was needed was a solution to the immediate political problem created by the July coup, and that the subdivision of the regions at this time would be impracticable and add to the instability of the country – its underlying concern almost certainly was to avoid any weakening in the region's own power base at that critical juncture.

There seemed little prospect of resolving these differences when the committee adjourned on 3 October, shortly after the outbreak of disturbances in the North, for consultation with their respective governments. The killings, moreover, had altered the political situation in and thoroughly traumatised the East. The Eastern Region government announced the expulsion of all non-Eastern residents (not Northerners alone) from the region 'in order to prevent the risk of reprisals' against them. When the Ad Hoc Conference was due to reopen in late October, the East announced its unwillingness to send its delegates while Northern troops were in the West, a position with which Chief Awolowo also concurred; and the meeting had to be postponed indefinitely.

In any case the committee had run into a number of other serious obstacles, partly the result of procedural difficulties,[2] partly because the political problems it had to try and solve were intractable. In addition to the altercation over the creation of new regions, it was still far from reaching accord on a distribution of powers between centre and regions. In broad terms,[3] it can be said that the East was holding out for some kind of confederation. For it envisaged a centre with some minimal responsibilities in matters like currency and communications; with coordinate responsibilities in foreign relations; and with no independent power to raise revenues; or to regulate

[1] It did not object in principle to the creation of new regions, but merely argued that the issue be deferred until the country's other political problems had sorted themselves out.

[2] For example, the fact that each delegation (and in some instances each individual) brought its own idiosyncratic constitutional proposals with it, rather than all working from a prepared draft; the fact that there were no 'Federal' representatives, meaning that the central government viewpoint had to be pressed informally on the delegations by the army and civil service; the fact that the delegates (though chosen in a loose manner by conferences of regional 'Leaders of Thought') were not representative, had no governmental power base of their own and had constantly to refer matters back to their regional governments for approval; and the fact that regional positions changed from day to day.

[3] It is not the intention here to go into the constitutional details. These are laid out in detail in *The Ad Hoc Conference on the Nigerian Constitution. Crisis, 1966*, vol. 3 (Enugu: Government Printer, 1966). A detailed account of the constitutional and political changes of this time is made by S. K. Panter-Brick in Chapter II of the book edited by him, *Nigerian politics and military rule.*

the movement of persons between regions. The army was to be cut up into regional forces coordinated by a central Defence Council, but not under the latter's day-to-day control. The remaining regions, on the other hand, eventually came to support rather wider powers and responsibilities for the centre, though to varying degrees. None, except possibly the Mid-West, provided for anything more than a weak federation, and they were all riven with contradictions. When the North, for instance, changed its position on the creation of more regions or states, it also modified its original proposals for a confederation modelled on the East African Common Services Organisation to give more weight to the centre. Yet it was still prepared to agree to an essentially confederal, regionalised army. Strangely, this was one of the matters on which all the delegations had been able to reach an interim agreement,[1] although it was later at Aburi to be the fundamental point of difference between the Federal army leaders on the one hand and Lt Colonel Ojukwu on the other.

For a poor view was taken by the army[2] of proposals to subdivide it, and there were strong feelings that 'the politicians would make a mess of things again', as one officer put it. Such sentiments can be seen in the adverse comments made by some of the Military Governors about the politicians and the Ad Hoc Committee at the Aburi meeting of military leaders in January 1967.[3] There were many military men indeed who felt that the problem should be solved by an offensive on the East. But this came to nothing, mainly because Lt Colonel Mohammed, whose fiery advocacy of invasion nearly brought him into conflict with Gowon's leadership, had by this time lost much of his support in the army.[4]

[1] The details of the interim agreement reached on this when the committee adjourned on 3 October are as follows: the army, navy and air force to be organised on a regional basis, the units in each region being composed entirely of indigenes of that region and their operative control being vested in their regional commanders; a Central Defence Council made up of equal representatives of each region would jointly control the army, but only in certain emergencies like external defence (not internal security); the office of Chief of Staff to rotate among the regional commanders; training facilities, depots, stores to be organised regionally, and with minor variations the police force to be organised in the same way. The Mid-West, however, though going along with the regionalisation of the army in respect of recruitment etc., took a different position with regard to the operative control of both army and police, arguing that provision should still be made for the centre to have adequate operational control over the regional army and police units.

[2] Except, of course, the Eastern Region segment. For obvious reasons the Northerners and those Easterners who had remained under the Federal command were the strongest opponents of regionalisation. But – at this time – most Western officers were also opposed to it, though some altered their positions later.

[3] For the criticism at Aburi of the committee and politicians in general quoted at length, see above, pp. 289–91.

[4] The Middle Belt officers and men in particular were not prepared to countenance any challenge to Gowon. One possible reason for Lt Colonel Mohammed's loss of support was that while he had supported a strong federation behind the scenes at the Ad Hoc Conference, it seems he had not shown great enthusiasm for the creation of new states or regions (though there is some difference in opinion among the sources of information on this point).

Although Gowon successfully withstood the challenge, he felt it necessary to take a firmer political initiative in response to army and civil service pressures. In mid-November, he adjourned the Ad Hoc Committee *sine die*. On 30 November, he made a radio broadcast announcing that 'my long term aim is the preservation of one Nigerian Army and one country';[1] that he envisaged a constitutional solution which would include the creation of at least eight and not more than fourteen new states or regions; that he would set up a new constituent assembly (presumably to supersede the Ad Hoc Committee); and that he would have the assembly discuss a prepared draft of the constitution on federal lines rather than allowing it to formulate its own proposals. He backed all this with the threat that 'if circumstances compel me to preserve the integrity of Nigeria by force, I shall do my duty by my country'.

Though Gowon's new proposals satisfied minorities demands as well as organisational pressures from the military, this was quite the wrong moment for them politically. They were, of course, rejected out of hand by the East, but what really killed them was their poor reception in the West. For this region since the autumn massacres had begun to shift its political position. A meeting of twenty-five Western 'Leaders of Thought', stage-managed by Chief Awolowo in mid-November, had drawn up a memorandum asking for the withdrawal of Northern troops from the West which they presented to Lt Colonel Gowon. Under pressure from Colonel Adebayo, army recruitment was started in the West and a number of soldiers of Yoruba origin in Northern units were called back to serve in their own region. Lt Colonel Hassan Katsina, however, had to be called down to placate the Northern troops serving in the 3rd Battalion at Ibadan to reassure them that they would not be withdrawn and to ask them 'to stay loyal to' the Western Region government.[2]

Meanwhile, political pressures were applied to secure the reopening of talks with the East. The outcome was a meeting of military leaders at a venue provided by the Ghana military government at Aburi on 4–5 January 1967. The agreements that were so hopefully reached at Aburi seemed at first to open the way for a negotiated settlement. Yet in reality they were flawed from the beginning, since all that the military leaders could agree upon was

[1] Text in *New Nigerian* (Kaduna), 1 December 1966. In the short term, however, he admitted that it might still be necessary for 'the bulk of the army in each Region' to be drawn from the people of that area.

[2] *New Nigerian* (Kaduna), 24 December 1966. A statement by Lt Colonel Hassan in his speech illustrates rather well the prevailing confusion in loyalties between the North and Nigeria as a whole (and also, it should be said between solidarity in the latter and the demand for new regions, of which Hassan was not a proponent): 'Those in the 3rd Battalion should note that they are Nigerian soldiers not Northern soldiers and should be prepared to serve anywhere in the country. But nor should they forget they are Northerners.'

a contract of unimpeachable but dangerous ambiguity.[1] The terms for the reorganisation of the military command and the Supreme Military Council were the nub of the problem. The formula of words that was reached vested control in all military policy matters, and over appointments and promotions in the armed forces and police, in the Supreme Military Council, the chairman of which was to be known as Commander in Chief and Head of the Federal Military Government. The Supreme Military Council was to determine 'any decision affecting the whole country' and, when it could not meet, all such matters had to be referred to the Military Governors of the Regions for their 'comment and concurrence'. There would be a Headquarters Organisation, on which the regions would be equally represented, and area commands in each region, which would be controlled during the period of military government by the respective Military Governors of the Regions 'in matters of internal security'.

A careful reading of the verbatim report of the meeting shows that in fact there was never, however, any agreement between Lt Colonel Ojukwu and his other military colleagues on the basic issue, namely how regionalisation of the army was to be reconciled with the functional imperatives of command and control.[2] Who was to be Commander in Chief and did his role as 'Chairman' of the Supreme Military Council give him normal powers of day-to-day command over the army? What were matters of 'internal security' and did the control of the Military Governors over the area commands in such cases entirely exclude the central high command from overall control, particularly in situations of emergency? Could matters referred to the Supreme Military Council for concurrence be decided by a simple majority or did they require the explicit agreement of each of the Military Governors? None of these questions was resolved, yet it is clear both from the verbatim report and from subsequent developments that each party to the bargain believed them to have been resolved in their own favour.[3]

[1] The full details of the agreements, which covered matters like the reconvening of the Ad Hoc Committee, the treatment of refugees and appointments in all the Federal public services can be found in the communique of the Aburi meeting, reprinted as Appendix 2.

[2] Some of the key parts of the discussion of command and control are reprinted in Chapter VI above. It will be clear from these that Lt Colonel Ojukwu did not envisage a Commander in Chief with any effective control over the armed forces in the regions, whereas all the other military leaders did envisage at least a minimum of effective central command; and that none of them changed their position during the course of the debate.

[3] A rapid perusal of the text of the final communique itself would on balance seem to favour Lt Colonel Ojukwu's interpretation, though it is by no means an open-and-shut case. One would expect this as he brought ready-made draft agreements for his colleagues to consider, whereas the latter were not so well organised. The legal quibble, however, is not so important as the fact that the terms of the Aburi settlement did not represent a genuine political agreement that all parties felt they could accept at that time or later. Subsequent recriminations as to the 'bad faith' or double-dealing of either side thus miss the point and do not do justice to the intentions of either set of protagonists.

On his return from the conference, Lt Colonel Ojukwu immediately gave a press conference in which he said that the military leaders had gone a long way towards confederation as a result of the meeting; and at the meeting of law officers called to tie up the loose ends, his legal representatives pushed the confederal case to its logical extreme.[1] This meeting and subsequent meetings of Federal and regional officials failed to get rid of the ambiguity and to reach any substantial measure of agreement. Lt Colonel Gowon was exposed to a penetrating critique of the agreements by his federal civil servants.[2] At the end of January, he too gave a press conference at which he stated that 'we definitely decided against regional Armies'. Lt Colonel Ojukwu began to accuse Gowon of deliberately sabotaging the agreements, with the histrionic rider that he was doing this to maintain Northern military occupation of the Western Region because 'the North wants to have a route to the sea and to do this it must maintain its domination over the West.'[3]

As it became clearer that he had not got what he anticipated out of the Aburi meeting, Lt Colonel Ojukwu felt his way towards an alternative strategy. This was to carry out a phased withdrawal from the Federation in the hope that he could generate enough momentum to detach the West and Mid-West as well. The object of the manoeuvre could either have been to force Gowon to accept some sort of confederal arrangement on the East's own terms, or to go right through to outright secession, carrying the rest of the south out too.[4] At the end of February, the Eastern Governor made a broadcast announcement that, if the Aburi agreements were not implemented by 31 March, his region would proceed to put them into effect 'unilaterally'. On that date he issued an edict that all revenues collected in the region which

[1] The report on the proceedings of the meeting of the Law Officers and of the subsequent meeting of the Secretaries to the Military Government is printed in *The meeting of the Nigerian military leaders*, pp. 71–105. The Eastern representatives attempted to argue that the Aburi accord gave each region a veto both on the executive acts and on the legislation of the Federal or central government; that this could lead to a situation of legislative vacuum in matters on which the regions could not agree; so that the regions should be given concurrent legislative powers in *all* matters previously reserved to the Federal government. This clearly pushed the logic of the agreements too far, and was out of step with Lt Colonel Ojukwu's first statements on his return from Aburi that the military leaders had agreed that the decrees of the Military Government which had 'detracted from the *previous* powers of the Regional governments should be repealed'. *Daily Times* (Lagos), 7 January 1967. The report of the meeting of the Law Officers underlines the very haphazard nature of the whole proceedings by calling attention to the fact that they 'had to refer back a number of questions for decision of the Supreme Military Council because we were handicapped by the fact that no authentic copy of the Accra agreements as such was available, and, in fact, some of the Law Officers came to Benin either on purely verbal instructions or with very sketchy instructions in writing'. *Meeting of the Nigerian military leaders*, p. 71.
[2] This is reprinted in Appendix 2, together with the Aburi communique.
[3] *West Africa* (London), 28 January 1967.
[4] Though it is not clear whether he envisaged all the regions going their own separate ways, or some kind of southern front of the type that the unfortunate Lt Colonel Banjo later tried to organise in August 1967.

were previously payable to the Federal government would be due henceforth to the Eastern treasury. In the weeks that followed, the East took a number of other steps towards autonomy, including the sequestration of Federal revenues collected in the region, taking over a number of Federal statutory bodies operating in the East, like the Nigerian Coal, Railway, Electricity and Broadcasting Corporations, authorising its Marketing Board to buy and sell produce outside Nigeria directly, instead of through the Nigerian Produce Marketing Company, and setting up its own Court of Appeal. The Federal government in its turn imposed strict control on foreign exchange transactions after an alleged purchase by the African Continental Bank in the East of £6 million against its holding of Nigerian currency. And it terminated all Nigeria Airways flights to the region, following which the East seized a grounded aircraft at Port Harcourt and another which was hi-jacked to the East from Benin airport. At the same time the Eastern government made informal approaches to the West and Mid-West, as well as emphasising their common interests with the East against the North in its public pronouncements and propaganda statements.[1]

This strategy came within an ace of succeeding. Successive drafts of a decree to put the Aburi resolutions into effect were put up by Federal civil servants and then modified under pressure from the East and West to fit a more confederalist interpretation of the agreements,[2] though still not enough to satisfy the East. On 10 March a meeting of the Supreme Military Council was held on 'neutral' ground in Benin to ratify the proposed legislation, but was not attended by Lt Colonel Ojukwu. The resulting Decree, no. 8 of 1967, conceded most of what the latter asked for, with the crucial exception that the Supreme Military Council would be permitted to take action with the concurrence of only three of the four Regional Military Councils in a state of emergency and in circumstances that would put the country's existence in danger.[3] It was rejected outright by the East, because

---

[1] It is fairly clear that Lt Colonel Ojukwu really did believe that he could make the West and Mid-West adopt common cause with him at this time: *viz.* his statement at a press conference with foreign journalists: 'How would you feel, being a Westerner, Governor of the West, with troops guarding your State House permanently, by the Northern soldiers? No matter what you feel intellectually, when it comes to the fact that your own life is in jeopardy you have to modify your public statements. The same goes for the Mid-West...It is for these people as much as it is for the East that I am making my resistance. I refuse to accept the North permanently dictating to Nigeria by virtue of their size. The day, I repeat it to you again, this people of the North accept that power at the centre should be shared, the crisis in Nigeria would end.' *Nigerian Outlook* (Enugu), 21 March 1967.

[2] The Western official ensured, for instance, that executive powers were entrusted to the Supreme Military Council as a whole, not the Head of the Military Government alone, as in the earlier Federal proposals.

[3] The decree vested all Federal legislative and executive powers as well as powers of appointment to top public service and military posts in the Supreme Military Council, which had to act with the explicit concurrence of all four Military Governors. The concurrence of only three of the

the emergency powers, if accepted, would limit the ultimate powers of self-determination by force if necessary which it wished to keep for itself.

As it became clear that the East was not compromising and was going ahead with its phased withdrawal, the West, and to a lesser extent, the Mid-West, began to detatch themselves too. Towards the end of March, Lt Colonel Ejoor and Colonel Adebayo both had informal meetings with Lt Colonel Ojukwu to obtain assurances that his threat to unilaterally implement the Aburi agreements on 31 March did not mean he would secede; though they pledged themselves against force if secession did occur. Shortly afterwards new Area Commands were set up in the regions to replace the old Brigade organisation, in accordance with the Aburi decisions on the regionalisation of the army, but this was not enough to satisfy the West whose demands that Northern troops be withdrawn continued. In late April the Supreme Military Council attempted to open the political dialogue again by reconvening the Ad Hoc Committee on the constitution. But the meeting had to be called off after Chief Awolowo had resigned from the Western delegation and refused to attend, claiming that the Northern soldiers in the West constituted 'an army of occupation'.[1] A meeting of Western Region Leaders of Thought was then convened at Ibadan on 1 May, at which Awolowo – flanked by Colonel Adebayo, Lt Colonel Olutoye and Major Sotomi[2] – made a delphic announcement that if the Federal government 'by acts of omission or commission' brought about the secession of the East, then his region would go with it too. Statements to a similar effect were also made by the Military Governor of the West, and the whole situation looked most ominous. Awolowo took a delegation of political dignitaries to Enugu to attempt to patch up a compromise with the East, but this failed to achieve anything.[3] By late May 1967 it was fairly clear that the East would secede, and it was not at all certain whether the rest of Nigeria would remain together if it did so.

Meanwhile, the Federal government was still exposed to pressures from the North and from the army against concessions that would weaken the

Governors, however, was required to declare a State of Emergency or to invalidate any regional legislation that impeded the executive authority of the Federation or endangered the continuance of federal government in Nigeria. The feeling among some Federal civil servants was that the new constitutional arrangements still conceded so much as to be difficult to work, and that without the emergency provisions they would be completely unviable.

[1] His other reasons for refusing to attend were that the Supreme Military Council had removed the military from the committee's terms of reference and that it was certain that the East would not attend.

[2] Yoruba officers who at the time were Military Governor, Area Commander (West) and CO of the 3rd Battalion, Ibadan, respectively.

[3] Most of these dignitaries could be said to have been relatively non-partisan in the conflict at the time. They styled themselves the National Conciliation Committee. Ojukwu seems to have rejected their mediation in part because of his strategy of forcing a confrontation and in part because he objected to the Easterners on the committee, like Dr Okoi Arikpo, who were advocates of the Eastern minorities.

Federation or the army, and in favour of the use of force against the East if it would not come to terms. Most officers in the Federal army did not hesitate to make known their dislike of the regionalisation of the army agreed at Aburi. After Decree no. 8 was promulgated Lt Colonel Hassan Katsina undertook a programme of visits to the military units in the North to explain the Supreme Military Council's decisions and was exposed to some very sharp criticism by his junior officers. These asked him why he 'had sat there like a blockhead' while the military leaders agreed to subdivide the army, and queried the decision to vest emergency powers in the Supreme Military Council at all, contending that these should have been left in the hands of the Supreme Commander alone.

In March 1967 after Lt Colonel Ojukwu had announced his decision to apply the Aburi agreements unilaterally, there was considerable feeling that he should be brought to heel by force, and Lt Colonel Hassan himself made a statement to the effect that the army could crush the East in a few hours if the Supreme Commander gave the go-ahead.[1] Some officers in Ibadan and Ikeja actually threatened to carry out an invasion themselves, but were dissuaded after informal delegations were sent down to them by their colleagues in the North. Similar pressures were building up prior to the East's secession at the end of May. When Lt Colonel Gowon finally gave in to demands that Northern troops be moved from the West the garrisons at Ibadan and Abeokuta refused to budge and Lt Colonel Hassan had to journey down again to plead with them to move. At first, it is said, they refused, and only agreed after Lt Colonel Hassan visited them a second time with Lt Colonel Akahan, now the Chief of Staff at Army Headquarters.

These pressures from the army derived both from the predominance of the Northerners in the military at this time, and also from the reassertion of its organisational interests remarked on earlier. The effect of the latter can be gauged from the fact that most of the southerners still holding regular Federal army positions (outside the East and Mid-West) shared the same views as their Northern colleagues in matters of military organisation,[2] and the invasion of the East.

On the other hand, discipline was still very shaky and the army was riven with insecurity and conflict, to the point that fragmentation always remained a latent possibility. In the Northern units, for instance, there were occasions when some of the better-represented Northern 'minorities' groups, like the

---

[1] *New Nigerian* (Kaduna), 9 March 1967.

[2] See, for instance, the case of Lt Colonel Olutoye, then CO, 2nd Brigade, Lagos, who went on record in early February as telling a military parade that he felt that regionalisation of the army was 'against the best interests of the country'. It is notable, however, that his views changed when he was posted Area Commander in the West and exposed to direct political pressure from Chief Awolowo.

Idoma and Tiv, found themselves under the same kind of verbal attack from their colleagues for 'monopolising' control positions as the Ibos had experienced in earlier days.[1] When the West under Awolowo began to threaten withdrawal from the Federation in May, Yoruba officers – particularly those in Northern units – began to feel very isolated and sought assurances that they would not be molested. In at least one instance the writer knows of, the insecurity was so acute that the Yoruba officers concerned would not at first accept their commanding officer's assurances because he came from a certain Northern minority tribe and they were sceptical as to whether *he* would be safe, let alone in a position to help them. At the end of May, when the Federal army started to pull out of the West, there were one or two Yoruba education officers in the North who panicked so much that they fled south for a few days.[2]

Though Lt Colonel Gowon's policy of playing a conciliatory waiting game may have had its political justification, it compounded all these problems of morale. Firm initiative was needed to dissolve uncertainty and the hankering after military action, but this the Supreme Commander did not provide until the end of May, when at last he judged the moment ripe.

It was evident to everyone by then that the East was on its way out, having rejected with 'contempt, levity and apathy',[3] last-minute offers of conciliation made through the good offices of the National Conciliation Committee, even though the Federal government lifted its economic sanctions on 23 May and withdrew troops from the West in response to the committee's appeals to it. On 27 May, the Eastern Nigeria Consultative Assembly mandated the East's Military Governor to declare a 'free, sovereign and independent state by the name and title of the Republic of Biafra'. Lt Colonel Gowon immediately assumed the initiative and forestalled the impending secession. He declared a state of emergency, assumed plenary powers and decreed the division of Nigeria into twelve states. Accordingly, on 30 May 1967, Lt Colonel Ojukwu finally declared the secession of the Republic of Biafra.

Meanwhile, Lt Colonel Gowon engaged in a vigorous political offensive, designed to secure the loyalty to the Federation of as many of Nigeria's nationalities as he could muster. The creation of six new states out of the old Northern Region and three out of the old East not only satisfied the demands of the soldiers and civilians of the Middle Belt but was aimed also at detaching the loyalties of the Eastern minorities. The latter were already

[1] See the specific examples given in Chapter VIII above.
[2] Though their example was not followed by any of the Yoruba combat officers, and they were later persuaded by Colonel Adebayo to return.
[3] The epithet is that of Cyprian Ekwensi, in *West Africa* (London), 3 June 1967. This edition and *West Africa* of 10 June give a useful diary of the last phases of the crisis.

represented in Lagos within the army[1] and by a number of politicians in exile. The support he won in these areas was later to be crucial in the success of Federal offensives in Ogoja, Calabar and Port Harcourt and the Rivers.

The adherence of the Western Region had also to be secured, and this necessitated the wooing of Chief Awolowo and Colonel Adebayo. On 25 May, plans were announced to withdraw all Northern troops from the West, to be redeployed in Lagos and Ikeja and on the Northern boundary at Jebba and Ilorin by the end of May, although the implicit threat of the coercion of the West if it fell out of step still remained. The creation of new states was a measure that Chief Awolowo had advocated all along, although it is significant that Lt Colonel Gowon did not attempt to cut into the former's power base by dividing up the Western Region in like manner to the East and North.[2] The master-stroke, however, was to invite Awolowo on 3 June to become Vice Chairman of the Federal Executive Council, and then to make him Commissioner for Finance, associating him closely with the military regime as its most powerful civilian adviser. The appointment of twelve civilians, one from each state, to the council broadened the regime's legitimacy[3] and recruited the political skills of leaders like Chief Awolowo, Chief Enahoro, Okoi Arikpo, Joseph Tarka and Aminu Kano, who were to prove invaluable in prosecuting the civil war, most especially in managing Nigeria's external relations and in relieving the military of some of the day-to-day tasks of government.[4] At this stage, however, the support of neither the West nor of the Mid-West was wholehearted, and this had to wait upon further developments, notably the invasion of the Mid-West by Biafra in August 1967.

The opening of military hostilities was preceded by a period during which the Federal government set up a naval blockade of the East, and there was a war of nerves between the Federal and Biafran governments and the oil companies. Up to the secession, the latter had paid rents and royalties to the

---

[1] There were still a number of Eastern minorities soldiers to start with and these were supplemented by a large number of recruits fleeing the East to join up, particularly from the Rivers area.

[2] Chief Awolowo had always advocated a subdivision based on the boundaries of the main ethnic 'nationalities' which would therefore leave the West intact (or preferably, from his point of view, enlarged to include Lagos and the Yoruba-speaking areas of the North, now Kwara State). The only modification made to the West's boundaries was the excision of a narrow strip along the coast to become part of Lagos State. Lt Colonel Gowon's tacit bargain with Awolowo has since become something of an embarrassment because of the reassertion of old political cleavages in the Western State and the appearance of demands for its subdivision into two or three new states.

[3] Again this was of crucial importance in realigning the Eastern minorities by associating some of their leaders like Arikpo and Wenike Briggs with the Federal cause. The appointment of Chief Enahoro was also to be of strategic importance in securing the loyalty of the Mid-West.

[4] Not that the military had involved itself much with these in any way, leaving them mainly to the civil servants.

Federal government, but had contributed to the East's foreign exchange reserves through wharfage and transport charges and the like. The Biafran government attempted after its declaration of independence to blackmail the oil companies to pay it oil revenues by threatening to take over their installations in the East, while the Federal authorities counteracted this by blockading all oil shipments from the East. The companies were in the uncomfortable dilemma of having to choose between paying royalties and rents to the Federal government, keeping them in 'suspense accounts' until the situation was clarified, or paying up to the East. In practice, however, only those with a *speculative* interest in new exploration rights or in taking over the installations of established concerns made substantial sums available to the Biafrans in the form of loans or advances (rather than as bona fide revenue payments), while the others waited upon political events.

It would be overstretching even a Marxist interpretation of history to say that oil was the root cause of the civil war. But given that the basic lines of cleavage were political, with their source in ethnic and regional conflict and in the fissure of the army, oil and the foreign earnings it produced were among the essential means of struggle. The Federal interest in Eastern oil needs no elaboration. And despite its many disclaimers to the contrary, it is clear that oil and access to the sea were two important reasons – though not the only ones – for Ojukwu's refusal to negotiate on new states or regions for its non-Ibo minorities. Estimates of the proportion of oil deriving from Ibo and non-Ibo areas of the East differ, with Eastern sources tending to stress that production in the former exceeded the latter and Federal sources the contrary.[1] Taking into account the rapidly increasing output of the Mid-West, oil in the Eastern minorities areas was certainly not the major portion of total *Federal* production; nor did oil yet provide a very high percentage either of Nigeria's foreign earnings or of its governmental revenues, even though it was rapidly growing. But for the ultimate survival of Biafra, access to such a major source of foreign exchange would have been crucial. Such considerations were clearly central also to the Federation's political strategy of wooing the non-Ibo areas, and to its naval blockade and the opening of a second front on the Eastern coast in the early stages of the war. Once there was an effective Federal presence on the shoreline, the companies with established interests in Nigeria unlocked their suspense accounts if they had them and put their full weight behind the Federal cause, though speculative funds from elsewhere still found their way to Biafra.

Actual hostilities did not break out until 6 July 1967, when Federal troops initiated an invasion of the East from the North. This was followed by the

---

[1] The difference depends on how one draws the boundaries of the Ibo areas, so that there is no really satisfactory resolution of the argument.

opening of a second front after a sea landing at Bonny on the sea approaches to Port Harcourt in the south. Meanwhile, the Mid-West remained in an uneasy neutrality, forced upon it by the fact that most of its soldiers were Ibo (even though the majority of its population was not) and by its vulnerability to invasion from the East. This neutrality ended, however, when the Ibo officers betrayed the Benin government and let in an invading force, led by Lt Colonel Banjo, on 9 August 1967. The opening of a new front by the Biafrans was a highly successful gamble in the short term, but in the long run was disastrous. The Mid-West Military Governor, Brigadier Ejoor, was forced into hiding. The combined East and Mid-West forces pushed right through to the borders of the Western State, where they threatened to cut Federal communications, which were then virtually unguarded. But the Federal Guard was rushed up from Lagos and checked the advance at Ore in the West, and within a few weeks, the invading forces had been pushed right back to the River Niger.

The political consequences of the Mid-West invasion were most inauspicious for Biafra. If there had been any doubts previously about the loyalties of the West and Mid-West to the Federation, these were now all abolished. During his brief stay in the Mid-West Lt Colonel Banjo attempted to make contact with military and political notables in the West and Mid-West and had held secret discussions with Brigadier Ejoor, with a view to overthrowing both Gowon and Ojukwu and disarming the entire Biafran and Federal armies, but all to no effect.[1] He then completely demoralised the Biafran army by withdrawing before the advancing Federal forces in the Mid-West. He plotted abortively against Lt Colonel Ojukwu; and was executed for 'treason', along with Major Ifeajuna and other radical allies on the Biafran side, in September 1967. Instead of creating a southern front against the North, the invasion resuscitated all the old fears and suspicions of the Yorubas and non-Ibo Mid-Westerners against the Ibos and re-emphasised their dependence for security upon the Federal army. A third front was opened and the Federal troops could concentrate all their energies on pinning the Biafran forces down within the narrow confines of the Ibo heartland.

POSTURES OF THE REGIONS

The above discussion has emphasised the forces taking the Federal government and the East into the civil conflict. We must now attempt to account for

---

[1] Ejoor reported the advances made to him by Banjo after he escaped to Lagos, but says he refused to consider the latter's suggestions. See *New Nigerian* (Kaduna), 26 September 1967. He says that Banjo had been angered by Ojukwu's orders to install Lt Colonel Nwawo as Military Governor of the Mid-West, which Banjo refused to do. Banjo also passed on intelligence reports which were used in the Federal government's invasion of the Mid-West.

the alignments of the regions in this time of fragmentation. Why did the North stay committed to the Federation and the East take itself out? Why did the West and Mid-West appear to waver in their position, but finally throw their support behind the centre? What were the relations of each region to the military?

THE NORTH

During this period, the North was undergoing structural transformations of considerable political consequence. The first of these changes was the destruction of the political hegemony of the old NPC and with it of the power of the Native Authorities. This was a result of the transfer of power to the military itself; of the reforms in the structure and functions of the NAs begun by the military administration;[1] and of the upheavals in May and September 1966 which demonstrated the NAs' loss of control in the urban areas. One early indicator of the shift in power was the refusal of Northern Leaders of Thought, at their meeting before the Ad Hoc talks in early September 1966, to elect the former General Secretary of the NPC, Alhaji Galadiman Pategi, as one of their representatives at those talks and their selection of radicals like Tarka and Aminu Kano instead. The culmination of these changes was the excision of the Native Courts from the NAs' jurisdiction and control and the banning of all NA personnel from politics, both measures being announced in February 1967.[2]

Secondly, out with the old politicians went their determination to run the North as a single political unit and thereby to control the political life of the whole Federation. This was partly because the ethnic and cultural minorities were in a strong position to assert their demands for new regions or states because of their well-entrenched position in the army; and partly because many of the new political leaders of the old North, like Aminu Kano, were willing to acquiesce in the subdivision of the North for complex reasons of their own.[3] The creation of new regions or states was not a practicable proposition unless some kind of effective political centre could be ensured. The demand for them arose, by a particular combination of circumstances, at a time

---

[1] The government of the Sardauna of Sokoto had already been effective in reducing the NAs' power vis-a-vis the NPC, thus preparing the ground for reform. The NPC, however, depended in the last resort on the interlocking of the NPC and the NAs at a local level and the recruitment of NA functionaries into regional politics. Military rule thus provided conditions in which more fundamental reforms could be initiated.

[2] The court reform was not actually started until April 1967 and then was phased over a year for administrative reasons.

[3] One of the reasons a number of 'dry North' politicians – particularly those from Kano – were prepared to agree to the creation of new states was that it was widely felt that their states now paid an undue proportion of the costs of the Northern Region in relation to the benefits in terms of jobs, university places, educational expenditure and the like, mainly because of their educational backwardness relative to the Middle Belt.

of waning influence for the old-style politicians, who preferred confederation or the secession of the North if the region as a whole could not be certain of controlling the county, as in the days of NPC hegemony.

The latter of the two changes had a dramatic public inauguration when the Northern delegation at the Ad Hoc Conference in September 1966 suddenly came out in support of the creation of more regions.[1] The question whether the North would be dismembered was not finally resolved, however, until Gowon's fiat in May 1967. Even the strongest advocates of new states in the North had not wished to see them created unless other regions (especially the East) were operated on too. Many of the radicals, civil servants and soldiers of the far North were all along ambivalent as to whether their purposes would be best served by vigorous reforms within the framework of the existing Northern Region or by permitting the latter to be divided, the former course tending, indeed, to be more popular in the few months following the failure of the Ad Hoc talks. In September 1966, Lt Colonel Hassan Katsina had appointed a Committee on Provincial Authorities to consider proposals for the devolution of some regional government functions to the provinces as a possible palliative to minority aspirations for self-rule.[2] On the anniversary of the first coup in January 1967, we find the Military Governor eulogising the late Sardauna of Sokoto (somewhat improbably) as being 'to Northern Nigeria what Gandhi was to India',[3] and resuscitating the Northern Nigeria Self-Development Fund, into which donations poured as a sign of renascent regional loyalties. At the same time, however, he was now quietly allowing the Committee on Provincial Authorities to cease meeting. A conference of Leaders of Thought at the end of January 1967 recommended that Nigeria should be divided into eleven to thirteen regions, and in May a joint assembly of the Emirs, Chiefs and Leaders of Thought of Northern Nigeria passed a resolution in support of the creation of new states, *whether or not* they were created in other regions also.

The same meeting of Emirs, Chiefs and Leaders of Thought also proclaimed itself in favour of a strong centre for the Federation. This was a position that had received steady support from most sections of the North, with the exception perhaps of a few traditionalists, from September 1966 onwards. The merits of an effective central government could be argued both by those like the minorities who wanted more regions or states and by proponents of a reinvigorated, reformed One North; the latter would still,

---

[1] The idea of secession, which had been seriously canvassed after the July coup, had been finally dropped at the Northern Leaders of Thought conference.

[2] On lines which had been suggested by the Hudson Report as far back as 1957, but set aside by the then NPC government of the region: R. S. Hudson, 'Commission Appointed to Advise the Government on the Devolution of Powers to Provinces: Report by the Commissioner' (Kaduna, 1957).   [3] *New Nigerian* (Kaduna), 16 January 1967.

as in the old days, be the only region with a reasonable chance of controlling the political decisions of the centre to its own advantage.[1] It is perhaps not surprising therefore that the Easterners were unable to disentangle these different strands of support for the Federal cause, and concluded that behind all of them, including the minorities position, lay the desire of the North to dominate again.

THE EAST

As will be evident from the earlier discussion, the East's overriding political goal from July 1966 onwards was to maintain control of its own means of violence and internal security arrangements, in order to minimise its dependence on Federal power. It is important, however, to note that in the interim period up to secession, neither of the two main strategies for achieving this goal – namely negotiating a confederal settlement which deprived the centre of all effective independent power or going on to outright secession – can be said to have been mutually exclusive. For – up to the final denouement in May 1967 – actions that could be directed by the one strategy could also be justified by the other. This makes it difficult to determine at precisely what point Lt Colonel Ojukwu decided to secede, though it is clear he must always have had this possibility in mind. As already shown, until February or March 1967 he seems to have been fairly confident that he could obtain what he wanted by negotiation; after that, with the failure of the Aburi initiatives, he forced the pace on secession but still hoped that it might eventuate in a settlement. This shift in emphasis was partly a matter of choice, following upon the misunderstandings created by the Aburi meeting. But it was also to an extent forced on the East by the fact that – pending a political settlement – Federal funds were still not forthcoming for the payment of its public servants, who had fled to the region and been absorbed there, or to cope with the vast problem of the refugees in general. Political and financial pressures, therefore, built up and the seizure of Federal revenues, assets and public agencies could be viewed as a response to these as well as a bargaining manoeuvre of the kind suggested earlier.

Regardless of shifts in strategy, however, it is clear that all the way through

[1] We emphasise that it was only the far-Northern radicals who could be expected to support the maintenance of the North together with a strong centre, because members of the NPC 'old guard' who wished to preserve traditional institutions were after July 1966 more disposed to feel safe within some form of confederal arrangement, isolating the North from the influence and responsibilities of the centre, as originally proposed in the Eight-Point Programme of the 1950s. There is evidence, however, that even the perspective of the traditionalists, including the emirs, had been transmuted by May 1967 to the support of the creation of new states and thus a strong centre, on the argument that the subdivision of the North was the only way to preserve traditional institutions in the 'dry' North from changes originating farther south in the diaspora and Middle Belt.

from July 1966, the East's Military Governor was consolidating his military position and political power base so that the option of secession would be available if he chose it. Alongside the old Battalion Headquarters at Enugu, he set up an embryo military command HQ on the lines of the Federal GHQ, with its A, Q and G Branches.[1] There is evidence of arms shipments as early as October 1966,[2] and these were almost certainly negotiated, if not actually begun sometime sooner than that. Recruitment also was started early on, though on this, again, it is difficult to give precise details. Foreign exchange was sought for, there were negotiations with oil companies and, somehow, the East managed to clear a request for £6 million in exchange through the Central Bank before the latter tightened its restrictions on such transactions in April 1967.

In the Ibo areas of the East the groundswell of popularity for the Military Governor personally and for the disengagement from Nigeria he was pursuing was such that there was relatively little need for him to exert himself in order to obtain legitimacy. Indeed, there were times when he seems to have acted as a restraining influence against demands for immediate secession, particularly after the September–October massacres. A strong focus for such demands at elite level was provided by Ibo civil servants and lecturers and students at the University of Nigeria, Nsukka, particularly those who had been driven out of or resigned from the University of Lagos and the Federal bureaucracies during the crises of 1966.

Ojukwu was undoubtedly the most politically motivated of all the Military Governors. Yet he made less use of established political figures than the others, partly because he had less need of them, partly because of popular rejection of the old political class. The East's was the only delegation at the Ad Hoc Conference not to include any politicians.[3] Both Dr Azikiwe and Dr Okpara were sometimes brought in to advise the Eastern government, but neither had the substantial power to influence decisions that was possessed by Awolowo in the West, Enahoro in the Mid-West or Tarka and Aminu Kano in the North. Instead, Lt Colonel Ojukwu tended to place reliance on a small circle of civil servants, lawyers and academics, like N. U. Akpan, C. C. Mojekwu, Eni Njoku, G. C. Onyiuke and the former Regional Governor, Sir Francis Ibiam. His relations with his senior army

---

[1] Visible in the Enugu office and telephone directories, with Lt Colonel Njoku as CO, Eastern Command Headquarters, Lt Colonels Imo and Ivenso as Deputy CO and Command Secretary and Lt Colonels Ude, Eze and Effiong as Principal Staff Officers, G, A and Q, respectively. Lt Colonel Ogunewe still commanded the 1st Battalion, at this time still the only official operative unit under this top-heavy command.

[2] At the end of that month a plane carrying arms for the East crashed under mysterious circumstances at Garoua, in the Cameroon Republic.

[3] Dr Eni Njoku had been a member of the Senate and chairman of the Electricity Corporation of Nigeria, but had given up these posts a long time before the January 1966 coup.

officers were not always happy: from the early stages his battalion commander at Enugu, Lt Colonel Ogunewe doubted the military wisdom of disengaging from Nigeria; Major Nzeogwu – soon to die at the front – like the officers, including Lt Colonel Banjo and Major Ifeajuna, who attempted a *putsch* in Biafra in September 1967, wanted revolution in Nigeria, not secession; and finally Ojukwu had to shed a number of top officers, including Lt Colonels Njoku, Imo and Ogunewe, during the civil war.[1]

Legitimacy at grass roots was sought through the continuous flow of anti-Northern and anti-Federal imagery described earlier on. Much of this was redundant in Ibo areas, where it was a celebration of existing feelings and beliefs and the opening of symbolic wounds served a psychological function as much as a political purpose. The flow of images was carefully coordinated with the publication of officially sponsored accounts of the facts and with the public hearings of the quasi-judicial Onyiuke Tribunal which was appointed in December 1966 to enquire into the massacres and the July coup. Changes in emphasis in Eastern policy were also accompanied by symbolic acts, like the release of the January conspirators as popular heroes, when confrontation began in March 1967.

One important audience for whom the publicity was intended were the Eastern minorities, the non-Ibo peoples of Ogoja, Calabar and the Rivers, whose support was strategic for securing the oil, access to the sea, and the justification of a secular Eastern or Biafran nationalism on territorial rather than tribal lines. Though some were convinced, the majority were not. The Eastern government attempted to satisfy demands for autonomy by developing a system of provincial administration which would give a measure of devolution of administrative (though not political) responsibility to the provinces in the region. But as early as September 1966 this ran into trouble, when Dr N. B. Graham-Douglas, a prominent Rivers lawyer, resigned as the East's Attorney General on this issue, and the related one of Lt Colonel Ojukwu's preparation of contingency plans for secession.[2] A conference of the Leaders of Thought of the Rivers people passed resolutions regretting his resignation and calling on the Eastern Governor to direct his representatives at the Ad Hoc Conference to come out in favour of the creation of new states or regions, including some in the East. In August and September 1966, three successive Constitution Committees were set up to study the question

[1] Though he finally found a Chief of Staff on whom he thought he could rely in Lt Colonel Effiong, one of the one or two Eastern minorities' leaders to stay in Biafra.

[2] For a somewhat biased statement of the minorities' case, see Dr N. B. Graham-Douglas' booklet, *Ojukwu's rebellion and world opinion* (London: Galitzine and Partners, 1968). His claim is that Ojukwu was making plans for secession as early as June 1966 and that the name 'Republic of Biafra' was coined just after the Northern coup. This is not inconsistent with the argument above that Ojukwu was holding a number of strategic options open from the July 1966 coup, and that one of these was secession.

of provincial administration and related matters. But a number of prominent minorities members did not cooperate and had to be replaced with more compliant representatives. The former included Dr Graham-Douglas himself, Okoi Arikpo[1] and H. Biriye, all three of whom turned up later in Lagos to put the minorities' case there.

The September–October 1966 massacres won round a certain amount of minorities' support to the Eastern government, but much of this was dissipated in the months that followed. Opposition to the official line tended to be expressed in a round-about manner, the onslaught upon the Easterners being blamed upon 'the Ibos who got us into trouble with the Northerners'.[2] The Eastern government – and the Ibo population at large – handled this crisis of confidence very clumsily. In the emotionally charged atmosphere of the time all signs of dissent were looked on as some kind of treason – witness the *Nigerian Outlook*'s reaction against Chief Murphy, a prominent Ogoja leader who went to Lagos to argue the minorities' case:

The criminal propensity of certain unstable former politicians are conditions most favourable to the real enemies of the East…A typical example is Chief Murphy …Our surprise is that Chief Murphy was never investigated. There are many more Murphys around not only in his Province but elsewhere.[3]

This inquisitional attitude did much harm to the Eastern establishment's cause. For example, after a number of incidents that had upset them the Kalabaris, at a meeting of the chiefs and people that was summoned by the Provincial Secretary in January 1967, rejected the latter's urgings that they should vote against the creation of new states and in favour of the proposed system of provincial administration. But the Eastern government forthwith announced over the radio that they had *accepted* the resolutions. This brought about a peaceful demonstration, on which the police opened fire. There were a number of casualties, and the incident led to much bitterness.[4] There were several clashes in other areas, and these became more frequent after the start of the civil war when the Biafran government relied more and more on repression to curb dissent and 'treachery' as it defined it. On

---

[1] Arikpo and Graham-Douglas indeed were the chairmen of the first two Constitution Committees. The Eastern government's allegations that the minorities' leaders who turned up in Lagos carried no weight in the East, therefore seems somewhat misplaced. Graham-Douglas was restricted in the East in the early part of the war and did not escape to Lagos until 1968.

[2] See the contemporary account of shifts in minorities' opinion by R. Horton, an anthropologist working in the East, in 'Reporting the Minorities', *Nigerian Opinion* (Ibadan), III, 3 (March 1967), 222–4.

[3] *Nigerian Outlook* (Enugu), 23 December 1966.

[4] Horton, 'Reporting the Minorities', gives details. There are also many examples in Graham-Douglas, *Ojukwu's rebellion and world opinion*, including some of repression and atrocities by the Biafrans in Rivers country during the civil war on quite a considerable scale, even taking into account his tendency to exaggerate.

balance, therefore, one can say that the Eastern government lost the battle of the minorities. There were, it is true, some who supported secession, but the lack of enthusiasm of most was such that Federal troops found it much easier to penetrate the minorities areas than the Ibo heartland, and the former became the Achilles heel in the Biafran defences.

THE WEST

The position of the West all the way through to mid-1967 was a very equivocal one, governed all along by two main political factors. The first of these was the search by the Yoruba people and their political elites for unity, because it was felt that their divisions in the past had both been disruptive in themselves and had hampered the West in its competition for resources at the centre. Among Colonel Adebayo's first actions as Military Governor in August 1966 were a pledge for 'Operation Unity' in the West and the holding of three unity conferences of university teachers, obas and chiefs and 'citizens and leaders of thought', at the last of which Chief Awolowo was elected with Adebayo's blessing as 'Leader of the Yorubas'.[1] The second factor, therefore, was the almost total ascendance of Awolowo and the old Action Group element in the region's political life, an ascendance which drew in even Colonel Adebayo and the other important military leaders in the region.

At first, Chief Awolowo tended to align the West, as during the Ad Hoc Committee meetings, behind a viable Federation and the creation of new states, a policy which both fitted his previously expressed political views and which would permit the Yorubas to fill some of the vacancies in bureaucratic posts and decision-making roles created by the Ibo disengagement. But after the second massacre in the North and Lt Colonel Ojukwu's announcement in October 1966 that all non-Easterners were to leave his region, his position changed sharply in the directions already indicated: namely to demand the withdrawal of Northern troops from the West; to come out in favour of more confederal constitutional arrangements; to drop his insistence on the creation of states if the East was unwilling to agree; and to affirm his determination that force should not be used to keep the East in the Federation, even as a last resort. The culmination of all this was his elliptical threat in early May 1967 to declare the West's independence if the East were to secede.

The reasons, however, that made Awolowo start to withdraw his support from the centre are difficult to disentangle. First, he seems to have calculated that after October 1966, the secession of the East was imminent and it would therefore be in the West's interests either to follow or to insist upon a very

[1] See *Nigerian Sketch* (Ibadan), 12 and 13 August 1966.

loose confederation;[1] though it is not easy to see how this is consistent with his later decision to stay with Nigeria when the East actually did secede.

Another factor was that Awolowo was engaged in consolidating his own power and that of his former Action Group supporters in the West. Yoruba unity was to be sought, not through conciliation of his old opponents, but by driving them out of political life, a policy which was to have unfortunate political repercussions later on. From November 1966 onwards, he exercised tight control over the composition of the Leaders of Thought meetings and excluded all who did not support him. His position was also strengthened by Colonel Adebayo's appointment of the Piper Commission to enquire into the conduct of the Western Region elections of 1965 and the Somolu Tribunal into the assets of public office-holders under the former Western Region government; both of which were a direct threat to Awolowo's former political opponents, the former supporters of Chief Akintola and the NNDP.

In addition, Awolowo gained a very effective hold on Yoruba military figures in the region. He influenced Colonel Adebayo by one means or another to change his position with regard both to the unity of military command and country and to the use of threat of force against the East.[2] Lt Colonel Olutoye went through a similar sea-change when posted as Area Commander to the West in early 1967. Of the successive commanders of the 3rd Battalion, Ibadan (both Yorubas) Major Ayo Ariyo was a known Action Group supporter and Major Sotomi soon became one. Only the Yoruba officers outside the region or with their own power base, like the Military Administrator of Lagos, Major Mabolaji Johnson, were able to evade his influence. One important reason for Awolowo's intensification of his contacts with Yorubas in the army as well as his demands for the withdrawal of Northern troops from the region was of course the fear that the latter could be used to unseat him.[3] This fear had been given some substance by Lt Colonel Mohammed's intrigues in November 1966.

Yet Awolowo's manoeuvres did not greatly improve his security. Northern officers and men remained in the majority at Ibadan and Abeokuta right up to the end of May 1967. In the crucial period from March to May 1967 the

---

[1] Awolowo's position is discussed in detail by B. J. Dudley, 'Western Nigeria and the Nigerian crisis' in Panter-Brick (ed.), *Nigerian politics and military rule*, Chapter V, which gives a more exhaustive account of the West's role in the crises of 1966–7 than that presented here.

[2] It is said that Colonel Adebayo was formerly a 'hawk' on the issues of national unity and the use of force to bring the East to heel. Some traces of his former position evidently remained in his private discussions with other military leaders in, for example, his support for an effective military command when closeted with his colleagues at Aburi.

[3] In mid-November Colonel Adebayo publicly alleged that 'certain persons' conspiring with 'persons from outside the region' had attempted to 'entice soldiers to react against their own government' and that, to the best of his knowledge, one immediate cause of the intrigue was the decision to appoint the Piper Tribunal to enquire into the administration of the 1965 Western Region general election.

top Yoruba officers in the West were in practice under restriction by their own Northern guards, who sometimes even determined who could and could not come to see them. Awolowo's own activities were under the intensive scrutiny of the Special Branch, a fact of which he made public complaint.[1]

Seen against this background, Awolowo's intransigence in negotiations with the Federal government and equivocation about whether to stay in Nigeria may seem in a slightly different perspective. It is plausible to argue that he made himself awkward mainly to improve the West's bargaining position at the centre. This suggestion gains support from the fact that he shifted his allegiance back behind the Federal position just as soon as he had secured appropriate concessions including the non-division of the West and his own elevation to the Federal Executive Council. If so, his was a chancy game which could easily have led to the secession of the West at the same time as the East, as originally threatened; an implication that Awolowo seems himself, nonetheless, to have accepted. That it did not do so is partly due to Lt Colonel Gowon's careful handling of the situation and preparedness to make concessions at the crucial moment.

Chief Awolowo's sheer lack of military power in the West must also have been a crucial element in his decision to stay in Nigeria, a suggestion which amplifies our earlier contention that it was the East's control of its own means of violence and of communication which made it possible for it to secede and indeed likely that it would do so. On the other hand, he did control the means of communication in the Western Region, exemplified vividly by the banning by the regional government of the *Morning Post*, the Federal government's own official newspaper, from circulation in the West and by the outspokenness of the two Ibadan newspapers, the *Nigerian Tribune* and the *Sketch*. And these he was able to use to great political effect in securing his position in the region.

THE MID-WEST

All the way up to August 1967, the Mid-West was in a very anomalous position. On the one hand, the majority of its population and its political leaders, like Chief Enahoro, were in favour of a viable Federation and the creation of states, because this seemed all along to be the best solution for such a small and ethnically heterogeneous region. It was the most consistent supporter of such a position in the Ad Hoc Committee; and its Leaders of

---

[1] In his letter resigning from the Western delegation to the Ad Hoc Committee, he accuses the Special Branch of fabricating the 'wicked lie' that he and certain Western Region politicians and soldiers were organising guerrilla training in the West. He also complains that 'it has been said times without number in authoritative government circles that I was in regular touch with Lt Colonel Ojukwu by phone calls and personal visits to perfect our joint position'. *Nigerian Tribune* (Ibadan), 25 April 1967.

Thought registered a strong protest of disappointment when the Ad Hoc Committee was not reconvened in early May 1967 because of the refusal of the East and West to participate.

On the other hand, its population contained a strong Ibo minority. And even more important, the majority of its army officers and men were Mid-West Ibos. After the July 1966 coup these were almost all concentrated at the small military station at Benin, the commanding officer of which, Lt Colonel Nwawo, was one of them.[1] There were no Northern troops in the Mid-West, in contrast to the Western Region, because Benin up to August 1966 had not been a regular military station; and unlike Ibadan and Abeokuta in the West, was not strategically positioned in relation either to Lagos or the North.

The Easterners, therefore, brought constant pressure to bear on the Mid-West Ibos to support them, even though this was somewhat at odds with the non-tribal, territorial identity they were trying to claim for their own region. During the Ad Hoc Committee negotiations, a meeting of chiefs and clan heads of the Ika-Ibos petitioned that they should 'be grouped with our kith and kin in Eastern Nigeria'[2] and received support in the *Nigerian Outlook*. Mid-West Ibos were specifically excluded by the Eastern Region government from its expulsion of non-residents of the region in October 1966. These two events drew a strong protest from Lt Colonel Ejoor against the East for its interference in the affairs of his region. But there was little he could do but remonstrate, even when the Easterners stole a Nigerian Airways plane from Benin airport in April 1967.

Accordingly, Ejoor attempted to deal with these conflicting pressures by articulating a posture of 'neutrality' in the conflict, differing in this respect from the politicians and Leaders of Thought of the region who were inclined to come down more clearly on the Federal side. At Aburi he was probably the most conciliatory of the military leaders towards Lt Colonel Ojukwu, and his representatives at the subsequent discussions of officials were instructed accordingly. Similarly he, with Colonel Adebayo, played an important role in acting as honest broker between the Federal government and Lt Colonel Ojukwu when the latter moved towards confrontation in March 1967.

When the East seceded and the war began, the Mid-West still remained

---

[1] There were six Ibo lieutenant colonels of combat status in the Mid-West (Nwawo, Okwechime, Nwajei, Trimnell, Igboba and Nzefili) and two non-combatants (Morah and Dunkwu). Lt Colonel Ejoor, the Military Governor, was the only high-ranking non-Ibo in Benin, though there were three temporary majors compared with two Ibos in this rank.

[2] *Nigerian Outlook* (Enugu), 28 September 1966. The 12 October edition of this newspaper castigated Ejoor for his allegations of Eastern interference in the Mid-West, saying that he did not represent the whole Mid-West because the Ika-Ibos opposed him. Other leaders of the Mid-West Ibos, however, were at pains to dissociate themselves from the above resolutions, because they felt the vulnerability of their position.

in theory neutral, though part of the Federation. The Military Governor still refused to have Northern troops in the region. Contingency plans were prepared for the eventualities both of an invasion from the East and of one from the Federation, though both plans were equally unrealistic because of the Mid-West's shortage of troops and armaments. Ejoor's hopes that his posture of neutrality and the personal loyalty to him of his Ibo contemporaries serving in the Mid-West would isolate the region from the civil conflict, turned out to be illusory, and the intrigues of the Biafran government with the Mid-West Ibo army officers paved the way for the Biafran invasion in August 1967.

CONCLUSION AND POSTSCRIPT

Historians have a knack of making the merely possible seem probable and the probable inevitable. Lest the reader assume from the description of events given above that the civil war was inevitable from the moment the Northerners staged their coup on July 28–29 1966 – that there was a veritable march of events – we should point out that right up to April or May 1967 there was always more than one possible outcome. In the first place, each of the protagonists in the political conflict held open a hierarchy of different strategies or options, none of them necessarily excluding the others and the emphasis as between which depended on the particular circumstances of the time and on the bargaining positions put forward by the others. Thus between 28 July 1966 and the civil war, the Northerners considered at different times the full range of options, including the secession of the North, a negotiated confederation or the Federation maintained, if necessary, by force. The first two options were more or less foreclosed after September 1966, though it is possible they could have been revived if, say, the West had carried out its threat to secede when the East did so. They also debated among themselves the question of whether the existing regions should be maintained or whether they would allow the North with the other regions to be carved up into a number of states, though this issue was never finally resolved until May 1967. Similarly, the Western Region held open the options of secession, confederation or Federation right the way through to the end of May 1967 (although, as we pointed out, there is some evidence that Chief Awolowo and Colonel Adebayo may have been holding open the former merely to improve their bargaining position *within* the Federation). Finally, we have suggested, Lt Colonel Ojukwu never made up his mind between secession or a confederal solution until March or April 1967. Although it was politically within his power up to October 1966, and possibly even after this, to opt for Federation, he chose not to do so. Had he, indeed, been a little more flexible and in March

1967 accepted the Federal interpretation of the Aburi agreements as put forth in Decree no. 8, he might have achieved the substance of what he wanted (*de facto* autonomy for the region) at a relatively small cost.

Events also have a degree of independence from the intentions of the participants in them: they have their own structure of possibilities. As they evolve, they undermine or remove some of the choices open to the participants and open others to them. Had the Northerners been able to seize the 1st Battalion at Enugu in July 1966, or had they invaded the East at any time up to October 1966 (or possibly even a little later), the latter region would never have had the option of secession. Had the September–October 1966 massacres not occurred, Lt Colonel Ojukwu might have been more pliable, the pressures on him to secede might have been less and he would have found it harder to create public support around his actions. Had Britain, the USA and the oil companies come out firmly on the side of the Federal government in February or March 1967, and brought pressure to bear on Lt Colonel Ojukwu, he might have been persuaded to accept Decree no. 8 (even though this 'strong' confederal solution might itself have turned out not to be viable in the long run). Had Colonel Adebayo and Chief Awolowo decided to secede with the East in May 1967, the Federal government would probably not have had enough political momentum to prosecute the war. Nor would it have had the political will or the means to do so had not the discipline and organisational coherence of the Federal army been gradually restored between July 1966 and May 1967; and had the army and the civil service not held out so strongly for an effective political centre. Finally, if Lt Colonel Ojukwu had not ordered the invasion of the Mid-West in August 1967, the political coherence of the rest of Nigeria would have remained in doubt and the war effort would always have been in danger of falling apart by reason of political cleavages in the Federation.

Yet as we pointed out at the beginning of this chapter, there were – between July 1966 and the outbreak of civil war – certain factors in the structure of the situation which rendered some outcomes more probable than others, which created a hierarchy of probabilities. The most important of these was that the events of July and August left Lt Colonel Ojukwu in charge of a battalion, the nucleus of an army, and in charge of the machinery of government and media of communication in the East. This expanded his range of choice at the expense of that of the rest of the Federation. It meant that he did not have to accept any kind of a Federal arrangement which deprived or threatened to deprive the East of control of its own security and its own means of violence unless he wanted to, which was unlikely because of the deep sense of insecurity he shared with the other members of the Ibo nation at that time. For this reason, one may argue, there were only three

337

outcomes which were genuine possibilities, namely an armed confrontation, the secession of the East followed by the break-up of the rest of the Federation (which Ojukwu seems to have been gambling on after March 1967) or a negotiated confederal solution (which might well not have been viable in the longer run), in that order of probability.

As for the war itself (though it is not intended to discuss it in any detail here), the pattern of conflict and the outcome seem to have derived from a number of factors, not least of which was the structure and organisation of the two armies themselves. First, there was the small size of the two armies – at its biggest the Federal army was never more than 150,000 to 200,000 men – which made it unlikely that there would ever be a rapid and decisive outcome. Secondly, there was the fact that both armies resembled each other in structure, tactics and mode of organisation – whether because of the sociological tendency of conflict groups to come to resemble one another,[1] or merely because the military elite of the two armies had been to the same military schools like Mons, Sandhurst or Camberley and did not know any different. This meant that the war was pursued with extremely conventional tactics (pushing down existing roads and communication routes, and artillery bombardments preceding every military advance). This was especially true of the Federal army, but the Biafrans also did not acquire the tactical and strategic initiative that one might have expected from a population supposedly mobilised for a 'people's war'.[2] Although they became fairly adept at infiltration, they completely failed to develop the kind of guerrilla organisation and strategy that might have won them the conflict.

For this reason, the Federal army's immensely greater firepower became the decisive factor. Indeed, it had to make up for a number of other organisational deficiencies. For the army's morale, discipline and tactical ability had been badly impaired, in part because of its disintegration in 1966 and in part because it had to expand so rapidly during the war, an expansion that was all the more difficult to accomplish because there was a shortage of experienced officers and nearly all the good NCOs were absorbed into the officer corps at the beginning of the war. Although combat experience may have made up for some of these deficiencies, the army had become a rather different kind of entity from that described in Part Two of this book.

[1] See Coser's reformulation of Georg Simmel's propositions to this effect in Coser, *The functions of social conflict*, Chapter VII, especially pp. 128–33. In the Nigerian case this would be a factor tending to *preserve* the existing structural similarity between the two parties, rather than actually creating it.

[2] See the discussion of guerrilla warfare and its fundamental difference from the positional warfare of conventional armies of the Sandhurst variety, in M. Elliot-Bateman, *Defeat in the East: the mark of Mao Tse Tung on war* (London: Oxford University Press, 1967).

Severe organisational problems beset both armies. Staff work was often poor, mainly a result of the great shortage of officers with the appropriate training. There was a serious problem of corruption.[1] Coordination between the Divisions in the Federal army was quite minimal, with sometimes disastrous effects. The warlords in charge of the Divisions, like Colonels Adekunle, Muritala Mohammed, Mohammed Shuwa and Haruna – particularly the two former – acquired considerable political power in their own right, built up their own networks of support in the officer corps and were very difficult to control or discipline. It is significant that the final phases of the war were preceded by the wholesale replacement of the Divisional Commanders in the field to make it possible for the new Chief of Staff, Brigadier Hassan Katsina, to achieve the required degree of coordination.

In these circumstances, the war might have remained in stalemate for much longer, were it not for three things. First, the circumstances which made it possible for the Federal military to keep up and increase its superiority in firepower, especially the Federal government's oil revenues and the arms supplies from Britain and the USSR. Secondly, the blockade of the former Eastern Region, which was made effective from the landings at Bonny and Calabar in the summer of 1967 onwards. Enormous as was its cost in human terms, the blockade was an essential part of the Nigerian strategy, and it was the demoralisation of the Biafran troops because of the shortage of arms, food and medicines – together with the improvement in Federal strategy – which provided the conditions for the Federal army's final success. The diplomatic victory of the Nigerians in preventing all but a few nations from recognising Biafra was crucial in the success of the blockade. But this also introduced complications, for it was mainly in response to diplomatic pressures that Major General Gowon permitted (mainly by default) the activities of the relief agencies in Biafra, which undoubtedly prolonged the war.[2] Thirdly, there was the political will of Nigeria for the war and the fact that the war itself on the whole reduced the nation's cleavages and developed a stronger sense of Nigerian identity. This was a crucial factor, because without political support Major General

---

[1] On the Federal side there were reports of the various commanders making money out of supplies and of officers even falsifying casualty lists, in order to draw the pay of dead soldiers. Corruption on the Biafran side also was reported by well-informed observers.

[2] In keeping the airfields and air routes open for arms supplies as well; in providing Biafra with foreign exchange (against the relief agencies' local expenditures); and in delaying the starvation and demoralisation of the Biafran army and population. *Politically* – if he was to continue the war at all – there was no alternative but for General Gowon to maintain as stringent a blockade as possible and to keep a very wary eye on the relief organisations, in spite of the human cost. Lest the writer be accused of condoning what some people have (somewhat precipitately) been calling genocide, it should be said that in his opinion *both* the Federal *and* the Biafran leaders contracted with violent means and bear responsibility for the consequences.

The way to secession

Gowon would neither have been able to carry out his diplomatic offensive, nor to make the blockade effective, nor to persuade the country's political and military elites to submerge their differences for the time being, nor finally to call forth the kind of sacrifices in economic resources and manpower which were needed.

APPENDIXES

INDEXES

Origins, training and promotions up to 1966 of officers in 1944 to 1961 cohorts

Cohort^a	Name	Train-ing^b	Staff train-ing^c	Region tribe^d	Com-mis-sioned	Total length of time of promotion^e from date of commission to the rank stated (months)						
						Lt	Capt.	Major	Lt Col.	Col.	Brig.	Maj. Gen.
1944	Bassey	NCO		E	1946	0	28	132	196	—	—	—
1947	Ironsi	NCO	psc, idc	Ibo (E)	1949	0	28	112	160	160	160	178
1947	Ademulegun	NCO	psc, idc	Yor.	1949	6	30	114	160	160	160	—
1948	Shodeinde	NCO	psc	Yor.	1950	0	41	125	150	177	—	—
1951	Maimalari	S'hst	psc (p), idc	N	1953	12	60	99	99	124	124	—
1951	Lawan	S'hst		N	1953				Discharged			
1951	Ogundipe	NCO	psc, idc	Yor.	1953	0	41	125	134	153	153	—
1951	Adebayo	NCO	psc, idc	Yor.	1953	0	48	106	106	121	—	—
1952	K. Muhammed	S'hst	psc	N	1954	24	72	107	107	132	—	—
1952	Largema	S'hst	psc	N	1954	24	72	108	108	—	—	—
1952	Nwawo	NCO		Ibo (MW)	1954	12	60	128	128	—	—	—
1952	Fajuyi	NCO		Yor.	1954	0	16	98	98	—	—	—
1953	Imo	NCO		Ibo (E)	1955	0	24	89	89	—	—	—
1954	Pam	S'hst	jssc	N	1955	11	59	86	93	—	—	—
1954	Kurobo	S'hst	psc (p)	E	1955	19	87	87	112	—	—	—
1954	Effiong	NCO		E	1956	0	18	84	99	—	—	—
1954	Njoku	NCO	psc (p)	Ibo (E)	1956	0	41	77	77	—	—	—
1954	Onuaguluchi	NCO		Ibo	1956				Died			
1954	Ojukwu	Grad.	jssc	Ibo (E)	1957	0	48	66	79	—	—	—
1955	Ejoor	S'hst	psc	MW	1956	8	56	79	93	—	—	—
1955	Banjo	S'hst		Yor.	1956	9	57	80	94	—	—	—
1955	Unegbe	S'hst	psc (p)	Ibo (MW)	1956	9	57	75	103	—	—	—
1955	Gowon	S'hst	psc, jssc	N	1956	9	58	75	88	—	—	—
1955	Okwechime	S'hst		Ibo (MW)	1956	11	59	75	111^f	—	—	—
1955	Madiebo	S'hst		Ibo (E)	1956	21	69	80	111^f	—	—	—

| | | | Staff | | Com- | Total length of time of promotion[e] from date of commission to the rank stated (months) | | | | | | |
Cohort[a]	Name	Train-ing[b]	train-ing[c]	Region tribe[d]	mis-sioned	Lt	Capt.	Major	Lt Col.	Col.	Brig.	Maj. Gen.
1955	Anwuna	S'hst	psc (p)	Ibo (E)	1956	23	75	75	112[f]	—	—	—
1955	Ekanem	NCO		E	1957	0	23	—				
1956	Nzefili	S'hst		Ibo (MW)	1957	7	55	68	101[f]	—	—	—
1956	Ogbonnia	S'hst	psc	Ibo	1957	—	Died	—				
1956	Nwajei	S'hst		Ibo (MW)	1958	6	42	48	—	—	—	—
1956	Olutoye	Grad.		Yor.	1959	0	29	51	82[f]	—	—	—
1956	Ekpo	NCO		E	1958	0	23	59	95[f]	—	—	—
1956	Trimnell	NCO		Ibo (MW)	1958	0	23	59	95[f]			
1956	Okonweze	NCO		Ibo (MW)	1958	11	36	74				
1956	Akagha	NCO		Ibo (E)	1958	0	18	59				
1956	Ogunewe	NCO		Ibo (E)	1958	0	59	59	89[f]			
1957	Katsina	S'hst	psc	N	1958	7	27	56	85[f]	—	—	—
1957	Eze	S'hst		Ibo (E)	1958	7	27	56	87[f]			
1957	Ezeogbana	S'hst		Ibo	1959	—	Died	—	—	—	—	—
1957	Okoro	NCO		Ibo (E)	1959	0	22	45	—	—	—	—
1957	Adigio	NCO		Ibo	1959	0	32					
1957	Brown	NCO		MW	1959	0	22					
1957	Okafor, D.C.	NCO		Ibo	1959	0	22					
1957	Okafor, D.O.	NCO		Ibo (E)	1959	0	22	63	—	—	—	—
1957	Ivenso	NCO	psc	Ibo	1959	1	34	60				
1958	Nzeogwu	S'hst	psc (p)	Ibo (MW)	1959	8	27	58	—	—	—	—
1958	Ude	S'hst	psc	Ibo (E)	1960	7	26	43				
1958	Chude-Sokei	S'hst		Ibo (E)	1960	7	26	56				
1958	Akahan	S'hst	psc	N	1960	7	26	53				
1958	Keshi	S'hst		Ibo ? (MW)	1960	11	35	53				
1958	Ochei	NCO		Ibo (MW)	1960	0	27	—				
1958	Dumuje	NCO		Yor. ?	1960	0	62	—				
1958	Ifeajuna	Grad.		Ibo (E)	1960	−6	24	44				
1958	Rotimi	Grad.		Yor.	1960	−12	18	46				
1959	Igboba	S.S.		Ibo (E)	1959	11	42	—				
1959	Sotomi	S.S.		Yor.	1959	14	41	71	—	—	—	—
1959	Obasanjo	S.S.		Yor.	1959	18	47	69	—	—	—	—
1959	Amadi	S.S.	psc (1966)	Ibo	1959	18	47	—				
1959	Adegoke	S'hst		Yor.	1960	4	21	51	—	—	—	—
1959	Adekunle	S'hst		Yor. (N)	1960	8	27	49	—	—	—	—
1959	Esuene	S'hst		E	1960	8	27	52	to Air Force 1965			
1959	Chukuka	S'hst		Ibo (E)	1960	8	27	—	—	—	—	—
1959	Udeaja	S'hst		Ibo (E)	1960	8	32	—	—	—	—	—
1959	Onwuatueg-wu	S'hst		Ibo (E)	1961	8	32	—	—	—	—	—
1959	Anuforo	S'hst		Ibo (E)	1961	7	26	43	—	—	—	—
1959	Bissalla	S'hst	psc (1966)	N	1961	7	26	—	—	—	—	—
1959	Ikwue	S'hst		N	1961	7	26	to Air Force 1965				
1959	Mohammed Shuwa	S'hst		N	1961	14	38	—	—	—	—	—

| | | | Staff | | Com- | Total length of time of promotion[e] from date of commission to the rank stated (months) | | | | | | |
| | | Train- | train- | Region | mis- | | | | Lt | | | Maj. |
Cohort[a]	Name	ing[b]	ing[c]	tribe[d]	sioned	Lt	Capt.	Major	Col.	Col.	Brig.	Gen.
1959	Muritala Mohammed	S'hst		N	1961	7	28	—	—	—	—	—
1959	Haruna	S'hst		N	1961	8	26	—	—	—	—	—
1959	Kalu	NCO	psc	Ibo (E)	1961	o	25	47	—	—	—	—
1959	Ogbemudia	NCO		MW	1961	o	36	—	—	—	—	—
1959	Ayo-Ariyo	NCO		Yor.	1961	o	27	50	—	—	—	—
1959	Daramola	NCO		Yor.	1961	o	36	—	—	—	—	—
1959	Imadomiwiyi	NCO		Yor.	1961	o	24	—	—	—	—	—
1959	Ochefu	NCO		N	1961	o	36	—	—	—	—	—
1959	B. Usuman	NCO		N	1961	o	36	—	—	—	—	—
1959	Afiegbe	NCO		MW	1961	o	?	—	—	—	—	—
1959	Iwe	NCO		Ibo	1961	o	30	—	—	—	—	—
1959	Nnamani	NCO		Ibo	1961	o	27	—	—	—	—	—
1959	Ademoyega	Grad.		Yor.	1962	?	19	—	—	—	—	—
1960	Aniebo	S.S.		Ibo (MW)	1960	18	48	60	—	—	—	—
1960	Kyari	S.S.		N	1960	18	48	—	—	—	—	—
1960	Ohanehi	S.S.		Ibo (E)	1960	11	42	—	—	—	—	—
1960	Agbazue	S.S.		Ibo	1960	14	—	—	—	—	—	—
1960	Omananyi	S.S.		N	1960	11	42	—	—	—	—	—
1960	Jalo	S.S.		N	1960	17	46	—	—	—	—	—
1960	Orogbu	S.S.		E?	1960	17	46	—	—	—	—	—
1960	Odiwo	S.S.		MW?	1960	16	41	to Air Force 1965				
1960	Obienu	S'hst		Ibo (MW)	1961	8	27	39	—	—	—	—
1960	M. Usman	S'hst		N	1961	8	27	to Air Force 1966				
1960	Emelifonwu	S'hst		Ibo (E)	1961	8	?	—	—	—	—	—
1960	Johnson	S'hst		Yor.	1961	2	23	—	—	—	—	—
1960	Aisida	S'hst		Yor.	1962	1	25	—	—	—	—	—
1960	Alao	S'hst		Yor. (N)	1962	1	?	to Air Force 1965				
1960	Ally	S'hst		E	1962	1	22	—	—	—	—	—
1960	Isong	S'hst		E	1962	1	24	—	—	—	—	—
1960	Obada	S'hst		MW	1962	1	25	—	—	—	—	—
1960	Onifade	NCO		Yor.	1962	1	25	—	—	—	—	—
1960	Ogunro	NCO		Yor.	1962	2	39	to Air Force 1965				
1961	Oluleye	S.S		Yor.	1961	16	45	—	—	—	—	—
1961	Okon	S.S.		E	1961	10	42	—	—	—	—	—
1961	Obioha	S.S		Ibo	1961	16	45	—	—	—	—	—
1961	Apolo	S.S.		N	1961	18	48	—	—	—	—	—
1961	Bamigboye	S.S.		Yor. (N)	1961	18	48	—	—	—	—	—
1961	Alabi	S.S		Yor. (N)	1961	18	50	—	—	—	—	—
1961	M. Adamu	S.S		N	1961	18	48	—	—	—	—	—
1961	Abisoye	S.S.		Yor. (N)	1961	18	48	—	—	—	—	—
1961	Obeya	S.S.		N	1961	18	48	—	—	—	—	—
1961	Danjuma	S.S.		N	1961	18	48	—	—	—	—	—
1961	Shande	S.S.		N	1961	17	—	—	—	—	—	—
1961	Okoye	S.S.		Ibo (E)	1961	27	—	—	—	—	—	—
1961	Armah	S.S.		Ibo? MW?	1961	27	—	—	—	—	—	—
1961	A. Abubakar	S.S.		N	1961	13	38	—	—	—	—	—
1961	G. A. Yakubu	S.S.		N	1961	27	—	—	—	—	—	—

Cohort[a]	Name	Staff Training[b]	Staff training[c]	Region tribe[d]	Commissioned	Total length of time of promotion[e] from date of commission to the rank stated (months)						
						Lt	Capt.	Major	Lt Col.	Col.	Brig.	Maj. Gen.
1961	Bajowa	S.S		Yor.	1961	27	—	—	—	—	—	—
1961	Oji	S.S.		Ibo	1961	27	—	—	—	—	—	—
1961	Iweanya	S.S.		Ibo	1961	27	—	—	—	—	—	—
1961	Idika	S.S.		Ibo	1961	27	—	—	—	—	—	—
1961	Ihedigbo	S'hst		Ibo	1962	3	27	—	—	—	—	—
1961	Uwakwe	S'hst		Ibo	1962	3	27	—	—	—	—	—
1961	Gbulie	S'hst		Ibo (E)	1962	3	27	—	—	—	—	—
1961	Akinrade	S'hst		Yor.	1962	3	27	—	—	—	—	—
1961	Eremobor	S'hst		MW	1962	3	27	—	—	—	—	—
1961	Anekwe	S'hst		Ibo	1963	2	—	—	—	—	—	—
1961	Nwobosi	S'hst		Ibo (E)	1963	2	—	—	—	—	—	—
1961	Egere	S'hst		Ibo	1963	2	—	—	—	—	—	—
1961	Remawa	S'hst		N	1963	2	—	—	—	—	—	—
1961	Olehi	NCO		Yor. ?	1963	7	—	—	—	—	—	—
1961	Tiku	NCO		N	1962	?	28	—	—	—	—	—

Notes

[a] For explanation how officers are divided into seniority cohorts, see Table 23, p. 134.

[b] Type of training: NCOs = former NCOs with short-service training; S.S. = direct entry short-service-trained officers; S'hst = Sandhurst-trained officers; Grad. = Graduates with short-service training.

[c] Type of staff training: idc = Imperial Defence College; jssc = Joint Services Staff College; psc = Staff College, Camberley; psc (p) = Pakistan Staff College, Quetta.

[d] Respectively: Ibo from East = Ibo (E); Ibo from Mid-West = Ibo (MW); non-Ibo East = E; non-Ibo Mid-West = MW; Yoruba = Yor.; and North = N.

[e] Only gazetted promotions are included.

[f] Promotions made between January and July 1966; any promotions after July 1966 are not shown in table at all.

APPENDIX 2

Extracts from documents concerning meeting of the Nigerian military leaders held at Peduase Lodge, Aburi, Ghana, 4th and 5th January 1967

1. COMMUNIQUE (those of meetings of 4 and 5 January combined)[1]
A meeting of the Supreme Military Council of Nigeria was held in Ghana on the 4th of January, 1967. Present were:

Lt.-Colonel Yakubu Gowon	Head of Federal Military Government and Supreme Commander
Colonel Robert Adebayo	Military Governor, West
Lt.-Colonel Odumegwu Ojukwu	Military Governor, East
Lt.-Colonel David Ejoor	Military Governor, Mid-West
Lt.-Colonel Hassan Katsina	Military Governor, North
Commodore J. E. Wey	Head, Nigerian Navy
Major Mabolaji Johnson	Military Administrator, Lagos
Alhaji Kam Salem	Inspector-General of Police
Mr. T. Omo-Bare	Deputy Inspector-General of Police

The meeting which was held in a most cordial atmosphere was opened with an address by the Chairman of the National Liberation Council of Ghana, Lt.-General J. A. Ankrah.

The meeting discussed a number of issues and took decisions. These included a declaration renouncing the use of force as a means of settling the present crisis in Nigeria and holding themselves in honour bound by the declaration. They also reaffirmed their faith in discussions and negotiation as the only peaceful way of resolving the Nigerian crisis.

On the powers and functions of the Federal Military Government the Council reaffirmed its belief in the workability of the existing institutions subject to necessary safeguards.

Other matters on which agreements were reached included the following:

(i) Re-organization, administration and control of the Army.
(ii) Appointments and promotions to the senior ranks in the Armed Forces, the Police, Diplomatic and Consular Services as well as appointments to super-

---

[1] *Communique, Declaration on use of force, and Statement on the Supreme Military Council* all extracted from *Meeting of the Nigerian military leaders held at Peduase Lodge, Aburi, Ghana, 4th and 5th January 1967*, pp. 67–9.

scale posts in the Federal Civil Service and the equivalent posts in the Federal Statutory Corporations.

On the question of displaced persons the Supreme Military Council agreed to set up a committee to look into the problems of rehabilitation and recovery of property. In this connection the Military Governor of the East assured the Council that the order that non-Easterners should leave the Eastern Region would be reviewed with a view to its being lifted as soon as practicable. Agreement was also reached that the staff and employees of Governments and Statutory Corporations who have had to leave their posts as a result of recent disturbances in the country should continue to be paid their full salaries up to the end of 31st March, 1967, provided they have not found alternative employment.

The Council agreed that the Ad Hoc Committee on the constitutional future of the country should be resumed as soon as practicable and that the unanimous recommendations of the committee in September 1966, will be considered by the Supreme Military Council at a later meeting.

The Council unanimously agreed that future meetings of the Council should be held in Nigeria at a venue to be announced later.

The entire members of the Supreme Military Council express profound regret for the bloodshed which has engulfed the country in the past year and avow to do all in their power to ensure there is no recurrence of the unhappy situation.

The Members of the Supreme Military Council place on record their profound appreciation and gratitude for the constructive initiative and assistance rendered by the Chairman of the National Liberation Council, the Government and people of Ghana.

Peduase Lodge,
Aburi, 5th January, 1967.

2. DECLARATION ON USE OF FORCE (issued with communique at Aburi meeting)

We, the members of the Supreme Military Council of Nigeria, meeting at Accra on 4th day of January, 1967, hereby solemnly and unequivocably:

   (i) DECLARE that we renounce the use of force as a means of settling the present crisis in Nigeria, and hold ourselves in honour bound by this declaration.
  (ii) REAFFIRM our faith in discussions and negotiation as the only peaceful way of resolving the Nigerian crisis.
 (iii) AGREE to exchange information on the quantity of arms and ammunition in each unit of the Army in each Region, and also on the quantity of new arms and ammunition in stock.

3. STATEMENT ON THE SUPREME MILITARY COUNCIL (issued with communique at Aburi meeting)

The Supreme Military Council now meeting in Ghana has agreed on the following reorganisation of the Army:

348

(a) The Army is to be governed by the Supreme Military Council the chairman of which will be known as Commander-in-Chief and Head of the Federal Military Government.

(b) There will be a Military Headquarters on which the Regions will be equally represented and which will be headed by a Chief of Staff.

(c) In each Region there shall be an Area Command under the charge of an Area Commander and corresponding with the existing Regions.

(d) All matters of policy including appointments and promotions of persons in executive posts in the Armed Forces and Police shall be dealt with by the Supreme Military Council.

(e) During the period of the Military Government, Military Governors will have control over their Area Commands in matters of internal security.

2. The following appointments must be approved by the Supreme Military Council:

(a) Diplomatic and Consular posts.

(b) Senior posts in the Armed Forces and the Police.

(c) Super-scale Federal Civil Service and Federal Corporation posts.

3. Any decision affecting the whole country must be determined by the Supreme Military Council. Where a meeting is not possible such a matter must be referred to Military Governors for comment and concurrence.

4. COMMENTS OF FEDERAL PERMANENT SECRETARIES ON DECISIONS AT ABURI MEETING (extracts from the document published by the Eastern Region government)[1]

MEETING OF PERMANENT SECRETARIES WITH MEMBERS OF
THE FEDERAL EXECUTIVE COUNCIL

Further to my letter No. 58783/63 of 18th January, I enclose herewith, for information, a copy of the comments on the 'Accra Decisions' of the meeting of the Supreme Military Council.

(Sgd.) S. I. A. AKENZUA
for Acting Secretary to the Federal Military Government

COMMENTS ON THE 'ACCRA DECISIONS' OF THE MEETING
OF THE SUPREME MILITARY COUNCIL
(Marked 'TOP SECRET')

Introduction

1. The implications of the decisions of the Supreme Military Council meeting held in Accra recently are commented upon *seriatim* in this paper.

[1] *The meeting of the Supreme Military Council: Nigerian crisis, 1966,* 6 (Enugu: Ministry of Information, 1967), 56–63. Though the Federal government repudiated this document when it first appeared, for obvious reasons, the writer sees no reason to doubt its validity.

Reorganisation of the Army

2. (*a*) The Title: 'Commander-in-Chief'. – Objections are raised to the use of 'Commander-in-Chief' which the Accra meeting agreed should be the new title for the Chairman of the Supreme Military Council and Head of the Federal Military Government on the grounds that:

(1) It would be a subtle way of either abolishing the post of Supreme Commander or declaring it vacant, to be filled by the unanimous decision of the Supreme Military Council; if the latter, there would be considerable instability caused by political and military manoeuvres to fill the post.

(2) The Accra decision transfers the Executive Authority of the Federal Military Government from the Head of Federal Military Government and Supreme Commander, (in accordance with Decree No. 1) to the Supreme Military Council. The implication of this is that the Commander-in-Chief would have no powers of control or dismissal over the Military Governors; a situation which is incompatible with Military administration.

(*b*) Establishment of Military Headquarters. – It is considered:

(1) that the establishment of Military Headquarters with equal representation from the Regions headed by a Chief-of-Staff amounts to confederation.

(2) that there is a need for clarification on the term 'Military Headquarters' as distinct from 'Supreme Headquarters'.

(*c*) Creation of Area Commands. – It is considered that the creation of Area Commands has the following implications:

(1) dividing the Nigerian Army into regional ones, without links with or effective unified control over the army by the 'Supreme Commander'.

(2) since area command would be under the control of Military Governors who can use the army for internal security, there is the serious political implication in respect of the creation of States in which the status of minorities cannot be guaranteed by the Supreme Commander.

(3) since under the constitution the operational control of the army is vested in the Prime Minister (and after 15th January 1966, in the Supreme Commander), the acceptance of the Accra decision would require the amendments to the Armed Forces Acts and the Constitution.

(4) no authority is vested with the power for the use of the army, for external attacks on Nigeria.

(*d*) Matters of Policy, etc., in the Armed Forces and Police vested in Supreme Military Council. – It is considered that the acceptance of this decision dispenses with the Army and Police Councils.

(*e*) 'Creation of Lagos Garrison'. – If the Lagos Garrison is intended to be the same status as 'Area Commands', it would imply that Lagos is regarded as another 'Area Command'. The Commander-in-Chief might not have direct control over any group of soldiers in any 'area' – a very vulnerable situation. Otherwise, the Lagos Garrison can only be interpreted as the Commander-in-Chief's 'Body Guard'.

350

(*f*) Preparation of Statistics by Military Committee. – This can be regarded as a useful exercise as long as there is unfettered and free inspection of all military operations in the regions.

Appointments to Certain Posts

3. There appears to be need for clarification as to the specific categories of officers for the appointment of whom the Supreme Military Council will like to be responsible. It is observed that:

(*a*) whichever category of officers is meant, the effect of this decision will tend to paralyse the functions of the Federal Public and the Police Service Commissions;

(*b*) if Regional Governors have power to appointments, the loyalty of Federal Officers would be to their regions of origin – meaning in effect that there will be no Federal Civil Service;

(*c*) the acceptance of this decision would also require, as the law officers have reported, amendments to those sections in the constitution dealing with appointment to Nigeria Police, Federal Public Service Commission and sections of various acts dealing with appointment in Federal Statutory Corporations;

(*d*) furthermore, it is observed that while Military Governors will have power to appoint, or approve appointments of Federal Government Servants, there is no corresponding power of the Supreme Military Council to even influence the appointments to senior posts in the Regional Public Services. This clearly makes the Federal Military Government subordinate to the Regional Governments.

Powers of the Federal Military Government

4. It is considered that the vesting of the Legislative and Executive Powers in the Supreme Military Council and the introduction of the element of Regional Military Governors' consent in the Federal Legislation will leave the Federal Executive Council with virtually no functions, and the powers of the Federal Military Government vis-a-vis the Regional Military Governments no longer exist. This view has been clearly expressed in the Report of the law officers meeting held recently in Benin; the relevant sections of which report are quoted as follows:

Section 69. – As regards the powers of the Federal Military Government vis-a-vis the Regional Governments, all the Law Officers, excepting those from the East, are of the view that effect would be fully given to the Accra decision in this regard by repealing section 3 of Decree No. 1 and restoring the provisions of the suspended section 69 with necessary modifications whereby the Federal Military Government will now have power to make Decrees to the following extent:

(*a*) With respect to the Federal Territory of Lagos on any matter whatsoever;

(*b*) With respect to the whole of Nigeria, or any part thereof (other than Lagos), on matters included in the Exclusive Legislative List and the

Concurrent Legislative List; provided that where there is an inconsistency between a Federal Decree on a Concurrent matter and a Regional Edict on the same matter, the Federal Decree will prevail.

Under this arrangement the Military Governors will have no power to make Edicts on matters on the Exclusive Legislative List but will have powers to make Edicts on matters in the Concurrent Legislative List on residual matters.

The view of the Eastern Law Officers is that the introduction of the element of Regional consent in Federal Legislation must necessarily modify the position as it was before January 17th in the sense that there will be a lacuna in the legislative activities of both the Supreme Military Council and the Regions where consent is not given. It appears therefore to be the intention of the Accra decision that such a lacuna should be filled by the Regions. With respect to matters on the Concurrent Legislative List, it is their view that the Regions can legislate without Federal consent and without any fear of repugnancy in relation to Federal law. With respect to matters in the Exclusive Legislative List, they have proposed that the Supreme Military Council be asked to elucidate the position. They have adopted this approach because the Accra decision does not appear to have made any distinction between both the Exclusive and the Concurrent Legislative Lists.

<h2 style="text-align:center">Section 8 of Decree No. 1</h2>

(*a*) This section deals with the composition of the Supreme Military Council and the Federal Executive Council...

(*b*) Subsection (v) of the section at present provides, *inter alia*, that the Supreme Military Council and the Federal Executive Council may act notwithstanding any vacancy in their membership or the absence of any member...

(*c*) It is understood that one of the Accra agreements is to the effect that all legislative and executive authority is now to be vested in the Supreme Military Council. It is not known, however, whether in the light of this decision it is still the intention to retain the Federal Executive Council as a body separate and distinct from the Supreme Military Council. If, however, the intention is to retain the Federal Executive Council then in regard to that body, some answers for the purpose of clarity and the avoidance of any doubts or argument in the future will have to be provided to questions similar to those already raised...

The questions raised are quoted:

(i) Whether it is the intention of the Accra agreement that a meeting of the Supreme Military Council will not be properly constituted and so cannot properly be held unless all the Military Governors are present.

(ii) Whether where all the Military Governors are present at a meeting of the Supreme Military Council decisions of the Council can properly be taken only with the concurrence or unanimity of all the Military Governors, or by a majority of the Military Governors, or else by a majority of all the members present.

(iii) Whether where one or more Military Governors are present at any meeting of the Supreme Military Council their concurrence in decisions taken at such a meeting will still be necessary before such decision can be implemented.

(iv) Whether all Decrees (whether affecting the whole country or not) are to be formally approved by the Supreme Military Council before they are signed by the Head of the Federal Military Government.

(v) In what manner should the concurrence of the Military Governors in the making of Decrees (in their capacity as members of the Supreme Military Council) be signified, that is, for instance, whether it will be enough for this to be signified orally in the course of a meeting of the Supreme Military Council or by writing under their respective hands or whether there should be a column in the Decree for the appending of signatures.

In the light of the implications of the Accra decisions as quoted above:

(a) the recommendations of the Law Officers should be adopted, i.e., the powers and functions of the Federal Government as contained in the Exclusive and Concurrent Legislative Lists should be restored;

(b) the Law Officers should confine themselves to only those decrees which tend to over-centralize the administration.

Composition of the Federal Military Government

5. The decision that the civilians should not be associated with the Federal Military Government for the next six months is incompatible with the various promises which the Supreme Commander has made to the Nation in this regard. Civilians including ex-politicians are closely associated with Military Governors in the running of the Regional Military Government. There is, therefore, a clear need to associate reputable Nigerians with the Federal Executive Council as previously recommended in the summary:

(a) A provisional Federal Government should be established immediately comprising –

(1) The Supreme Commander of the Armed Forces (Chairman).

(2) The Head of the Navy, Army, Air Force, Police.

(3) Three civilian members each from the East, Mid-West, North, West and one from Lagos.

(4) Attorney-General of the Federation.

(b) The civilians must be people who were not actively involved in politics in the past five years, of undoubted integrity and independent character.

(c) They will, on oath and by their instrument of appointment, be debarred from seeking political office for at least five years.

(d) They will be appointed by the Supreme Commander and the Head of the Federal Military Government himself.

(e) The civilian members will be assigned Portfolios as Commissioners.

Soldiers in Detention

6. It is considered that the determination of the fate of the soldiers in detention should be done after assessing the possible reactions of the rank and file in the Army. This is necessary to avert any adverse repercussions.

Ad Hoc Constitutional Conference

7. It is considered that the 'Accra Decisions' – in so far as they tend towards strengthening the Regions at the expense of the Federal Government and hence towards the setting up of a Confederal System of Government – are incompatible with the unanimous decisions of the Ad Hoc Constitutional Conference. It seems more advisable, therefore to stick to previous recommendations and advice to the Supreme Commander, *viz:*

(*a*) that the Ad Hoc Constitutional Conference should stand adjourned indefinitely;

(*b*) that the immediate political programme announced to the nation on 30th November, 1966 by the Supreme Commander should be implemented and the country must be so informed.

'Problems of displaced persons'

8. It is suggested that:

(*a*) When the meeting of Permanent Secretaries of the Ministries of Finance resumes, the principle of revenue allocation should not be discussed as it was not mentioned in the minutes of the Accra Meeting.

(*b*) The decision to continue to pay salaries till the end of March, 1967, does not take into consideration economic factors which are linked with it. For instance, the railways are not fully running and cannot earn enough revenue with which to pay their servants who are not working. The Posts and Telegraphs is in the same plight and the Federal Ministry of Finance has indicated its inability to make additional financial provision for this purpose. Secondly, it does not make sense to include daily paid workers among those whose salaries should continue to be paid. The decision should therefore be reconsidered.

(*c*) That there is no reason to leave out the Military Governor of the North from sending representatives to discuss the problem of the recovery of property because Northerners who left the East also left their property behind.

Summary of Conclusions and Recommendations

9. (*a*) If the adoption of the title Commander-in-Chief declares the post of Supreme Commander vacant, serious instability would result from political and military manoeuvres to fill the post.

(*b*) The creation of Area Commands without any unified and effective Central control of the Nigerian Army has serious political implications: internally, because of the vulnerable position of the Commander-in-Chief or Supreme Commander and the status of minorities; externally, because no single authority is vested with the power to use the Army for defence against external aggression. Acceptance of the Accra meeting's decision would require amendments to the Armed Forces Acts and the Constitution.

(c) To avert possible repercussions, the determination of the fate of soldiers in detention should be done after assessing the possible reactions of the rank and file of the Army.

(d) The decision to appoint or approve appointments of Federal Public Servants, will not only paralyse the Federal Public and Police Service Commissions, but will also create Regional loyalties among Federal Public Servants.

(e) The decision that displaced persons should continue to receive their salaries till the end of March, 1967, should be reconsidered for economic reasons.

(f) The vesting of executive powers of the Federal Military Government on the Supreme Military Council with the introduction of the element of consent of the Regional Military Governors makes the Federal Military Government subordinate to the regional Military Governments and this amounts to accepting Confederation. The powers of the Federal Government as contained in the Exclusive and Concurrent Lists should be restored as recommended by the law officers.

(g) The Ad Hoc Constitutional Conference should stand adjourned indefinitely and the immediate political programme announced by the Supreme Commander to the nation on 30th November, 1966, should be implemented.

(h) There is a clear need to associate reputable civilians with the Federal Executive Council as previously recommended and the nation should be so informed.

INDEX OF NAMES

Abubakar Tafawa Balewa, Sir
    assassinated January 1966, 21–2, 31, 34–5; chooses Ironsi as GOC, 243; fails to deal with Western Region crisis, 1965–6, 219, 250; handles military with caution, 104, 230, 243; myths surrounding death of, 267, 271; plays down intelligence reports, January coup, 18; political role as Prime Minister of Federation, 211–13, 216–17, 227 n, 288
Adamu, M. P. S.
    background and military career, 345; conspirator, July 1966, 65, 67 n, 70–1
Adebayo, R. A.
    absent in January 1966, 44; background, 112, 343; military career, 99 n, 129, 175, 240–1, 299 n, 343; Military Governor, Western Region, 106, 195, 291, 296, 316, 320, 323, 332–7; political opinions, 291; professional outlook, 149
Adekunle, B.
    background, 344; division commander, civil war, 107, 157, 339; military career, 125, 175, 344
Ademola, Sir Adetokunboh, Chief Justice, Federation of Nigeria
    part in negotiations, July 1966, 67
Ademoyega, A.
    background, 43, 48, 345; conspirator, January 1966, 18, 28; military career, 28 n, 36, 126 n, 135, 174–5, 240–1, 345
Ademulegun, S. A.
    assassinated January 1966, 23, 32, 35, 42, 51, 84; background, 112, 343; commander, 1st Brigade, 32, 104; military career, 99, 166, 175, 186 n, 240–1, 343; political links, 42, 104, 107, 241–2, 250; rivalry with Ironsi, 239–40, 243; role January 1966, 19
Ahmadu Bello, Alhaji Sir, Sardauna of Sokoto
    assassinated January 1966, 23, 31–2, 34–5, 84, 267; attitude of Northerners to death of, 58, 267, 271, 327; links with military, 42, 104, 242; nominees for GOC not chosen, 243; as Premier of Northern Region, 211 n, 223–4, 326–7; recruitment drive for Northern officers, 185, 244; role January 1966, 19–20, 41; support for Chief Akintola in Western Region crisis, 1965–6, 19–20, 41–2, 250
Akagha, F. E.
    background and military career, 175, 344; role January 1966, 23–4, 26–7, 29; under Ironsi regime, 56, 60
Akahan, J. R.
    background, 185, 344; military career, 51, 56–7, 175, 321, 344; professional outlook, 109–11, 119; role July 1966, 67 n, 71, 259
Akilu, Alhaji Ali
    heads interim administration of North, January 1966, 266; under Ironsi regime, 60 n, 266–7, 277
Akintola, Chief S. L.
    assassinated January 1966, 21, 32–5; and census, 213–14; and Kano riots 1953, 210; links with military, 242; myths surrounding death of, 267; as Premier, Western Region, 212–14, 218–19; role January 1966, 19–20, 41; and tribalism, 214, 223, 228; and Western Region election crisis, 1965, 19–20, 41–2, 218–19, 250; and Western Region emergency, 1962, 212, 249
Alao, S. A.
    background and military career, 175, 345; conspirator, July 1966, 63, 65, 67, 70–1, 76
Ankrah, J. A.
    at Aburi meeting of military leaders, 289–90; and National Liberation Council in Ghana, 30–1
Anuforo, C. I.
    assassinated August 1966, 91 n, 305; background and military career, 30, 133, 175, 192, 240–1, 344; conspirator, January 1966, 18, 28, 35

357

Index of names

Anwuna, P. A. O.
    background and military career, 344; professional outlook, 153, 282; role and survival January 1966, 29n, 45–6, 52; under Ironsi regime, 53, 277, 282

Arikpo, Okoi
    civilian commissioner, June 1967, 323; and Eastern minorities, 331; and National Conciliation Committee, May 1967, 320n

Awolowo, Chief Obafemi
    in Ad Hoc Committee, 311, 313–14, 332; attacks Anglo–Nigeria Defence Agreement, 232; Banjo attempts intrigue with, August 1967, 41; civilian commissioner, June 1967, 323; controls Western Region after August 1966, 106, 296, 316, 320, 332–4; imprisoned after Western Region crisis, 1962, 212, 218; January conspirators plan to make President, 42, 285; release from prison refused by Ironsi, granted by Gowon, 256, 296; threatens to withdraw West from Nigeria, 316, 320, 322, 332–4, 336–7, wooed back by Gowon, 323, 334

Azikiwe, Dr Nnamdi
    absent January 1966, 24; attempts to obtain military backing for constitutional *putsch*, 1964–5, 215–17, 237–8; consulted by Ojukwu, 329; links with military, 104, 112, 238; removed by Ojukwu as Chancellor, University of Nigeria, 269n

Banjo, V. A.
    background and military career, 36n, 175, 343; discusses intervention during 1964 election crisis, 238; executed for plotting against Ojukwu, September 1967, 41, 146, 325, 330; political links, 39; role in invasion of Mid-West, August 1967, 40–1, 146, 325; role in January 1966, 26, 28–9, 36, 39, 44–6

Bassey, W. U.
    background and military career, 56, 91n, 133n, 147n, 186n, 343; survival January 1966, 24, 26n, 32, 45; survival July 1966, 66n

Biobaku, Dr S.
    dispute over appointment as Vice-Chancellor, University of Lagos, 217, 228

Chukuka, I. H.
    background and military career, 30, 36, 133, 141, 174n, 175, 240–1, 344; conspirator, January 1966, 17, 28, 35

Danjuma, T. Y.
    background and military career, 175, 345; conspirator, July 1966, 63, 65, 67n, 71, 74

Dike, Dr K.
    and tribalism, 278

Effiong, P.
    background and military career, 175, 343; Chief of Staff of Biafran army, 329–30; and minorities in Biafra, 330n

Ejoor, D. A.
    attempts unsuccessfully to secure Mid-West neutrality in civil conflict, 105, 133, 195, 305, 320, 325, 335–6; background and military career, 92n, 99, 175, 299n, 343; Banjo attempts intrigue with, August, 1967, 41, 325; discusses intervention during 1964 election crisis, 238; as Military Governor, Mid-West, 195, 254–5, 277n, 296, 335–6; political beliefs, 277n, 281–2, 285, 290–1; professional outlook, 128–9, 133, 153–4, 281–2; survives and assists Ironsi, January 1966, 20n, 22, 26n, 45–6

Ekanem
    assassinated, August 1966, 69; background and career, 344

Ekpo, E.
    background and military career, 175, 313, 344; and Eastern minorities in federal army, 313

Ekwensi, Cyprian
    Director of Information, Eastern Region and Biafra, 301–2

Elias, Dr T. O.
    removed as Attorney General by Ironsi, 268; member Ad Hoc Committee, 313n

358

Enahoro, Chief A.
in Ad Hoc Committee, 311, 313; civilian commissioner, June 1967, 323; imprisoned, 212; release from prison refused by Ironsi, granted by Gowon, 256, 296; self-government in 1956 motion, 210; support for Federation and minorities, 334–5

Enahoro, P.
editorial comments on North under Ironsi, 261; writes about violence, July 1966, 304 n

Eze, A. O.
background and military career, 344; escapes assassination, July 1966, 304; in nucleus Biafran army, 329; professional outlook, 126

Fajuyi, F.
assassination, July 1966, 52, 65, 91 n; background 112, 343; on leave, January 1966, 20, 44–6; military career, 175, 343; Military Governor, Western Region, 254, 256, 261–3, 271 n; political opinions, 289

Galadima, Alhaji Tako
Minister of State, Army, 242, 244–5

Gbulie, B. N.
background and military career, 30, 133, 175, 346; conspirator, January 1966, 18, 28

Gowon, Y.
advises against intervention during 1964 election crisis, 238 n; agrees to Decree no. 34, 266; aids Ironsi, January 1966, 22, 25; assumes power, July 1966, 68, 83, 147–9, 298–9; authority rejected by Ojukwu, 68, 77 n, 105, 147–50, 298–9, 304, 317–18; authority routinised, 75, 105, 304–5, 315; background, 112, 129, 181, 184–5; chief of staff under Ironsi, 53, 56, 254, 259, 269; conciliatory posture in civil conflict, 302–3; convenes and dismisses Ad Hoc Committee, 311, 313–16; handling of autumn 1966 massacres, 305–10; investigations into January 1966 coup, 53; leadership holds Federation together, 312, 316–18, 321–5, 334; military career, 99, 175, 192, 269, 343; and minorities, 221, 313, 322–3; orders military burial for Nzeogwu, 128; political opinions, 291–2; role in July 1966, 11, 30, 62–3, 65, 67–71, 259; on shortcomings of military regime, 114, 306; takes Nigeria into civil war, 322–5, 336–7, 339–40

Haruna, I. B. M.
background and military career, 175, 345; division commander, civil war, 339

Ifeajuna, E. A.
background, 39, 47, 104, 344; conspirator, January 1966, vii, 17–18, 21–2, 27–8, 35; escapes to Ghana, 22, 35, 42 n, 43 n; failure to carry through coup in south, 22, 35, 44, 47; and Maimalari, 18 n, 35, 158; military career, 30, 35–6, 104, 135, 175, 240–1, 344; executed for plotting against Ojukwu, August 1967, 40–1, 325, 330; political opinions and links, 36, 39–43, 286; professional outlook, 121–2, 125, 158, 247, 286

Igboba, H.
aids Ironsi, January 1966, 27 n; background and military career, 56–7, 344; escapes to Mid-West July 1966, 335 n

Imam, Alhaji Ibrahim
opposes unitary constitution, 270

Imo, U. O.
background and military career, 46, 56 n, 147 n, 299 n, 343; in nucleus Biafran army, 329–30; survives January 1966, 46, 52

Inuwa Wada, Alhaji
links with Northern soldiers, 59 n, 112, 310 n; Minister of Defence, 103, 242

Ironsi, J. T. U. Aguiyi
assassinated July 1966, 63, 65, 68–9, 91 n; assumes power, 25–6, 252; attempts to unify Nigeria, 60–1, 259, 264–6, 272, 275–7, 286–7; attitude of Northerners to, 61, 243, 257, 266–70, 272; background, 112, 253, 343; ignores minorities, 194, 269–70; military career, 99 n, 100–1, 166, 175, 186 n, 191 n, 234, 238, 240–1, 243, 253, 343; political opinions, 104, 203, 252–4, 276–7, 280–7, 291–2; political shortcomings, 49, 53, 101, 194, 203, 252–3, 236–9, 265–6, 276–8, 288, 292; and politicians before January coup, 18–19, 46–7, 191 n, 238–43, 250–1; professional outlook, 92–3,

104, 132, 157, 250, 291–2; regime of, chapter XI, 280–1, 283–9, 291–5; relations with other officers, 166, 239–40, 253; succession to, 147, 298–9; survives and stages counter-coup, January 1966, 21–9, 31–4, 44–7, 83; and tribalism, 28, 46–7, 51–2, 56–7, 60, 104, 257, 259, 268–9, 277

Johnson, Mabolaji
at Aburi meeting of military leaders, 148–9, 258n, 290–1; background and military career, 175, 345; escapes influence of Awolowo, 333; Military Administrator of Lagos, 254, 258n; political opinions, 290

Kano, Alhaji Aminu
in Ad Hoc Committee, 311, 313; civilian commissioner, 323; influence in North after July 1966, 106, 326; leader of NEPU, 214; overtures to Ironsi ignored, 256, 269–70
Kano, Emir of
appointed Chancellor, University of Nigeria, by Ojukwu, 269n; attempts to halt Northern massacres, 272
Katsina, Emir of
slander of by East, 301–2; sons of in army, 112
Katsina, Hassan Usman
background, 112, 184–5, 269, 283; military career, 56, 112, 175, 192, 339, 344; as Military Governor of North, 27, 52–3, 60, 254, 257–9, 263–4, 266–7, 269, 271, 274–7, 309–10, 326–8; omitted from July 1966 conspiracy, 63, 71, 259; and political alignment of North before civil war, 316, 320–1, 327; political opinions, 52, 259, 266, 276, 283–4, 286, 289, 291, 294–5, 316n; professional outlook, 126, 129, 149, 276, 289; role and survival January 1966, 21, 23, 26–7, 29–30, 46, 266; trouble-shooting in army, 1966–7, 309n, 316, 321
Keshi, A.
background and military career, 104, 344; role January 1966, 23n, 26
Kurobo, G.
background and military career, 56n, 92n, 102n, 175, 343; role and survival January 1966, 20, 29n, 45–6

Largema, A.
assassinated, January 1966, 21, 26, 32, 45; background and military career, 175, 343; political links, 19–20, 242; reaction of Northern soldiers to death of, 26, 51, 57; role January 1966, 19–20

Maimalari, Z.
assassinated January 1966, 21, 32, 35, 42, 45; background and military career, 99n, 133, 175, 192, 232n, 240–1, 246, 343; as commander, 104, 157–8; favoured by Northern politicians, 243, 246; and Ifeajuna, 18n, 35, 104, 158; myths among Northern soldiers about death of, 51–2, 68–9, 84, 267, 271; plays down reports of coup, 18n, 25; political opinions, 107, 239–40, 250; professional outlook, 250; quarrels with Ironsi, 239–40; role Western Region crisis, 1962, 42, 249
Mojekwu, C. C.
in Ad Hoc Committee, 313n; advice to Azikiwe in 1964 election crisis, 216n; advisor to Ojukwu, 329
Mohammed, Kuru
assassinated January 1966, 21, 32, 35, 45; background and military career, 32, 99n, 175, 192, 240–1, 343; reaction of Northern soldiers to death of, 51
Mohammed, Muritala
advocates invasion of East, 304–5, 313, 315; advocates secession of North, 61; authority rivals Gowon's, 71, 75, 304–5, 315; background, 111–12, 345; conspirator, July 1966, 63–5, 70–1, 75; division commander, civil war, 107, 339; military career, 57, 175, 345; political links, 59, 111–12, 310n, 313, 333

Njoku, H.
background and military career, 99n, 299n, 343; commander 2nd Brigade under Ironsi, 56n, 147n, 175, 257n; in nucleus Biafran army and jettisoned by Ojukwu, 329–30; role and survival January 1966, 21–2, 25–7, 45–7, 52; survival July 1966, 65

Njoku, Dr Eni
  in Ad Hoc Committee, 313 n; advisor to Ojukwu, 329; appointed to tribunal investigating May
  1966 massacres, 275; replaced as Vice-Chancellor, University of Lagos, 217, 228
Nwawo, C. D.
  absent January 1966, 43; background and military career, 343; role in Mid-West invasion, 1967,
  133, 325, 335–6; takes Nzeogwu into custody, 27
Nwobosi, E. N.
  background and military career, 30, 133, 141, 175, 346; conspirator, January 1966, 21, 28, 33, 35
Nwokedi, F. C.
  advisor to Ironsi on national unification, 257 n, 264, 268, 270
Nzefili, M.
  background and military career, 344; escapes to Mid-West, July 1966; temporarily in charge 4th
  Battalion after January coup, 26, 56
Nzeogwu, C. K.
  attitudes to authority, 24, 27, 30–5, 83; background and military career, 30, 36, 38, 133, 141, 175,
  240–1, 344; blames associates for failure of January coup, 35, 44, 47; conspirator, January 1966,
  17–18, 20 n, 23, 27–8, 30–5, 44, 56, 102; death in war and burial, 128; interim administration,
  Kaduna, January 1966, 23–4, 27, 254, 266, 280–3; opposes Biafran secession, 40, 330; political
  opinions and links, 32–3, 36, 39–42, 254, 280–7, 292; professional outlook, 125; surrenders to
  Ironsi, 26–7, 31, 83; and tribalism in January coup, 44, 47–8, 50

Obienu, J.
  assassinated July 1966, 64; background and military career, 46, 56, 192, 345; role January 1966,
  21, 26, 30, 46
Ogundipe, B. A. O.
  abroad January 1966, 44, 91; background and military career, 66, 91 n, 99 n, 175, 239–41, 243,
  246; fails to re-establish control during July 1966 coup, 65–6, 68, 147–9, 299
Ogunewe, D. S.
  background and military career, 56, 175, 344; doubts about Biafran secession, 329–30; keeps
  control 1st Battalion, Enugu, July 1966, 66, 75, 329
Oji, O.
  background and military career, 175, 240–1, 346; conspirator, January 1966, 17–18, 22, 28
Ojukwu, O.
  background and military career, 36, 39, 99 n, 112, 129, 175, 343; Biafran secession and civil war,
  part in, 303, 318–19, 322, 324–30; considers intervention during 1964 election crisis, 17, 135,
  328; handling of Eastern minorities, 330–2; image as regional rather than tribal leader, 195, 296,
  330–2; keeps control Eastern Region, July 1966, 66–7, 75, 304; as Military Governor, Eastern
  Region, under Ironsi, 254, 277 n, 281–2; plot against, September 1967, 325, 330; political links
  and opinions, 112, 282, 284, 288, 290–2, 312 n, 329; posture toward North after July 1966 coup,
  77, 127, 299–303, 306–9; professional outlook, 127, 129, 147–50, 281–2, 329–30; rejects Gowon's
  authority, 68, 77 n, 105, 147–50, 298–9, 304, 306; role and survival January 1966, 21, 24, 26–8,
  45–6; role July 1966, 61, 65–7; strategies in constitutional negotiations, 303, 311 n, 314–15,
  317–22, 324, 328, 336–8; use of propaganda, 300–2, 309 n, 330–1
Okafor, D. O.
  assassinated August 1966, 69, 91 n, 305; background and military career, 36–7, 104, 141, 175,
  240–1, 344; conspirator, January 1966, 17–18, 20, 28, 35, 46, 135; failure to carry coup through
  in south, 22, 25–6, 44, 47
Okigbo, Dr Pius
  economic advisor to Ironsi, 257 n, 294 n
Okonweze, G.
  assassinated July 1966, 64; background and military career, 56 n, 175, 344; role January 1966, 22,
  26 n, 52
Okoro, I.
  assassinated July 1966, 66; background and military career, 56 n, 175, 344; role January 1966,
  23 n, 26, 29 n; under Ironsi, 60, 257, 277
Okotie-Eboh, Chief, F. S.
  assassinated January 1966, 21–2, 35, 267; Minister of Finance, 224

Index of names

Okpara, Dr M. I.
advisor to Ojukwu, 106, 311, 329; Premier, Eastern Region, 213; survives January 1966, 22, 32, 35, 43-4
Olutoye, O.
aligns with Awolowo, 320-1, 333; background and military career, 299 n, 320 n, 344
Onwuatuegwu, T.
background and career, 30, 36, 133, 141, 174-5, 240-1, 344; conspirator, January 1966, 18, 23, 28, 35
Onyiuke, G. C. M.
advisor to Ojukwu, 329-30; Attorney General under Ironsi, 257 n, 268
Osadebay, D. C.
Premier of Mid-West, survives January 1966, 32, 35, 43

Pam, J. Y.
assassinated January 1966, 21, 32, 35, 45, 51; background and military career, 99 n, 175, 192, 343; professional outlook, 119, 152

Ribadu, Alhaji Muhammadu
as Minister of Defence, 103, 236-7, 242-3; and regional quota, 188-9, 243-4, 246

Sardauna of Sokoto
see Ahmadu Bello, Alhaji Sir
Shodeinde, R. A.
assassinated January 1966, 23, 32-3, 35, 45, 51, 84; background and military career, 112, 175, 186 n, 240-1, 343
Shuwa, Mohammed
background and career, 56, 175, 344; division commander, civil war, 157, 339; role July 1966, 67 n, 71
Sultan of Sokoto
attempts to halt Northern massacres, 272; Ironsi seeks support in North through, 269

Tarka, J.
in Ad Hoc Committee, 311, 313; civilian commissioner, 323; leader, Northern minorities, 106, 270, 313-14, 326; overtures to Ironsi ignored, 256, 267 n, 269-70

Ude, G.
background and military career, 344; conspirator, January 1966, 18, 23, 28
Udeaja, E.
background and military career, 30, 133, 174-5, 344; conspirator, January 1966, 28
Unegbe, A.
assassinated January 1966, 21, 32, 45, 47; career, 99 n, 175, 343
Usuman, B. M.
background and military career, 345; conspirator, July 1966, 65, 67, 70-1

Welby-Everard, Sir C.
advises against Ironsi as GOC, 243; declines Azikiwe's instructions, 1964 election crisis, 237-8; as GOC, 38 n, 169 n
Wey, J. E.
declines Azikiwe's instructions, 1964 election crisis, 237-8; political opinions, 148-9; under Ironsi, 254
Wey, S. O.
Secretary of Military Government under Ironsi, 255 n, 257 n, 268 n

INDEX OF AUTHORS

Abrahamsson, B., 236n, 237n
Abrams, P., 154n, 160n
Ambler, J. S., 302n

Barnard, C. L., 3
Bascom, W. R., 114n, 168n
Bauer, P. T., 207n
Becker, H. S., 12n
Blackburn, R., 84n
Blau, P. M. and Scott, R. W., 85n, 103n, 131n, 143n
Bohannan, P. 220n

Clark, J. Pepper, 42n
Cohen, R., 168n
Colas, J. N., xiii, 28n
Coleman, J. S., 108n, 190
Coleman, J. S., 188n, 207n
Cooley, C. H., 193n
Coser, L., 190n, 338n
Crozier, M., 150

Dahrendorf, R., 145n
Demeter, K., 128n
Dent, M. J., xiii, 22n, 25–6n, 42n, 47n, 59n, 66n, 67n, 69n, 220n, 243n, 246n, 270n, 288n, 309n
Deutsch, K. W., 6n, 9n, 201n
Downs, A., 101n
Dudley, B. J., xiii, 25n, 42n, 208n, 222n, 224n, 226n, 273n, 333n
Durkheim, Emile, 171–4

Easton, D., 7n, 9n, 201n
Ejindu, D. D., 27n, 281n
Elliot-Bateman, M., 338n
Ezera, K., 208n

Fallers, L., 114n, 167n
Fanon, Franz, 39
Festinger, L., 126
Finer, S. E., xiii, 4–5, 94n, 260n
Foster, P., xiii, 111n, 115n
Furnivall, J. S., 206n

Geertz, C., 114n, 177n, 193n, 194n, 207, 222n, 280n
Gottschalk, L., 11n

Gouldner, A. W., 164n
Graham-Douglas, N. B., 330n, 331n
Grusky, O., 170n
Guttsman, W., 127n

Halpern, B. J., 94n
Heider, F., 48n
Hobbes, T., 299
Hochuth, Rolf, 279
Hodgkin, T., 206n
Horton, R., 331n
Huntington, S. P., 5–6, 101n, 247n

Jahoda, G., 120n
Janowitz, M., xiii, 5–6, 36n, 93–4n, 99n, 104n, 118n, 119n, 124, 126n, 202n, 236n, 256n, 260n, 279n
    and Little, Lt Colonel R., 85n, 145n, 153n, 154n
Johnson, J. J., 94n

Katz, D., 276n
Keatley, P., 19n
Keay, E. A., 255n, 265n, 293n
Kerr, C. and Siegel, A., 108n
Khan, General M. Ayub, 172–3
Kilson, M., 168n
Kim, C. I. E., 131n
Kornhauser, W., 108n, 221n, 271n

Lasswell, H., 287n
Lawson, R., 248n
LeVine, R., 48n, 188n
Lenin, V. I., 49
Lerner, D. and Robinson, R. D., 94n
Lloyd, P. C., 178n, 207n
Luckham, A. R., 8n, 242n
Luttwak, E. N., 19n, 49n, 59n

Mackintosh, J. P., 208n, 209n, 216n, 227n, 232n
Mao Tse Tung, 39, 338
March, J. G. and Simon, H. A., 101n, 285n, 295n
Marx, Karl, xi, 39, 324
Mead, G. H., 193n
Merton, R. K., 85n, 173n, 174n
Miners, N. J., xiii, 184, 233n

Index of authors

Mitchell, J. C., 193n
Morgan, R. W., 124n

O'Brien, C. Cruise, 248n
O'Connell, Fr J., xiii, 208n, 309n
Odumosu, O. I., 208n
Okedeji, F. O., 121n
Okot p'Bitek, 125n
Otley, C. B., 104n, 112n, 119n, 127n

Panter-Brick, S. K., xiii, 40n, 59n, 315n
Parsons, Talcott, 84n, 119n
Perlmutter, A., 152n
Phillips, C. S., 232n
Plotnikov, L., 178n
Putnam, R., 7n
Pye, L. W., 2n, 94n

Roethlisberger, F. J. and Dickson, W. J., 131n

Schwartz, W., 68n
Selznick, D., 287n
Shils, E. A., 119n, 131n
    and Janowitz, M., 143n, 206n
Simmel, Georg, 108, 189n, 338n

Sklar, R. L., 96, 207n, 212n, 216n, 221n, 226n, 258n, 273n
Smelser, N. J., 52n, 70n, 84n
Smith, M. G., 14n, 114n, 167n, 168n, 222n
Smock, M. C., 222n
Smythe, H. H. and Smythe, M. M., 111n
Solarin, Tai, 20n, 41–2n, 50n, 284–5
Soyinka, Wole, vi, xi, 115

Thomas, W. I., 193n

Van Doorn, J. A., 132n
Vatikiotis, P. J., 131n

Warren, W. H., 227n
Webb, E. J., 12n
Weber, Max, xi–xii, 85n, 145n, 150–1, 161, 164
Whitaker, C. S. Jr, 224n
Wood, D., 89n
Worthy, J. C., 158n

Young, C., 190n

Zolberg, A. R., 1–2n, 63n

INDEX OF SUBJECTS

Aburi, meeting of Nigerian military leaders at, 11, 52, 147–50, 258 n, 289–91, 296–7, 298–300, 312, 315–19, 328, 335, 337, Appendix 2

Action Group, *see also* Awolowo, Western Region
in civilian politics, 96, 209–12, 214–19, 249–50
and January coup, 19, 42, 84, 249–50, 285
resurgence under military rule, 106, 332–3

Ad Hoc Committee on the Nigerian Constitution, 186, 290–1, 309–10, 312–16, 320, 327, 330–2, 334–5, 348, 354

Age-structure, of Nigerian Army
compared with other elite groups, 77–99, 101
consequences for authority, 164–7
distorted after January coup, 53–4
effect of indigenisation on, 164–5
relation to other variables, 7, 87

Anglo–Nigeria Defence Agreement, 231–2

Anomie
defined, 171 n, 172 n
mobility in army and, 168–76
modernisation and, 2

Armies and civil–military relations, compared with Nigerian
African, 19, 88–90
American, 99, 104, 124, 126 n, 236 n, 145 n, 153 n, 154 n, 170 n
Argentinian, 5
British, 3–4, 112 n, 119–20, 122, 127, 236 n, 151, 154, 160, 166–7, 247, 338
Chinese, 338 n
Congolese, 190 n, 247–8
Dominican Republic, 5
Egyptian, 131
French, 90, 202 n
German, 6, 127–8, 131 n, 143 n
Ghanaian, 49
Greek, 5
Israeli, 152 n
Japanese, 6
Latin American, 7 n, 94 n
Pakistani, 172 n
South Korean, 131–2
Swedish, 236 n, 237 n
Syrian, 6
Turkish, 6, 94 n

Army, Nigerian, *see also* age structure, authority, boundaries, brotherhood, civilian control, cleavage, cohesion, cohorts, command, coups and mutinies, culture, discipline, education, elite, format, functional analysis, hierarchy, honour, indigenisation, initiative, military, mobility, Non-Commissioned Officers, Other Ranks, peer groups, primordialism, professionalism, promotions, recruitment, revolt, security, seniority, size, skills, socialisation, social system, solidarity, staff, status, strain, structure, training

general: assumption of power by, 25–6, 252; and civilian riots of 1966, 273–4, 305–10; and civil war, 93–4, 97, 338–9; composition, ethnic and regional, *see* ethnicity, region; expenditures, 89, 235–6; numbers, *see* size; operational experience, 88, 231–6, 247–51, 338–9; organisational support for Federation before civil war, 296–7, 311–13, 315–17, 321–2; politicisation of, 17, 36–42, 48–9, 51–60, 103–8, 226–9, 230–1, 237–51, 257–9, 267–8, 275–8, Chapter XII, 298–9, 304–7, 309–10, 312–16, 320–3; subdivision on regional lines proposed, 105–7, 315, 317–18, 320, 338–9, 348–51

Area Commands, 105–7, 320, 329, 333, 335

Battalions, general: command changes after January coup, 56–7; dispositions, xiv, 101–2, 105–6, 155, 306, 316; loyalties to, 139–40; movements in January coup, 20–4, 26–7, 33–4; rotation, 102, 275

1st Battalion, Enugu: not involved, January coup, 22, 33–4; not involved, July coup, 66–7, 75–6; nucleus, Biafran army, 105, 304, 328–9, 337

2nd Battalion, Ikeja: controlled by Ironsi January, 25; part in July coup, 64–6, 305; use in Western Region, 1962, 42, 249

3rd Battalion, Kaduna: in Congo, 249; in January coup, 23, 27; in July coup, 66; transfer to Ibadan after July, 106, 155, 316, 333

4th Battalion, Ibadan: not involved, January coup, 20, 22, 33–4; in July coup, 64–5, 71, 275, 305; NCOs incensed by killing of commander, January 1966, 26, 51; in Northern riots, 305–6; transfer to Kaduna after July 1966, 155, 305–6; use in Western Region, 1962, 249

Index of subjects

Army, Nigerian (*cont.*)

5th Battalion, Kano: careers of conspirators intersect in, 28, 141; not involved, January coup, 21, 24; in July coup, 66, 71; mutiny of, October 1966, 305–9

Brigades: in January, 18–19, 23, 28, 32–3; in July, 64–6, 71; organisation of, xiv, 56–7, 101–2, 105–6, 155

Depot, Zaria: careers of conspirators intersect in, 28, 141; in January coup, 23–4, 29, 36; in July coup, 66; links with Northern schools, 187

Federal Guard: establishment, 234; in January coup, 20–2, 28, 33; in July coup, 64–6; NCOs of incensed by January killings, 22, 25–6, 51

Garrison, Abeokuta: in July coup, 62–4

Lagos Garrison Organisation: in January coup, 21; in July coup, 65–6

Nigerian Defence Academy: establishment, 232, 235, 246; training at, 109, 135, 156–7, 159–60, 246

Nigerian Military School: careers of conspirators intersect in, 28, 141; establishment and training at, 132, 234–5, 244; in January coup, 18, 23, 28, 30, 32–3, 36, 38

Recce Squadrons: establishment and dispositions, xiv, 235

1st Recce Squadron, Kaduna: in January coup, 22, 23, 27; in July coup, 66

2nd Recce Squadron, Abeokuta: in January coup, 21, 30, 33–4; in July coup, 64–5

Assistance, military

granted to: Tanzania, 237; Congo, 237, 247–50

sources of: and civil war, 338–40; diversification in, 231–2

Authority, military, *see also* command, coups and mutinies, hierarchy, initiative, legitimacy, revolt, status

authoritarianism and, 154–7

charismatic and rational–legal, 3, 150–3, 159–62, 291–3, 304

cohesion related to, 85–7, 143–4, 227–9

crisis of, in Nigerian Army, 1–3, 9–10, 13, 53–4, 86–7, 304–10

effect of rapid indigenisation on, 164–8, 170, 173–6; *see also* indigenisation

factors maintaining, 13, 137–8, 143–5, 159–62, 179–80

fragmentation of, regional and ethnic, 1–2, 104–8, 204–5, 289, 295–7

hierarchy related to, 147–51, 153–62; *see also* hierarchy

'ineffectiveness in specific instances', 3, 161–2

initiative related to, 145–6, 150–3, 161–2, 291–3; *see also* initiative, revolt

maintained in midst of rebellion, 30–, 68–75, 83; *see also* coups and mutinies

revolt against, 145–7; *see also* coups and mutinies, hostility, revolt

routinisation of, 3, 74–5, 146–7, 304–5

subordinates and, 85–6, 150–3

Behaviour

hostile: *see also* anomie, coups and mutinies, riots, strain, violence; instances of, in military, 22, 25–6, 34–5, 68–70, 158–9, 304–6, 309; and organisational strains, 68–70, 83–4, 108, 138–9, 157–9; and political strains, 51–2, 60–1, 83–4, 221–2, 271–3, 307–10; and primordial imagery, 57–8, 60–1, 76, 84, 193–4, 196–7, 222–3, 271–2; *see also* primordialism

mass: in civilian society, 5, 271–3, 307–10; *see also* riots; in military, 1, 5, 68–9, 77, 83–4; *see also* coups and mutinies, myth, revolt

non-rational, 84: *see also* hostile behaviour

Biafra

army of, 91–3, 97, 105, 207, 329–30, 338–9

civil war and, 338–40

declaration of independence of, 332–5, 336–8

political background to secession of, xii, 67–8, 75, 105–8, 192–7, 201–5, 208–10, 219–29, 277–8, 288–91, 295–7, Chapter XIII

Boundaries

concept of, 7–9

ethnicity, region and, 43–50, 76–9, 143–4, 177–80, 192–7, 295–7

feedback of political environment on, military, 17–20, 36, 41–2, 52–3, 57–61, 201–4, 230–1, 252, 257–9, 265–78, 298–300

fragmentation of, military, 43–61, 76–9, 104–8, 196–7, 204–5, 227–8, 277–8, 289, 295–7, 298–300

fragmentation of, civilian bureaucracies, 217–18, 227–8

maintenance of, military, 85–6, 101–5, 107–9, 126–30, 132, 136–40, 143–4, 177–80

Nigerian Army's, 101–9

Britain

High Commissioner of advises against Northern secession, July 1966, 67

legacy of in Nigerian military, 1–4, 88–90, 95–7, 101–3, 109, 117–22, 126–7, 132–7, 154–6, 160, 163, 166–8, 230–4, 237–40, 247, 338

military assistance of, 231–2, 339

non-political tradition of army of, in Nigeria, *see* civilian control

British Army Council, as delaying indigenisation, 163, 231–3

Brotherhood
  army as a, 86, 92–3
  fratricide and, 6, 60, 75–6, 83, 85–6, 108, 127,
    138–9, 299–300
  peer groups and, 85–6, 132–9
  solidarity and, 108, 132, 136–9, 180, 284
Bureaucracies, federal, *see also* civil service,
    Nigerian Railway Corporation, universities
  'tribalism', ethnic arithmetic and, 49, 193,
    214, 217–18, 227–9, 277–8, 329

Cabinet (Federal Council of Ministers)
  decisions relating to military, 232–7, 242–4,
    249–50
  political role of, 211–13, 218–19
Career
  lines in Nigerian Army, 94–101, 111–12,
    122–3, 132–6, 139–41
  lines, effect of indigenisation on, 4, 168–76,
    233, 238–9
  of military elite compared with January
    Majors, 174–6, 238–41
  mobility, peer groups and, 139–42
Case Studies, limitations and problems of, 7, 13
Civilian control, of the military
  colonial heritage of neutrality in, 1, 88, 103–4,
    127, 215–16, 230–4, 237–41, 243, 247
  control of ethnic composition of, 48–9, 185–6,
    189–92, 225, 243–6
  defence and foreign policy, military lack of
    influence in, 88–9, 230–8
  dispute over control of, during 1964 election
    crisis, 215–17, 237–8
  objective and subjective control, 5–6, 230–1,
    247
  police, control of compared with military, 8,
    103, 108, 242
  preserved by cleavages of military elite, 239–
    40
  professional interests of military and, 3, 5–6,
    25–6, 48–9, 107–9, 127–8, 202, 230–1,
    247–51, 279–80
  undermined by civilian regime's loss of
    legitimacy, 17, 20, 36, 41–2, 201–2, 219–20,
    225–7
Civil–military relations
  approaches to, 4–7, 10
  in Nigeria after coups of 1966, *see* military
    regime
  in Nigeria before coups of 1966 *see* civilian
    control
Civil Service
  Eastern: influence in Biafran secession, 106,
    329–30
  Federal: age-structure and education of,
    compared with military, 96–8; corporate
    support of, for Federation under Gowon,

1966–7, 106, 312–18, 337; critique by, of
    Aburi agreements, 318, 349–55; regional
    balancing applied to, 229, 269n; role of
    under military government, 106, 254–7,
    261, 264, 268–9
  Federal and regional: regionalisation of, 1954,
    210; unification of, by Ironsi, 264–6, 268–9
  Northern: influence of under military, 24,
    263, 266–7, 277, 326; role of in May 1966
    riots, 266–70, 272
Cleavage, *see also* cohesion, conflict, peer
    groups, primordialism
  consistent and cross-cutting: concept of,
    189–90; in Nigerian Army, 10, 85–7,
    140–4, 186, 189–97, 204–5;
  lines of, between Federation and Eastern
    Region/Biafra, 298–303, 324–5
  in Federation, reduced by civil war, 339–40
Clientage
  between military and politicians, 192, 239–
    42
  in military, 2, 12, 54, 103–4, 112, 166–8
  political and ethnic, in Nigeria, 207, 209–10,
    217–18, 224–6
  regionalisation of wanted by Ojukwu, 296
Cohesion, *see also* authority, cleavage, soli-
    darity
  and cleavage, in army, 83–7, 102–3, 107–8,
    140–4
  collective honour and, 127–30
  peer groups and, 132–41
  political beliefs of officers, importance in,
    284–5
  military, political order dependent on, 6–7,
    204–5, 298–9, 305–10, 312
  size of army and, 92–4
Cohorts, Seniority
  term defined, 134
  term used, 36–8, 47–8, 78, 133–5, 174–6,
    183–4, 189–92
Colonial tutelage
  emergence of army from later than other
    institutions, 230; *see also* Britain
Command, *see also* authority, discipline,
    hierarchy
  effective, rather than hierarchical, 147–50,
    166–8
  hierarchy, routine and, 150–9, 160–1
  lines of, undermined by turnover, 168–70
  relations of, and military government, 258–9,
    288–9
  style of, 154–8, 160, 167–8
Commissions and Tribunals of Enquiry
  Coker Commission, 212, 225, 282
  under military government: Eastern Region,
    330; Federal, 264, 269, 277; Northern
    Region, 264; Western Region, 333

Communications
feedback of to military government restricted,
201, 203–4, 255–9, 277–9
output of in military government inadequate,
52–3, 257–8, 268–9, 305–6, 310
system of in military, 102
Community, *see also* primordialism of identity
interest groups and, 178–9, 206–7, 222
resilience of in Nigerian politics and social
life, 206–7, 219–25
Conflict, *see also* cleavage, coups and mutinies,
political competition, primordialism, revolt,
riots, 'tribalism'
dynamics of, in military, 107–8, 144–7,
159–62, 171–8, 196–7
societal dynamics of, 201–5, 219, 221–9
Congo (Kinshasa)
consequences of Nigerian participation in
UN contingent in, 27, 102, 234, 237, 247–
50, 286
Conspiracy
beliefs in a feature of Nigerian military coups,
19–20, 41, 52–3, 59–61, 69, 84
beliefs in before May and October riots, 267–
8, 211, 307–8
emphasis on in East before secession, 302,
331–2
networks of by-pass formal hierarchy, 59–60,
259
organisational requirements of, 49–50
Constitution
arrangements for Independence and the,
207–11, 219, 231–2
discussions concerning, September 1966 to
civil war, 312–21
Eight-Point Programme of North for, 210,
328n
military government and the, 254–5, 265–6
unitary constitution introduced by Decree
no. 34 of 1966, 264–6, 270, 272
unitary constitution repealed by Gowon, 304,
311
Corruption
attitudes of military to, 248, 282–3
measures of military regime against, 262–4,
277
under civilian government, 17, 202, 207, 209–
10, 212, 215, 218, 224–6
under military regime, 113–14, 339
Coups and mutinies
African, 1–2, 19, 90
in Biafra, attempted, 1967, 40–1, 325, 330
general, 4–7, 13
of January 1966, 1, 9, Chapter I, 83–4, 219;
civilians in, 18, 39, 42–3; consequences of,
24–5, 51–8, 91–3, 104, 108; ethnicity and
region in, 26–7, 43–50, 246; failure of,

22–7, 33–5, 46–7; Ironsi's counter-coup,
24–7, 46–7, 252, 267; motives for, 6, 17–20,
36, 38–42, 44, 48–50, 142, 203, 246, 250–2,
280–1; organisation and disorganisation
in, 17–18, 20–4, 27–31, 42–3, 46–7, 49, 131,
146–7; participants in, 27–8, *see also*
Majors; political background to, 17–20, 34,
36, 41–2, 201–4, 218–19, 226–9, 243–51;
victims of, 43–6
of July 1966, 1, 9, 11, Chapter II, 83–4, 219,
252; consequences, 66–8, 91–3, 104–6,
298–300, 304–10, 336–8; ethnicity and
region in, 55–63, 76–9; motives for and
political background to, 51–3, 57–61, 78–9,
266–78; organisational strains and 53–8;
organisation and disorganisation in, 61–6,
68–75, 108, 131, 304–5; part played by
junior officers in, 58–61, 70–4; part played
by Other Ranks in, 51–3, 59, 68–70;
victims of, 65, 69, 76
of Mid-West Ibo officers, 1967, 325, 335–6
mutinies: attempted, Yaba, 1952, 233; attempted, Kaduna, soon before July coup,
64; of 5th Battalion, Kano, October 1966,
305–9
Culture, *see also* elite, honour
corporate, of officer corps, 126–30, 136–9, 160
image and reference groups of officers, 115–22
instability of cultural image, 109, 130
traditional, interaction of with military, 112–
13, 138, 166–8

Decrees, of military government
angry rhetoric of, 293
Decree no. 1 of 1966, 265–6, 352–3
Decree no. 33 of 1966, 263, 284
Decree no. 34 of 1966, 58, 76, 253, 255–6,
261, 264–6, 272, 276, 284, 287, 294,
311
Decree no. 8 of 1967, 319–21, 337
Decree on Indian Hemp, 253, 283, 293
Public Officers (Investigation of Assets)
Decree, no. 51 of 1966, 264n, 277
Rent Control Decree, no. 15 of 1966, 294
State Security (Detention of Persons)
Decrees, 256n, 262, 263n
Suppression of Disorder Decrees, 256n, 262,
293
Tribunal of Enquiry Decree, no. 41 of 1966,
264n, 277
Definition of the situation
examples of, 60–3, 145, 178, 186, 193–6,
221–4, 308–9
sociological tradition of analysis by, 193n
Diaspora, Hausa–Fulani
defined, 181; *see* minorities, Northern
Region

Diplomacy, *see also* military assistance
of African states, 88–90
civil war and, 300–3, 323–4, 339–40
of Nigerian civilian regime, 231–4, 237, 247–50
Discipline, *see also* authority, command, hierarchy
legacy of indiscipline after 1966 coups, 146–7, 305–9, 321–2
and political style of military regime, 258 n, 281–2, 291–5
survival of, in January coup, 22–7, 30–1, 35
survival of, in July coup, 63, 67–74, 298–9, 305
system of, in Nigerian Army, Chapter VI
violation of, in coups, 146; *see also* coups and mutinies, revolt
Dissonance, cognitive
concept of, 126
used in relation to: brotherhood and fratricide, 108; political behaviour of Ironsi, 259; political motives of January conspirators, 41–2; status position of officers, 126–8
Dualism, structural
of centre and periphery in Nigeria, 206–8
in ex-colonial societies, 2, 206 n
and political conflict in Nigeria, 221–4

Eastern Region, *see also* Biafra, Ibos, minorities, region
dismantling of, 220–1, 313, 322–3, 330–2
emphasis on region rather than ethnicity before secession, 194–5, 296, 302, 329–32
military government of, under Ojukwu, 254–5, 262, 264, 274 n, 281–4, 296, 328–32
politics of, under civilian regime, 19–20, 43–4, 208–9, 212–19, 241, 258
propaganda of, *see* propaganda
secession of, *see* Biafra
Eaton Hall, 133, 235 n, 253
Education, *see also* elite, socialisation, status, recruitment
and entry to officer corps, 95, 187–8
and Northern officers, 184–6, 122–3
of officer corps, compared with other elites, 96, 122–3
and status strivings of officers, 115, 122–5
Elections
Federal, of 1959, 211
Federal, of 1964, 42, 131, 135, 212, 215–17, 224, 226, 231, 237–8, 243
Northern Region, of 1961, 226
Western Region, of 1965, 17, 19, 218–19, 227, 249, 333
Elite, *see also* education, status
British military, status position of compared with Nigerian, 112, 119–20, 127–8

image of Nigerian officers, 109–11, 115–26
January conspirators as an, 36–9, 42
military, compared with others, 96, 98, 111, 114–15, 117, 119, 122–4
military ruling, narrowness of, 253–9
openness of Nigerian, 111–14
Emirates, *see also* Hausa–Fulani, Kanuri, Native Authorities
Northern Region, 77–8, 90, 114, 167, 180–6, 209, 222–4, 273, 307, 310, 326–7
Ethnic
arithmetic in Federal bureaucracies, 228, 244–5, 268–9
balance of army upset by January coup, 54–8
differences in achievement motivation, 178, 188
Ethnicity, *see also* primordialism, 'tribalism'
in coups of 1966, 26–8, 43–58, 61–3, 76–9, 84, 177–8, 194–7, 246; *see also* coups and mutinies
and organisational strains, *see* strain, primordialism
and promotions, 48–9, 191–2, 245–6, 268
and recruitment, 9, 87, 182–9, 243–5
ties of, lack stability, 186, 194–6
Expenditures, military, 89, 234–6

Federal Defence Council, 231, 234
Federal Executive Council
establishment and composition of, 254–5, 257, 351–2
politicians included in, 323, 334
Federal Military Government
establishment and legal basis of, 24–7, 254–5, 258 n, 265–6
becomes National Military Government under Ironsi, 264–6
reverts to Federal Government under Gowon, 304, 311
Federation, sources of support for before civil war, 296–7, 310–15, 320–3, 327–8, 330–2, 334–5, 336–7
Feedback, *see also* boundaries, communications
concept of, 9
and military regime, 201–4, 252
Format
changes in, of Nigerian Army, 102–7
organisational effects of, 8, 85–6, 107–8
political effects of, 6, 8, 93–4, 102
Functional analysis, *see also* social system
examples of latent functions: of authority, 145; of career mobility, 139–40, 170; of charisma and initiative, 145–6, 150–3; of civilian control, 230–1; of the gentleman ethic, 127–8; of hierarchy and routine, 159–62; of peer groups, 142–50; of pri-

Index of subjects

Functional analysis (*cont.*)
    mordial cleavage, 143–4, 196–7; of size,
    90–4; of transfer of British military
    organisation, 3; of unity in format, 107–8
    functional imperatives: of internal security
    create strains in military, 202, 247–51;
    taking Nigerian Army into civil war, 106,
    312, 315, 317, 321–2
    use of, 7–8, 85–7

Generalised beliefs, 52; *see* myths
General strike of 1964, 17, 214–15, 226–7, 237,
    249
Gentlemen, officers and, 12, 86, 109–11, 116–18,
    126–30, 160; *see also* elite, honour, status
Ghana, coups and military regime of, compared
    with Nigeria, 49, 146, 204, 256

Hausa–Fulani, 77–8, 181–3, 208–9; *see also*
    Emirates
Hierarchy
    control through, 154–8
    and initiative, 86, 145–6, 150–3
    precedence in, 31, 147–50, 160, 298–9
    and revolt, 145–6, 158–9
    shape of, 154–5, 158
Honour, *see also* gentlemen, status
    collective: and authority, 160–1; and gentle-
    men image, 126–30; and mess life, 136–9,
    180; and political beliefs and behaviour of
    military, 122, 180, 203, 279–80; and status
    position of officers, 122, 127–30
    individual, as motive for career choice, 128–9

Ibos, *see also* Biafra, Eastern Region, Mid-West
    Region
    collective insecurity of, 60–3, 217–18, 277–8,
    300–3, 329–30, 337–8
    creating own stereotypes, 270–2, 274, 301–2,
    330–1
    effect of quotas and employment restrictions
    on, 48–9, 57, 217–18, 225, 227–9, 243–6,
    329
    exodus from North of, 300–1, 307–9
    in Ironsi government, 257, 264, 267–9, 277–8
    in January coup, 26–8, 43–4, 47–9, 77
    massacres, civilian of, 271–4, 301–2, 305–10,
    329–30; *see also* riots
    massacres, military, of, 64, 66, 69, 75–6
    in military hierarchy, 9, 47–8, 55–7, 189–90
    and nationalism, 48–9, 104, 177–80, 192,
    194–5, 269, 284
    Northern fears as object of, 51–3, 57–8,
    60–1, 62–3, 69, 84, 86, 142–3, 192, 213–14,
    223, 228–9, 267–9, 271, 302–3, 307–8
    population and social organisation, 208,
    223–4

recruitment and promotions, military, of,
    186–92, 245
    and regional/Biafran identities, 194–5, 296,
    329–31
    Yoruba hostility, as object of, 213–14,
    217–18, 223, 228–9
Identities
    latent social, 178–80, 192–7, 202–3; *see also*
    ethnicity, primordialism, region
    military, 177–80; *see* culture, gentlemen,
    honour
Idomas, 196, 220, 322
Images, *see* culture, elite, myths, propaganda,
    stereotypes
Imperial Defence College, 97, 240–1, 253, 343–6
Indigenisation, of military
    delayed and begun, 90, 230–3, 238–9
    effects on: age structure, 98, 164–6; career
    mobility and promotions, 168–76, 191–2;
    civil–military relations, 103–4, 233–4,
    238–43; distribution of skills, 95, 97–101;
    ethnic balance, 188–92; responsiveness to
    social environment, 112–13, 127–8, 166–8,
    178–9
    rate of, 163–4, 239, 245
Initiative, *see also* authority, hierarchy, revolt
    control of, 153–62
    functions of, 150–3
Institutions
    fragility of, 1–2, 227–9
    traditional: and allocations in the modern
    context, 2, 206–7, 220–2, 224; ethnicity
    not identical with, 177n, 193–5, 222–3;
    links with regional identity of North,
    180–4, 223–4, 326–7; *see also* Native
    Authorities; status in, *see* status norms
Integration, political, related to military co-
    hesion, 204–5, 298–9; *see also* cohesion,
    legitimacy
Intelligence, military, 18, 93

Jihad, tradition of evoked, 244
Joint Action Committee, *see* trades unions

Kanuri, 77–8, 181–4; *see also* Emirates

Legitimacy, political
    decline of: under civilians, 5, 17, 201–2,
    226–7, 247, 250–1; under Ironsi regime,
    202–4, 252–3; *see also* military regime;
    undermines military authority, 202–4,
    247–51
    dependent on military authority, 147–50,
    204–5, 268–9, 291–5, 298–30, 304–5
    and political attitudes and skills of military,
    280, 287–97
Legislation, military, 126–7, 160–1, 238n

Majors of January 1966
Ironsi's treatment of, 27, 52–3, 267
professional background of, 30, 36–8, 132–3, 135, 140–2, 174–5, 240–1
subsequent fate of, 69, 305, 325, 330
Mass
behaviour, *see* behaviour
society, Nigeria as a, 221–2, 271
Massacres, *see* coups and mutinies, riots
Middle Belt
defined, 181; *see* minorities, Northern Region, United Middle Belt Congress
Mid-West Region
army recruitment and, 186–9, 245
creation of and identity, 195, 212, 219–20
Ibos in, dilemmas of, 91–2, 105, 129, 133, 195, 335–6
invasion of, 105, 107, 132–3, 146, 325, 335–6
neutrality of before civil war, 105, 334–6
Military Governors, of the regions, 195, 254, 257–9, 262–4, 269, 288–9, 295–6, 327–9, 332–3, 335–6
Military intervention in politics, 4–7, *see also* civil–military relations, coups and mutinies, military regime
Military regime, *see also* Federal Military Government, political beliefs of military
under Ironsi: alienates North, 52–3, 57–60, 266–78; attempts to legislate unity, 58, 264–6, 275–7; inertness, 52–3, 252–3, 256–7, 275–7; initial legitimacy, 252, 260–1; lacks political roots, 253–9, 269–70, 274–7; overthrow of, 64–8, 277–8; reforms of, 262–6, 277; structure, 254–5
under Gowon: abdicates to the politicians, 311–16, 320; begins civil war, 323–5, 336–40; East declines authority of, 298–304, 314, 316–22, 328–9; fails to control violence, 304–10; reasserts authority, 316–25; relations with regions, 311, 316–17, 319–20, 325–36
Minorities
Commission, report of, 219n
Constitution defines position of, 208–9, 219–21
demands result in creation of Mid-West state, 212, 219–20
demands result in creation of twelve states, 79, 186, 221, 322–3, 326–7
Eastern: in army, 186–90, 195, 313; delineated, 186, 219; detached from Biafran secession, 313, 322–3, 330–2; uprising mooted, January 1966, 19–20
emphasise national over regional identity, 195–6, 313–14
Northern: in army, 77–9, 181–6, 194–5, 313; part in Northern riots, 309–10; resurgence

under Gowon, 79, 186, 313–16, 326–8, 322; turned aside by Ironsi, 269–70
Mobility
career, between military postings: develops solidarity, 87, 139–41, 170; effect on ethnic ties, 102–3, 178; and peer groups, 139–41; undermines authority, 87, 168–70
patterns of, social, in Nigeria, 111–12, 122–3
promotional, *see* promotions
Mons Officer Cadet School, 37, 74, 95–6, 120, 123, 133–6, 159–60, 240, 338, 343–6
Myths, *see also* primordialism, propaganda, strain
exaggerate coherence of conflict-groups, 60–3, 77
indicate strain, 84, 145
in January coup, 19–20, 35, 41
in July coup, 51–3, 57–8, 60–3, 68–9, 76–7, 271–4
and measures to prevent rumours, 274
in Northern riots, 267–9, 307–8
project organisational insecurities, 69, 85, 139, 145, 158, 161, 196–7
project political insecurities, 193–6, 221–3, 267, 271–2, 307–8
propaganda uses of, *see* propaganda
and 'tribalism', 177–8, 192–7; *see also* 'tribalism'

National Conciliation Committee, 320, 322
National Council of Nigerian Citizens (NCNC), 41–2, 84, 96, 106, 209–17, 258
Nationalism
and attempts to legislate national unity, 264–6, 272, 287
civil war and, 339–40
fragmented, 58–9, 289, 295–7
motif in January coup, 31, 39–40, 284, 286–7
precedence of over primordial ties, 180, 195–6, 296–7
Native Authorities, 213, 221, 224, 263, 272–3, 326–7
Newspapers, 11, 213–14, 259–61, 270–1
Nigerian National Alliance (NNA), 214–18
Nigerian National Democratic Party (NNDP), 19, 59, 77n, 212, 214–19, 250–1, 258
Nigerian National Development Plan, 209, 236, 294
Nigerian Railway Corporation, 49, 179, 193, 210, 214, 218, 228, 246
Non-Commissioned Officers (NCOs), *see also* Other Ranks
indigenisation of, 122, 163, 166–8
part in military coups, *see* Other Ranks
recruitment of to officer corps, 95–6, 133–6, 166, 186–7

Index of subjects

Non-Commissioned Officers (NCOs) (*cont.*)
  relations of with officers, 2, 22, 26, 58–9, 70,
    87, 157–8, 160–1, 166–8, 179
  socialisation of Nigerian, by British, 121–2,
    154–8
  tensions between ex-NCOs and other officers,
    140–2, 166, 179
Northern Elements Progressive Union (NEPU),
  214, 267, 269–70
Northern Peoples Congress (NPC)
  in civilian politics, 24, 41, 96, 209–17, 220,
    223–4, 231, 236, 242–4, 250–1, 258
  networks survive under military rule, 59, 77 n,
    252, 257–8, 263, 267, 270–3, 309–10, 326–7
Northern Progressive Front (NPF), 214, 216
Northern Region
  in army, 57–8, 70, 77–8, 128–9, 167–8, 174,
    180–92, 220; *see also* recruitment
  behind Federation before civil war, 106, 312,
    320–1, 326–8
  dismantling of, 79, 186, 194, 220–1, 313,
    322–3, 326–8; *see also* minorities
  dominance of, in Federation, 41, 44, 208–17,
    219, 226, 242, 250
  Hudson Report on devolution in, 295 n, 327
  images of, 62–3, 69, 77, 194, 223–4, 269,
    301–3
  and January coup, 19–20, 23–4, 26–7, 28 n,
    32–6, 41–7, 219
  and July coup, 51–3, 56–7, 71, 75–9, 84,
    128, 168, 184–6, 295, 304–5, 336
  military government of, under Hassan
    Katsina, 25, 27, 52, 257–61, 263–78,
    326–8
  'Northernisation', policy of, 213–14, 225,
    259, 268, 273
  political identity of, 58, 78–9, 180, 184–6, 194,
    223–4, 270–3, 307, 316 n
  political strains in, 210, 213, 219, 221–2, 261,
    266–7, 271–2, 277–8, 307–10
  politicians of the, and the army, 48–9, 59,
    103–4, 111–12, 236, 241–6, 250, 310
  reforms in, under military, 263–4, 326–7
  rejects Ironsi's unitary constitution, 58,
    264–9, 272
  riots in, *see* riots
  secession of considered, 62–3, 67–8, 210, 272,
    336

Oil, 209, 324–5, 330, 337
Organisation of African Unity, 88, 237
Other Ranks, *see also* NCOs
  military position of, 161, 167–8, 245
  and part in January coup, 22, 25–6, 31, 33,
    35–6
  and part in July coup, 51–2, 57–60, 64–6,
    68–70, 75, 77, 83, 85, 175

Pakistan Staff College, Quetta, 97, 232 n, 241,
  243–6
Parliament
  Federal House of Representatives, 210–11,
    216–17, 222, 232–3, 245
  Federal Senate, 34, 244
  Western Region House of Assembly, 212, 249
Patronage, *see* clientage
Peer groups, 10
  and career mobility, 139–41, 170
  as common feature of military organisation,
    131–2
  data concerning, 13–14
  and ethnic and regional cleavage, 47–8, 87,
    142–4, 186–91
  in January coup, 27–30, 36–8, 47–8, 83,
    132–3, 135–6, 140–4
  in July coup, 70–4, 83, 135–6, 142–4
  and solidarity, 86, 132, 138–9
  as source of cleavage, 10, 85–7, 131, 135–6,
    140–5, 189–91
  and status norms, 85–6, 132, 137
Planning, attitude of military to, 293–5
Police
  army takes on functions of, 202, 248–50
  civilian control of, compared with army, 103,
    242
  education of, 95–7
  hold the ring in Enugu during July coup,
    66–7, 75
  in military government, compared with
    Ghana police, 256
  numbers and training of, 273–4
  and part in controlling Northern riots, 108,
    250, 272–4, 306, 310
  Report on January coup, 18, 32, 53
  structure and boundaries of, compared with
    army, 8, 102–3, 108
  support of for Federation before civil war,
    312, 334
  under Ironsi, 254–6, 275–6
  use of for political control by civilian
    politicians, 218–19, 226–7, 249–50
Political beliefs, of military
  collective honour and, 107, 230–1, 127–30,
    278–9
  elusiveness of, 279–80, 293–7
  internal security role and, 202, 230–1,
    248–51
  leadership and, 150–3, 276–7, 291–5
  military rule and, 252–3, 260–1, 276–7, 280–1,
    287–97
  themes in: achievement, 48–9, 122–5, 245,
    283–4; anti-corruption, 39–40, 113–14,
    248, 262–4, 277, 282–3; anti-politics, 107,
    203, 230–1, 248, 260–1, 263–4, 284–6,
    288–91; nationalism, 31, 39–40, 121–2,

Political beliefs, of military (*cont.*)
195–6, 264–6, 276–7, 286–7, 296–7, 315;
self-discipline, 160, 281–3
Political class
emergence of, 207–8, 209–10
disillusion with, 17–18, 215, 226–7
Political competition
course of, 210–21
diminishing resources and, 225–7
imposes political choices on military, 201–2,
230–1, 237–8, 249–50
objects of, 209–10, 224–7
Political environment
concept of and characteristics in new states,
2, 4–9
in Nigeria: *see* boundaries, dualism, legitimacy, political competition, political order,
primordialism
Political order
breakdown of, 218–20, 247, 249–50, 272–4,
305–10
credible violence, military cohesion and,
204–5, 273–4, 298–9, 305
and legitimacy, 226–7, 247, 262, 274; *see also*
legitimacy
Political parties
banning of, 263–4, 284
coalitions among, 210–12, 214, 216–17
competition among, *see* political competition
lacking institutionalisation, 227
and the military, 19–20, 41–3, 231, 236,
242–4, 250–1; *see also* politicians
and Northern riots, 210, 267, 272–3, 309–10
and patronage, 209–10, 214, 217–18, 224–5
and violence, 212, 215, 218–20, 226–7, 250–1
Politicians
compared with military as rulers, 101, 257–8,
287–8
distrust of military for, *see* political beliefs
interference of in military matters, 48–9,
230–1, 242–6; *see also* civilian control
and linkages in military, 40–4, 59–60, 103–6,
202, 238, 240–3, 246, 310; *see also* political
parties
re-emergence of after July coup, 311, 316,
320, 322–3, 326–7, 329, 332–5
Population
censuses of 1962 and 1963, 212–14
figures for Nigeria, 208, 213
Primordialism, *see also* ethnicity, region,
'tribalism'
and boundaries of military, 60, 109, 178–80
as central to argument of book, 10, 177–8,
196–7
defined, 177, 193–4
as not superseding organisational ties, 77,
142–4, 179–80

of identity, 178, 192–6, 222–3, 296
and the military coups of 1966, 1, 84; *see also*
coups
and political conflict; *see* 'tribalism'
of projection, 178, 193–7, 221–4, 295
as symbolising other cleavages, 3, 9–10,
86–7, 142–4, 174, 189–94, 196–7, 228–9
Profession, military
image of, unstable, 109, 130
and politics, 48–9, 231, 244–5, 248–50
Professionalism, military, 3–7
and cultural image of officers, 109–11,
122–30
and political neutrality, *see* civilian control
and skills of Nigerian officers, 94–101; *see
also* socialisation, training
Promotions
after January coup, 56–7, 268
fears of bias in, 48–9, 124–5, 191–2, 245–6,
284
as motive for January coup, 38, 48–9, 174–5,
191–2, 246
speed of disorganises career lines, 97–100,
143, 170–6
Propaganda
of Eastern Region/Biafra, 11, 19n, 62–4, 64n,
69n, 72–3n, 77n, 300–3, 309n, 319,
330–1
effect on research of, 10–11, 61–3
Federal, 62, 302–3, 339
Northern, 61, 270, 307–8
Western, 334

Radicals, cooption of by military rulers, 256,
311, 323, 326, 332
Radicalism, political
in civilian politics, 214–17
of January Majors, 39–43, 330
and military rule, 280–1, 291–4
Recruitment, *see also* indigenisation
different attitudes of ethnic groups to, 2,
188–9, 225, 244–6
from North, 182–5
qualifications for entry, *see* education
and reasons for choice of military career,
128–9, 233–4
regional quotas on, 103, 185–6, 188–9, 202,
210, 230–1, 243–6, 283
schools and, 184–5, 187–9, 244
social background and, 111–14
uneven regional and ethnic pattern of, 9,
186–9, 243–5
Regions, *see also* Eastern Region, Mid-West
Region, Northern Region, Western Region
dismantling of, 322–3; *see also* minorities
interests poorly represented under military,
257–9, 288–9

Index of subjects

Regions (*cont.*)
and military cleavage, 76-9, 86-7, 185-6,
189-91
nature of ties to, in military, 77-9, 180-6,
192-6
resurgence of under military rule, 266-78,
311, 325-36
Regionalism
in civilian politics, 208-10, 223-4
and political beliefs of soldiers, 286-9,
295-7
Research
multivariate analysis in, 7-8, 13-14
problems of, 10-14
Revolt,
civilian, *see* riots
military: against authority in 1966 coups,
34-6, 64-6, 68-70, 74-5; *see also* coups;
and boundaries/solidarity, 85-6, 107-8;
expressed in primordial imagery, 3, 68-9,
143-4, 196-7; *see also* primordialism,
'tribalism'; generated by authority relations, 3, 9, 68, 74, 85-6, 145-7, 150-3,
157-62; generated by mobility, 171-6; *see
also* mobility, promotions; and routines,
159-62
Riots
Kano, of 1953, 210, 214
Northern, of May 1966: causes, 62-3, 196,
221-2, 253, 266-73, 307-8; effects, 58-60,
259, 261, 274-8, 300-2; handling of, 257,
272-5; the riots, 272-3
Northern, of September/October 1966:
causes, 196, 221-2, 299, 307-10; effects,
300-3, 310, 314, 316, 329-32, 337;
handling of, 108, 204, 292, 299, 305-7,
310; the riots, 305-9
Tiv, of 1960 and 1964, 17, 202, 220, 222, 231,
237, 247, 261
Western Region, of 1965, 19, 41, 202, 219,
222, 231, 237, 249-51, 261-2
Royal West African Frontier Force, 88, 90,
231
Rumours, *see* conspiracy, myths

Sandhurst, Royal Military Academy, 30, 36-7,
47-8, 74, 95-6, 120, 132-6, 140-2, 155-6,
159-60, 187-8, 192, 240, 338, 343-6
Secession
of Eastern Region, *see* Biafra
of Northern Region, considered, *see* Northern
Region
of Western Region, considered, *see* Western
Region
Security
external: role of army in, 88, 234, 236-7,
247-9

internal: effect of role on army, 202, 231,
247-51; role of army in, 202, 218-20,
226-7, 237-8, 247-51
Seniority
cohorts, *see* cohorts
principles, military: and hierarchy, 137, 160;
and the political debate, 147-50, 298-9;
and promotions, 191-2
Size, of military, 88, 91-4, 163, 234-5, 273-4,
338
limits capacity to rule, 90-3, 253-4
no obstacle to intervention in politics, 89-91,
94
Skills, distribution of in military, 94-100
Sociability, prescribed, and the army officer,
116-18, 126-7, 136-9, 180
Socialisation
childrearing and, 2
and cohesion/solidarity, 132-3, 136-40
and collective honour, 122-30
disrupted by mobility, 171-6
external reference groups and, 118-22, 129-
30
military, 10, 13, 94-101, 109, 115-17
Socialist Workers and Farmers Party, 40,
215
Social system, military as a, 7-10, 83-7; *see
also* boundaries, functional analysis
Solidarity, *see also* brotherhood, cohesion, peer
groups
and career mobility, 139-41, 168-70
and conflict, 6, 60, 85-6, 107-8, 299-300
and the officers mess, 136-9
and peer groups, 132; *see also* peer groups
and primordial ties, 177-80
and relation to cohesion, 85-6, 92-3
and status position of officer corps, 125-30
Sources of data, 10-13
Staff
functions in Nigerian Army, 93, 101-2
and line, 99-100, 153-5
training, 97, 99-100
Staff College, Camberley, 38, 97, 100, 239-41,
253, 343-6
Status
discrepancies: among officers, 164-6; between officers and NCOs, 166-8
norms: convivial reinforcement of, 137;
functions in regard to authority, 159-62;
of Nigerian traditional societies, and the
military, 112-14, 167-8; and peer groups,
132, 142-4; and seniority, 147-8, 160
position, of officers: compared with elite
reference groups, 109, 115, 124-6; in
Nigerian status structure, 109, 111-14,
122-4, 129-30; Northern, 185-6; upheld
by collective honour, 109, 111, 126-30

374

Strain
concept of, 84–7, 145
organisational sources of: authority relations in military, Chapter VI; *see also* authority, discipline, revolt; consequences of January coup, 53–8; distortions in age structure, *see* age structure; lack of professional experience, 94–101; the military image, 107, 280, 287–97; *see also* political beliefs; mobility, *see* mobility, promotions; peer groups, 140–4, *see also* peer groups; uneven ethnic/regional recruitment and promotion, 186–92, *see* also primordialism; unity in format, 107–8, 299–300, *see also* brotherhood, boundaries, solidarity
political sources of, 58–61, 84, 196–7, 201–5, 221–9, 266–73, 277–8, 299–300, 307–10
projected in primordial imagery, 86, 193–7, 221–2, 228–9, 300–3
Structure, of army, 1–4, 7–10, 85–7, Chapter III, 153–8, 231–6; *see also* boundaries, social system
Study Groups on Constitutional Review, National Planning, National Unity
establishment of by Ironsi, 264–5, 268–9, 274
Supreme Military Council
discussed in constitutional negotiations, 316–20, 349–53, 355
establishment and composition, 254–5
under Gowon, 305n, 316–17, 319–21, 347–9
under Ironsi, 52–3, 254–8, 265–6, 274–6, 289
Symbolic, *see also* myths
commitments, by military regime, 252–3, 265–6, 276–7, 292–3
deprivations and threats, 61, 253, 266–7, 271, 308
evocations of primordial ties, 193–7, 228–9; *see also* primordialism
humiliations and wounds, 301, 303, 330

Tiv, *see also* minorities
in military, 77–8, 181, 195, 321–2
riots of 1960 and 1964, *see* riots
social and political organisation, 220, 223
Trades Unions
and general strike of 1964, *see* general strike
Joint Action Committee of, 215–17
and the military, 285
Traditional institutions
and allocations in modern context, 2, 206–7, 220–2, 224
ethnicity not identical with, 177n, 193–5, 222–3
links with regional identity of North, 180–4, 223–4, 326–7; *see also* Native Authorities
status in, *see* status norms

Training, of Nigerian officers, 95–7, 133–6; *see also* socialisation
Transfer, institutional, 1–4, 86–7; *see also* Britain, indigenisation
'Tribalism', *see also* ethnicity, primordialism
accusations of, 28, 44, 52–3, 60–3, 84, 177–8, 193–5, 214, 217–18, 228, 267–9, 271, 295, 303, 307–8
attempts to disclaim, 180, 194–6, 296, 334–5
in bureaucracies, 214, 218, 227–9, 244–6
and ethnicity, 177–8, 192–4, 295
in January coup, 28, 40, 43–50, 84, 177
in July coup, 52–3, 56–8, 60–3, 76–9, 84, 295
minorities and, *see* minorities
opposed by military, 40, 264, 284, 286–7, 295
political origins of, 9, 193–7, 204, 209–10, 213–14, 217–25, 227–9

United Middle Belt Congress (UMBC), 214, 267, 269–70
United Progressive Grand Alliance (UPGA), 42, 210, 214–18
USSR, military assistance of, 339
Universities
Ahmadu Bello, 59, 125, 185, 187, 220, 257, 268, 272–3
of Ibadan, 193, 260, 262, 278
of Lagos, 49, 179, 193, 210, 217, 228, 246, 262, 329
of Nigeria, Nsukka, 262, 269n, 329

Violence
civilian: *see* riots
military: *see also* coups, hostile behaviour, revolt; August to October 1966, 304–9; in January coup, 21–3, 31–6, 39, 43–7, 83–4; in July coup, 64–6, 68–70, 76, 83–4; culmination of political processes, 204, 219, 221–2, 226–7
the contract with, xii, 31–3, 339n
control of the means of, 105–6, 204–5, 298–300, 303–5, 329, 333–8

Western Region
civilian violence of 1965–6 in, *see* riots
cocoa price and, 212, 218, 226
elections of 1965, *see* elections
emergency of 1962, 211–12, 237, 249
political alignments under civilians, 208–20, 225–8, 249–50
political position under Adebayo, 105–6, 296, 311, 313–16, 319–23, 325, 332–4, 336–7
political position under Fajuyi, 59, 76, 254–6, 261–4, 278
restoration of order in, by military, 261–2

Index of subjects

Western Region (*cont.*)
 secession of considered, 320, 322–3, 332–4, 336–7
 White Paper on the new political alignment in, 214, 217–18, 228

Yorubas
 in January and July coups, 28, 39, 42–6, 48, 76–8
 in military, 76–8, 106, 113, 181–90, 195, 245, 320, 322, 333
 in North, 76–8, 181–6, 220–1, 223; *see also* minorities
 political alienation of, 212, 218–19, 221–2, 226–7, 332
 population and social organisation of, 180, 208, 222–3